The UNTOLD JOURNEY

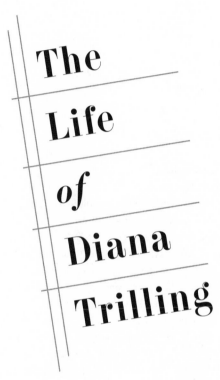

The Life of Diana Trilling

NATALIE ROBINS

Columbia University Press
Publishers Since 1893
New York   Chichester, West Sussex
cup.columbia.edu

Library of Congress Cataloging-in-Publication Data
Names: Robins, Natalie S.
Title: The untold journey : the life of Diana Trilling / Natalie Robins.
Description: New York : Columbia University Press, 2017. | Includes
bibliographical references and index.
Identifiers: LCCN 2016040242 (print) | LCCN 2017000065 (ebook) |
ISBN 9780231182089 (cloth : alk. paper) | ISBN 9780231544016 (electronic)
Subjects: LCSH: Trilling, Diana. | Authors, American—20th century—Biography.
Classification: LCC PS3539.R55 Z85 2017 (print) | LCC PS3539.R55 (ebook) |
DDC 818/.5409 [B]—dc23
LC record available at https://lccn.loc.gov/2016040242

Cover design: Julia Kushnirsky
Cover photograph: Thomas Victor

For my son, Noah Lehmann-Haupt

For my daughter, Rachel Lehmann-Haupt

For my grandson,
Alexander Louis Lehmann-Haupt

CONTENTS

PREFACE

Upon entering the apartment at 35 Claremont Avenue, in the Morningside Heights neighborhood of New York City, a visitor does not at first notice the group of Italian and French prints hanging above a rose-colored silk settee that had been a wedding gift, nor, sitting on a corner shelf in the living room, a gleaming gold watch, which instead of passing from father to only son had passed from father to youngest daughter. Nor does one take in the portrait of the young Henry James that stands on a banquet in the adjoining dining room. One notices instead the somberness and the fine coat of dust on an antique mahogany desk, which holds a massive lamp—and magnifying glass—and all but dominates a room that makes no concession to modern times. It is three o'clock on a warm October day in 1996. The heavy brocade drapes are already drawn, closing out any views of the avenue that in so many ways represents the essence of the Upper West Side and Columbia University.

"She's expecting you," the visitor is told by a friendly, poised woman wearing a bright white nurse's uniform. "Go right on back."

"Back" is the bedroom Diana Trilling shared with her husband, Lionel, for forty-six years. To get there, one walks along a well-polished wooden floor past the cheap pine-board-and-bracket bookshelves that dominate the long hallway. Volumes by Freud, Dickens, Wordsworth, Henry

Adams, James Agee, and many of Lionel Trilling's own books—his studies of Matthew Arnold and E. M. Forster; his most celebrated book, *The Liberal Imagination*; and his novel, *The Middle of the Journey*—line the shelves. Diana Trilling's books are there, too: *Claremont Essays, Mrs. Harris, The Beginning of the Journey.* In fact, all ten of Lionel Trilling's books are likely somewhere in the packed shelves, as well as Diana Trilling's six books. Stuck here and there among the hundreds of volumes are galley proofs, magazines, pamphlets, textbooks, and occasional photographs.

Diana Trilling is lying on a metal hospital bed set up in the middle of a room I have never been in before. I kiss her forehead, and she smiles at me. She is bedridden and knows she is dying, of non-Hodgkin's lymphoma, and she knows also that I was diagnosed with a less aggressive form of this cancer a year earlier. But we do not talk about illness. It is not any form of denial that keeps us from this subject (we've always been able to talk candidly) but rather her unspoken but very clear insistence that she go on living in the moment. And so, at her request, I read aloud several essays from the 100th Anniversary issue of *The New York Times Book Review.* After I finish the review of Freud's *A General Introduction to Psychoanalysis,* she closes her eyes. I say, "It's probably time I leave." She nods. Five days later I return to read more to her. She is much weaker, and I don't expect to stay long. But she wants to hear more and more, even after briefly closing her eyes. "I should leave," I say. "No, not yet," she answers. I see that once again she is not resisting death but telling me she still has some points of living to explore. "Just sit here," she says. And I hold her hand for over an hour, and feel a strength as strong as steel.

———

I first met Diana Trilling in 1988, when I interviewed her about her husband's FBI file, which I had applied for under the Freedom of Information Act for inclusion in my book *Alien Ink: The FBI's War on Freedom of Expression* (1992). I had heard her referred to many times as one of the very last of the notable midcentury New York Intellectuals—one who was equally notable for being extremely difficult—and had been warned she'd probably be pretty intimidating. I somehow felt I could handle that characteristic if it showed up (which it never did), but I was certain she'd have passionate reactions to every piece of paper I put before her. And she did. Lionel Trilling was admired as one of America's most influential and original literary critics, often fêted worldwide. Diana Trilling—herself an eminent social and literary critic, as well as the editor and/or author of six books and hundreds of book reviews and essays published in dozens of prominent magazines—too often lived in the shadow of her more celebrated husband, one whose courtly manners seamlessly matched her own sense of the importance of correct public conduct. But I knew also from many people that she was fiercely independent and called herself an "old-time feminist."

When I told her that her husband's file had begun in 1937, she very quickly interrupted me. "That's very stupid of them. Why as late as that? He was a member of the National Committee for the Defense of Political Prisoners; 1932 to 1933 was the period of his most ardent commitment— he was never a member of the Communist Party, never a member *at all*. He was a fellow traveler." She told me that she would be questioned from time to time by agencies other than the FBI about people whose security clearance she guessed had come under suspicion. "They were very intelligent," she said of these interviewers, "and they knew an enormous amount about me!"

When I said that the next reference in her husband's file wasn't until 1944, seven years after the first one, she was extremely curious. "What did they have?" she asked, almost breathlessly. I told her the page was mostly blacked out except for the words "The Revolutionary Workers League." Without a word she picked up the phone, which was on a well-worn mahogany coffee table in front of the silk settee where she was sitting. She dialed a number, and after a brief greeting she mentioned someone she called "the last living Trotskyite." There was some muted chitchat and then she shrieked into the phone: "He's been a professional revolutionary all his life." She then brusquely asked the person she was talking to, "When were you divorced? Lionel wasn't friends with him after you were divorced. By 1944 he wasn't on anything with him." A few seconds later she ended the call, and after hanging up the phone, she looked pleased. She said nothing to me about the conversation, but I could tell she knew I had grasped the gist of what she was saying—that she and her husband had joined some so-called innocents clubs in the 1930s and that was that. Members of these clubs believed they were working to oppose fascism, but in reality their purpose was to undermine the West and pave the way for Communist control.

I told her that her husband's FBI file contained a 1947 review of his novel, *The Middle of the Journey*, that had appeared in the Communist *Daily Worker*. I said that according to the file, the FBI wanted to see if the book could give Alger Hiss and his lawyers information for his defense. (Whittaker Chambers, a former Communist, had accused Hiss of being a Soviet spy, and Lionel Trilling's novel depicts a character based on Chambers.) "They are feeble-minded," Diana Trilling roared. I then read her the perplexing last line of the book review: "it leaves the reader with one impression and that is that the CP is an innocent front for another sinister force." "Well, it's true," Diana Trilling replied softly. Her face looked almost rapt. "It's true." She explained no further.

We sat and talked for more than an hour—probably closer to two— about social upheavals from the 1920s to the 1990s and sensitive political arguments that marked each decade of her long life; every writer or editor she had ever known seemed to come into the conversation. She mentioned Allen Ginsberg, Lillian Hellman, Mary McCarthy, William Phillips, William F. Buckley Jr., and William Jovanovich. She was surprised, even slightly offended, I sensed, that the FBI had no references in the file about her own volunteer work in 1933 with the Committee for the Defense of Political Prisoners or, that same year, the Scottsboro Boys case. She wondered why the bureau wasn't interested in these matters because "of [Lionel] being associated by marriage with me and by friendship with many people." I explained to her that I could request the files only of dead writers, and that she would have to request her own file, and that I was sure she had one.

She told me that she and her husband had always been anti-Communist liberals and that their position was rarely understood, especially by their literary friends. Looking pensive, she commented that William F.

Buckley's anti-Communism had nothing in common with hers. "Right-wing anti-Communism has very little in common with what I believe," she said. She was not a neoconservative. Later, responding to a question I had asked about whether the FBI influenced the way that writers wrote their books, she resolutely said, "No." She told me that although many people believed that the FBI had destroyed the Communist Party in America, she did not. "It was one factor of many," she said. "The CP self-destructed." Such judgments, especially about people and books, were, I would learn, an essential part of her nature. Although she was a feminist, she did not believe in women's liberation, because as she wrote, it created an unnecessary complication and friction with men. In expressing all her opinions, she was sharp as a blade and didn't seem to care if her conclusions were popular or fashionable or even brash-sounding. She followed the path of her mind to the end of its every thought, usually landing square on a spot where logic and imagination merged. She had made her share of enemies, and she was not always liked by her husband's Columbia University colleagues. But both friends and foes recognized that she had an exquisite brilliance, and they considered her unique among women of her generation. Still, women especially sometimes judged her harshly, even those who called her a friend. There were many reasons to dislike her, they would whisper, but the real question was, why despite all did they love her?

As we were ending our interview, I asked Diana why the government had investigated her and her husband in 1964 and 1965. She said that in 1964 they had gone to England for a year, when her husband had been a visiting professor at Oxford, and that in 1965 President Johnson had asked him to represent the United States at T. S. Eliot's funeral. "Later they wanted him to be a cultural attaché in England or France," she said; "they wrote to Columbia and asked if they would mind letting him go. I considered it because I wanted to go to Europe."

—◦◦◦—

Our conversations continued and soon were part of many dinners with my husband. At one she described a party she attended in 1937, and she spoke as if it had happened the evening before. Her ailing eyes, bulging from disease and near-blindness, still managed to convey both pride and indignation. She said that for the very first time she had not retreated to a room with the other women but instead had followed the men to the library, where they were going to light up cigars and sip brandy. She lingered at the doorway, unseen, and listened to the men talk, mostly about politics. She decided that one day she would be in that room—with other women present. There would be no after-dinner separation of the sexes.

Women did not have to behave as men to succeed, she said; men were their companions "in the same hard business of being human." She spent her life trying to prove that assumption, even though in an unpublished book called "The Education of a Woman," she wrote that "commonly women are judged to be less generous than men, but they have reason to be: they are liable to so many more kinds of failure." Women frequently had to prove themselves in ways men did not. "It's not easy," she concluded, "not as the writing wife of a well-known writing husband." She always felt she deserved to be more front-and-center.

She worked every single day, writing even harder after she became a mother at the age of forty-three. She was what could be called the first "family feminist," pursuing her ambitions but at the same time putting her child and husband on equal footing with her career, one that positioned the couple as leading members of the so-called Family of New York Intellectuals. Yet she would tell an interviewer, in a never-before-cited tape recording, that although she considered hers "a great marriage, it was not one of the great love affairs." She and Lionel "were a neurotic pair," she confessed, a couple "that in later decades got known in the world as the most beautifully self-contained, calm and harmonious figures."

———✦———

Diana Trilling's life—one full of secrets, contradictions, and betrayals—chronicles social, political, sexual, and literary changes over the decades of the twentieth century, enormous changes she lived through and was in almost constant conflict over. Despite going through her "own private hell," she found a path into many rooms that once excluded her by using words that seem to shimmer with candor and wisdom. Her work could be breathtaking and innovative in a way that only a person with her sensibility could create.

She wrote a memoir called *The Beginning of the Journey*, and her husband wrote a novel called *The Middle of the Journey*. This book tells *The Untold Journey*.

Note: All quotations by Diana Trilling using "Diana said" or "Diana noted," etc. without further explanation are from previously unpublished tapes she made in the 1980s with Christopher Zinn. These tapes, which I regard as "oral history," contribute to my belief that a biography should be part oral history, part interpretation, and part storytelling. The transcribed tapes are all housed in the Diana Trilling Papers at the Rare Book and Manuscript Library at Columbia University.

All other Diana Trilling quotations are from documents identified directly in the text or further clarified in the source notes. DT also made a series of tapes in the 1970s for a book of interviews she never published; these tapes, once housed in the Oral History Research Office at Columbia, are now transcribed and located in her archives.

The UNTOLD JOURNEY

1

ESCAPE INTO FICTION

Pop. Pop. Crrrack. The handsome briarwood Dunhill pipe, flung from the fifth-floor window of a two-room apartment at Number 1 Bank Street in Greenwich Village, New York, landed smack on the sidewalk, its once tapered form in pieces that scattered into the gutter. It had been the man's favorite pipe, so later he "puddled around" the street, as his wife described it, looking for the parts in the hope of fitting them together again, which never happened. It was too far gone. A lost cause. As was, evidently, a comic mystery play the man's wife had cowritten that had caused the man to call it "vulgar babble" after reading it aloud in the presence of one of his college friends, and further caused the man—Lionel Mordecai Trilling—in a fury—to hurl his pipe out the window in front of his bride of one year, Diana Rubin Trilling. She had cried and cried. "I didn't think you would cry," her husband's best friend, Henry Rosenthal, a rabbi, in fact the rabbi who had officiated at the wedding of "Di" and "Li," had sheepishly told her before leaving the apartment.

"They thought the air was polluted by the play," Diana Trilling later noted. "It was a terrible fight, which left me seriously discouraged. It had a bad effect on me, and it was one of the least worthy things I've ever known Lionel to do."

The play was about a Jewish clothing manufacturer with a passion for suspense stories who solves a murder in his apartment building on West End Avenue, and Diana and her Radcliffe pal Bettina Mikol Sinclair had written it mostly for their own amusement. Neither had considered writing as a career, and both knew their play wasn't very good, even though through connections (Bettina was married to Upton Sinclair's son, David) they discovered a well-known theater agent, Leah Salisbury, who liked it enough to forward to a London producer, who in the end turned it down because "the type of artist[s] necessary for the principal characters are not to be found in this country at ordinary salaries." In other words, Jewish actors cost more money. Two years later, Salisbury sent the play to a story editor at the Jewish-owned Paramount Pictures who thought it clever but ultimately pronounced it "too light." And that was that for the twenty-character *Snitkin*, whose last line of dialogue, spoken by Mrs. Snitkin, read: "I'm asking you, what does a woman know what a man has to suffer in this world!" Both inexperienced playwrights were pondering such questions. Radcliffe had offered them some small practical answers but not the big, philosophical ones they longed for.

Diana Rubin had entered college in 1921. She was just sixteen. "In those days all you had to do to get into college was pass your college entrance exams," she later wrote. "I certainly didn't feel I'd been touched by the hand of God because I was admitted to Radcliffe. I picked it out of the telephone book." This was not exactly true. She had read about it in her high school library and liked that it was near Boston—and near Harvard.

She was one of three Jewish women in her freshman class and the only one to admit to being so. She was a novelty, so much so that one of her dorm mates asked her to come and meet her parents, who lived in nearby Concord, because the family had never before known a Jew. (She didn't go.) Ancestry was often a topic at dormitory meals, where after saying grace—"Oh Lord, we thank thee for these and for all Thy gifts, for Christ's sake, Amen"—the students ate their food at tables covered with white damask and lace doilies and were served by waitresses in black uniforms, white caps, and aprons. (Maids regularly cleaned and polished their dormitory rooms.) Diana said that at dinner she was often "tempted to interpose my rude boast: no, my ancestors hadn't sailed on the *Mayflower*; my father had peddled macaroons on the Staten Island ferry, a different test of seaworthiness." Over time such verbal temptations would be voiced—even pompously, some would later say— although Diana's witty remarks were her way of making up for the conventional sense of humor she felt she lacked, the writing of *Snitkin* notwithstanding.

She was firmly middle class, and her family very comfortably well-off—they even had a chauffeur, although mainly because neither parent could drive—until the stock market crash of 1929 ruined her father's women's hosiery business. His showcase factory—Merit Hosiery Corporation—on Long Island was said to be one of the first all-glass plants in America, a factory with music piped throughout its four stories, a medical office with a nurse on site, and a large cafeteria providing hot meals for all the employees.

The Rubin family moved several times, from an apartment near 225th Street in the East Bronx, where Diana was born in 1905, to a spacious house in Larchmont in Westchester County, New York, that had a yard with peach and plum trees tended by a part-time gardener and even a flock of chickens, cared for by Mrs. Rubin. "My mother with her own beautiful hands chopped off the heads of the chickens she prepared for dinner—she was a gifted cook," Diana said; "our Larchmont household was much more a European than a Westchester home, much more rural than suburban. Pickles and sauerkraut were stored in barrels in the cellar. We ate spareribs and tripe and stews made out of the innards of large animals. . . . When it snowed—and often the snow was so heavy that the bell tolled at the town firehouse to announce that school would be closed—my mother rose early to clear a path from our porch to the street for my father." A few years later the Rubins moved to an even bigger house, in New Rochelle, because that town had a Jewish population (which Larchmont did not). In 1914, when Diana was nine, the family moved again, to another large house at 935 Ocean Parkway in the Midwood section of Brooklyn (to be close to a braid factory Joseph Rubin had recently set up in Bush Terminal, the first industrial complex in New York to house a multitude of warehouses and manufacturing plants). And finally, in 1922, when Diana was in her second year at Radcliffe, the family settled in an elegant apartment at 498 West End Avenue near Eighty-Fourth Street, on Manhattan's Upper West Side. The Rubins were now part of well-to-do metropolitan Jewish society.

Joseph Rubin, raised in a Warsaw ghetto with study of the Talmud his sole education, had left Poland at eighteen to avoid military service. To reach the boat that would take him to America, he had to hide under the thick straw in a peddler's cart to avoid being seen by border guards. It was not difficult because he was small, just five feet, one inch. Rubin was a little odd-looking, with a head that seemed too large for his small frame. He arrived on Ellis Island penniless, and because he spoke no English, the only job he could find in immigrant-filled New York City was one selling fresh-baked cookies. He needed no words for that; the rich almond aroma of the macaroons spoke for him.

Diana wrote that she was her father's favorite child because he played with her "more precisely than he did with her siblings" (an older sister by five years and brother by three years) and that although her father could be a bully to just about everyone who crossed his path (he once told her when she expressed an interest in singing that he'd build her "a stage in the toilet"), she was, in fact, devoted to him because he was one of the most intelligent people she ever knew. She said also that he was the most ardent believer in the power of the mind over the body she would probably ever come across in her lifetime. From her father she learned at a young age that she was smart, really smart, and that she had something neither of her siblings had: a special kind of intelligence that, her father taught her, was connected to feelings and imagination. Young Diana Rubin learned also to be sensitive to seemingly contradictory situations. She figured out how to cope with—and even rise above—inconsistencies others couldn't handle. She knew her parents were dedicated to the well-being of their three children, yet the word *love* was never used around them except, she would later recall, "in irony or mockery." She knew as a young girl that a dark band of mistrust held the family together. "Fear was my accustomed state as a child," she later said, "a condition so prevailing that it's a wonder that it left room for my other emotions."

She suspected that her mother was threatened by her youngest daughter's intelligence. "I was locked in a kind of negative confirmation of her poor opinion of me," Diana said. "My mother became a little paranoid toward my father and me, and she believed my father was bribing me to say certain things to put me on his side."

Her mother, Sadie Helene Forbert, was an orphan who lived with an older married brother she worshipped and a loathed sister-in-law so parsimonious she bought teacups with ridges at the bottom so her guests would think they were stirring lumps of sugar. Forbert, a lithe, seductive beauty who loved to sing, had also come to New York at eighteen but from the Polish countryside, far from the dark and crowded Jewish neighborhoods of Warsaw. She earned a living by modeling in New York's garment district—she was a perfect 36-24-36—and eight years after her arrival she met Joseph Rubin through her brother. She was at first put off by Rubin's lack of height—when he sat his feet didn't even touch the floor—but she was soon captivated by his mind. After her marriage she and her new husband moved to California and lived in the Chinatown section of San Francisco, where Joseph sold straw braid from their tiny apartment, and Sadie created elaborate women's hats from the braid that remained unsold. She had given up modeling because she grew tired of rebuffing unwanted advances, even though she continued to have admirers—maybe even more than admirers—up until her death at fifty-three of an anemia that was incurable in the 1920s.

When Diana picked Radcliffe, Mrs. Rubin was puzzled by her daughter's choice. What about nearby Adelphi? (At the time the college was situated in Brooklyn, not Long Island.) Why did she have to go away to college? In truth, she wanted her daughter to be done with her education, to stay in New York under her supervision, and to find a suitable husband. But Joseph Rubin prevailed on his wife, and the teenage Diana went up to Cambridge.

She was not at first a serious student. Halfway through her first year she was failing all her courses, not only because she was not studying but also because she didn't even see a reason to go to her classes. Fortunately, one of her professors—Charles Homer Haskins, one of the country's first experts in medieval history and a longtime adviser to President Woodrow Wilson on government affairs (he was present at the Paris Peace Conference of 1919 where the Treaty of Versailles was drawn up), looked up her high school record. Professor Haskins discovered that Diana had attended the rigorously academic Erasmus Hall High School in Brooklyn, the first secondary school to be chartered in New York State, and realized his student was capable of outstanding work. (Her brother also went to Erasmus, but her sister went to a commercial high school where she learned to be a secretary.) Professor Haskins warned Diana she'd flunk out if she didn't start making an effort. Out of sheer politeness, she took his advice.

She majored in art history (as at most colleges in the 1920s, the study stopped short of modernism) and thought she could eventually work in a New York museum, the Frick or the Metropolitan. She was not going to graduate immediately into marriage as most young women did. A similar-minded friend suggested that a private gallery or even a bookstore would be a suitable place to work. Her father, a socialist at the time (he would eventually become a Republican), didn't understand what art history could do for his daughter's future and wanted her to become what he would have liked to have been: a political journalist. Nevertheless, if art was really what she wanted, he recommended with his typical crude bluntness that she sweep floors in a Manhattan art gallery "to learn the business."

Diana had become something of a star in the art history departments of both Radcliffe and Harvard, although it hardly mattered: her Jewish name would bar her from desirable jobs. But a favorite professor who happened to be Jewish—Paul J. Sachs, the creator of one of the first museum courses in America—asked her to become his assistant at Harvard's art museum, the Fogg. (Sachs's maternal grandfather had founded Goldman Sachs, and his father was one of the original partners.) Diana turned her professor down, as she did his suggestion that she start a Fine Arts department at Mount Holyoke College. She told him that she needed to return to New York. Her mother had been ill for many years, and her condition was worsening, and she did not have long to live. But the real reason she wanted to return to West End Avenue was that she was not ready to become independent.

Diana had wanted to sing in the Radcliffe Choral Society (she had minored in music, having inherited her mother's good singing voice) but didn't make the cut and later quipped that "they refused to have a Jewish chorus line." She was, however, allowed to sing in a small independent choir that often performed before special lectures. She recalled that "religious bias was the given of anyone's experience as a Jew in America in my girlhood and young womanhood, annoying but manageable." Her father had wanted his children to learn about being a Jew and had given them casual Sunday school exposure, as well as some perfunctory involvement in certain holidays.

Diana always found a way to deal with whatever life brought her, from the limitations of her parents to the constant teasing, often bordering on the sadistic, she received from her siblings, even her brother, Samuel, once throwing tennis balls at her treasured porcelain tea set, breaking every cup and saucer, or Cecilia tossing her younger sister's cherished, if eccentric, collection of ledgers and account books into the basement furnace, reducing them to ashes.

When Diana's mother told her she must not ever try to surpass her brother and sister, she listened as she was trained to even though her every fiber resisted such advice. "I raged all the way to submission," she later wrote. Her mother's order of "don't win a tennis match with your brother when he visits your summer camp" made her arm and hand tremble so much that it took years for her to play the game again successfully. During her only experience riding, when her brother brought his horse next to hers, she knew she must not attempt to gallop ahead, so she fell off the horse. "I brought with me to college and took away with me from college a fear of success that could never be matched by my desire to succeed," she insisted; yet Diana would look for ways to counter such inhibitions, which never completely stopped her from reaching for something she wanted, even when it involved a mere object. As a child, when she discovered that her mother had removed her picture from her father's watch (she said her mother considered her homely), she made up her mind that someday she would own the watch despite tradition holding that it belong to her brother. In fact, it became the only family keepsake she wanted. Many decades later, when she received her bittersweet prize, she saw it still as a triumph over a treachery.

In spite of everything, Diana respected her mother for many things—her lack of vanity, her elegant simplicity, and her meticulous work ethic, which extended to embroidering the family's tablecloths and napkins, canning all the fruits and vegetables, and scrubbing the crevices of furniture with a toothbrush. "My mother just didn't look like other women—she wouldn't have dreamed of using colored nail polish. She didn't go to beauty parlors except very rarely," Diana said. "I don't know where she found her clothes, but they had no relation to anything anyone else wore. She wasn't the least bit interested in being in style, but was just innately one of the most elegant people. She wasn't boastful." Diana was perplexed that her mother had no friends independent of her father, not even among the neighbors. And Diana could not ever feel the warmth she saw her friends sharing with their mothers. Her mother thought she was selfish. They shared no common ground, no hobbies or interests. Her mother had discouraged her even from reading because she thought her daughter would discover in books a life beyond the one her parents had provided her; reading might turn Diana from her family.

She took only two courses in literature at Radcliffe: a semester of Tolstoy and a yearlong course on romantic and Victorian poetry, taught by John Livingston Lowes, a Coleridge and Chaucer scholar. She wrote what she considered her best paper for him, a comparison between Swinburne's epic poem *Tristram of Lyonesse* and Matthew Arnold's narrative poem *Tristan and Iseult*. She later said that "contrary to Radcliffe habit" she did only a minimum of secondary reading but applied herself "diligently to the texts," adding that "the project strangely excited" her. She received only a C-minus for her work and said that when the paper was returned to her, "it looked like an illuminated manuscript, the margins were so richly decorated with the instructor's queries about my right to the opinion I expressed. 'Source?' he demanded. 'Source?'

'Source?' I should have written, 'Me,' under each of these queries and confronted the instructor with his implied charge that I was using without acknowledgment ideas that weren't my own, but I was unable to do this at the time."

She was troubled about the study habits of her fellow students, noting that "if the authorities saw the state the girls work themselves up to they would cut out exams altogether." She included herself, of course: "Studied all day for my Fine Arts exam. I'm simply crazy about that one, too. Honestly, these are the awfulest [sic] days I've ever lived through. A continual state of nervous strain. . . . Slept almost all morning. Studied all afternoon and evening until 12:20. It's a great life if you don't weaken. I'll be a wreck by the time these exams are over."

In general, she thought her education was much too focused on the historical instead of the critical, though she did learn to apply high standards to whatever she studied, most likely as a result of her membership in the Debating Society, where she argued her positions with a ferocious righteousness. She also knew from an early age that she had a capacity for abstract thought. Diana often drove friends and relatives mad with her unforgiving emphasis on logic, an attribute acquired partly as a response to her mother's habit of dodging the truth by telling white lies. So in her childhood, when her mother would announce, "there are no cookies," and Diana knew there was indeed a cupboard full of them, she would confront her mother, who would then respond, "Well, it doesn't make any difference if there are or are not any cookies; you can't have any." Such twists of logic drove young Diana into a frenzy. When her brother and sister went off to grade school, Diana, still at home, would "tag at her mother's heels" and ask, "Mama, what should I do?" Her mother would tell her with a straight face, "Put your head out of the window and holler, 'fire!'" That sort of treatment made her desperate, she recalled. As she grew up, she learned to calm herself by framing her world with logic—all words, phrases, sentences, and punctuation had to make the strictest sense, or she would be forced back into what she considered an irrational universe.

Diana managed to defy her mother by reading constantly. At a bookmobile near her summer camp, she had bought with her own money a volume of Rudyard Kipling's poems, the first book she had ever purchased. Her father liked to collect books and bought dozens of leatherbound volumes from a door-to-door salesman. But Diana was warned not to dirty them or wrinkle their pages and was told to wash her hands before touching them. With all these deterrents, she let the books—by Mark Twain, Balzac, Hugo, Moliere, and George Eliot, among others—remain in the family's two glass-fronted mahogany bookcases. (Her father dipped into them only occasionally.) Instead, Diana snuck copies of her brother Sam's Rover Boys books, an adventure series involving three brothers at a boarding school; the stories were full of antiauthoritarian pranks and mischief and often featured the latest turn-of-the-century inventions like cars and airplanes. At the local library she read George Barr McCutcheon's popular Gaustarkian romances (so named after a fictional country in Eastern Europe), stories that told of strange conspiracies among royalty. She read Mark Twain and came to know Louisa May Alcott's *Little Women* by heart. For what she called its "sexual excitation," she read the novel by Theophile Gautier *Mademoiselle de Maupin*—based on a colorful seventeenth-century singer and swordswoman. "Sex was volcanic in the mores of my girlhood," she added; "it roared its path over the virgin land." So Diana also read to discover what she had not yet discovered firsthand, or had heard about in her high school's Twenty-Nine Lessons in Home Hygiene, a course given by the American Red Cross. And then there was also the book her father had brought back for her brother and sister from The Battle Creek Sanitarium in Michigan, the institution run by Dr. J. H. Kellogg, the brother of the creator of corn flakes. Joseph Rubin had become a disciple, believing that the body needed proper diet and adequate exercise and that 90 percent of disease started in the stomach or bowels. For weeks he insisted that the family eat only dates, figs, olives, and nuts, until Mrs. Rubin put a stop to it.

The book her father had brought from Battle Creek, which Diana discovered and read in secret, was one she called "Sexology" but was actually titled *Plain Facts for Old and Young: Embracing the Natural History and Hygiene of Organic Life*, and it included twenty-five chapters with headings such as "Sexual Hygiene," "Unchastity," "The Social Evil,"

"Results of a Secret Vice," "Treatment for Self-Abuse and Its Effects," "Diseases Peculiar to Women," and "Diseases Peculiar to Men." She later said that its "compendium of horrors" made it "the blackest book I ever read" and that it "reflected the peculiar sexual misery" of her childhood. During her growing up, all aspects of sex were considered an area of medicine and, more specifically, of disease.

Diana worried that she'd become blind or insane from merely reading Dr. Kellogg's book. It bothered her even when her mother encouraged kissing games among her young friends. Was she trying to cause harm to her daughter and her friends?

Diana continued reading other books, and despite her father's conveying to her that criticism was "a sorcerer's art," she honed some early skills in a diary she kept in 1922, when she was seventeen. Filling in two sections at the end of the diary—"Books I Read" and "Remarks"—she had several things to say. Of John Galsworthy, who would win the Nobel Prize ten years later, she noted, "didn't finish it," not saying which of his books she meant, but most likely it was *The Forsyte Saga*. She wrote that Booth Tarkington was "fairly good," again not spelling out which books she had in mind—no doubt either *The Magnificent Ambersons*, which won a Pulitzer Prize in 1919, or *Alice Adams*, which won a Pulitzer in 1922. She said that Joseph Hergesheimer, cited in 1922 by *Literary Digest* as the most important American writer, was "disgusting but well-written." Stephen Vincent Benét, the poet, short-story writer, and novelist, she judged as producing "word pictures." Nothing more was pointed out.

Keeping a diary enabled Diana to record her thoughts frankly, spontaneously, and privately, in contrast to the often daunting formality she had to put up with at Radcliffe. In addition to the strict meals, where a change of clothes for dinner was the iron rule, the young women were served tea or coffee from ornate trays set up in the parlors of the dormitories. Some students even handed out printed calling cards to their professors. All dormitories had mandatory quiet hours. Amid such rituals the message was clear: the purpose of their education was only to "increase their domestic efficiency." Questions like "I'm asking you, what does a woman know what a man has to suffer in this world!"

were considered useless. The practical was the goal. Even though women had had the vote since the Nineteenth Amendment was ratified in 1920, "onward and upward" for Radcliffe women was only achievable with methodical skills applied to family and home.

The young women were even taught that instead of rinsing each plate separately when washing dishes, they were to stack them all together in a rack and rinse them with just a single pot of boiling water. Diana recalled that "to ease this chore, they were told to recite Shelley and Keats to themselves at the sink." She paid attention to this advice, just as she practiced the etiquette she was taught as a child. She had never rebelled against such guidelines; she continued to see them as leading her to a life of quiet dignity that she had begun to envision for herself. She had thought matters out for herself and decided that self-respect had been missing from her upbringing, despite her parents' focus on manners.

There was one minor rule Diana always ignored: students were required to wear hats when walking around Cambridge, but she and her two closest friends refused to do so. She even debated the issue in the college newspaper, although the classmate on the side of covered heads won the day. Still, Diana relished the chance to speak her mind or, in this case, to write publicly what was on her mind. It seemed natural that she would eventually be asked to cover college events as a stringer for a Boston newspaper; it was not her first such job: at Camp Lenore, a summer camp in the Berkshires on Lake Ashmere in Hinsdale, Massachusetts, that she had attended as a young girl, she had been the editor in chief of its small mimeographed weekly. In her senior year at Radcliffe Diana became an associate editor of the class yearbook.

But it was fine arts that interested her the most. The study of the visual seemed safer to her. Writing? Full of danger, no matter its pull on her. She could still sometimes hear her mother's admonition about reading, too. Nevertheless, it was at Erasmus High School that she first learned to tune out her mother. In high school Diana had been what she called "a cultural yearner." She and some classmates had formed an all-girls club to read poetry—Sara Teasdale, Amy Lowell, and one or two of Diana's own attempts. They listened to classical music and opera while smoking cigarettes and drinking a combination of ginger ale and grape juice they were told could make them tipsy. The club also took a small political step, organizing a new party that ran an African American boy for class president. Although he lost, his candidacy made a bold statement in 1919 Brooklyn, the same year race riots broke out in twenty-six cities across America.

At Radcliffe Diana didn't show much interest in politics, although she once "ushered at a Bolshevist meeting but only stayed about half an hour." She later joined the Liberal Club. She also joined the Dramatics Club, where she was once cast as a wooden pole in *The Tempest* (she decided she was not offered a speaking part because she was Jewish).

Diana had her first glimpse of war when she and her family were traveling in Germany in 1914, right before the beginning of World War I. Diana was nine, her brother twelve, and her sister fourteen. Around this time Diana decided she couldn't survive without a middle name so she let people think that her full name was Diana Deeana Rubin. She'd tell anyone who would listen. The family had almost been stranded in Berlin during a summer vacation Mr. Rubin insisted must not be cancelled, no matter what the stirrings in the world. It was a charged time; everyone was on edge until Mr. Rubin decided they should return home. He had trouble getting them passage to New York, spending several days canvassing steamship lines, until he finally managed to get them on a train that would take them to Holland and to a connection in Liverpool on a ship called *Olympic*. Diana and her siblings wore tiny American flags in their buttonhole to show their neutrality. The train ride was a misery after Joseph Rubin left their carriage to get his family some sandwiches from a station vendor and misjudged the length of the stop. The train chugged off apparently without him. Diana, the youngest, was in a panic. She badly needed to use the bathroom but was afraid to leave the compartment, so she waited, as she had trained herself to do at home in Brooklyn because she was afraid to go upstairs to the bathroom on the unlit second floor of their house. Mrs. Rubin, who was left without money or the family's single passport, tried to charm the conductor into helping them until he promised that at the next station he would send a telegram to the American embassy. Meanwhile, Diana and her brother tried to console themselves by continuing their new game of talking in pretend German. Mrs. Rubin stood by the open door of their compartment. She would not sit down. Suddenly, Mr. Rubin entered the car with his arms full of paper bags filled with sausages and beer. He explained that he had been on the train all along but had missed the entrance to their car when he got back on and had had to jump quickly onto the nearest empty one, which happened to be at the rear of the train. The episode left Diana with the nascence of what would much later evolve into a multitude of phobias. Fear of abandonment was high on a long list. Yet the experience also saw the emergence of a youthful political conscience, which would not fully blossom until she was a young adult.

Diana remembered a nun who rode in their compartment showing the family two bullets she had hidden in her long black vestment; one was blunt, the other sharp, and she told the children that "the sharp bullet was Allied and merciful and the German bullet slow, designed to torture." The crossing to America was particularly stressful because the ship was blacked-out to prevent a submarine attack.

Once safely home, Diana and her grade-school friends at PS 99 in Brooklyn knitted scarves and filled books with thrift stamps. These stamp albums marked the beginning of a lifelong fascination with such ledgers.

On many Saturday mornings she went with her father to his factory, where she helped wind braid. She saved walnut pits, which she was told were needed to produce the material for a special kind of mask for soldiers. All these combat-related activities, nerve-racking for most people, brought the young and fearful Diana an unexpected happiness. It was "the last and best carnival of a long holiday season," she later wrote, adding that as peculiar as it seemed, and probably because she was far, far from the battlefields, she was not afraid of the bloodshed. But it would still be years before her political conscience would awaken her into action.

By the end of the war, fourteen-year-old Diana—dressed in dark cotton stockings, flat shoes, a navy middy-blouse, and pleated skirt, her long hair cascading down her back, her face plastered with spit curls on her cheeks, and a speck of black paper pasted at the corner of one eye to fashion a beauty spot—had begun to show a daredevil side. She discov-

ered the relative safety of flirting. She put Dr. Kellogg's book aside. She
and her girlfriends would rent a flat-bottom boat in Brooklyn's Prospect
Park Lake and pick up boys by rowing close to—and sometimes even
ramming—boats filled with suitable young men. A year later, after sup-
per, she began sneaking out of the house in the dark to walk along Ocean
Parkway to try to pick up men. At her summer camp, where she eventually became a counselor, Diana and a friend hitched a ride on their day
off with two young men who stopped their car for them. The boys had
more than friendship on their minds. Diana and her friend managed to
jump out of the car when the driver stopped for gas, and they ran to seek
shelter in a nearby car; its middle-aged occupants quickly understood
their dilemma and drove them back to the camp.

Radcliffe turned her into a prude, and she suffered what she characterized as "acute sexual embarrassments," even during the birth of some
kittens belonging to the house mistress's cat that everyone had assumed
was a male. The scene in her dormitory also brought back distressing
memories of the time a maid had killed, on orders of her mother, the
kittens of the family cat, Doncie, because she had decided to give birth
on the regal dining room rug. The maid had crushed the tiny beings
with a thick, long-handled kitchen broom, a sight and sound Diana said
she never forgot. While she was still in grade school she had joined the
Society for the Prevention of Cruelty to Animals after a teacher had
passed out buttons for the group. She found the will and the means to
confront her mother. "Now I can have you arrested," Diana said to her
mother, who laughed in her face.

A Radcliffe dorm mate who had married in her junior year was not
allowed back because, as the dean told the other young women, the new
bride had now had "the most important experience in a woman's life"
and would be subject to inappropriate questioning. Diana began to be
haunted again by the memory of Dr. Kellogg's book and did what many
of the other girls did to avoid thinking about sex: they overate. Between
regular meals they had such snacks as egg-salad sandwiches and hot
fudge sundaes with whipped cream, which they prepared in the dormitory's kitchenette. "Our concern with food was more compelling than
our concern with ideas," Diana said. "It was our sexual appetite we were

trying to appease." The body held danger. Be very careful, Diana had once read, a warning she had now thoroughly absorbed. At her summer camp when she once complained that she had a pain in her side, the nurse told her she had a strained ovary. The young camper had no idea what an ovary was.

When Diana was twenty-one, she had a disturbing encounter when one of her mother's admirers, a friend of her father's, followed her into a coatroom, where he assaulted her and ripped her dress apart before she managed to escape. Years later she realized that this attack was an underlying reason for her despondency after graduation. It was not only her mother's death that year or her fear of independence that caused her depression. It was also the sexual molestation by her father's friend. Who could she trust? she asked herself.

She had not felt freed by her mother's death; instead, she found herself bewildered. She was a year out of college, and lost. She had stayed in bed nearly every day and rarely dressed when she did get up. Nothing could rouse her, not even the chance to join some Radcliffe classmates at a movie theater in Times Square to see *Don Juan*, starring John Barrymore, the first feature film to use the Vitaphone sound system, in which a phonograph record played as the movie was being projected.

The grand apartment on West End Avenue, which she hated for being pretentious, and was embarrassed to give as her address, held little of interest that she could see. Despite being the first college graduate in her family, she saw no future for herself. She felt trapped, although one thing gave her some solace: books. She later wrote that "my escape into the world of fiction saved me."

After her depression lifted, Diana resolved to change the course of her life dramatically. She would forget trying to be an art historian. Instead, she would study to become a singer—an opera singer, in fact—and her stage would certainly not be one built in a toilet, as her father ("a little Napoleon," she sometimes called him) had dismissively predicted. She surprised even herself with her new choice. The day before her mother died, she had been asked to sing to her in what Diana called her mother's "last bid for continuing life." Diana sang very softly—in a tiny whisper— as her mother listened, and though she said she never "found a path" to her mother, on her deathbed she had. She found an idea for a career.

Diana's college diary gave her a needed emotional outlet—one that reflected a side of her personality she could never show at home. When a fellow student tried to commit suicide, Diana at first wrote calmly about it, deciding it must have been an accident when she was cleaning a gun, but then she conceded that "I was so scared I couldn't fall asleep." She was afraid that she, too, would attempt suicide. Still, several pages later, she scribbled that she was "rather in love with my French professor, a dear." So much for lingering suicidal thoughts. She confessed to being miserable when her best friend got engaged. She described the clothes a blind date was wearing, adding, "I don't know whether he's wild or not. I didn't know what kind of line to give him." She noted that someone else had called her for a date and given her different names. She cut another suitor "dead" when she passed him in Harvard Square, said that still another had "abominable table manners," and claimed another made her "sick. He's such a baby." Still another "bought a bag of gumdrops which he ate in the street. Ugh!" A week or so later she concluded "no more blind dates for me."

Diana also admitted, "There are so few people here whom I care a snap about." She mostly meant boys. She often dated a "Joe," whom she didn't like very much, writing that "he held my hand and put his arm around me, which ruined everything. Men. So damn stupid, I feel nothing but contempt." Still, she told her Radcliffe friends that the kind of man she wanted to marry would have to equally love "tea-dancing" at the Plaza Hotel and sitting in the top balcony at Carnegie Hall. Where could she find such a person, someone she could also trust and pin her hopes on?

2

UNDERTAKINGS

Tonite met Diana. Disliked her at first but even in dislike I felt attracted. She is perhaps the first girl whose being in my arms made me feel triumphant and joyous. Perhaps this is because she is aware of and admits her body and because she has the mechanical trick of being able to talk about anything—risqué jokes etc. We sat and drank but sobered to rationality and there was real tenderness and grace between us. She is the first woman I have actually and unmistakably desired and the first woman the taste [sic] whose kisses was not afterwards perplexing and obnoxious. Hers are somehow still sweet and tempting.

—LIONEL TRILLING, JOURNAL ENTRY, CHRISTMAS 1927

A year after her mother's death, Diana accepted the kind of date with which she said she was finished: a blind date. A friend from high school, Pauline ("Polly") Elizabeth Rush, and her new husband, Clifton Fadiman, known as "Kip," thought it would be amusing if only "for the sheer joy of euphony," to get a "Di" and a "Li" together. Polly told Diana she couldn't wait to see what would happen.

The foursome met at Mario's, an atypical speakeasy in the west forties of Manhattan situated in a shabby brownstone that had once been a
boardinghouse. The hideaway nightclub was unusual because it also
contained a popular family-style Italian restaurant, so even though
there was a peephole in the front door in order for the owner to know
exactly who he was selling his illegal liquor to, everyone who knocked
on the door was allowed to enter. The liquor served at Mario's was considered safe by its frequenters, unlike the tainted alcohol served at other,
more furtive, places around the city. The night "Di" and "Li" met—
Christmas Eve, 1927—they weren't there for the spaghetti and meatballs
but just for the Bullfrogs, a drink made of gin, apricot brandy, and gren-
adine. And they had plenty of them.

Liquor had never been kept away from Diana or her siblings. Even as
children they were allowed sips, and generally more than sips, an odd
practice in such a strict household. (Lionel Trilling's parents were not
drinkers at all, except for the sweet wine served at their Passover table.)
When Diana was at Radcliffe, her mother once sent her a roast chicken
along with a "flask" of gravy (but whiskey was actually in the flask).
Mailing a cooked chicken from New York to Massachusetts was bizarre
enough, but adding liquor? Diana said she never understood her parents' relaxed attitude toward alcohol. She quickly buried the container
in her underwear drawer; if it became known what she was hiding, she
could have been expelled. (She eventually tossed it into the trash, and it
remained her secret.)

Diana had continued to be listless for a year after her mother's death;
she called her state "a crisis of being," although she had decided to
change careers. That decision had made her life seem more organized,
although she was enervated and unable to proceed with further plans.
But creating a semblance of order always served her well. Socially, she
had no dates until the Fadimans suggested one. She'd go; perhaps getting out would help lift her blues.

Both Diana Rubin and Lionel Trilling were twenty-two when they
met. After their first date, which lasted until twenty minutes before
midnight, Diana and Polly left Mario's (the men stayed on) to go to

St. Patrick's church a few blocks north on Fifth Avenue between Fiftieth and Fifty-First Streets to attend the midnight Christmas service. Polly was more intent on the religious service than was her childhood friend, who went along for the spectacle. Diana later said that she was embarrassed by Polly's genuflecting, which she thought was not only going on too long but also not being done correctly. She hoped that Polly wasn't going to try to pass as a gentile, or even act like one, as so many of her Jewish friends at Radcliffe did. Her irritation grew, because she wanted to return to Mario's to spend more time with her date, even though Polly divulged on the walk over to the church that she and Kip didn't think Diana and Lionel would like each other. Diana tried and tried to get Polly to hurry up. It seemed that she was always demanding something of Polly and occasionally teased her to get her way. In school, when Diana sat behind her in class, she would dip Polly's long blonde hair in her inkwell. "I wanted awfully to be blonde," Diana later admitted. She'd try at least to make Polly's curls more like her darker hair.

Drinking and more drinking would soon become a ritual for Di and Li. They would alternate between Bullfrogs and Alexanders, a cocktail of gin, crème de cacao, and whipped cream. "We drank these liquid desserts before meals and again after meals, through long evenings," Diana later said. Because of her family's attitude toward drinking, she felt free to arrive back at West End Avenue thoroughly drunk. One evening she, Lionel, and the Fadimans returned to the Rubin apartment and raided Joseph Rubin's preprohibition liquor closet, to which his youngest daughter had the key. She put every available bottle on her family's round dining room table, and the foursome took a taste from each one. Mr. Rubin walked in on them in the midst of this "undertaking," as Diana later called it, adding that her father "was very charming about it. He said, 'tsk, tsk,' and walked out."

Diana's sister, Cecilia, who was also living at home, and would be for most of her life, had a slight curvature of the spine regarded by the family as a considerable handicap (and they always let her know). She also suffered from Tourette's syndrome, although the disorder was not correctly diagnosed until she was an adult. But she grimaced much of the time, made peculiar noises, and moved her hands and arms in an erratic, convulsive manner. Lionel later noted in his journal that she was "an ugly caricature of Diana and that she frightened him."

During the late-night drinking episodes of her younger sister, Cecilia was usually asleep in their shared bedroom. Despite her impairment, she was able to help in all the housekeeping duties (there was only a part-time maid). Both young women tried to make things as pleasant as possible for their widowed father, even though they would fight and even bite and scratch each other almost daily. (Such contentiousness continued into their middle age, despite odd moments of tenderness and generosity between them through the years, starting when Diana became frightened at night in one of the Westchester houses and her sister comforted her. In 1921 Mr. Rubin insisted that Cecilia accompany Diana to Radcliffe to make sure she settled in properly and contentedly.)

Soon after his wife's death, Joseph Rubin thought of moving his family to a new apartment because West End Avenue held too many sad memories. Diana offered to help find a new home and in fact found one she thought would be perfect. It was in Gramercy Park, was large but still unusually cozy, and even had a fireplace in the living room. But Mr. Rubin thought it was too expensive, although Diana knew that was not the real reason he turned it down. She decided that her father was made uncomfortable by the offbeat neighborhood—that it was not suitably middle class. The family remained on sedate West End Avenue.

The Rubins always had a full-time maid and, because of it, the children were slightly spoiled. Mary, the maid, was Polish like their parents, and Polish was the only language spoken at home until Mr. Rubin returned from his factory, when they all shifted to English. (He did not speak Polish, just Yiddish. He wanted English to be the only language of his family. Still, his children became bilingual at early ages.)

Diana's brother, Sam, who had flunked out of Cornell—he had partied too much at his fraternity and had passed a few bad checks his father hadn't authorized—was working in the braid factory and also briefly living at home, although he had no particular household responsibilities. He was about to get married. Despite her brother's scholastic failure, Diana considered him "very, very brilliant. He had an extraordinary power of organizing," she said. He was a complicated young man, more interested in status and show than anything else. "He wanted recognition as a power person," Diana later wrote, adding that he manifested a "never-to-be-conquered rage" that began when their mother "disappeared" for several months when Sam was three and Cecilia five. Years later Diana found out that her mother had had a nervous breakdown soon after she was born, a circumstance that would help explain some of Mrs. Rubin's peculiar feelings toward her youngest daughter.

In high school, where Sam ran with the so-called fast crowd, he often passed Diana in the halls without acknowledging that he knew her, and he called himself "Stanley Roberts" to avoid being known as a Jew. (Later in life he converted to Presbyterianism.) And although his relationship with his younger sister was always thorny and aggressive, in their later years he showed moments of empathy. Diana would write that while she turned complex, knotty emotions into phobias and illness, her brother just wove his frustrations and anger into the "fabric of his character."

A few months after meeting Lionel, Diana accompanied her father and Cecilia on a two-month business trip to South America. Diana was never sure what business her father had that kept them away from home for so long, but she thought it had something to do with steamship business with W. R. Grace & Co., which owned a line of freighters running from New York to various ports in South America. Some of these ships had passenger service. The Rubins traveled in such an ocean liner; it could not navigate shallow harbors, so the three of them would be taken ashore in a large motorboat. Diana later wrote that "early each morning, in Peru and Chile, in Buenos Aires, in Rio, promptly after he'd have his breakfast, my father would take off in his search for Jewish names on storefronts." He was looking for "connections between these wanderers in strange lands and their relations in New York, Troy, Mobile, any or everywhere in the United States." She knew these side trips weren't part of his main business, but what else he was doing and why, she never understood.

Although Joseph Rubin was no longer a practicing Orthodox Jew, he observed special holidays like Rosh Hashanah, Yom Kippur, and

Passover with his family, and Diana remarked years later that her childhood Seders never had any "festive spirit." These Seders were held in the small, dingy apartment that belonged to a paternal aunt, in the Brownsville section of Brooklyn, a mostly Jewish area. The rooms, with the smell of garlic permeating the air, felt like a foreign country to the young Diana. Her aunt spoke no English, just Yiddish. She had arrived in America before her brother Joseph, along with her father and two other brothers, all of whom remained Orthodox. Joseph was the only renegade. Diana learned to understand what she called "a primitive Yiddish"—as well as "a primitive German—by guesswork and association."

She took great pleasure in her paternal grandfather, who had once been in the millinery business. She said that his broad shoulders and heavy beard made her think of Moses as depicted in the stained glass window of a temple in New Rochelle. But he was not demonstrative with his grandchildren, never hugging or kissing them. When he would visit them, he refused to sit at their non-kosher table; instead, he would sit away from them, eating a tomato, sardines, and a large chunk of rye bread served to him on a cut-glass plate. He would use his own pocketknife to lift the sardines from their can. (Although Campbell soups were readily available in all the New York food stores, canned foods were still a relatively new concept, and Diana's mother did not trust anything in a can and never used them.)

Even though Joseph Rubin considered himself basically nonreligious, when the family moved to Brooklyn, Diana started attending Sunday school (and was confirmed at twelve). Her father even became a board member of the school. Still, she was the only one of her friends not to have Chanukah lights, or even to receive presents. (She concocted a list, though, telling friends that a new pair of shoes or even basic white socks or an ordinary petticoat were gifts.) There was also no Christmas tree. But at Radcliffe she had attended temple from time to time. ("It was lovely," she wrote in her diary, noting that during the High Holy Days, she "fasted all day.")

Diana said that she was raised as "an American who also happened to be a Jew." Her religion was always "a source of self-respect and moral incentive," she said with pride. This fierce and passionate attitude would allow her to accept with ease and pleasure the devout religious rituals that she would soon observe at Lionel Trilling's kosher home, where candles were lit every Friday night.

Writing in his journal, shortly after meeting Diana, Lionel remarked that "I forgot to mention the very amusing fact that last night one of the most dominant components of my emotion with Diana was her Jewishness. I was conscious of it in my arms—and liked it." At some later point he reflected that "being a Jew is like walking in the wind or swimming; you are touched at all points and conscious everywhere." On this the young couple would always agree.

Diana never questioned her father about his search for Jewish names when they were in South America. Her thoughts were elsewhere. She and her sister spent much of their time exploring and sightseeing by themselves. They had no chaperone. They wandered the streets, and sometimes Diana went off with young men she had met on the ship. "I started to pick up all sorts of odd characters," she admitted. Years later she said that "these men I was going around with were always being measured against somebody waiting in New York."

She meant, of course, Lionel Trilling.

Diana kept a travel diary in which she frequently tried out political ideas, theories she had never examined while at Radcliffe. But during the trip, revolution was on her mind, even though it had been ten years since the Russian Revolution and nine since the end of World War I. A civil war was going on in China, one that would last for decades, and she heard details about it from her father and people they met on the ship. But her father—who always freely discussed his progressive and other views in front of her, and was at heart a frustrated political commentator—was her main guide. (The only magazine he subscribed to was *Political Science Quarterly*, started in 1886 by a Columbia University professor, John W. Burgess.) Joseph Rubin talked about the French Revolution being a middle-class revolution, not a proletarian one at all. He spoke of the Cossacks raiding the Jewish shops and apartments in Warsaw when he was a boy and how perilous his life had been and how fearful he was of the Cossacks' military prowess. Diana's father, in favor of a socialist state, told her he had seen enough anti-Semitism to last a lifetime. All the same, he was opposed to fighting: Jews used their brains, not weapons. Still, Diana wrote in her diary, "we will gain nothing by revolution. Revolution means reaction and counter-revolution. We must feed the corruption—irritate the festering pores of society—until we eat ourselves up. At the expense of the people? Yes, the people are poisoning the lives of their children's children. They must be destroyed. We will create for these children a new life—out of chaos will come a new creation." Her father's influence was a forceful one. Words were becoming her bullets.

Much of the time on the South American trip, Diana had worried she would never see Lionel again. She had been thoroughly enjoying their budding friendship, even though she was concerned that she wasn't literary enough for him or that he wasn't, as she later put it, "sufficiently solid" for her. She meant "rich." (Joseph Rubin, worried about the financial future of his daughters, had once joined a golf club specifically to find wealthy husbands for them.)

Lionel's father, David, had been a tailor who became a not particularly shrewd manufacturer of fur coats for men. The family was not well-off but always had just enough money—they had a part-time maid and at one time a full-time one—until the stock market crash in 1929. David was the son of a rabbi and had come to America from Bialystok when he was just thirteen. The story was that he was sent away because he had shamed the family by messing up his Bar Mitzvah speech. But in America there were no such blunders; he read books and found a wife who read books, a woman who, in fact, remembered the details of every volume she read. They read poetry to each other every night, not at all like Diana Rubin's parents.

David Trilling was "a splendid dancer," Diana was told, although by the time she met him, he had given it up, as he had swimming. "He wouldn't have gone near cold water," so extreme had his anxiety about his health become.

One of Lionel's bachelor maternal uncles, Hymie, was a rich enough lawyer to own paintings by Picasso, Modigliani, and Cezanne. (Some were bartered for legal work; others he "bought cheaply at auctions," Diana said.) With two other lawyer brothers, Larry, also a bachelor, and

Izzy, who was married, Hymie owned a sixty-six-foot sloop called the *Zinita*, with which the young Lionel seemed obsessed and had even hoped one day to write about. Lionel, as the oldest nephew, was in line to inherit his uncle's fortune.*

When Lionel Trilling met Diana Rubin, he was a part-time instructor at Hunter College. After receiving his master's degree in literature from Columbia University in 1926 (he graduated with honors the year before), he began a yearlong teaching fellowship at the University of Wisconsin. In 1924, as an undergraduate, he had begun keeping a journal soon after publishing his first poem, "Old Legend; New Style," in *The Morningside*, Columbia's literary magazine, where he also published an essay on Emily Brontë's poetry. In 1925 he and some college friends began publishing essays and stories in the *Menorah Journal*, an English-language American-Jewish magazine begun in 1915. He published book reviews, essays, and short stories there for the next six years. His friend Kip, who also graduated from Columbia in 1925 (although he was a year older), had been an English teacher at the Ethical Culture School in New York, and then in 1927, when he and Polly introduced Lionel to the woman he would eventually marry, Kip had become a junior editor at a new publishing company, Simon and Schuster.

Diana recalled that at the time she was fixed up with Lionel, "Kip was already not exactly a loyal husband. In those days most of us didn't of course believe in sexual conformity. We'd have thought, or half thought, that conventional marital loyalty was retrograde." Kip later told Diana that "sex was amusing in those days because it was so difficult." He meant, she said, that the places to have it were hard to come by. Diana remarked that up to that time, "necking was the great sexual activity of our period."

Diana often went out on what she called "nonromantic" dates with Kip, even though she was also seeing Lionel. It didn't seem to matter that

---

* Diana later said that Uncle Hymie's art collection (if it actually existed) was so secret that no one knew about it, and none of it was ever shown in galleries or museums. She said also that because he didn't buy most of the pieces from dealers, there are no records pertaining to them.

Kip was married to her close friend. She later conceded that "it never occurred to me to think that wasn't a nice thing to do because I knew that Polly was doing the same thing with somebody else." Diana would also go out to lunch every now and then with Lionel's college friend Henry Rosenthal, and Lionel would have lunch with Henry's wife, Rachel, although one time Diana became jealous and decided to make an appearance at their scheduled lunch date. Lionel mentioned in his journal that "the other night, I having said that before marriage I felt I could have any woman though now I do not, Rachel turned to me and said very downrightly, 'I could never have loved you,' and went on for several minutes explaining that Henry was hard—'all elbows'—and I was soft etc. Was this revenge for my sexual indifference to her?"

Diana said that when she and Lionel "were married and technically faithful, we flirted with each other's husbands and wives. . . . We were hovering around the bed rather than hopping into it." Flirting was refreshing and safe, and talk about sex, which went on constantly, was standard; "we were conversational sex maniacs," she quipped many years later.

While living in Madison, Wisconsin, Lionel hardly dated at all, although his journal mentions one woman "whose acquaintance was an experience compensatory for the year." In another entry he refers to a second woman very briefly on a list of twenty-one items of "'Madison Memorabilia: 5. Alice's face. 6. Alice's hands.'" The next entry reads like fiction: "in the afternoon he gave a good class, spurred to vivacity by the fact that she had come to listen. . . . Later he met her, took her to tea, then lazed in a canoe. . . . Her scent still clung to his nostrils, his lips were a little bruised. . . . She had been even more passionate than he—yet she could laugh more readily. He was gently glad for all the kisses. His arms were grateful for her slenderness, and he could feel burning intermittently the spot on his neck she had kissed. . . . Yet she was not what he wanted."

Whether the woman who caused Lionel's bruised lips was real or not, at the time, writing fiction was on his mind much more than women. Still, the very next journal entry reads: "He who is afraid of love worships virginity in women." He would soon show no such fear. Diana and Lionel would be considered by their friends—mostly her Radcliffe friends—daring for their background and time, even though it would be more than two years before they slept together; still, they would be the first to do so before marriage, Diana said. (They used the apartment belonging to Henry and Rachel Rosenthal.) "I had not only been terrified that my father would discover what we were doing," Diana said, "but I suffered a sense of sin—I differentiate this from guilt, with which I was also burdened." Dr. Kellogg hovered nearby.

When Diana had returned from her lengthy South American trip, a package was waiting for her at the dock. It had arrived too late to be given to her before she and her family set sail. It was a bon voyage present (an established custom at the time whenever a friend or relative was leaving on a trip) from Lionel: Stendhal's *The Charterhouse of Parma*. She later wrote about the gift: "Lionel had begun my literary education." In fact, before 1927 she had never heard of Stendhal, not even at Radcliffe.

As his parents had done for each other, Lionel would sometimes read poetry to Diana. One evening he read her T. S. Eliot's *The Waste Land*, which Diana said she didn't understand in a way she could explain. Her logic failed her. But because Lionel read the poem so well, its meaning came through to her. He had an extraordinary ability to illuminate words and ideas by his very demeanor. "I loved Lionel's seriousness and I wanted to be serious, too," she later wrote. Aside from her father, she had never met anyone with a mind as bright and creative as Lionel's—she was sure he possessed genius. And because of his guidance, she was learning to believe in her intuition, as well as in a future with Lionel.

Lionel was not as confident at first. Despite observing that Diana "had the mechanical trick of being able to talk about anything," he later wrote in his journal: "Note on D after seeing her at dinner: she is still desirable, simply, and a splendid woman; also I suppose is a more or less educated and sophisticated woman, idiosyncratic etc. But evidently not much beyond that. Her body is lovely to touch but her laugh and her voice irritate me and her talk does not stimulate but rather represses, although I do not think her stupid but rather lazy."

Lionel's family of avid readers, especially his doting mother, Fannie Cohen Trilling, always had considerable literary aspirations for him.

When he was just six years old, his mother told him he would go to Oxford for his PhD, and she made sure he would remain healthy until that time—every single day he had the same lunch: a lamb chop and a baked potato served with milk at just the right warm temperature. When Lionel went off to summer camp for the first time, his mother and her two spinster sisters, Deborah and Della—a third sister, Maude, did not join them—moved to a nearby boardinghouse to keep an eye on him. Fannie Trilling, born in London, used to part her young son's hair on the right side so he would look like the Prince of Wales. Lionel wore a coat made of squirrel fur his father made specially for him. He would never be cold. As a child he read compulsively, while dressing and undressing, at meals when he was alone, and in bed at night with a flashlight. He was always treated as an only child, although he had a sister, Harriet, who was seven years younger. (While Diana's relationship with Harriet would often be very rocky, she later wrote that her sister-in-law was "more intelligent than anyone she knew in the academic world.")

Fannie Trilling was not pleased that her son had gone off for a year to a teaching fellowship in Wisconsin; she had wanted him to stay in New York, where they lived on Central Park West and 108th street. Five years earlier, in 1921, even though Lionel had preferred Yale over Columbia, his mother had gone to the dean at Columbia to beg for her son's acceptance because his record in math at DeWitt Clinton High School did not point toward the bright future she knew was before him.

"He had a fierce mind, a fierce intelligence," Diana said. "He pressed hard, hard, hard on any idea that he dealt with, trying to force it to yield up its meaning." She was thrilled with his mind's complexity, even awed by it. Fannie Cohen Trilling once told her daughter-in-law, "the one thing I'll never forgive you for, Diana, is if you do anything to interfere with Lionel's career." Diana knew that would never happen. She'd see to it.

Radcliffe tamped down any early feminist stirrings in most of its students—women could talk all they wanted, as long as they remembered their place. Women were to be wives first. Men needed to put their careers first, even when the women in their lives were more competent. Diana later said that "the women in my father's family . . . had their fates made for them by men who had nothing but their sex to recommend them as providers" and that this had been communicated to her when she was very young through "weary contempt" by her female relatives "for the husbands to whom they were bound." Observing this "contempt," she concluded, would be "the roots of such feminism as I would always profess."

Diana's 1927 and 1928 engagement books, which she religiously maintained and stored away safely (especially after her sister burned her first collection of scrapbooks and vouchers), record many dates with Lionel: "Lionel here"; "Lionel at Polly's house"; "Theatre with Lionel—formal clothes"; "Tea with Lionel"; "Lionel here to lunch and tea"; "all afternoon and eve with Lionel." She documented the life-threatening scarlet fever Lionel contracted shortly after her return from South America.

The engagement books also record her schedule for singing lessons, for which she said her father refused to pay. Her father—despite everything—had always encouraged his girls to earn a living in case the men in their lives failed them. Nonetheless, Joseph Rubin did give Diana a generous weekly allowance. But soon after returning from South America, Diana found a job through a Radcliffe friend with the National Broadcasting Company as an assistant to a writer-producer of a radio program called *The Gold Spot Pals*. The "pals" were a group of children who, along with a singing policeman and an organ grinder with a monkey, went on walking adventures all around New York City, from Coney Island to the tip of the Bronx, to advertise their durable "Gold Spot" leather shoe soles. Diana babysat the child actors, and the job paid enough for her to have two singing lessons a week, as well as to have some fun. She said that she "met some of the men that were around the radio station and that I'd go out to parties with them—these were pretty much drinking parties."

Without her father knowing, Diana could have used her allowance for some of her lessons, but she acknowledged that the real reasons she went to work (aside from following his work ethic dictate) were to force herself out of the apartment, to get away from her sister, and to prove that she was not emotionally dependent on her family. The latter would be the hardest of all for her to do, although she succeeded in making her sister think she had. But in truth the only real independence she showed was in her diary or in some of the other writing—stories and poems—with which she toyed halfheartedly, where she could be as brave as she dared. She was even able to overcome her father's latest way of expressing disapproval—silence. And when not silent, he sometimes spoke too much. His arrogance had become worse than ever since his wife's death. If Diana asked what he thought of a particular dress she was wearing to work, he might shout, "You look dreadful." Diana began to rationalize that such insults were her father's way of expressing love, and as she later wrote, "The communication of love by insult is a very Jewish trait."

The page in Diana's engagement book for Tuesday, December 4, 1928, just one year after she met Lionel, notes: "Lionel calling for me at studio."

She had invited him to hear her sing.

When she first began her lessons, her teacher suggested that she concentrate only on opera. Despite her certainty in switching careers to singing, Diana wasn't certain about this direction; however, after she learned that Lionel loved opera, her choice became clear. She practiced every day until sweat covered her whole body. She worked harder than she ever had in her life. Her teacher told her she got goose pimples up and down her spine just listening to Diana's voice and that her talent was extraordinarily strong and sensitive. Soon Diana even risked showing off, as her parents had called it (although inexplicably, as a young girl, they liked her to perform—singing as well as playing piano or violin—in front of relatives). All three siblings took piano and violin lessons. Diana was the only one who sang.

Diana discovered she liked an audience, even an audience of one or two. At her summer camp she had often serenaded her bunkmates with Russian folk songs, and at Radcliffe she would frequently sing for her dormmates.

Lionel was thoroughly pleased—and a little surprised—by his girlfriend's talent. She was not just a run-of-the-mill entertainer for her family—a nineteenth-century-style social entertainer. She had professional skill. (Lionel's sister had a good voice, too, but not on Diana's level.) Diana was exhilarated by his response, and when she later told her teacher what he had said, the reaction was not what she expected to hear. Her teacher was very put out. She finally calmed down enough to ask Diana why in the world she needed the approval of a boyfriend. Diana burst into tears, because she knew her teacher had recognized her pupil's "indefensible dependency," as Diana later called it.

How would that dependency affect a future with Lionel? Would she be able to curb the tendency, even though she did her best to hide it with a determined—often gritty—attitude?

She would meet his family and he hers. Joseph Rubin had met Lionel casually when he came to pick up Diana on West End Avenue or came to tea. But they had not had a long or meaningful encounter.

A year after their first date at Mario's, Lionel invited Diana to his family's Passover Seder. She later said that she could remember every detail of that evening, including what she wore—"a lovely, lovely dress"—although its description went no further.

As she entered the Trilling apartment and walked into the living room, she was introduced to all the maternal aunts and uncles by Lionel's mother, who seemed ill at ease. Diana walked silently past the relatives, all of whom turned their backs on her. "I traveled the room without one person holding out a hand to me," she later said. What had she done wrong?

Lionel said nothing, so Diana followed suit, and they sat quietly at the Seder table, although not next to each other. The Seder service went on and on, with no one looking at or addressing her. She was not asked to read any passages from the Passover Hagaddah. She did not yet exist for them.

But once Fannie Trilling realized her son was serious about "the bold-featured" (as she called her) young woman she believed might be a potential heiress, and even before the couple announced their engagement, she started to plan their wedding. Actually she had her fifteen-year-old daughter, Harriet, do some of her early bidding. If Fannie Trilling couldn't put a halt to her son's relationship, at least she'd try to control it. So there were arguments about the guest list, and eventually it was decided that only the immediate family would be present. She hectored Diana even about her trousseau; her son must sleep on only pure linen sheets, and Diana, with unusual bravado, told her she planned to buy the cheapest sheets she could find. By now Diana had learned that Lionel's father had always liked her and had in fact been taken with her at first sight but had been shy in expressing his feelings at the Seder. Diana found out also that the Trillings rarely spoke to each other anymore. There was no more poetry between them.

Diana's introduction to Lionel's family was similar to her introduction to his *Menorah Journal* friends. "I'd never known people who were educated but had such bad manners," she said. "They treated me like dirt." In fact they thought Lionel's choice of a wife looked too well-to-do because she was wearing such striking clothes, including a fur coat.

As for Lionel's more thorough introduction to her family, Diana said that from the very beginning her father hadn't "liked or disliked Lionel." She later said they just could never reach each other. "Two dammed fools can't get married," he exclaimed at one point. Joseph Rubin would have preferred that his daughter marry someone like Kip, who was involved with books and made a decent living. But an English instructor who wanted to write novels? And in what Diana referred to as his "most fatherly remark," her father told his daughter that her intended needed to have his kidneys checked because he went to the bathroom far too often. Diana did not reveal that Lionel did so to escape conversations with his future father-in-law. Diana found it impossible to describe Lionel's qualities to her father—"his power of person and mind"—so she stopped trying. She always felt that in their early years, she alone had recognized Lionel's promising future.

Surprisingly, Diana's brother, Sam, and his new wife made no comments about Lionel. But Cecilia did. She took Lionel aside to warn him that her baby sister had a big appendix scar. Indeed, while at Radcliffe Diana had had an emergency operation, and her mother, in her one and only visit to the college, had come to minister to her daughter when she was recuperating. Diana's main memory of this unusual visit was that her mother wore an exquisite hand-pleated black chiffon dress, one of the most striking dresses she had ever seen in Boston or Cambridge.

On another occasion, while Lionel was waiting in the Rubin living room for a date with Diana that didn't involve drinking (once they decided to marry they resolved to cut back on their consumption because marriage was a solemn business), Cecilia had even more to say to her future brother-in-law. When Diana appeared after ten minutes or so, and Lionel told her she looked beautiful, Cecilia told him, "My sister is not beautiful; she has an interesting face."

Everyone in the Rubin family was on the whole pleased that Diana was to be married, although Diana herself halfheartedly wished that her older sister could have been married before her. (This was not to be, until Cecilia was in her seventies and married a fellow resident at her nursing home. Diana was not elated.)

When Lionel finally told his mother that he and Diana had set a date—June 12, 1929—for their wedding, Fannie Trilling had a noteworthy reaction, despite all her scheming and preplanning.

She fainted dead away on the living room floor.

3

PROLEGOMENON

For me this marriage is, without sentimentality, gush or woman-worship, the expectation of the completest fulfillment. I want it to be not the completion or augmentation of a life but the pattern in which my life is to be shaped—and a starting place, a foundation, a great tool: it contains—[or may] or should—the greatest part of my emotional, moral, and spiritual-religious actually—activity. I want it to carry it along with me. I want indubitable permanence for it—accepting its changes and variations as they come. I place so much in it: all beauty and excitement. It has absorbed all my desire for glamour and sexual adventure. Already it has cleared away from my sight so much that had obscured it.

—LIONEL TRILLING, JOURNAL ENTRY, SPRING 1929

More than a handful of people invited the young couple to dinner to celebrate their engagement—"their expectation of the completest fulfillment," Diana called it. It was asparagus season, so there was asparagus—too much of it, as it turned out—at every meal. It was everywhere they went. Asparagus, asparagus. Diana said that her husband-to-be joked that "the minute you got married, you get asparagus" and that he later commented, "We've made a capitulation to society and this is the price we pay for it; we become social beings and have to accept all these dull invitations." She said that "he wasn't being funny. He was saying something serious about social membership as opposed to the wishes of the individual."

And the wishes of the individual went mostly unheard. Diana later realized that "the wedding had not been mine, nor had it really been Lionel's." Because of her guilt over marrying first, Diana allowed her sister to be in charge of planning the menu for the dinner to be held in the apartment on West End Avenue after the late-afternoon wedding ceremony. Diana said that Cecilia was such a bad judge of food that when she volunteered to plan meals at a camp for underfed children, the campers went on a hunger strike. And then there were the guests they hadn't planned on inviting. The chuppah, or canopy, under which the couple would say their vows needed to be held by two nonblood kin, so to perform the job, Diana had to invite a friend of her father's she barely knew, as well as the man who seemed to be Cecilia's latest boyfriend, basically strangers at her wedding. But it had to be that way, and Diana reluctantly went along.

The food "arrived in disguise," Diana later wrote. "The melon wedges had become battleships with smokestacks contrived of maraschino cherries and with little American flags waving at their prows. The carrots, pared and molded, sat in baskets like brightly colored Easter eggs. The dessert was a dramatic bombe. Above a wide billow of ice cream and spun sugar appeared the face of a doll bride. This confection was passed from guest to guest; one served oneself by shoving the spoon under the skirt of the bride." Diana was appalled by this final indulgence. It called to mind the image of a doll she was given on her fifth or sixth birthday, a doll that was as tall as she was and, in fact, was presented to her dressed up in one of her own favorite dresses. The doll had a rosebud mouth (the kind that Lionel's mother wished her new daughter-in-law possessed) and had longer eye lashes than the birthday girl had. "Her thighs and knees and ankles were jointed like mine; so was her head jointed to her neck—she could be made to sleep and wake, lie or sit, maybe she said mama . . . and reach out for an invisible love. I hated her," Diana later wrote, continuing with a final insult: "My mother said I was not to play with her because she was not any ordinary doll—she was not to be broken." But at least the wedding bombe had no cruel rules attached to it and melted over time.

The orthodox ceremony was performed by Henry Rosenthal. It would be his first wedding. Before he became a rabbi, Rosenthal had seemed such a promising novelist that his Columbia University friends thought he would be an American James Joyce, although the novel they praised when he read aloud from it was never published (nor even finished).

A few moments before the vows were to be spoken, Joseph Rubin disappeared into a bathroom for a long time. Diana waited alone in her bedroom, as Henry had instructed her, holding the very special, new-to-the-marketplace bronze roses she was going to carry into the living room. Her father, it turned out, was sulking one last time, telling himself that perhaps a writer could make some sort of living after all. He meant his future son-in-law, not his daughter. For a wedding gift he gave the couple what he thought they needed most: a check for $5,000 (which would be more than their annual income for many years thereafter).

Lionel waited with Henry in another room for the ceremony to begin. He was wearing a custom-made suit chosen from a dark cloth that, unbeknownst to him, had been cut from a larger sample that contained red stripes undetectable in the small swatch he saw, so the finished suit incorporated oversized stripes that made him look like a barber pole. His new wife later called it his flag suit. He never wore it again. But that hardly mattered. In a diary entry he wrote, "I think of suits I will get, ways of getting them—tailor-made or at what store, price, color, etc. the same with shoes, raincoats." Lionel Trilling liked to shop. Diana later reflected that it was a way of maintaining a connection to his father, who had what she called "artistic feeling about tailoring." She said that her father-in-law once told her that he "often lay awake nights pondering a new method for cutting the collar of a jacket."

Once married, the "grotesque" dinner (as Diana later described it) eaten, the young couple entertained a few close friends (who had not been at the immediate-family-only ceremony and multicolored dinner) with cake and champagne. The Fadimans were there, as were Diana's playwriting friend Bettina Sinclair and her husband, David.

Diana and Lionel then spent their wedding night at the landmark Fifth Avenue Hotel, an ultraluxury hotel between Twenty-Third and Twenty-Fourth Streets built in the mid-1800s on a site that had once been a stagecoach stop. In the morning Joseph Rubin, well over his brief tantrum, had his car and driver pick the couple up and take them to Easton, Connecticut, sixty miles from New York, where they had rented a cabin for the entire summer, one that was quaint but unpainted. Diana continued to feel guilty about marrying before her sister, so as she and her new husband were driven up Fifth Avenue toward the road leading to Connecticut, she had the driver stop at Lord and Taylor's department store so she could buy a thank you gift for her sister. Lionel also decided to get his seventeen-year-old sister, Harriet, a gift, even though she had hardly helped, except, as Diana later wrote, as "a nuisance, her mother's humorless messenger"—both before and after the engagement and wedding.

"We launched our marriage in guilt," Diana said. "Everyone had to be listened to, apologized to, thanked for giving us permission to live our lives. On our first day of marriage, starting our honeymoon, all we could think of was propitiation: how to win back our families, how to win their forgiveness for deserting them."

The cabin the couple rented, at the suggestion of friends, belonged to Jim and Winifred Rorty; Jim was a poet and advertising writer, and later a political activist, as was his wife. The cabin, on a deserted dirt road, had no electricity, only kerosene lamps, and, of course, no refrigeration (there was a daily delivery of ice). The walls were made of beaverboard. There was a two-burner stove that used bottled gas. The property had a well, and Lionel strung up an outdoor shower for them to use; water from the well was also pumped into the kitchen. (There was a working toilet.) There was no telephone and no neighbor within earshot; their landlords were a quarter of a mile north of them, and another family a half mile below them. They had no car and used the Rortys' phone to order groceries, which were delivered to the foot of the hill near their cabin. They stored milk and butter in a bucket lowered into the well. The

Rortys let them pick all the vegetables they needed from their garden in exchange for weeding it.

It was rustic living to be sure, and while Diana had once delighted in the relatively primitive life at her summer camp, she did not particularly relish it with just two people, even though the cabin's interior held some surprises. Crisp white organdy curtains hung at every window, and the Early American–style bed had white organdy ruffles surrounding it. There was a fancy dressing table in the bedroom, and the Rortys had left several jars of expensive creams and perfumes on it. The bathroom was papered with bright pink wallpaper. Still, the place was a bit of a let-down because Diana had once fantasized a European honeymoon. But Lionel objected to such a trip, saying he had to study for his PhD exam (which was not until many months later, in January 1930). Diana saw his reluctance to travel as an excuse to remain close to his family, as well as justification for him to forgo pleasure. She maintained that the decision not to travel on their honeymoon "laid a pattern of nonpleasure in his life."

She explained that they were "too close together, too alike, in emotional insecurity." She meant their emotional dependence on family. But she also "felt I was being betrayed for something I couldn't put my finger on—Lionel was acting on behalf of something other than his or my best interests." Whatever it was, Diana said she had no adequate language for it and believed she never would. For her entire life she would search for the words so she could unravel her long and lingering sense of betrayal that focused on Lionel's actions.

In an unpublished book, she recalled that she "was not brought up to expect life to be easy." This was conveyed to her "wordlessly," she said, adding that "to be reared in the belief that there is little that you have the right to look for in this world other than what comes to you by happy accident, to be conditioned from earliest memory in such an all-embracing minimalism of expectation, is subtly and permanently disabling. Fight as you may for more than comes to you by chance, your weapons have no edge."

Diana and Lionel both wrote short stories that honeymoon summer. Diana didn't think of herself as a writer, or if she did, it was strictly as an amateur one; yet she felt comfortable writing, as when she easily won a literary prize at her summer camp. Diana's honeymoon story, "Mornings in Florence," was about a young Jewish American woman living in Florence who picks up a young man in the Uffizi and shares a summer of romance with him. She liked the story well enough to send it at the end of the summer to Elliot Cohen ("a fantastically powerful person," she later described him), the editor of *The Menorah Journal*. A few weeks later, he invited her to come to his office to discuss the story. Diana was thrilled. They had a long talk about many things, but Cohen, who was very close to Lionel, never once brought up the story. Neither did Diana. She later found out from a mutual friend that Cohen had admired it, especially the ending, yet he never published the story, and never explained why. His lack of encouragement stung bitterly, and Diana always felt that the publication of that story would have made an incomparable difference in her life. (Cohen, a brilliant but troubled man, ended up killing himself in the late 1950s.)

When not studying and reading, Lionel, who would become a part-time editor at *The Menorah Journal* later in the year, also wrote a short story. It was based on a snake that lived under their Easton cabin, although he never told his wife about the actual snake until they were safely back in New York.

The snake was a copperhead, and Lionel took to holding a long stick whenever he walked across the meadow to the well house; he was shielding himself from other snakes by whacking the stick back and forth in the tall weeds as a farmer might do. He would not allow Diana to sit on a blanket in front of the cabin, and because he didn't tell her why, an atmosphere of fear soon invaded their honeymoon.

The isolation of their cabin bothered Diana. Its atmosphere reminded her of the stories Mary, her family's Polish maid, had told her and her siblings, stories that became, Diana said, her "language of terror," when every creak of the furniture or floor became a possible death trap. Diana also thought of the bizarre neighbor who lived next door to her in New Rochelle. Diana would later describe this woman, Mrs. Raffael— called "Bobolinka" by her mother—as looking "as if she had been made up for the part of a deranged old lady in a play: skinny, beak-nosed, unkempt, her dirty white hair falling thinly to her shoulders in a cruel parody of girlishness. She was living out her old age irremediably alone."

In Connecticut Diana began to hear strange thumping noises at night or before dawn, and not until the end of summer did she find out that deer sharpened their horns on their well house and that the heavy scratching was the ominous sound that had been troubling her sleep. Lionel was troubled, too—by the snake—but Diana later said that he always hid his fears better than she did. (During their honeymoon he went into Manhattan specifically to buy an antivenom, although he told his bride the trip was for another reason.) He had a "deceptive exterior," Diana later explained, although "neither of them went around complaining." They went about their living without a fuss. So Lionel continued his reading and studying as if he hadn't a care in the world. He slept like a baby. And he wrote the snake story, which he showed to Diana when their honeymoon was over. She later wrote that the story, which he never published, was not exactly about the snake but instead was used as a symbol of evil. "It was a story of sexual jealousy, and Lionel's jealousy of anybody I knew before I knew him, and had originally been generated by a snapshot Lionel came across of me with a friend in South America," she said. "I remember it as the most brilliant writing Lionel ever did, but it was morbid to a pathological degree: there had been nothing in that South American relationship to justify his extravagant feeling. A prolegomenon to depression, the story greatly worried me for our future."

The story was often revised, but not enough to satisfy its author. Two years later, in 1931, he gave his wife a copy on her birthday inscribed: "To Diana—for her birthday—again—after a long time with more love."

What had changed in the story that it could now be a birthday gift?

Not the beginning. "It was impossible. Impossible. It was impossible. It could not go on. Every moment was an orgasm of defeat and he awoke from sleep weary."

Nor the ending, when the snake makes its very first appearance.

The story explored ideas—even perplexing concepts like "orgasm of defeat"—more than it did characters. It would move Diana to ask her husband that if he planned to become a novelist—and he did—then why did he need to pursue a PhD? And she also meant, why did his studying have to interfere with their honeymoon? Lionel told her that a novelist could no longer be only a man of feeling but that he also had to be a man of the mind. He would teach and write—and would probably not be as financially successful as Kip, but he'd try. "No one can give me anything anymore," he wrote in his journal in late 1929. "Essentially, I think, I am settled in sad stability and what I most want is fact and explanation."

For a few weeks that summer, Polly and Kip rented a house about eight miles from the Trillings' honeymoon cabin. They had no car either, and the four friends occasionally walked the distance to visit. Diana was distressed to learn that one weekday when the Fadimans were at their apartment in Manhattan, upon their return to Connecticut they discovered that a trespasser had been in their house. They discovered the intrusion after Polly opened her underwear drawer and found that the contents of a can of spaghetti and tomato sauce had been dumped into it. Upon hearing of this incident, Diana's sense of isolation and unease intensified.

There was no piano in the cabin, of course, so Diana practiced scales and sang familiar folk songs. She noticed during the summer that her voice was occasionally strained and frequently cracked, and she became concerned. One afternoon in the middle of the summer Jim Rorty came by to say there was a fire in a pasture a few miles away—would Lionel join him in helping to put it out? Lionel went with the landlord, and Diana, left behind, said she began trembling. Fiercely trembling. Her heart was racing, and in an instant she realized she was in dread of being left alone. Such trembling had never happened to her before. She was frantic. She ran out the door to a boulder not too far away from the cabin and climbed up it to see if she could see any hint of smoke, but she saw nothing; the fire was too far away. Her trembling continued. Slowly, she began to sing the Valkyrie from Wagner's Ring Cycle in the loudest possible voice, "as if to fill the countryside and dispel my loneliness," she wrote years later. She sang and sang, and her voice did not break. It was as smooth as ever, and she gradually began to feel better.

Singing would be her refuge and comfort.

Before leaving for Connecticut, the Trillings had signed a lease for a two-room apartment in a new building on Bank Street, in Greenwich Village. The Trillings were among "Number 1's" first tenants, and neither Diana nor Lionel thought the small, tan structure was attractive or especially desirable. But they liked its prime location and offbeat ambience; indeed, the building was constructed on the site of Willa Cather's third Village home. Edmund Wilson lived right across the street. He was then an editor at *The New Republic* and would not publish the first of his important books, *Axel's Castle*, until 1931.

As a Radcliffe student, Diana had always loved to visit the Village with her friends and act and dress as if she belonged there. Her mother would strenuously object to her daughter's colorful dresses and big heavy silver jewelry. Diana was happy that she and Lionel could begin their life together in a place where so many artists and writers lived.

The rent was affordable: $90 a month. They used Joseph Rubin's gift to buy many furnishings, and Lionel's Aunt Blanche, the wife of his Uncle Izzy, knew some Spanish and Italian wholesale antique dealers and helped Diana with her purchase of a seventeenth-century dark oak table, high-backed dining chairs, a green velvet sofa, a cherry wood desk, a large satin-covered club chair, rugs, drapes, glasses and dishes, and of course, a bed—a studio bed. Joseph Rubin was outraged that his daughter had not bought a full bedroom set and told her so. In fact, they had a heated fight over the issue, and Diana later wrote that she had the feeling her father "was trying to promote the sexual life in some way. Or maybe just the opposite." But the young couple wanted their two rooms to be interchangeable as either living rooms, dining rooms, or studies, and they wanted the bed always to look like a sofa. Deciding on the green velvet fabric took weeks and weeks, Diana said. "We were in a condition I later found out was called 'compulsive doubt.'"

There was enough money also for a small grand piano, so Diana could continue her singing. They were in Bohemian paradise, but they continued to live as if they were on West End Avenue, and their friends noticed and spoke of it behind their backs. They were not careful with the little money they had. Diana, who had stopped working at NBC, no longer received an allowance from her father. She had saved $1,000 from her past earnings and hoped to use her art history background to buy some paintings by the young Peter Blume and Utagawa Kuniyoshi as investments, but Lionel did not approve of her plan. (Blume would later gain recognition for his meticulous portrayal of social themes, and Kuniyoshi would become one of the last great masters of woodblock prints and painting.)

Diana had plenty of clothes from before she was married and particularly loved a beige fur coat that had been made to order for her, although she "loathed" the gold-brown braid embroidered with her initials in the lining of the garment. "The coat became a great point of attack" among their writer and editor friends, she said; it announced her middle-class values in a "vulgar way." She added that she also "loathed these people who made such a symbolic thing out of it, even though I partially shared their judgment." But she understood that she and Lionel now lived in the Village and were expected to be less conventional, and eventually she saw the coat's inappropriateness and gave it away.

Lionel made $45 a week in his job as a part-time editor. From time to time he made extra money by giving $10 talks to local women's clubs about "Joyce, Proust, Wyndam Lewis and the Modern Spirit." Diana later said that "the ladies always knitted while he was lecturing, and then they would serve coconut layer cake with hot chocolate or one time hot dogs with hot chocolate. It was always the most incredible experience. He said nobody knew what he was talking about." Nonetheless, Diana said she urged Lionel to raise his fee from $10 to $15, because they really needed the money, but the ladies balked at the increase, and that was the end of the lectures. "He was terribly upset for having listened to me," Diana said, because he was always "under a terrible strain to make more money, more money." The same had been true when he was in college, when he worked as a genealogist. Diana said that Lionel "made up genealogies for people who paid large sums to some genealogical publisher. . . . He would go to the library and he would find out a little bit about their families, and then he would make up a beautiful story about their pasts because that was the only thing they wanted to buy."

The Trillings were soon broke all the time and had to begin selling wedding gifts, starting with a set of silver demitasse cups and several ornate silver bowls and trays. Still, Diana later emphasized that "I never knew poverty, but by my middle class standards we were poor." And she said, surprisingly, "I enjoyed very much the challenge of this."

While Lionel read, studied, and wrote book reviews for *The Menorah Journal*, Diana busied herself with bookkeeping; she created separate envelopes to keep track of all their money. She also kept a daily expense book that noted every single purchase they made—$2.35 for two tooth-brushes and tooth powder; ninety-five cents for a powder puff, compact, and cold cream; and seventy-five cents for a haircut. She experimented with cooking and became quite inventive, especially with curries and stews. She usually kept to a budget, although once or twice she used their entire week's allotment for food to buy a rib roast. (All the same, Lionel's mother believed that Diana was not feeding her son enough wholesome food.) But Diana usually watched for food specials— especially fish, which she could buy for eight or nine cents a pound. She found that she could feed the two of them and a guest now and then for $5 a week. She soon became an excellent cook and thoroughly enjoyed preparing food—from shopping to serving.

At one point Diana and her brother's wife began an interior decorat-ing business—The Sutton Company—that didn't do very well, mostly because Diana and her sister-in-law had clashing tastes. What's more, Diana did not particularly like to shop for home goods. Clothes, yes, as her husband did, although once to Lionel's horror—after all, it was al-most his entire week's wages—she bought a $35 hat at the upscale Bonwit Teller, where she had bought most of her clothes as a young girl. (But Lionel could be a big spender, too, and shortly after they were mar-ried bought them box seats at the opera.)

Diana would not indulge herself extravagantly for many years to come; when the shopping urge hit her again as a young bride, she bought two dresses for less than $5 apiece at the more affordable Macy's. "I counted on having those dresses for a long time," she said. But she loaned one of them to a friend—"not a close friend"—who wanted to wear something nice for a job interview, and the acquaintance's nervousness caused her to perspire so much that the dress was ruined. "My heart was broken," Diana remembered.

She continued singing, mostly for her intended career but sometimes just for entertainment. In moments of playfulness she would don a Japanese kimono she had received as a gift once and in a squeaky voice sing *Madame Butterfly* to her husband. They would giggle and laugh. Living in the Village brought out the most amusing frolicking, she liked to say.

But in October—on "Black Tuesday"—the stock market crashed. The Great Depression hit America hard. Most industries were affected. There was loss of revenue and, of course, unemployment. Within a year Joseph Rubin was wiped out. He had put up all his personal savings as collateral for a bank loan to expand his hosiery factory, and after the crash his securities became worthless. The bank took over the business and put Diana's brother, Sam, in charge. But he did not command the respect that his father had—the employees disliked him—and, most important, he broke the union; still, the factory limped along until "the whole business disappeared," as Diana later reported. She also said that her brother just didn't use his mind "adequately," and he wasted the "power he had—much the same kind of mind that I and my father have."

Joseph Rubin, with Cecilia to care for him, had very little money left and could not afford to live the way he was accustomed to, and he and Cecilia moved to a small apartment on the East Side. Despite his grave financial condition, he did his best to give Diana and Lionel $10 a week toward their food allowance. Once he even stopped by their apartment with bagfuls of groceries he could ill afford. "He bought us everything luxurious in sight," Diana said, "strawberries and asparagus, all the out of season foods my mother used to buy when money didn't have to be counted."

Joseph Rubin soon developed a heart condition, which Diana believed was caused by stress, although he had had rheumatic fever as a boy. He died in 1932, after which Cecilia somehow managed to give her sister and brother-in-law $85 a month from the small inheritance left to the siblings. Cecilia had a big heart, after all.

Eventually Lionel, with his meager earnings, had to help his parents, whose savings were used up. The elder Trillings moved several times, finally settling in a small apartment on 113th Street between Broadway and Amsterdam Avenue. Lionel broke off relations with his extended family of aunts, uncles, and cousins shortly afterward. "They were increasingly hostile as Lionel grew up," Diana explained. "They made trouble through Lionel's mother. They put pressure on Lionel's mother that she couldn't withstand, and then she would bring these pressures to bear on us." Diana never explained further; still, she said she wanted to try to make things right, and she invited Lionel's unmarried aunts to Bank Street for lunch. "When they came to the door, I said, 'Do you want to take off your hats?'—I said this as a courtesy but—apparently I was supposed to say 'Take off your hats,' which showed I was welcoming them into my house." They were beyond insulted. And they later told Lionel's mother they never wanted to speak to Diana again. Diana gave up trying to be friendly, and relations deteriorated, with Lionel even telling his wealthy Uncle Hymie he didn't care if he ever saw *him* again. The family turmoil was never clarified further nor, in fact, discussed again. Lionel's father had long ago severed ties with his brother, Harry, and that break was never mentioned in the family. It was as if David Trilling was always an only child.

Diana had observed that Lionel's father was kicked around by his wife's family, and she said, "I felt sorry for him." Diana had become quite fond of her father-in-law. One late afternoon he stopped by their Bank Street apartment as Diana was preparing dinner, and she invited him to stay. David Trilling asked his daughter-in-law what she was cooking, and she told him chicken soufflé, although it was really tuna soufflé. "He ate it with great appetite," Diana recalled, "and he went home and told Lionel's mother what a great cook I was. She called me and said, 'What did you give father that he's talking about?'" But Fannie Trilling somehow instinctively knew Diana hadn't made the soufflé out of chicken and said so, but also agreed that if Diana had told him it was tuna, he wouldn't have eaten it. Diana liked this particular "naughty" quality in her mother-in-law, "even when I didn't like her." Her dealings with Fannie Trilling steadily improved over the years. In fact, Diana wrote in an unpublished book that "in a moment of pained reflection" Fannie Trilling once told her that if psychoanalysis had been available when she was young, it would have made all the difference in the world to her marriage.

One time Fannie Trilling visited Diana late in the afternoon, and when Lionel arrived home and found his mother there, he seemed flustered. After she left, he told Diana, "Look, I'm going to have to ask you not to have your mother-in-law here quite so often." Diana later recalled that his response made her very uneasy, and she worried that Lionel would soon get very angry with her. How could she resolve this? Suddenly she realized he had said "your mother-in-law!" She "did a double take" and the episode became what she called "a weighted joke" between them, especially after she realized that Lionel was, in fact, jealous of her growing rapport with his mother.

Lionel began teaching at Hunter College in the evenings, and he somehow managed to give his parents $100 each month. Diana tried to persuade her mother-in-law to start a business with the tasty jams and marmalades she made for family members, but Fannie Trilling refused and "took to her bed." Somehow the elder Trillings found the money to pay for Harriet's tuition at NYU, and even to pay for a part-time maid—all with their son's contribution—and to make matters worse, Fannie Trilling hoarded her mother's diamonds and refused to sell them to ease Lionel's great burden, although Diana later learned the diamonds were used to pay for Harriet's education.

Lionel also tutored rich boys who wanted to learn to write novels. But in the end Diana and Lionel left Greenwich Village and moved to a cheaper apartment at 160 Claremont Avenue, where the rent was $50 a month. The neighborhood was dreary, and miles away from their precious free-spirited Village, but at least they weren't living in a Shantyville or selling fruit on street corners, like so many other New Yorkers. "Every day you read in the paper about people jumping out of windows and this was really true; they did," Diana said. "Or you saw . . . in Riverside Park, little sheet metal huts that people were trying to live in [during] the bitter winter weather. They'd try to warm themselves over fires in little tin cans."

In the spring of 1930 Diana's health began to break down. Shortly before her condition worsened, Fannie Trilling, trying hard to be on good terms with her daughter-in-law, became concerned that Diana looked pasty-faced and wan, so she would sneak her into her kosher kitchen and insist she eat a specially buttered roll before their regular Friday evening meal. Diana was deeply touched at her willingness to break the food laws by offering her butter but did not have much of an appetite.

Diana went to see more than one doctor, each of whom told her she was basically healthy despite her symptoms—no appetite, weight loss, no strength in her arms and legs, clammy and shaking hands. "And my heart was beating wildly all the time," she said. She was simply adjusting to marriage, she was told, and she needed to rest more and refrain from too much sexual activity. Joseph Rubin, thoroughly mystified by an illness that involved no germs, sent Sam to tell Lionel that perhaps Diana was suffering from sexual excess and that perhaps Lionel's own health was also at risk.

Finally Diana, who firmly believed that the early negative treatment from the extended Trilling family "took its toll on her health," went to the doctor who had treated her mother. The doctor diagnosed hyperthyroidism, an overactive thyroid condition that could be successfully treated with iodine, which caused the thyroid—the butterfly-shaped gland in the lower neck that regulates the body's metabolism—to shrink. Lionel asked this doctor about Sam's sexual concerns, and the doctor wisely told him to tell his brother-in-law to mind his own business. (All the same, Lionel later told his wife that "in his whole life" he "had never known anyone with a better mental mechanism than her brother.")

Diana went to the New England Baptist Hospital in Boston for several weeks to have the iodine treatment, and then afterward to the nearby Lahey Clinic, world famous for its thyroid care. She had a private room and a private nurse because she couldn't bear to think of herself as a ward patient. (The Trillings would spend decades trying to pay off the bills until finally the hospital forgave the debt.) Lionel rented a cheap room in Cambridge and had only a dollar a day left over for meals. He lived on bananas and the food from Diana's hospital tray. (She still didn't—couldn't—eat.) The iodine treatment was not successful, so she was operated on at Lahey for the partial removal of her thyroid gland. There were, in fact, two operations because the surgeon believed his patient was not strong enough to continue the first time, so he stopped the operation. A nurse told Diana she almost died.

No one from either the Rubin or Trilling family was able to afford travel to Boston, which the young couple understood. But Diana was lonely—and felt betrayed again—even with Lionel right there. She was also miffed that Lionel's young sister, Harriet, who was a junior counselor at a summer camp, seemed completely oblivious to Diana's dangerous condition and her brother's precarious situation. Harriet, very unhappy at camp, would call her big brother incessantly for advice and never ask about Diana. Lionel was patient and always listened to his sister's woes.

Diana quickly understood what was behind her loneliness and sense of being abandoned. She did not feel as protected by Lionel as she wanted, needed, or expected to. She wanted to be his only concern. Was he not strong enough to tell his sister that Diana was now his number-one responsibility and that he had to preserve his energy to care for her?

She feared she knew the answer.

After a lengthy hospital stay Diana's vulnerability lessened, and her strength returned, but not her total health. She convinced herself that she was going to die young. She often thought of her childhood illnesses, when wearing a camphor bag inside her blouse was all that was needed to ward off germs. But she was now far from such folklore. She and Lionel went back to Connecticut to recuperate, although they didn't stay in their honeymoon cabin but instead in another, even smaller, one.

Diana soon learned that her voice was in jeopardy. The two surgeries had affected the nerves to her larynx, as well as her vocal chords' ability to produce high notes. The result was that the quality of her singing voice changed considerably. Her singing career might come to a halt before it even had a chance to begin. Lionel, trying to reassure her, told her she could always write about singing, its technical characteristics, and the challenges in balancing strength and delicacy. He told her there was a similarity between singing and prose style, without explaining further what exactly he meant. But Diana wanted to sing, not write about theories or her inability to sing; moreover, Lionel was the critic-in-training. She was not. But she put all these thoughts aside—even her newest one in which she admitted to herself that while she craved dependence on Lionel, she feared that he was going to become dependent on her.

Later, she jotted down a note to herself about her operations: "came through w/a few phobias, but lived." She also developed bulging eyes, an abnormality in her appearance that she learned to ignore over time.

4

ISOLATION AND DESPERATION

In Diana the dominant quality is justice. It motivates, uncon-
sciously, all her life and from it comes all her sweetness.

—LIONEL TRILLING, JOURNAL ENTRY, UNSPECIFIED MONTH IN 1930

One year after her surgeries, Diana said that despite everything that had happened to her and everything she worried about, she felt completely understood. This mattered more than anything else in her life. Lionel had recognized early on that her need for righteousness and a fairness organized around an underlying logic was connected to a sense of self that had been formed in her childhood. Furthermore, that she and he were alike in this respect made their union solid in a way that could enable both to endure whatever life brought them, even though logic sometimes eluded Lionel. "I wanted everything wonderful for Lionel far more than for myself," Diana said, "and Lionel was precisely the same: he wanted everything for me too before he wanted it for himself. . . . There was absolutely literally nothing that I couldn't talk about with Lionel and have a completely understanding response, and I think he felt the same way whether it had to do with the way we gossiped or the way we thought about the most serious issues in life. We talked the same language, and that was from the day we met."

Lionel used the word *sweetness* as Matthew Arnold, the subject of his first book, used it in the phrase "sweetness and light"—for the intelligence and beauty that art and culture bring to one's life. Lionel, who told Diana early in their relationship that she was more confident than she knew, understood that for better or worse Diana was the partner he needed in life to bring him his own sweetness and light.

But first, things deteriorated.

Diana began having panic attacks. She would wake up at night in terror, and Lionel would hold her close. She later said that even though he preferred not to talk about things when he was upset—which was the opposite of how she was, "he was really one of the strong people of this world . . . in his quiet way." He would tell Diana, "Don't let's formulate things too much. Let's not articulate things too much. It fixes them."

But very soon her fears escalated, and Diana became afraid even to leave her Upper West Side neighborhood. At one point she thought her panics were from something she had eaten, but she quickly saw what a foolish notion that was. She sometimes felt that if only Lionel had agreed to a European honeymoon, her travel phobia, as she soon called it, might not have developed the way it had. But most of the time she blamed her thyroid operations for bringing on multiple phobias, which ranged from a fear of strangers to a fear of flashing lights.

In time Diana was unable even to stay home alone. "I was always trying to arrange to have someone with me in order to free Lionel," she said, "but if there was no one with me, Lionel couldn't go up the street for a pack of cigarettes without my getting in[to] a panic." She later confessed that "even when he was right there with me, I'd often have panics."

She decided to see a neurologist, who first asked if she had normal sexual desire (she thought the question "silly") and then eventually prescribed Luminal, or Phenobarbital, a barbiturate that had been manufactured in America by Bayer since 1912. (The drug was originally a remedy for seizures but later began to be used as a sedative.)

Singing practice failed to calm her down because she was wary of straining her now delicate vocal chords. Lionel did his best to stay by her side when he could, but he had to teach and earn a living for them. In 1930 he began writing book reviews for *The New Republic* and *The Nation*, as well as continuing to write for the literary section of the *New York Evening Post*, where he had appeared since 1927. He also taught a course at the New York Junior League, the women's group founded in 1901 to encourage volunteerism.

Diana, not depressed, just deeply troubled, wanted—needed—to do something useful. But what could that be? she asked. She could not assert herself in a way she thought she should, even though, with the help of Luminal, she managed to plan inexpensive tea parties on Sunday afternoons for their close friends, although she said that "we didn't have that much of a circle with whom we felt close." But she found that despite her gloom, she could still take some pleasure in cooking and planning. "It's always been my recourse when life gets too bad for me; I start cooking," she said years later. "I always feel that if I can get people to come and eat, then I'll have some company."

At a market on Broadway she'd buy a chunk of liverwurst and mix it with a big slab of cream cheese and have a spread that cost fifteen cents. And she'd make a big tuna salad—because most fish was cheap—and also serve red caviar, which cost next to nothing because people believed it was not suitable to be eaten. Shrimp was inexpensive, too, so she'd make a large casserole of curried shrimp, which she would serve with coconut. "People always had a good time at our house," she said, "better times than they ever realized."

Despite their precarious financial situation, Lionel and Diana occasionally splurged. Diana later told some devoted friends and neighbors, Thelma Ehrlich Anderson and Quentin Anderson,* that once in a while she and Lionel would go to a Broadway show.

---

*   Quentin Anderson, the son of playwright Maxwell Anderson, would become an important Columbia University cultural historian and literary critic, and Thelma Ehrlich Anderson was a social researcher who worked for various government agencies, as well as for private research companies.

She revealed that during one intermission when they went out to have a cigarette, they returned to their seats and saw "a totally different set of characters on the stage." She said that they "had actually walked back into the wrong theater" and that "that was the kind of thing that was constantly happening the first year we were married."

She confided to the Andersons that Lionel was "not practical in some ways even though he was generally terribly attentive to all the details around us." Nonetheless he had allowed them to mistake one Broadway theater for another in the area.

Before they were married, Diana said, Lionel had ordered opera tickets and then discovered he had no money to pay for them. She came to the rescue and paid out of the allowance from her father she had luckily set aside.

Lionel could be a little deceptive. Diana described a time during the Depression when she and Lionel had been out for a walk, "and then we took the crosstown bus. Lionel was carrying a walking stick and the bus was very crowded. A great big workman obviously, [sic] he was wearing work clothes—got up very kindly, gently took Lionel's arm and offered his seat. Lionel very quickly saw what the man had thought, since he was carrying a stick, that he might be a little lame. Lionel accepted this. He didn't say, 'No, you sit down.' He sat down right away and thanked the man and then when we got off the bus, he limped off the bus. And then never carried the stick again."

Several months after being prescribed the sedative, Diana was able to take the 183-mile train trip to Saratoga Springs, New York, where she and Lionel were to be in residence at Yaddo, a four-hundred-acre artist retreat founded in 1900 by philanthropists Spencer and Katrina Trask. Kip had recommended them for the residence. Both Trillings thought that getting away from New York would be therapeutic. Diana could sense acutely the isolation that people felt as a result of the Great Depression, and she would later say that the 1930s were so awful because of both the isolation and the desperation. And although unspoken, she felt those two aspects in herself, as well.

Because they were short of money, they had sublet their apartment and hoped to be able to stay at the all-expenses-paid Yaddo for the entire summer. Lionel expected to work in earnest on his PhD dissertation on Matthew Arnold. (He had received his master's in 1926 for a thesis on the minor romantic poet Theodore Edward Hook.) In New York he had worked on the Arnold thesis in fits and starts but was often blocked. "When he was supposed to be off working in the library, he was at the movies, watching double features," Diana later discovered, adding, "that was an escape in a period of great depression." He had a novel in mind also. Diana told the Andersons that Lionel had told her that "a novel is a different thing than it used to be" and that "a novel, now, is the novel of ideas." And, she went on, "he meant Thomas Mann," adding that "he was a great admirer of Proust, and as a human being he is very like a Proustian." Quentin agreed.

But at Yaddo Lionel "was like a well-recommended graduate student," Diana remarked; "this professionalism of the artist class or the writing class hadn't dawned yet." Yaddo "was run like a house party."

Diana thought of herself as just a tagalong, although she still hoped to slowly build up her voice over the course of the long summer despite the medical obstacles she faced. It turned out that the quirky director of Yaddo, Elizabeth Ames, had not promised the Trillings residence for the entire summer but just for June and July. She told Lionel she would keep them in mind for August. Mrs. Ames also seemed taken aback by Diana's wish for "intensive studying" of her voice and said she could only offer her a place to sing in an old farmhouse three blocks from the mansion, mentioning that a new highway was being built along that road, and the noise might be a problem for Diana. Mrs. Ames asked Lionel to have Diana write her directly, which she did a few days later. Mrs. Ames replied immediately that she had now found a place on the estate for Diana to sing as long she practiced after 4:00 p.m. She also unexpectedly offered Diana a writer's studio, which was a piece of good fortune because Diana decided that if she couldn't make operatic singing a career, she'd use the summer as an experiment to see if some form of writing could become a "substitute" career.

As it happened, the singing practice did not go well because Diana was so afraid of destroying her voice altogether. She began to work on a second play about marital infidelity, which developed out of all the "obsessive" talk on the subject among their friends in New York. Surprisingly, Diana said that she had "determined" that it "was clearly the male of the species who would preserve the monogamous institution." She later decided that after three revisions, although she had a gift for dialogue, she didn't know anything about a play's construction. *The Young Wives Tale* was as unsuccessful as *Snitkin* had been.

But what had caused such a turnaround in Elizabeth Ames, causing her to offer Diana two studios? Diana would contend it was no turnaround at all, just the second act of an "intrusive, selfish woman of little heart driven by jealousy of any young woman who had a husband." Mrs. Ames, she said, had a "bitter resentment toward those whom she considered more fortunate than herself." Indeed, several weeks into the residency, Diana felt the full brunt of Mrs. Ames's biting displeasure. A photographer in residence at Yaddo asked Diana to come to his studio at eleven in the morning so that he could take her picture in the proper light, but this request violated Yaddo's rule of no visits to other studios until after 4:00 p.m. Mrs. Ames found out about Diana's infraction and told her she would have to leave Yaddo immediately. She was to pack up and go and not return for a month. Lionel was allowed to remain, which he did because he was desperate to get work done on his Arnold thesis.

Diana reluctantly returned to New York and lived with her father and sister for two weeks and then with the Fadimans for another two weeks until her suspension from Yaddo was over. She returned to Yaddo with great trepidation, and her fearfulness became stronger than ever, especially when a now mustached Lionel greeted her at the train station. As she later wrote, "in the next months and years any change in my familiar circumstances, even a sudden shadow across a window or an unanticipated sound, filled me with terror. . . . Lionel could shave off the offending mustache but he could not keep the world unchanged for me."

And the world did change quite suddenly for both Trillings when they met Sidney Hook, who had studied under John Dewey while getting his PhD at Columbia and who was also staying at Yaddo that summer. At the time, he taught philosophy at New York University (where he would remain for decades) and had recently become a Marxist, believing that capitalism needed to be replaced first by socialism and then by Communism. At Yaddo he introduced Diana and Lionel and quite a few other guests to Marxism and its vision of a workers' state, then to Communism. "He was a fantastic debater," Diana said. But no one joined the party; rather, they were just sympathizers, or fellow travelers, which many writers, artists, and intellectuals became as a result of the financial crisis around the world. "By 1931, we were ripe for conversion," Diana said. "You walked on the street and you saw lines of people waiting for milk for their children . . . people picking over the garbage in garbage cans trying to find something to eat . . . so you thought, this is what happens under Capitalism. It has failed."

She said that almost all of the writers at Yaddo that summer— Malcolm Cowley (then an assistant editor at *The New Republic*), Max Lerner (then an editor at the *Encyclopedia of the Social Sciences*), Marc Blitzstein (who was working at Yaddo on his soon-to-be-world-famous pro-union musical *The Cradle Will Rock*)—"joined the proletariat in asserting its claims to the product of its industry. The working class was going to own the means of production, and they would have the benefit of what was produced, and so in that sense there was always the positive, a working class."

Diana said that because she and Lionel were teenagers at the time of the Sacco-Vanzetti case in 1920 (in which two suspected anarchists were accused of murder), they were only bystanders during an investigation that "had mobilized a great part of the intellectual community, and was probably the first time anybody [in that community] had taken a stand on any public issue in this country." But at Yaddo they were more than ready to take an active political stand, and the years 1931 to 1933 were crucial in their political education.

They joined a front group, the National Committee for the Defense of Political Prisoners, which had been founded in June of 1931. Theodore Dreiser was a leader, and other writers who eventually joined included Lincoln Steffens, John Dos Passos, Josephine Herbst, Sherwood Anderson, Malcolm Cowley, and Edmund Wilson. Eventually the group came to blows over Hitler's rise. Some members followed Trotsky's view that Hitler had to be stopped. Trotsky, a revolutionist and major figure in the Communist Party, who founded the Red Army, would be assassinated in 1940 on Stalin's orders because of his belief in internationalism and his long-lasting opposition to Stalin's ruthless policies. Other members of the Committee for the Defense of Political Prisoners followed the strict Communist Party line that the chief danger was not Hitler or Stalin but the rise of a democratic socialism that would achieve its goals through gradual reforms. "They had been absolutely certain that Hitler was going to be defeated and that there was going to be a rising of the German proletariat," Diana told her new friend Elinor Rice Hayes, a novelist and biographer. She added that "they were indoctrinated up to the teeth with the idea that it was worse to make a united front with social democracy than to have Hitler come to power."

Trotsky had promoted socialism and Communism globally, while Stalin favored its expansion only in the Soviet Union. Brute force was his main weapon. Trotsky's main "weapon" had been his intellect. "We were all seduced by Trotsky because he was such an intellectual," Diana told Elinor; "he wrote such good history, he wrote such good prose; and he made fun of Jewish dentists in the Bronx."

She told Elinor that Lionel had wanted to write a play about Trotsky's secretary, who had betrayed him. "He thought that in writing a play like that, he would be able to say what he came slowly but surely to feel, that between Lenin [the premier of the Soviet Union from 1922 until his death in 1924] and Trotsky and Stalin, who was to choose? Stalin was a maniac, and Trotsky was the architect of large murderous plots."

Elinor answered that Trotsky didn't have the paranoid character that Stalin had, although all three of them "were just as much for violent revolution and just as committed to anything that justified their ends. Lenin was a violent, and in my terms, an evil man. I think Trotsky was, too. But I think one has to discriminate in the quality of the men."

The Trillings and their friends debated day and night and went to meetings. Diana said that she and Lionel, and Elinor and her husband, George Novak, would sit in a row together at meetings on Sixteenth Street and Irving Place and "stand up and sing the International with clenched fists raised in the air." Diana and Elinor liked to think of themselves as revolutionaries, although Diana admitted they never actually felt like ones—they felt more like "masqueraders" because there were no "clenched fists" at the end of meetings, which was not true. Diana was ashamed of her fists and quickly forgot that she had once declared: "This is unforgettable for me, the four of us with our fists held in the air . . . and I often think, suppose this had been my child, I'd have found it unendurable."

The two friends decided to work together in service to their—but more Elinor's—political beliefs. "I wanted something to do," Diana said. "I hadn't been well . . . [and] I needed something to occupy me."

With the help of Luminal, Diana was able—and, more important, motivated—to work as a secretary for the National Committee for the Defense of Political Prisoners, in its office off Fifteenth Street, near Union Square. "I got myself deeply involved in political activity on the basis of a nonpolitical drive. I did have a political conviction, but what drove me downtown was the drive to have an occupation." She said she thought of the committee "as an instrument, a helpful tool in my life."

But the work wasn't exactly what she had in mind. Elliot Cohen, who had left *The Menorah Journal*, supervised the office, and he didn't take the women seriously. According to Diana, even though Cohen was "in a high theoretical position, he was planning strategies; he was the real politico. . . . He was also just a fellow traveler, so what it really comes down to in some odd way was male chauvinism. I mean, they took this kind of lead over us because they were men, and they knew about the theoretical aspects, and we only knew about licking stamps." She meant herself and Elinor, who also worked in the office.

Lionel, who was very glad his wife's phobias were under enough control to allow her to leave the neighborhood, had very little time to be politically active. In 1932 he became an instructor in Columbia's English department; his salary was $2,400 a year. In his journal he wrote that political activity could be an impediment "to my getting to write. The question, would I engage in these activities if I had not the friends I have? No. I think not." Yet his introduction to Communism fueled the idea for the novel he conceived (but never wrote) at Yaddo. He noted its political implications in his journal: "In the Yaddo novel: the two older women, the lady Communist and the lady romantic and the aspirations of the two younger women." He also wrote in his journal: "How little the Marxist literature dealt with the idea of class. For that we have to go to Forster, Arnold, James!"

Elinor pointed out to Diana that they were "two bourgeois girls who insisted on keeping records of everything." They were just doing the housekeeping, or as Diana put it, "we house kept." It was a painstaking task that the men didn't appreciate. "They just thought we had brought our ugly, foolish, time-wasting, motion-wasting middle-class habits into their paradise," Diana said.

But Diana and Elinor insisted on keeping records, and as Diana explained to Elliot Cohen, "you can't just collect the money; you have to have cards and records of who sent the money, their addresses, the date the money was received, the amount." She said that he and the other men "looked at us as if we were out of our minds," but in the long run they saw that because of the new methodical system, the office was actually running more efficiently, and it became clear that "they were raking in the money" because they kept careful track of all the amounts.

The men really took notice when the National Committee for the Defense of Political Prisoners got involved in working for the Scottsboro case.* Diana said that "we really got started on keeping good records and creating a Prisoner's Relief Fund." Indeed, Diana also remembered that trouble began with the Communist Party when she and Elinor studiously followed the trail of the money. Elinor said that the committee "took the money we collected and used it to send people out to a Communist Party meeting in the Middle West somewhere. They did not use the money for the specific purpose it had been intended." Diana recalled that "the families of the Scottsboro Boys were being denied this relief

---

* The Scottsboro case, in which nine black teenagers were falsely accused of raping two white women—their accusers were men who appeared to have blatantly racist motives and no evidence that the teens had committed the crime—was one of the causes célèbres of the 1930s. The case not only involved extreme lies but had a history-making number of trials, convictions, retrials, and reversals. Five of the young men had charges against them dropped in 1937, and one was pardoned in 1976. On November 22, 2013, *The New York Times* reported that the Alabama Board of Pardons and Paroles voted unanimously to pardon the last three men—"closing one of the most notorious chapters of the South's racial history."

money and food because they were black, because these boys had been arrested and accused of rape. Everything was being done to harass their starving families, and so I sat down and wrote a most moving letter on the basis of these facts . . . and sent it to a list of people whose cards I had in my middle-class way collected." But, she said, "one day a letter came from the state attorney's office in Alabama . . . saying that I had used the mails to defraud. The letter said I was wrong and that food had been sent to the families—that so many bags of flour, so many bags of sugar-dried egg powder and so on—*had* been given to the families of the Scottsboro Boys."

Diana didn't know who or what to believe. "I was terrified," she recalled. "But the only thing that I was more than scared was furious. I was in a blind rage. . . . I had signed a letter saying they didn't get any flour or sugar." So she asked some party officials and was told, she said, "what difference does it make, Comrade? Essentially you were telling the truth. It doesn't make any difference, a bag of flour, a bag of sugar. These people were being persecuted." But Diana couldn't tolerate such reasoning or her role in writing the original letter about the families not receiving any relief, so, she said, she "marched out of the office and went downstairs, took out the file, wrote a very careful letter in which I said, 'Every fact that I put in my previous letter was a lie. I didn't tell these lies purposely.'" Diana offered to give everyone his or her donations back, because they had not gone to the Scottsboro families but to other party activities, but she said no one asked for any money back because she had been honest about what happened, and "some people included more money. That was for me a turning point," Diana told Elinor, "because I said, 'For what purpose do you tell your lies, when your lies have even no practical usefulness—when you lie just to lie?'" Diana realized that "if you had to lie in order to make a revolution, then I think I didn't want to have a revolution. It was more important to me to tell the truth."

But for a while, in working for the Scottsboro cause, Diana enjoyed her trips to Harlem, where she rang lots of doorbells and solicited contributions (although Lionel worried about her being out in the evenings). "We got W. C. Handy to do a great big benefit performance, also Cab Calloway. The [concert] was one of the greatest evenings of my life," she said, adding that Handy told her, "If the Scottsboro Boys are found guilty I will write a blues that nobody can dance to."

Diana later explained how politically disillusioned she and Lionel had become and how Communist-front groups or "innocents' clubs" existed all over the world. The two of them had begun to see "how the rule from the top [of the Communist Party] was passed down to underlings . . . the innocents . . . the used ones . . . the idea that you have to break eggs to make an omelet, which was commonly the excuse being offered for all the criticisms that one might raise of the Communist Party, was not finally satisfying to us. . . . My politics have never been radical—I have an intellectual position. . . . I wouldn't want a violent revolution for anything in the world." She had come a long way from her strong words about the need for revolution written in her diary when she was a young woman in South America with her father and sister.

Diana said that she and Lionel just never "accepted the aesthetic of the party," and she added that they also "didn't like to think of those opposed to Communism as enemies." Nonetheless, she had many a fight with Bettina Sinclair, her college and playwriting friend, who was an early anti-Communist. Bettina and her husband, David, both socialists, had lived in the Soviet Union for a year (supporting themselves primarily with rubles that had accrued and not been allowed out of the country from Upton Sinclair's book royalties, which they had permission to collect). The young Sinclairs were appalled by the squalor and the abysmal class distinctions they saw in the Soviet Union, plus the lack of fairness they witnessed, and the scarcity of every necessary household product. Diana said she "took every word Bettina said to be a vile, vicious slander" and at first didn't believe a word of her stories. She decided Bettina was a reactionary. Then in 1933 the poet E. E. Cummings published his prose poem *EIMI*, which dealt with his visit to the Soviet Union in 1931, and Diana said that they were all "delighted to have literary proof" of their opinion about Bettina, because "Cummings' book had a portrait of a young American couple based on Bettina and David," and he "was making fun of them because they were so naive and wide-eyed." She therefore "took great pleasure in that as confirmation that David and Bettina were ludicrous characters; their reports not to be credited." But in truth the poet, in a book described as impenetrable and incomprehensible by one reviewer, was writing about his disappointment with the Soviet Union, especially its lack of artistic and intellectual freedom. Cummings actually agreed with the Sinclairs' assessment of life in the Soviet Union.

The Trillings had also occasionally attended New York chapter meetings of the John Reed Club, a cultural organization that had been started in 1929 by members of the *New Masses* magazine and was controlled by the Communist Party. (The club was named after the controversial activist and journalist who had written the celebrated firsthand account of the Bolshevik revolution, *Ten Days That Shook the World*.) In 1934 the *Partisan Review*, founded by William Phillips and Phillip Rahv, was begun as a publication of the John Reed Club, but the magazine "quickly freed itself from Communist control," as Diana later described its evolution, and "began to function as an independent Marxist publication." She went on to comment that "with the wide general disillusionment with the revolutionary ideal, the magazine considerably altered its radical position, moving from orthodox Marxism to a more congenial left-liberalism."

Liberal—in a particularly special sense opposed to both nineteenth-century libertarianism (maximizing individual rights and minimizing the role of the state) and left-wing liberalism that favored radical change—became Diana's chosen term. And years later she said that a confusion "grew up from the early thirties between fellow-traveling Communists and Liberals" and that she came to her anti-Communism "on the basis of my liberalism. I feel that the first tenet of liberalism has to be that it is opposed to any form of despotism; therefore, it had to be opposed to Communism as soon as Communism showed itself to be a despotism."

By 1933 the Trillings, along with their mentor, Sidney Hook, were thoroughly appalled by Joseph Stalin's abuse of power and had become anti-Communists. "We didn't see the working class around us very much," Diana said. "What we saw was a lot of middle-class young people who were speaking on behalf of a class that wasn't represented very much in our view. Who was this working class in whose name we were making this revolution? What we began to see," she said, "was the effort [by the Communists] to woo and rule the opinion-forming class . . . the people in the public eye: the people of the theater, the people of the movies, the people in publishing houses, the people on newspapers, the opinion-forming university people, people who were in a position to influence opinion. . . . The middle-class intellectuals were being mobilized to make a revolution in which they invoked the name of the proletariat."

Shortly before Diana quit the National Committee for the Defense of Political Prisoners (which she had joined in 1931) and she and Lionel left front groups behind them forever, she unwittingly almost became part of a political conspiracy that formed an intriguing chapter in American history.

Whittaker Chambers, who had been an acquaintance of Lionel's when they were students at Columbia, approached Diana and asked her to be a courier (or in espionage-talk, a "Dead Drop") in his work as a Soviet spy. He wanted Diana to accept and hold on to secret documents for him. As she later wrote in her memoir, *The Beginning of the Journey*, "I was enormously flattered that he thought me capable of such an assignment, and I was ashamed to refuse him." But, as she explained, "by the time [he] called me for my decision, we had broken with the Communists. It was a very, very strange period. So Whittaker said, 'I know your answer,' and I said, 'I would like to tell you my reason,' and what I wanted to tell him was I didn't want to betray my country. He thought it was because I was mad at the Communist Party." Diana had heard from one of her friends that Chambers also needed, for reasons she didn't know, information about Columbia's large-scale tunnel system— some of the underground passageways dated from 1885—and Diana certainly didn't want to have anything to do "with something like that," she said. "Maybe he would have maps of fortifications or military information." Her mind went wild with speculation about any covert attack plans he might have had in mind.

According to Diana, Sidney Hook maintained that it was Lionel who had been asked to be the clandestine courier. In a letter to Diana, Hook even reminded her that she had once told him that "Lionel was naively agreeable to the proposal but you decidedly not," he wrote. "Your language about Lionel's good will and naiveté was rather emphatic." But Diana said that Sidney Hook was entirely mistaken and that *she* was the one Chambers asked, but, most important, no Trilling was ever a spy.

As Diana later made plain, "We were closest to the workings of the Communist Party in this country at the moment when two things were happening simultaneously. These two things were that Roosevelt had been elected, and Roosevelt was beginning to pull the country together. We're talking about 1932–33, that we were going to have the beginning of something that would be a rescue operation. . . . There was an election in November, and by March of the next year we were totally disillusioned by the [Communist] party. . . . We stayed very close, of course, to all the activities of the Stalinists for the rest of the decade of the thirties. We were aware of every move they were making and of how damaging it was to everything we valued in world affairs—how damaging it was to the cause of democracy and freedom and human life in Europe, and how the Communist Party was really influencing our own American administration, not in American policy but in foreign policy."

Diana said that after the innocents' clubs were out of their lives, she wholeheartedly agreed with what Elinor Hayes said to her: "'Never again is anybody going to lead me by the nose into any political position.'" And Diana went on: "I remember saying Amen to this. Never was anybody going to manipulate me that way. . . . It was like a set of Russian dolls: you have this manipulation within another manipulation within another manipulation."

5

THE REST OF OUR LIVES

*Two people within three days told me I am aloof, restrained,
removed, coldly at ease, snooty, high-hat, proud-seeming, confident, superior. This is really amusing when I think of the shy
puppy-dog constantly within me.*

—LIONEL TRILLING, JOURNAL ENTRY, SOMETIME BETWEEN SEPT. 1926
AND SPRING 1929

I n the late spring of 1933 Diana and Lionel moved from 160 Claremont Avenue to a two-room garden apartment—it was actually two
steps below street level—in a brownstone at 15 East Seventy-Seventh
Street, between Fifth and Madison avenues. It was more expensive but
cheerier for Diana than Claremont Avenue, and Lionel had privacy to
work in what Diana described as a "cell-like extension of the kitchen."

Diana had hoped her new surroundings would raise her spirits, but
every so often Lionel's sister, Harriet, would come to visit at lunchtime
and find her sister-in-law still in bed. Diana sometimes tried to fill up
her days by writing short stories, but she could never rid them of what
she called her "intrusive supervision." The stories were stilted, and she
had too little faith in her intuition.

Diana had written a poem at Yaddo and liked it enough to send to her new acquaintance Malcolm Cowley. He wrote her that he would give it to *The New Republic*'s poetry "czar" but that "the chances are exactly seventeen to one that he will reject it, even with the note of intercession I wrote, but I want to say for the record that I enjoyed it immensely." (The poem was rejected a few weeks later.)

The Trillings stayed on Seventy-Seventh Street for just eighteen months (the neighborhood was just too expensive) before moving back to the more affordable and manageable Columbia area. They found an apartment on 114th Street between Amsterdam Avenue and Morningside Drive, where they remained until 1936, when they moved yet again—this time to a dark and confining first-floor apartment at 620 West 116th Street. But it was close to Riverside Drive, so in warm seasons they could sit on the grass in Riverside Park across the street and look at the lights flickering in New Jersey and boats gliding up and down the Hudson River. "It was cool there," Diana remembered; "a breeze coming off the water made it [a] little cooler. Sometimes we sat there for hours."

Diana hadn't enjoyed the outdoors so much since her tranquil days at Camp Lenore as both a camper and a counselor (she taught archery, basketball, and drama). One of her greatest pleasures as a camper had been the dancing classes held on the sweeping lawn in front of the director's house. Diana loved leaping around in the open air with the sun beaming down on her body, knowing her mother would probably disapprove. Despite getting lice one summer, for which her hair had to be covered in a black salve thick as tar, she had only good memories of being outdoors so much. But the freedom she felt at the camp had once led to an urban accident at home: she had wanted to show off that she could ride a bicycle with her feet on the handlebars and her arms spread out like a bird's wings, and the result was that she fell and knocked herself unconscious. And she had revealed to her father, who was "utterly incompetent in all physical things," she said, that after all, she was no better than he.

In 1934, as the Trillings approached the age of thirty, life had hardly any joy for the couple. "We were funny; we laughed a great deal because we were funny people," Diana said. "Lionel was an extraordinarily witty man . . . so we clowned, we laughed, we had parties, we went to parties . . . but we [weren't] having pleasure or adventure."

She later told Thelma Anderson that they "were a very unpositive couple." Still, every now and then she and Lionel managed to cobble enough money together to rent houses for a month in the summer, first in Babylon and then in Amityville, Long Island. The house in Amityville was so primitive it had only an outhouse, yet there were nearby posh tennis courts that they used so often they developed what Diana called "tennis fever." She had managed to overcome the trembling she had once had when she served to her brother. Lionel rediscovered fishing, a sport he had enjoyed as a boy with his Uncle Hymie. "He really loved that," Diana said, "and it was an occupation in which he didn't have me to take into account." (Later, under the guidance of Quentin Anderson, Lionel became a fairly accomplished flycaster, and they frequently went on trout-fishing weekends together.)

"We were living our lives in preparation for a serious place in life," Diana said. "I was, of course, one of the lost young women of my generation." She had no career. And in the beginning Lionel was also adrift. "Some people thought he just wasn't going to make it, despite the determination that he communicated to people. . . . Some people thought that he was too mild to be a force in the world. . . . But I was the only person who knew he would make the most impact as a writer." Diana wanted to share in that "impact"—participate somehow in its development—but she could not see how this could ever happen.

The neurologist who had prescribed Luminal to Diana also suggested she try hypnosis, and as she later wrote in *The Beginning of the Journey*, "the doctor to whom he sent me was youthful, agreeable, and attractive. He wanted to make me well. But he knew little about the dark art." Not only did his attempts to hypnotize Diana fail, but so did his attempt at psychoanalysis, because, as she wrote, "a hint of the illicit was entering our relationship. This frightened and excited me." The hypnotist-doctor actually asked her out on a date—a *date*—which Diana improbably accepted. They met in a speakeasy (not Mario's, where Diana and Lionel first met). "The date was a disaster," she nonchalantly went on, saying no more about him but making clear the so-called treatment ended, but not before he "fixed me up with other men." These dates were not for analysis. They were plain and simple trysts.

In the early 1930s, psychoanalysis was not exactly a mainstream medical therapy, although it had gained many followers among writers and intellectuals. It had grown up in the 1910s and 1920s, when the first person to translate Sigmund Freud's work into English was Abraham Brill, a 1903 graduate of Columbia University's medical school. He was also the first practicing psychoanalyst in America; he founded the New York Psychoanalytic Society in 1911 and later the American Psychoanalytic Association.

Psychoanalysis in the United States was thus launched.

Diana first heard about the new "talking therapy," as most people called it, from a Radcliffe friend and was intrigued. Her unfortunate encounter with the hypnotist-doctor did not stop her from trying again, this time with a classmate of Lionel's. There was no sordid dating involved. But the young doctor, Nat Ross, also proved to be unconventional, to say the least; he invited Diana to stay with his family in their brownstone in Greenwich Village, while Lionel was in class. And then, in 1934, Lionel also became his patient. Neither Diana, Lionel, nor Dr. Ross recognized at first how reckless this was, and the treatments ended only because the doctor decided to return to school for more training, which he clearly needed.

Diana moved on to a Dr. Paul Schilder, who she later learned had received no formal psychoanalytic training. But she remained in treatment with him for five years—until he died in a car accident—later confessing that she had followed his orders, as well as the hypnotist's, because she felt like a powerless child—so much so that she let herself go on dates with other men despite the fact that she was a new bride. Even though Diana acknowledged that she and her women friends were "all for sexual variety," she understood that they were "only half-joking." The men," she said, "were furious at us" for the way we talked.

Diana concluded that Lionel assumed she was at a doctor's appointment when she went off on her outings.

At Dr. Ross's house, when Diana stayed there in the afternoons, she witnessed bedlam: food left on tables, chairs, and rugs; pets urinating and defecating any place they chose to; and the doctor's infant daughter crawling right through the mess. Freud himself had warned a colleague that he worried that he was bringing a plague to the United States. Could Americans handle psychoanalysis?

Dr. Schilder forced Diana to face her fears by making her roam around Manhattan alone and to confront her fear of heights by spending time in a penthouse. She somehow found the courage to go along with these instructions because it was as if her father, in his role as intimidator, was controlling her. Dr. Schilder also discussed Diana freely with Lionel, telling him she was making great progress. But most radically of all, he invited Diana and Lionel to accompany him and his family on a trip to Canada, which they accepted. Diana reported that just being in her analyst's company (his wife was also a psychiatrist—as well as an alcoholic) lessened her fear of travel.

In the 1930s Lionel read all of Freud's works, which Diana did not, although she eventually read his seminal book, *Civilization and Its Discontents*. She applied what she read—and had previously known about—to real life, which, she said, Lionel never did, except his "concurrence in Freud's tragic view of life," which for her husband didn't derive from recognition of death—but "perhaps it started with sex—the need to sacrifice the unrestricted pursuit of desire in order to maintain the family." She explained that "Lionel's interest in analysis wasn't so much clinical as literary. He didn't think of analysis as a field of medicine but as a study of human behavior, even perhaps a study of civilization, a study in culture. He never applied the insights of analysis to the people he knew, as I do." And she added, with amusement, that they eventually "protected each of their Freuds from the other."

Lionel, she said, "never talked to anyone about his own analysis, not even to his closest friends." She said that everyone simply took it for granted that the reason her husband knew so much about psychoanalysis was "because he had a neurotic wife." But, she said, Lionel "was in analysis over just as an extended period of time as I was. The difference was that his symptoms weren't of a kind to show in public, like mine." She meant her phobias that couldn't be hidden—especially her fear of heights. Diana agreed that "in an important sense Lionel was right to keep his analysis secret, at least at first. He was making his career in the university, and in the period when he first went into treatment, analysis was very suspect in the universities; it was thought to be some kind of dark science."

Before Lionel had become an instructor at Columbia, in the fall of 1932, he continued to teach in the evenings at Hunter College to make more money; he taught both an undergraduate and a graduate course. He was paid by the hour, and if he missed a class, there was no income, which the couple desperately needed since they were always in debt, despite borrowing from friends. After Diana's father had died in December of 1932, they had also received a small inheritance of $5,000 from his nearly depleted estate, but in addition to everything else, they now had psychoanalysis bills. They stretched and stretched their income— Lionel's salary at Columbia was $1,800—as far as it could go. It was time for Diana to try to help out in some way.

Diana later wrote in a letter, "There came the evening when Lionel had the flu and couldn't manage to get up from bed. In our desperation we decided I'd take the sessions at Hunter for him, though I had had no training." Still, she'd try to be a substitute teacher. She said that she read aloud a story of Katherine Mansfield for the undergraduate course and then led a discussion, which went well. "But," she said, "the graduate assignment that evening was Ruskin. I had never read the essays and I wasn't allowed to fake: there were three girls in the class, one of whom not only had an acute intuition of my ignorance but also of the fact that I was married to her handsome teacher and obviously didn't deserve to be." And one particular student, Diana emphasized, "gave me a very bad time and made me a permanently honest reviewer afraid to skip a sentence."

Later, Diana spoke much more freely about the evening at Hunter, where despite everything, she said she had her first experience in literary criticism. Lionel had encouraged her and had told her she would do just fine, and he liked her idea of reading Katherine Mansfield to his students. But Diana confessed how "Lionel's face had darkened because he was worried about the graduate course. So he said, 'Quick, read it on the bus going down.' And he picked out an essay by Ruskin and he said,

'Teach it.' So I said, 'Yes.' Like an idiot I got on the bus and hadn't gone two blocks before somebody got on whom I hadn't seen for ages, and we talked all the way downtown."

As for the student who gave Diana a bad time: "I had known all year," she said, "that this girl had a crush on Lionel. I could tell from the way the stories he brought home to me about this girl in class. . . . She was smart. And she knew more than I did. A feeble-minded graduate student knew more than I did. I knew nothing. Zero. . . . There I was. I started to dither. . . . She undertook to make me suffer . . . and succeeded perfectly. I mean, I have never been put through such a wringer. It was a nightmare. . . . I was so miserable and so scared."

Diana wanted never to teach again. The experience also brought to light her jealousy, unfounded, but fueled by her sense of inferiority; she was just someone who "didn't deserve to be married to the handsome teacher."

She began to have bad dreams, worse than she had ever experienced, and they all had the same theme. She dreamed she was supposed to be in an opera performance, but had never practiced for it on the stage or even with the orchestra, or that she was taking an exam for which she had never studied, or that she was trying to get to a railroad station, or a restaurant, and kept getting lost. Anywhere, everywhere, Diana continued to feel alone and abandoned. Having Lionel around so much lessened these feelings most of the time, and she rationalized that at least it kept her husband at his desk and his books. "He didn't waste himself on running around," she said.

After the death of Diana's second analyst, a friend helped her find a new doctor through Dr. Bertram Lewin, the president of the New York Psychoanalytic Society, who told her, as she wrote in *The Beginning of the Journey*, that she "was as innocent of analysis as the day [she] was born." So was Dr. Lewin, it would seem, since the analyst he recommended—a Dr. Ruth Brunswick—turned out to be a morphine addict, albeit one who had studied with Freud himself. But as Diana pointed out, "Freud had himself been addicted to cocaine . . . for the better part of a decade, . . . [so] to put Dr. Brunswick's reliability to question because of her drug habit would be tantamount to questioning Freud's reliability."

Dr. Brunswick exhibited peculiar behavior. As Diana described it, "she broke as many appointments as she kept, often at the last minute when I was about to leave the house. When we did meet on schedule, she could squander my whole hour in silly chatter or in doing her shopping on the telephone. 'No, of course my slacks don't have to have a fly front! Why does a woman need a fly front?' she burbled on the phone to a salesgirl at Saks Fifth Avenue while I waited on the couch for her return to business." Dr. Brunswick told Diana that she was the only patient she behaved this way with, and she did so to try to break through Diana's hardened emotions. Often Dr. Brunswick would spend the time lecturing on psychoanalytic theory, as if they were in a classroom; in fact, one such lecture helped Diana to discover, on her own, she said, the source of one of her phobias. (Oddly, she never mentions which one.) Diana stayed as Dr. Brunswick's patient for five years, at least getting, she says, "a first glimpse of psychoanalysis."

And always, Diana and Lionel talked. "We never stopped talking," she said, "except at breakfast. Lionel couldn't stand the sight of me because I was talking. I started talking the minute I got out of bed. Lionel did not." Also, Lionel did not like Diana talking about him to others. She often tried to defend him during testy discussions with friends. "I can take care of myself," he would tell Diana. "I do not have to have my wife intervene to protect me."

With her political activities behind her, or about to be, Diana tried to figure out what else to do with her life. Singing was no longer an option. Nor was writing plays, short stories, and poetry. Lionel's career wasn't going anywhere, either. She felt as if they had thrown away the early years of marriage to "illness and responsibility, and dreariness and neurosis." She was angry that because of her relationship with her parents and siblings, she had learned "total sacrifice" but had not figured out any "strategies of living and working with others." She knew bullying, and that was one reason she jumped into arguments—to protect Lionel from what she had suffered. She felt compelled to look after him, often as a pretense of demonstrating to him how to protect *her.*

Lionel had developed some physical problems when they were first married. He had back trouble. "He had it in some measure all his life,"

Diana later said. "He always had a 'back' as they called it. We don't say we have 'a stomach' or 'a heart,' but you have a 'back.' He sometimes wore a heavy leather and metal girdle. When we were in our first year of marriage, this was terribly, terribly difficult . . . and sometimes he had digestive problems."

Still, Lionel continued teaching and struggling with his Matthew Arnold dissertation, which was overdue. "He was writing badly, limping along . . . floundering, and his adviser, Emery Neff, rejected each draft," Diana said. "All his life Lionel worried that he was an insufficient scholar. He worried that he didn't know Greek; he worried that he hadn't been properly trained in philosophy; he worried that he didn't have enough skill in modern languages. This was a great burden to him when he was working on the Matthew Arnold."

In 1936 Lionel underwent a crisis at Columbia. Diana almost couldn't believe what happened to her husband. As she described the events, "he was told he was being let go, that he would be happier elsewhere. He said, 'No.' He wouldn't be happier elsewhere, but they said yes he would, and so he came home with this terrible report, and it just climaxed all our expectations for ourselves." Diana was stunned. "That's what life was like," she said. "It was just horrid. . . . Lionel thought he 'was the very model of failure, the very model of defeat.'" How could she properly reassure him when she felt the same way about herself?

Lionel told her, she said, that "'they weren't firing me because I was a Jew or a Marxist or a Freudian. They were groping for things to say because they thought I was nothing. They just thought I didn't add up to anything. . . . I had the stamp of failure on me, and I invited their cruelty. I invited their aggression; also I gave them no promise. They had to find language in which to express it, and it had some significance that they chose Freud, Marx, and Jewishness as things that discredited me, but that is not why they fired me.'" (Diana later explained that Lionel had been told that his appointment had been "put through without the democratic consent of the department," that actually there "was no fault in his teaching," and that Emery Neff had told Lionel that his "sociological tendencies had hidden his literary gifts in the thesis as in the classroom.")

Soon, Diana said, Lionel did something totally out of character. He roared into Columbia, and as Diana proudly recounted, told them, "'You can't fire me. I'm going to be the best person you've ever had in this department.'" She said, "It was like madness . . . going from one office to another. Lionel yelled and swore in Emery Neff's office, and Neff said, 'Shhhhhh,' and jumped and closed the transom so that it couldn't be heard outside." Diana said that Neff was very shocked that Lionel was talking that way. "It must have been very, very much of a surprise to them that Lionel was taking this view of himself," she said, "because it was just the opposite of the view they all had of him. And they all fell for it. They all said, 'Well, look, he's got a lot of skills, maybe he has something going for us.' That's the way he interpreted it to me, to himself. Lionel said, 'You know, I've destroyed this image of me as the passive person who is just going to sit here and fail, and they bought my new picture of myself, just as they had bought my earlier picture of myself.'"

After the Columbia crisis Diana said her husband "was an absolutely changed man. . . . He told this story to everybody. Lionel didn't keep this a secret once it happened. . . . He had had this amazing showdown at Columbia."

Lionel was even able to get back to work on his Arnold dissertation. Sidney Hook, the Trillings' Yaddo mentor, later insisted he had been the person who had encouraged Lionel to fight back at Columbia. Diana disputes this: "Lionel was incapable of acting on other people's impulses." This would not always prove to be the case.

Diana said that Lionel "got right into the heart of the book and wrote. He wrote one chapter; he wrote the next; he knew where he was going . . . and then every single day proved him to be more and more a different person."

This happened because of more than just what Lionel had been able to achieve with his "amazing showdown."

It happened because Diana, too, had been changing, and had discovered a new gift—that she was a very capable judge of writing.

Diana became her husband's editor. "I was always working on the Arnold manuscript, from the first bad versions right on to when he was really on the final haul," she said. "It got to be my joke that what Lionel was writing over and over again was that England had had an industrial revolution yet the roads were bad, because what he was doing was not writing about Arnold but about the political and social conditions of England in Arnold's time. . . . Lionel hadn't yet integrated all this material with the work of Arnold himself," and that's why, she said, all the early drafts were rejected by his adviser. "There were days when he sat in front of his typewriter unable to produce a word. He never gave up and eventually he'd break through the barrier."

Diana went over the Arnold manuscript so many times, she said, "that by the time the final version went to press," she knew the book by heart. She said that she "had gone over and over and over [it], saying insane things like 'this paragraph has to have two more sentences. Somehow it's not full enough. This paragraph needs to have something lopped off it.'" She knew it was "a rather odd way to talk to a writer. But the material was there," she said. And she knew what to do with the material. "I'm not saying I wrote the book. I'm not claiming credit for the thought," she said, "just for its presentation. I made the thought, Lionel's thought, clearer, more understandable, more graceful, better balanced. I made the book go forward at a proper pace."

Diana said she never changed the fundamental character of Lionel's writing in editing him as much as she did. She "just pulled the ideas out of him." And while she said he was grateful for her help, nonetheless, "sometimes he would go into despair at her criticisms and say he couldn't do it." Once Lionel showed her "with amusement how she had rewritten a page of Arnold." He was entertained, she said, and quipped that 'I couldn't keep my hands off anything, could I?'"

But always, Diana emphasized that the ideas were there in the thesis, and "I never contributed the ideas." She only made them more coherent and better organized.

She also created the index for the book, a task that greatly satisfied her bookkeeping inclinations. She discovered many changed words and punctuations in some of the quotations used in the book, which Lionel thought didn't matter, but Diana was "stubborn" (her word) and insisted on checking every single quote. They hired a young man to find the many books from which all the quotations came, and, as Diana said, "Lionel had a great instinct for then finding [most of] the necessary quotes [from the trove of books]. He could open a book to the passage he was looking for—it was a most extraordinary gift." She also said she "wouldn't have dared to do the work if Lionel hadn't been right there to consult," yet "sometimes we'd spend the whole day searching for one sentence. We both were searching. . . . We were soaked with sweat. . . . There was not one quote that didn't have an error in it." She continued:

If anyone wanted to, they could have destroyed him with this. There would be the most inconsequential thing, and there was something wrong with every single quote. At the end of chapter 1, Lionel said, "Well, thank god that's done, now we can stop." I said, "That's chapter 1 that's done, but there's the whole rest of the book," and he said, "The rest is all fine." And there we were right back in the beginning again. I yelled. I said I wouldn't leave the office . . . and we got through chapter 2 in a few days. At the end of chapter 2, Lionel said, "Now it's all right. Everything is fine." Now it never bothered me that Lionel made these mistakes because, after all, when he took those notes, he didn't know whether he was going to use them. They were notes for him to write from. He didn't know he was going to quote them. But that once having shown that there were errors, not to be able to accept that—it was the largest act of literary denial in the technical, psychoanalytical that I've ever seen. With every chapter he denied that this was a reality. He never, to the end of his life, admitted this. Around once a year we fought about this. I think probably around once a year we came near [to] killing each other on this. Because I would say, "It's just like what you did on the Arnold. I don't care that you made mistakes. I care that you denied that you made the mistakes and that I had to fight like this to make you clean up your mistakes." "Oh," he would continue and say, "I didn't make any mistakes. You're just trying to make it out that I made mistakes." And this went on like this for the rest of our lives.

Diana had found an occupation: "being Lionel's helper this way," as she put it. She was not surprised he respected her judgment as he did because on the most minor of scales he had been an admirer of the letters she wrote him before their marriage (if not, afterward, of her play *Snitkin*), as well as the discussions they often had long into the night about books and politics. Lionel had once suggested, of course, that she could turn to writing if her singing career did not work out.

And despite all her insecurities, Diana understood—as did Lionel—that she had a very special gift as an editor of words—just as a musician knows he or she has a gift for chosen sounds. She had, she now knew, "a natural feeling for prose not her own—how to make it better." And she also knew that Lionel deeply believed in her editing skills, even though he didn't want the world to know of her revisions.

Diana lamented that Lionel destroyed the manuscripts she worked on so they wouldn't be among his papers. She said that he "left earlier versions on which for one reason or another I hadn't worked, [but] wherever there was a really notable amount of my handwriting, he destroyed the manuscripts." And she further divulged that her "rewriting of Lionel's manuscripts, not only the Arnold, but all his manuscripts, was most extensive." (Years later, Lionel told the editor Elisabeth Sifton that Diana had taught him how to write and that "she knows when a paragraph should end.")

Still, "whatever our unconsciouses were doing to us," Diana explained, "every conscious commitment was honorable and trustworthy, on both sides. I've never been able to find in our relationship—and this is probably the most remarkable thing—a single instance of competitiveness with each other or putting the other's welfare before our own."

It was complicated, Diana and Lionel Trilling's language and behavior, and *complicated* soon became one of their necessary words.

6

THE GREATEST SERVICE

*My debt to my wife Diana Trilling is greatest of all; I cannot
calculate its full sum, for it amounted to collaboration; at
every stage of the book she was my conscience, and there was
scarcely a paragraph that was not bettered by her unremitting
criticism and her creative editing.*

—LIONEL TRILLING, PREFACE TO *MATTHEW ARNOLD*

When Lionel's book on Arnold was finally published in 1939
(the manuscript had been finished the year before), it contained a gushing tribute to Diana. Her "creative editing"!
Her husband's "conscience"! Her "collaboration"! Whatever reason
he had for throwing out the drafts of his wife's editing didn't mean he
wasn't very grateful for her help; it more likely meant he was made uncomfortable by his first drafts, as well as feeling ashamed of needing so
much help.

And he hoped Diana's role could remain his secret despite the book's
dedication, which in general is recognized by knowledgeable readers to
be a place for hyperbole and thus not always to be taken that seriously.

Lionel also kept his depression—"his emotional darkness," as Diana called it—a secret from others. "It was well-hidden from public view," she said, "and it predated our marriage."

"He had his secrets and his cunning with which to subvert his upbringing and devise a tolerable destiny," Diana explained. "Which of us was sicker?" she asked herself. "I would have to leave it to the doctors to say, but my symptoms were certainly more colorful. . . . Every marriage is a conspiracy of health and ill health. Ours was both." But Diana was now part of Lionel's present destiny, one he could control, so he could toss out those embarrassing early drafts.

A friend who had gone to library school told Diana that the drafts of a manuscript that go to the publisher or to the printer are probably the most valuable versions and that perhaps Lionel was saving only those copies. But Diana would have nothing to do with that explanation; she knew that he just didn't want the world to know of her extensive editing. Despite her disappointment in not being part of a lasting paper legacy, she firmly believed that her husband "was unique in his lack of resentment for the work I did for him." Clearly, his enthusiastic dedication attests to that conviction.

Matthew Arnold was published by W. W. Norton, and Lionel was asked to contribute $250 toward its production, a sum he had to borrow from friends. (The book was published also in England by George Allen and Unwin.) "You couldn't get a PhD without publishing," Diana said. "You had to publish first. You had to have a professional publication of your thesis, and you had to deposit a hundred copies or seventy-five copies in the library. You had not only to write the damn book, you had to go through all the torture of finding a publisher for it." (The first reader at Norton who recommended the book for publication happened to have been the writer Eleanor Clark, once briefly married to one of Trotsky's secretaries and later to Robert Penn Warren.)

Publication gained Lionel an assistant professorship at Columbia and a small raise. The book was highly praised by none other than the university's president, Nicholas Murray Butler. (The often controversial leader had once been an admirer of Mussolini and Hitler, and he had complex feelings about Jews.) Yet when the time came for Lionel to gain permanent status, he became the first tenured Jew in Columbia's English department.

The Trillings were invited to a lavish white-tie dinner party at the president's residence on Morningside Drive, and Diana saw the invitation as "marking the end of [a] decade of despair." After a formal dinner there was dancing, and Mrs. Butler took Diana aside and whispered to her, "You must go and dance, dear. You mustn't be so serious." Naturally, she obeyed. She was not going to spoil a grand and entertaining evening.

The book on Arnold had been their life for nearly ten years, and Diana believed her husband's "wonderful study of the 19th Century" was a "triumph." There were criticisms, but in general the reviews were very positive. Edmund Wilson wrote in *The New Republic* that the book was "probably too long" and found the summing up of Arnold's poems and essays "occasionally a little dull." (It had been Wilson who encouraged Lionel to write about Arnold in the first place.) F. R. Leavis called the book "disappointing" in *Scrutiny*, a literary periodical he had cofounded to help sustain rigorous intellectual values. Lionel Trilling's book was "disappointing because its intention is clearly so admirable," Leavis wrote. Still, Leavis agreed with Wilson's overview that the book "is a credit both to [Trilling's] generation and to American criticism in general." Edward Sackville-West wrote in the *Spectator* that it was "the most brilliant work" of English language criticism in the 1930s. William Phillips, soon to become a close friend of the Trillings, wrote in *Partisan Review* that the book is "one of the best works of historical criticism produced in this country."

From the moment she had met Lionel, Diana was fascinated by the literary profession; in fact, she soon realized that the intellectual atmosphere of Lionel's "kind of writer," as she characterized it, was just the sort of orbit in which she wanted to move. But she stood, she said, "at the borders of the literary community" and felt as if she was way off course. Once at a faculty club dinner a member of Lionel's department came up to her to ask if she had been her husband's typist on his Arnold book, adding, "How could a wife do more than that?" She thought he was just being "mischievous" since he had a "twinkle in his eye," but she could also tell he was curious if she had really done—and been—what Lionel wrote about her in his dedication. "The idea that a woman had really worked on every single word and phrase in a man's book is really very unattractive to men," she said.

In 1934, two years before his crisis at Columbia, Lionel, still an instructor, had begun teaching a joint colloquium with Jacques Barzun every Wednesday evening. The Barzun-Trilling colloquium was intended for upper-classmen and involved reading some of the great literary works of Western civilization—Plato's *Republic*, Homer's *Iliad*, and Dante's *Divine Comedy*. Barzun, a historian who was called "a man of letters of the people," had entered Columbia when he was sixteen years old, and he graduated in 1927, two years after Lionel. Barzun and Trilling weren't great friends while undergraduates—Barzun thought that Lionel had "affected a sort of Bohemianism" and was " stand-offish." (Lore Dickstein, the literary critic, said that her husband, Morris, a historian and literary critic, as well as a former Trilling student, told her that many of the undergraduates considered Lionel "a very icy person.")

Barzun later told Diana that the book on Arnold was "a masterpiece of intellectual biography." He later wrote that "whoever is willing to let the long roll and retreat and fresh surge of Trilling's thought carry him from outset to destination will find it is clear, firm, undeviating despite its wave-like movements, and unambiguous in its delivery of the particular complication it proposes to establish."

Barzun developed a lifelong friendship with both Trillings and said that in his relationship with Lionel he did not remember a single moment of irritation at anything said or done despite being the more impatient of the two. Lionel once asked Barzun to help him create a contest to be conducted by the *New York Evening Post* that required readers to identify selections from some of the great books. Barzun would receive $200 for his efforts (he needed the money) out of the $1,000 Lionel asked for and received from the newspaper. Diana said that "the two of them became a pair of maniacs let loose among our bookshelves. They had knives, scissors. . . . They'd grab books off the shelves and start ripping the pages out. For a while, until we replaced these sources, you couldn't pick up a book in our house that hadn't been mangled. (There is no record of when, or if, the contest was ever printed.)

Barzun and Trilling helped to bring the practice of cultural criticism to America. It was "a genre making its way, cuckoo-like into the nest of scholarship," Barzun wrote. In England F. R. Leavis had stressed in his book, *For Continuity*, published in 1933, the importance of having well-trained, university-based intellectual leaders to help uphold culture and literature. Diana said that "Lionel's Columbia generation taught each other, and they worked it all out. It was the birth of criticism in this country. They were the founding fathers," just as Leavis was the founding father of a new rigorous literary criticism in Britain.

In 1934 Barzun said, "It was still risky for the young to write and publish 'outside' [the university] say a book review in a weekly journal of opinion" (as they both did). He said that Lionel, "without trying, made disciples, and of the best kind—not expounders of a system or repeaters of catchwords, but scholars, critics, teachers, who were awakened from dogma by Lionel's 'Word,' or who were caught on the wing of an idea, perhaps casually thrown off, and nurtured the germ into a free-standing plant. . . . His teaching was, by the nature of his thought, a reshaping of the mind, not an indoctrination."

Both men were greatly influenced by the Pulitzer Prize–winning poet and critic Mark Van Doren, who began teaching at Columbia in 1920 (following his older brother Carl, a Pulitzer Prize–winning biographer, who became a member of the faculty after he earned his doctorate there in 1911). As Diana wrote, "For years any Columbia undergraduate with literary ambitions brought his poems and stories to Mark Van Doren for criticism. Lionel did; all his hungry friends did." She said that Van Doren set an example for academics who wanted to write, showing that they could bridge both worlds.

Barzun said that he and Lionel "read and discussed all of each other's writing in first draft." He "had some hint" of Diana's important work on the manuscripts but nothing more than that. It was never discussed. He knew, of course, that both he and Diana believed in Lionel's extraordinary gifts.

"It's like an echoing chamber," Diana explained about her husband's prose; "he can stay with an idea and let it resonate and reverberate," while in her own tentative writing attempts she believed she moved too fast and didn't give her ideas "their full day." She said that "Lionel always had the gift for the work. What he didn't have was the ability to use his gift." She said that she had discovered that she could "preserve the individual quality of another person's writing yet make it better."

Barzun had been recently divorced when Diana first met him. He moved to the Trillings' apartment building on 114th Street and "was in our house more than he was in his own," Diana said. She recalled that for a time he wanted to work in the same room with Lionel; "he loved companionship, and he said why couldn't they set up their desks next to each other. This was a great problem for Lionel because he didn't like that close a companionship while he was working, and he didn't want to hurt Jacques's feelings. This was a little bit difficult to handle, but he handled it. But they were together a great deal."

And most important, Diana said, "I didn't get any 'What are you doing moving in on your husband's literary life?' from Jacques, not at all."

She said that when Barzun married his second wife, Mariana, which he did while living on 114th Street, "it was a little more difficult. Mariana was a difficult woman to get on with; she was a person of very limited intelligence and very, very odd Boston ideas. I mean, the century had moved on without taking Mariana with it." Diana went on to say that Mariana "was a leftover of the Boston I had known when I had been at Radcliffe, a Boston in which it meant something to be a Lowell. She was a Lowell . . . and she was constantly walking on eggs with me because she was always meaning not to say something anti-Semitic and so something was always blurting out. She was a most awkward, blurting out kind of woman for all her breeding. . . . One time she said to me, 'The difference between you and me is that you have really good manners.' I thought it was the most endearing thing she ever said. . . . She had a kind of openness of that sort." (In later years they became very good friends; "I was devoted to her," Diana said.)

A year after Lionel began coteaching the colloquium, even though he was still an instructor, his schedule became crowded with meetings with students and members of his department. Five years later, after Lionel was promoted, his schedule almost burst at the seams. "Everybody wanted him to write for them," Diana said—*Partisan Review, The New Republic, The Nation.*

In a chatty letter, Diana's college friend, Bettina Sinclair, wrote Diana: "Have you given any thought (tons of it, no doubt) to how you are going to spend your time while Li is out bread winning?" Diana couldn't tell Bettina, as close as they were, about her main occupation as Lionel's editor or how much confidence that role had given her. She did mention she was trying to do some writing and was sending her work to magazines. But she did not mention she was trying to overcome her childhood admonition that writing held danger.

Cleanth Brooks Jr., the cofounder of *The Southern Review*, rejected a story called "The Namesake," but he praised its "good writing" and asked to see more of her work. Kip Fadiman, who became the book editor of *The New Yorker* in 1933, passed along "a little sketch" called "Eight to Nine" to an editorial assistant, after telling Diana, "It's touching and so *woebegone*—as who isn't." The sketch was rejected as "a little too slight," although the assistant asked: "Won't you please try us soon with something else?" The three-page sketch, told from the point of view of an eight-year-old girl who mimics her mother's clothes and flirtations, starts with her stretching out her small sweater to create a long and stylish "hobble skirt," a kind of skirt so narrow it causes a woman to totter, and ends with her succumbing to a schoolgirl crush on a fellow ocean liner passenger during a family trip to Europe. As Diana wrote, "With the sweater around my legs and a Spanish shawl draped over my ferris waist [a corset garment created in the 1900s by the Ferris Bros. Company] revealing only my bare shoulders and arms I could easily be mother in an evening dress. Mr. Briggs was very tall, much bigger than father, and even mother whisked her hair into place when he came up on deck." But alas, at the end of the voyage Mr. Briggs never says goodbye. Still, Diana wrote, "I am sure Mr. Briggs loved me, too." After the family was safely home, the girl still hoped he would show up. But only a bicycle did—a gift from her parents. Quickly switching her allegiance from Mr. Briggs to a new boy on the block, the girl decides to race him, and instead of getting him to fall in love with her expertise, as is her plan, she falls off her bike, as Diana had done in real life decades ago. In her story "the nice little boy had carried me into the house all by himself," whereas back in Brooklyn no one had come to Diana's rescue. The woebegone story was never published anywhere.

She tried *The New Yorker* again with a six-page story called "Only Emma." The opening line reads, "We had always had someone to do Miss Emma Twickham's job at Camp Sansouci and I don't think it was because she was to be the camp disciplinarian that we all took such an immediate dislike to her." Diana was escaping into fiction again, this time to the camp where she said she first began to understand that she was more intelligent and had greater perception than any of the other members of her family. ("Only Emma" was rejected, but sixty years later, Diana would immortalize the real place, Camp Lenore, in a long non-fiction piece published in *The New Yorker* the summer of 1996, a few months before her death.)

She continued to write poems, although none were published. All of them spoke of a passion awaiting release:

OH BE BRAVE

Summon the wind with your whistle
Bend the tall tree at your touch
Much that is loud is pretending
Much that you fear is defending

SAD PORTRAITS OF LADIES

She stands upon the fading grass
All regal in her I-ness
She scatters love like autumn seed
Largesses-ness suits a Highness:
The Queenly eye and you-ly touch
However, do not get her much.

Diana tried to use her wit in a poem written sometime before 1933 that she sent to Malcolm Cowley at *The New Republic*. It was rejected:

LITERARY WIFE

Which dress will you wear tonight
When you come to my house to sit and talk of
Edmund Wilson?
Of D. H. Lawrence and significance
Virginia Woolf's relations, insignificance?
Or shall it be the coming revolution?
The unemployed apples are rotten with the worms of discontent
This country's ripe for juicy murder
—The juice of conversation's dry, completely dried;
We need cafés, liqueurs,
—More sexual exhibition. Without sex
Conversation dies at birth:
The American woman dies at marriage.
—What kind of house shall it be?
In Brittany—in Italy?
O sun of Guggenheim, shine down upon us three:
We try so hard to save; my father always said
I should have studied economics.
—Oh, for God's sake, take Polly:
Polly has a part-time maid
A part French maid has she
Who prepares escallopine
(avec marrone purees)
And goes to Toscanini
Every other Thursday.
Only the early Beethoven does not pall.
Let's search the soul of gaiety for awhile
Let's spawn a Mozart, forget our counterpointed Freuds
Our art has overboiled.
Let's talk of gastronomics.

In 1939, after ten years of marriage and no children, she decided to write a series of more than twenty children's poems. All were rejected by the McCall Corporation, which published *McCall's* magazine, as well as two short story magazines, *Blue Book* and *Red Book*:

I AM TWO

When I was under two years old
The question what to wear
Was very simply answered:
I didn't really care.

ANIMAL LESSON

Kangaroos and owls
Don't wipe their hands on kitchen
Towels
Camels are most suspicious
Of people who eat out of dishes
But an owl hoots
A kangaroo jumps
And whoever heard of a camel with
Mumps?

Diana also wrote a children's book called *Beppo*, about a canary who "had a big chest and wore boots" and didn't tweet-tweet but only sang "muh-muh-muh-muh." This, too, never found a home. Sometime in the late 1930s Diana tried her hand at a short memoir called *The Prodigious Trip*, about a time when she and her sister and brother gave a concert to celebrate their parents' fifteenth wedding anniversary. Diana and Cecilia alternately played the piano, and Sam played the violin. "It was a mad idea," Diana wrote, and they played and played until their grandfather insisted they stop. The memoir was left unfinished.

In the early 1940s she decided to write what she called a "simplified" version of Kenneth Grahame's classic *The Wind in the Willows*. This never found a publisher in part because, for reasons known only to her, she took the drama out of the story by making one of the main characters, "Mr. Toad," just a minor one.

Throughout the 1930s and into the 1940s Diana and Lionel remained in psychoanalysis. "The expense was frightful," she said. Lionel's salary was less than $4,000 a year. It was a stressful time for both Trillings, and Diana's would-be writing career was going nowhere (even though most women during this period did not pursue careers).

Lionel's journal indicates that after the publication of his book on Arnold, he began to have a new problem, a sexual problem. It was impotence. But at the time, Diana had troubles of her own she had to worry about. Lionel also continued to have problems with his back. He wrote in his journal that "there was mention made by L [his analyst, Dr. Rudolph Lowenstein], or me, I forget—of the beginning of my sexual difficulties at the point of my beginning to be successful [i.e., with the publication of *Matthew Arnold*]." (A decade later, Trilling would explain more in his journal about his ambivalence toward his achievements, noting his "intense disgust with my official and public self, my growing desire to repudiate it. . . . I used the phrase *lese mageste*—I felt that this crime had been committed against me and the use of the phrase seemed to carry great meaning, summing up that part of my childhood that was dealt with as if it were privileged, royal. There is the sense in which this was literally true—in which I was thought of as a prince.")

Lionel's impotence was disturbing and most likely only one reason for the couple's not having had a child for nine years. It was also a reason for Diana's sublimating her need for a child into verses. She was now thirty-four years old.

I WANT MY OWN NAME

> If my name is Freddy and Dad's name is Freddy
> Now how can I tell us apart?
> If Mother calls "Freddy" and I answer "ready"
> Is that a mistake at the start?

TIPPY

When Tippy was a baby
Her head was almost bare
I'm told she had a little fluff,
You'd hardly call it hair;
She hadn't pretty ringlets
To tie up with the pain
She had to wear a bonnet
That tied beneath her chin;
She never had a shampoo
Her mommy says "why bother?"
A little oil will do as well
For babies, as a lather.

Another poem about Tippy ends—

I'd like to have a birthday
A birthday now and here;
I'm much too in a hurry
To wait another year.

But "Tippy" and Diana would have to wait.

Her doctor after Dr. Ruth Brunswick was a William Dunn, her first non-Jewish psychoanalyst. As Diana wrote in *The Beginning of the Journey*, "He was not a conspicuously astute physician. He frequently reminded me that it was not necessary for an analyst to be as quick-witted as his patient. But he was gentle and kind and conscientious and, in wonderful contrast to his predecessor, he was unfailing in his attention—until he died of a heart attack."

Some essential work had been started in dealing with what she referred to as her "pent-up unexplored passion of my infant love for my father" (Diana was serious in her use of psychoanalytic jargon), but there was not enough progress to suit her. Nonetheless, she would say that psychoanalysis did her "the greatest service," even though she ultimately thought that Dr. Dunn evaded the real issue: that her love for her father, which gave her the "capacity for love," also gave her a "lasting fear of rejected love."

Diana often bristled at her husband's criticizing what he called her lack of manners. She enjoyed the freedom of putting her feet up on a table or chair because she had not been allowed to do that as a child. But Lionel didn't like it either. "Please put your feet down; don't sit like that," he would tell her. "That was not good for me," Diana groused, although to win Lionel's approval she always took notice.

"If you want to call my wish for Lionel's approval a weakness, okay, it was a weakness," Diana admitted. "Certainly as an aspect of my dependence on him it was an enormous weakness. In its very nature the dependence was pathological. But an ingredient of my desire for his approval was my loyalty to him and the feeling that he had something very special about him with which I wanted to ally myself and which I of course wanted to advance. That doesn't mean that I didn't think I was important or that I didn't want a great deal for myself too—but I did feel secondary in the sense of putting his powers first."

It had been much the same with her father—admiring, worshipping, really, even in the face of his barbs about her singing. Yet, as she wrote in an unpublished book, "Were I to choose someone with whom to work in the underground, someone to rely on to the death, who would never betray a trust, of all the men I have known in my life my father would be my first choice."

Diana often thought about something the pitiful Dr. Brunswick had told her. In addition to the analyst's peculiar behavior in the office, she sometimes spoke to Lionel on the phone, as a previous analyst had also done. Diana learned that during one conversation Dr. Brunswick mentioned some appointments Diana had broken, and Lionel had been so concerned that he told Dr. Brunswick Diana's behavior "was an emergency with her neurosis." At the next session with Diana, Dr. Brunswick told Diana what her husband had said. "What makes him think that you are anymore an emergency than he is?" she asked her patient. "You're no more an emergency than he is."

Diana was not happy with this statement. In fact, she said it shocked her. It shocked her not because an analyst had once again been unprofessional and spoken to her husband, or that Lionel had said what he did, but that "anybody dare say that Lionel was as much a neurotic emergency as I was." It meant he "lacked the strength to protect me," and she added, "the fact is that nobody was allowed to say a word in criticism of Lionel, least of all myself."

7

THE NATION CALLS

I did not speak [to his psychoanalyst] of the accusation that D had made a few years ago of my assumption of a role of superiority, of haughtiness, of indifference or condescension to her. . . .

—LIONEL TRILLING, JOURNAL ENTRY, JUNE 1952

Out-and-out frustration had caused the newlywed Lionel to throw his favorite pipe out the window of their Bank Street apartment after the unpleasant aftermath to his criticism of Diana and Bettina's play, *Snitkin*. Diana always thought that her husband had been excessive in his expressed hatred of the play she and Bettina had written just for fun. Why had he also resorted to a tantrum and wrecked his pipe? Every now and then Diana thought of something that her mother-in-law had told her in what she assumed was jest but that, she later came to understand, was said in utter seriousness. Fannie Trilling had warned her that if Lionel ever got into a rage with her, Diana "was to take a bottle and hit him on the head." Diana later learned that Lionel's father, David ("who was too narcissistic in his later years to have a relation with anybody except himself and his health") had "furies."

In fact, in one outburst he had reached over and torn his wife's blouse almost to shreds.

Diana said Lionel had an obsession that was crucial to some of his "emotional difficulties," and this was "his belief that all of his problems had been created by me."

Soon after the pipe episode, a pattern of outbursts began. Diana said that Lionel exploded at her "sometimes for an hour, sometimes many hours, days, even weeks. . . . His face would be all contorted and gray and he'd just be at me." And she later admitted that "this kind of anger that Lionel directed at me lasted the whole of his life, really, although he never tore or broke things, or even screamed. But he could be fiercely angry and verbally cruel to me, very cruel. . . . He'd keep working at it, tormenting me with accusations. . . . And for a long long time, far longer than it should have, it absolutely undid me."

Lionel would tell his wife that she was ruining his life and that his marriage was terrible. She called such talk "his encapsulated madness."

"As soon as he had me in a complete state of collapse," she said, "he would come over and want to make up. I was pulp and he was purged. . . . It made him suffer, and it made me suffer," she added poignantly. "There was a terrible misuse of me," she said.

Even though she and Lionel were never "in love"—in storybook love—she said candidly, they loved each other, yet it wasn't a "romantic marriage." "But we were deeply, deeply devoted to each other's interest and well-being," she said. "We never thought anything was being taken away from us by being married to each other; it was only something being added to."

Still, she said that "when Lionel and I were angry at each other and feeling we couldn't stand to be married to each other any longer, which happened frequently, we would have the feeling 'Let's get divorced. Come on. Let's get rid of this marriage. Enough already.' And we were very sincere when we'd say that. But you know, there was no more chance of our having done that than fly—we were so terribly married to each other."

Yet over time she realized that her husband "really did have a thing going about women. He hated women at certain moments and in

certain situations. . . . I suppose every marriage has something in it
that people don't talk about."

In their case it was three "elephants" in the room. The "furies," the
impotence, and Diana's major contribution to Lionel's work.

When not in a rage, Lionel often gave his wife the silent treatment,
the tactic Diana's father had sporadically used on her. Even at meals
Lionel sometimes refused to talk, and as Diana wrote in *The Beginning
of the Journey*, he often seemed "angry at his food. He pushed a potato
away from him on his plate as if it were his contemptible enemy—I had
seen [Lionel's father] make the same gesture." Diana later commented
that, paradoxically, David Trilling was always a negative image for
Lionel and that "the whole of his life was not to be like his father . . . who
had no sense of obligation to his household." She added, "The moment
David Trilling stopped being the main and only support of the family,
he stopped being any support and could only think of his private requirements. He would come to wheedle money out of Lionel for his drug-
store bills. . . . He gave me the creeps." And, Diana said, by the time she
came on the scene, David and Fannie mostly communicated through
their children.

With his outbursts well-hidden from public view, Lionel "lived his
life and could be very charming," Diana said. It was why she had once
called him deceptive. No one knew what was going on in his head and
in his home, and Diana continued to contribute to their life in ways that
enabled her husband to write. "There were days and days when Lionel
sat in front of his typewriter unable to produce a word," she said. "He
never gave up, and eventually he'd break through the barrier," with her
help. She knew that she did more for Lionel than other wives of writer
husbands did. It was the right thing to do and what she knew was expected of her. It wasn't exactly giving in to the total sacrifice she had
learned as a child, but it was close to it.

Diana sometimes thought of Lionel's "furies" as his aiming his "depression at me." She said that she considered his three different analyses
"largely unsuccessful"; nonetheless, he "indeed wanted to be cured of
his depression. . . . It was extremely painful. He wanted to be rid of it.
He wanted to be cured of his writing block. He had great difficulty

writing through most of his life, but he never subscribed to that modern idea that neurosis is health and a validation of one's creative gifts." And, she emphasized, "he did not let his own clinical experience color his assessment of Freud's contribution to thought." (Years later, Diana said that he even acknowledged "grudgingly" that his mother's excessive coddling that caused him "miseries," as well as her obsessive dreams for his literary success, might have spurred him on, and "in all his dealings with women, certainly in his dealings with me, his unadmitted early love for his mother was, I think, a stronger factor than his reasonable complaints against her.")

In 1937, two years before his book on Arnold was published, Lionel began writing for the new, Communist-free *Partisan Review*, a magazine whose strong intellectual and cultural influence would last for decades. It was edited by William Phillips and Philip Rahv, two men who had first met at meetings of the John Reed Club. Both men, and their wives, would become close friends of the Trillings.

Diana, gratified by her husband's accomplishments, nonetheless began to feel very uncomfortable at the *Partisan Review* parties they attended. Her views were overlooked in discussions by and large because she was not a writer, at least not a published one. "If you went in as a wife, which I did in the early years of my married life, they [the parties] were hell," she later told the writer Patricia Bosworth. Mary McCarthy, who was listed on the masthead of the first issue of *Partisan Review*, wrote an occasional theater column for it, and at the time was living with Rahv, especially snubbed Diana. McCarthy focused all her attention on Lionel. But Lionel did not enjoy being in her spotlight. "What makes an intelligent woman suppose that the way to attract a man is to be rude to his wife?" Lionel asked Diana, as she reported in *The Beginning of the Journey*. She later made clear that despite everything, "Lionel never got upset about anything that happened to himself the way he got upset if something went wrong for me, and I felt that way about him." This was because of "their extraordinary mutuality," and "extraordinary alikeness." They had fierce and spirited minds and a powerful sense of loyalty that transcended their acute emotional difficulties.

Mary McCarthy, along with the political theorist (as she liked to be known) Hannah Arendt, and later on, the critic and novelist Elizabeth Hardwick, and the historian Bea Kristol, writing under her birth name Gertrude Himmelfarb, all had "honorary membership" in *Partisan Review*, Diana told Bosworth. And "they all weren't friendly at all," even though Himmelfarb and Diana would, for a long while, become pretty good pals. But in general, in the late 1930s, and for several decades after, there was no sisterhood. As for Arendt, Diana said that she "never said hello to me in her whole life. I guess she wanted to go to bed with Lionel. That was usually the reason when women weren't pleasant to me."

The parties "were primarily political," Diana told Bosworth, although intense flirting, the initiation of affairs, and heavy drinking all tied for first place. "Every time you went to a party you were flirting, flirting, flirting," Diana later elaborated. "Whether you did anything about it or not, that was what you were there for. Parties were for sex. They were for exploration," although she and Lionel considered themselves part of "the famous puritanical group." She did not name the other members.

The men were dubbed "The PR Boys," the women "The PR Girls." The "Boys"—Rahv, Phillips, Elliot Cohen, Meyer Schapiro (the art historian), and the writers Max Eastman, F. W. Dupee, and later Alfred Kazin and Delmore Schwartz—always led, while the "Girls," even if published writers, always took a secondary role. There was very little loyalty or patience among them all and a great deal of competitiveness and envy. The gatherings could be exhausting, and if the party included dinner, afterward the men usually retreated to another room for cigars and brandy while the women stayed behind, gossiping, sharing political news, dabbing at their lipstick, or sometimes helping to clean up.

One late afternoon in January 1941, the phone rang in the ground floor apartment at 620 West 116th Street. The drapes were already closed, although the apartment was always dark and gloomy-looking. Lionel, just home from his class, picked up the phone, which was on a table in the hallway leading to the back of the apartment. Diana listened to her husband's end of the conversation from the entrance to the kitchen, where she was standing. She understood at once that he was talking to Margaret Marshall, the literary editor of *The Nation*. She quickly surmised that Marshall was asking her husband if he had any candidates who might be interested in writing unsigned reviews of novels for the magazine. As soon as Lionel hung up the receiver, she walked over to him, smiled, and surprised herself by asking if she would be a suitable candidate. She wanted to be in the running. Lionel immediately agreed that it was a very good idea, though he mentioned that Marshall had a graduate student in mind for the job. He said he would speak to her but insisted that if Diana didn't work out for some reason, she should receive "no preferential treatment."

Diana liked the fact that the reviews would be unsigned so she could still cling to her father's ever-haunting proscription "against any form of self-display" (excluding family concerts with her siblings, and her aborted singing career, which her father had once callously proclaimed belonged in the toilet.)

At her next psychoanalytic hour Diana mentioned the potential *Nation* job, emphasizing her pleasure and relief at having unsigned reviews. There would be no fear of showing off. She was safe from harm. Dr. Ruth Brunswick, listening carefully for a change, suggested that perhaps Diana was hiding behind her father in an attempt to cover up her real objective, which was to have her name all over the magazine. Diana very quickly recognized the truth presented to her. "I always felt secure about my intelligence," she said, "much more secure than I felt about my exhibitionism . . . and I didn't have any doubt in my ability to do the work for *The Nation*."

There was one other matter—her name. Diana Rubin? Or Diana Trilling?

While married, she had once or twice signed her name to documents as Diana Rubin, but she felt more comfortable with *Trilling*. Lionel agreed that if she got the job (and she did), she should use *Trilling*. But some of the "PR Boys" had something to say to him privately: wouldn't she be an embarrassment to Lionel? Diana's insecurities had already translated into a haughtiness they disapproved of. They were dead serious about their objections. Lionel dismissed their warning and looked the other way, as he always did in such cases.

So at the age of thirty-six Diana began a career that seemed at first a whim but would become the "sustaining," she said, focus of her life.

And by 1942, the same year that her hostile acquaintance Mary McCarthy published her first novel, *The Company She Keeps*, Diana would have her own signed column, which, as a matter of fact, she had asked for, and Margaret Marshall had immediately agreed to.

Diana continued with her own writing, but now did mostly short sketches. She tried *The New Yorker* again, with a piece about eccentric bus conductors. She was told in February 1941 that "it is hardly substantial enough a piece" and that, anyway, they "try to steer somewhat clear of [that type of] piece." A year earlier she had tried to get an agent, Nanine Joseph, to handle a novella she called "We Must March My Darlings" (which in 1977 would become the title of a book of her essays). Joseph wrote her that although she was "desperately sorry" that she couldn't take on the work, she believed that Diana had "a real idea here that is lost under words, many more words than necessary, so that nobody comes alive. . . . I think part of the difficulty is, as I said, you can't see the forest for the trees. . . . There's too much in it that you have put in to clarify things for yourself, but which in the end, obscured the reader."

Diana's need to map out every step of any argument—the kind of logic that gave her strength (and that annoyed the "PR Boys"—and some of the "Girls"—in conversations with her when she used "many more words than necessary") would stand her in good stead for book reviewing. But it was also stopping her from successfully writing fiction. ("I'm much too over-conscious, I suppose. I can't draw on some stream of unconscious feeling and let it go at that. I think that's how the novelist works," she later said.) Nonetheless, she went on trying and wrote a short story called "The Sale of a Work of Art," about a painter attending a Washington cocktail party, "the kind of person who *does* things instead of talking about them." The painter meets a very rich woman who wants to buy one of his works and appears very excited to do so, but the next day at the time when they are to meet at his studio, the buyer insultingly sends her ten-year-old daughter to choose any painting of *her* choice. The story was never published.

Diana decided to concentrate on her column, "Fiction in Review." It appeared in the "back of the book," as the Arts section was called, and was regarded as being anti-Communist, while the front section of the magazine was judged pro-Communist. "I was part of the spirit and politics of the back," Diana said. James Agee, who in 1941 had published *Let Us Now Praise Famous Men*, wrote about movies for the "back" after he left his position as the film critic for *Time* magazine; Clement Greenberg, an editor at *Partisan Review*, became *The Nation*'s art critic in 1941. F. W. Dupee and Delmore Schwartz wrote about poetry. From time to time Mary McCarthy contributed theater pieces. David Riesman, Eric Bentley, C. Wright Mills, and Reinhold Niebuhr reviewed nonfiction.

The novels—four to eight at a time—were sent to Diana's apartment (she never went to the magazine's office on lower Broadway), and she would go through every one of them and then decide which ones to write about. When she chose the books to review, she sat down and read every single word of each novel; sometimes she read them twice. At first she was a very slow reader, and then gradually she sped up. She worried constantly that she might overlook a very good book by an unknown writer.

Her first full-length review was of H. G. Wells's novel *You Can't Be Too Careful*. Wells was already famous for his scientific romances—*The Time Machine* and *The War of the Worlds*, as well as his nonfiction on world history and sociology. Of *You Can't Be Too Careful*, which would be his last novel, Diana wrote, it is "announced as a return to storytelling but actually it is a reformer's field day in which the story of Edward Albert Tewler is only a pretext for Wells to range the whole of modern English life, scolding, satirizing, waving the banner for science and education." Although she said the novel added nothing new to what Wells had said in the past, she applauded his desire to have "wise men settle the ills of society."

Shortly afterward, she reviewed *Marling Hall*, a novel by the once wildly popular Angela Thurkill, who wrote about the English upper class. Diana wrote that, while "advertised as a pleasant bundle of froth, Angela Thurkill is in fact a grim little person. For all her gentle voice, she is one of the great haters on the contemporary fictional scene. She hates sex, the movies and the lower class, except an occasional half wit [sic] mechanic." Margaret Marshall cut the review extensively, telling Diana that "Angela isn't worth so much space." Marshall had also asked Diana to make her comments "lighter and sharper, with more scorn and less anger." The revised review drew praise from the poet Louise Bogan (the poetry editor of The New Yorker, who would become the country's Consultant in Poetry in 1945). Bogan asked Marshall to "congratulate D. Trilling for me for the job she did on Angela Thirkel [sic]. Someone once gave me an AT to read on a train, and to my horror I found myself involved with a beady-eyed (spiritually!) English upper class vixen with venom in every pore. A 'grim little person' is wonderful."

Generally, Marshall edited Diana only lightly but often tried out theories and new ideas on her. At one point Marshall decided the magazine reviewed too much fiction and thought about just having a listing of relevant new novels. She also wondered if it was possible "to see, in general, more textual criticism of novels. One gets it only in reviews of poetry, and even only occasionally, and of course, it can be overdone." Diana was bewildered and hurt that Marshall thought she neglected "matters of style" and was asking her to change her "way of writing." In fact, Diana believed that she was being fired, especially since earlier Marshall had wondered if Diana "was being too sociological and insufficiently literary." (It would turn out that Randall Jarrell was the person who believed Diana was too sociological, and he had said so to Marshall.) But Marshall, herself, was specifically concerned that in Diana's review of Edmund Wilson's story collection Memoirs of Hecate County, although the review was "very good," Diana "hadn't said anything about the writing." Marshall accepted that Diana had explained that because Wilson's writing "varied so much in quality" she couldn't "get into it." But Marshall persisted, telling Diana that "the fact that the writing varied so much in quality was a principal and pertinent matter for discussion particularly in a review of a book by Wilson." But almost immediately the entire matter was laid to rest because Marshall decided that her "reservation was unjustified" because she fully understood that Diana's "main emphasis has been on the ideas—social and moral—in the novels you have reviewed, and that ideas are your primary interest." In fact, she was sorry she had brought the whole issue up because Diana had "her way of writing about fiction, [and] it's a good way and a distinctive way, and I like it." (Inked in next to this sentence were the words "Will you please believe me?") She continued to reassure Diana that she had not been trying to "eliminate" her; "that's the last thing I want to do."

Diana said that she always considered herself "a reporter with critical ideas rather than as a critic." And though her honesty often stabbed, and her praise seemed like a tickle, she continued "her way of writing about fiction."

She called Waugh's *Brideshead Revisited* "incoherent" and boring, causing one of her readers to comment that her review shows "the most violent prejudice" and that "undoubtedly Miss Trilling disapproves of Proust who mirrored a completely decadent society or Dostoyevsky whose characters are hopelessly enmeshed in a dying social order."

Diana wrote that she had never considered Sinclair Lewis a great novelist, and in reviewing his *Gideon Planish*, she found it "unimportant, sloppy, and even dull." However, she praised his "sweetness of temper" and his "boyish idealism," adding, "of which he is so boyishly ashamed."

Although she wrote that she is "antipathetic to historical novels," nonetheless, she could "heartily recommend the historical novels of Howard Fast," who had "taste and talent." (Two decades later his publisher would ask her to read a new novel by Fast, *Power*, for a fee of fifty dollars. She agreed to do this, providing her opinion was not quoted. There is no record of what she thought of the book or why the publisher needed an outside opinion.)

Diana continued to wield her logic. Elizabeth Hardwick's *The Ghostly Lover* earned "a poor score; it lacks drama and even a coherent story direction; many of the characters are not given their narrative due; there is no unity of prose rhythm; a large part of the book is dull reading." (Years later Hardwick remarked that she had never thought much of any of Diana's reviews.)

Marshall gave Diana a chance to write an occasional long essay, and on one occasion she chose to write about Alice James, the sister of Henry and William, who died at forty-four. Alice, an invalid all of her life, possessed an "extraordinary intensity of her will," Henry wrote of his sister and the journal she kept, also commenting later, in a letter from which Diana quoted, that Alice might have been a "feminine 'political force,' if her health had permitted." Diana described Alice James's journal as the "record of a life from which the elements of equality and reciprocity have so long been absent." She said that "Alice, too, can write that wonderful educated James prose with its incandescent accuracy and then its sudden flight of homeliness." Diana brought in a favorite subject— psychiatry—when she wrote, "by what miracles of accident or strength the two older brothers were able to rescue themselves as they did still remains an investigation for psychiatry." By this she meant the depression that the elder James had had, as did his five children. Trilling wondered if the birth order is a clue to the "fierce range of private symptoms." She was looking in literature for clues to Lionel's depression.

In reviewing *The Way Some People Live*, John Cheever's first collection of stories, Diana said they "are even more talented than the average stories" printed in *The New Yorker*, and she managed to write a treatise on the short story in general. She said that reading Cheever's stories "is a bit like holding a conversation in a language in which one has been well-schooled but in which one is still not fluent. . . . The best . . . are strongly-worded hints rather than completely communicated statements." She went on to lecture that "even more than our novelists, our present-day writers of short fiction not only choose inarticulate characters to write about but refuse to be articulate *for* them. It is an artificial limitation and wholly self-imposed, of a piece with the time-limitation in the contemporary short story. The sooner it is got rid of, the better for this branch of fiction."

Continuing to write about short stories, she reviewed a collection of Latin American stories and novelettes (they were all "promising") that included an introduction by Katherine Anne Porter. This time Diana included a discourse on artists in her review: "*Good* artists lie less than other people—bad artists probably lie rather more than less," she wrote. In a letter Porter told Diana that she herself did not "recognize the existence of the 'bad' artist. If he is 'bad,' that is, unserious, untruthful,

sentimental, he shouldn't be called [an] artist." Diana relished such ex-
changes; she saw them as keeping her "critical ideas" in circulation.

She did not like to review books by people she knew, although she
praised (in another magazine) Elinor Rice Hays's novel *Mirror, Mirror*
for its "uncommon approach" to "problem women" and Philip Rahv's
Discovery of Europe for being "as instructive as it is entertaining" and
said his prefaces were "models of lucid condensation."

After she began her full-length column in *The Nation*, she worried
that Mark Van Doren (who had recently written her that "you are doing
not only valiantly in your fiction reviews but brilliantly") would think
it peculiar that his novel *Tilda* was done in a brief, and not in a full-
length, column. Diana wrote in a note to Marshall: "Won't he think
that I did it, if he knows that I used to do the fiction briefs, and suppose
that it was some sort of purposeful distinction. . . . I'd be very grateful
if you'd explain it to him when you see him, or drop him a card or even
send him this note if you want to." Diana knew how important Van
Doren was to Lionel. She need not have worried, not only because
Van Doren understood the situation but the review he received from
her was an excellent one. The novel was called "a warm, simple, tender
love story," and "the characters are completely natural, so natural that
they seem capable of walking out of the pages of the book and continuing where their author left off. And the nicest thing about it is the way
the reader becomes gradually involved in the un-folding of the plot."

Diana's reviews gathered as much criticism as praise. She was accused
of making "sweeping and untrue indictments of the democratic writers
of the left" and then "of flirting with fascism," and sometimes of showing too much personality and not using artistic standards. One reader
accused her of attacking Catholicism; then another, the Rector of the
Grace Episcopal Church in Anderson, South Carolina, said he considered her reviews "to be absolutely within and true to Christian catego-
ries. They are almost theological." She decided she must be doing something right.

By 1943 she had received offers to review books for other magazines,
including *The New Republic*, the *Kenyon Review*, and the *New York
Herald Tribune Weekly Book Review*. In the summer of 1943 she was

also asked to read some manuscripts (she received fifteen dollars for each) for Viking Press. Pascal "Pat" Covici wrote that her "reports are extremely intelligent and lively reading. If only the manuscripts you rejected were half as good. That two people, you and Lionel, should both wield so fine and sharp a pen is one of the modern miracles. And I still love miracles."

8

NOT MERELY A CRITIC'S WIFE

Most of the book was written, as I well remember, in a concen-
trated rush, and although much of the enthusiasm and pleasure
of its composition is to be attributed to my liking for the sub-
ject, I have no doubt that I was benefited by the special energies
that attend a polemical purpose.

—LIONEL TRILLING, PREFACE TO *E. M. FORSTER*

In November 1943 Diana received an unusual letter of praise from
an editor at *PM*, the leftist daily newspaper published in New York.
Anita Berenbach wrote that Diana's reviews hit her "between the
eyes, and were so profound, and so veracious, and so well put!" She
added that a recent piece by Lionel of *A Choice of Kipling's Verses*, edited by and with an introduction by T. S. Eliot, was confusing and that
he "rather got himself into the woods." Summing up, Berenbach commented that "I like the kind of criticism that navigates its point and then
enlarges on it. Certainly a critic wants to be fair, but it is not fair for a
critic to be confused. Do you think Mr. Trilling might borrow some
acuity from you?"

The *Partisan Review* Boys and Girls, had they known of the letter, would not have been pleased. Lionel Trilling lost in the woods? Diana herself was left perplexed—disturbed, really—by the remark. Even though her star was rising, and their "friends" now made her feel as if she was at least worth listening to and was no longer wasting their time, she was, after all, just the wife. Diana really wanted it that way.

Or did she? Her analysis was taking her mind to new heights, even though her body, with its fear of heights, could not conquer them.

Lionel's book on E. M. Forster was published by New Directions in 1943. Amazingly, he wrote it in just six weeks. As Diana said, he "had such an uneven way of performing. He could spend weeks and weeks at certain times in his life, just looking at a blank page and writing the same thing over and over again. But he could also do some of the most difficult things very fast indeed. . . . With New Directions . . . he felt sure of himself, felt sure of his audience."

Diana did very little editing directly on the pages; instead, they talked things out. " 'No, that isn't what I'm saying,' he'd tell me, and I'd answer, 'What's wrong with it?' and he'd try again and finally I'd say, 'Why don't you just say that?' And he would."

Diana continued, "Maybe I helped form his rhetorical style. I don't know whether I did or didn't. But there is no question in my mind that when I went over his work, the prose was improved." She said that the Forster book revealed "the basic direction of his thought at the time, or, at least, one of its strands: his concern for the insufficiencies in the current practice of liberalism." This, too, was the direction in which Diana steered her own literary criticism.

Diana's sister, Cecilia, had been staying with them while recuperating from an operation to have some toes amputated. (The sisters got along better as they got older, as Diana did also with Harriet Trilling.) Lionel gave up his study for his sister-in-law and rented a room from a widow in their building who had a large apartment. "He stayed there for long hours each day," Diana said, "which was fortunate for him as he couldn't stand being near my sister." Diana said that she "tried to work at home in our living room as I always had, but my sister listened from down the hall, and if I stopped for even a moment, she would call me in coy admonition: 'Diana, I don't hear your typewriter.'"

Sometimes, Lionel helped her the same way she helped him. Diana said that when she occasionally got stuck on a review, he would sit next to her when she was at the typewriter and ask what she wanted to say. Lionel would coax her, "'Well, come on, suppose we say it this way,'" and then, Diana admitted, "I'd start screaming! 'No, that isn't what I want to say at all.'" But, she conceded, "Out of that might come something."

"In the 40s," Diana said, Lionel "was feeling his oats. Nobody wanted him for anything in the 1930s. Now suddenly, everybody wanted him, and I had a place, too. I wasn't that failed opera singer. I was a successful book critic."

Between reviews Diana continued to think of writing projects. For inspiration she often listened to Puccini as she wrote. In 1944, with the blessing of Pat Covici, who was very interested in luring Lionel to Viking Press, she considered organizing "an anthology of childhood." She told Covici that she had discovered that there was "almost no correlation between an interesting adult life and an interesting childhood—or rather between an interesting childhood and the ability to capture its import in maturity." She said that as far as she was concerned there were only two people who could combine childhood recollections with great insight and great literary skill—Stendhal and Henry James. Others to be included in her proposed book were Tolstoy, Yeats, Goethe, Edith Wharton, Helen Keller, and, curiously, P. T. Barnum. Despite her research and serious interest in the project, it never was completed; however, a warm relationship developed between Covici and both Trillings, and they often socialized.

In the following year, 1945, Diana wrote an article titled "The Psychology of Plenty," about an idea that Reinhold Niebuhr had heard during a recent tour of wartime Europe, that rationing should continue after the war. Diana wholeheartedly agreed and wrote that it was "a healthy idea," saying that Americans "take our abundant supplies of food for granted." She wondered "how many Americans have thought of the relation between the word *ration* and the word *rational*," and she went on to write that "we *ration* food so that everyone will have his fair share. This is the *rational* approach to the problem of distributing our food."

She did not find a publisher for her essay.

Every now and then Diana experimented by sending out work under the pseudonym Margaret Sayles. One short story, "The Marriage of Elsie and John," was about a wedding reception (not unlike her own) and irritable relatives who had not been invited to the actual ceremony. The story mentioned a browbeaten sister, enormous amounts of uneaten food, a mother and father who no longer slept in the same room, and an abandoned puppy. It was a depressing four-page tale that barely mentioned the bride and groom, although it somehow managed to shout that the wedding should never have taken place. The story was never published.

But Diana persevered. After she had published her long essay on Alice James, Edmund Wilson told her she must not write reviews anymore but should continue to write long essays. Diana, ten years younger than Wilson, was flattered by this advice and by the fact that he was helping a new writer with that kind of encouragement.

In 1945 Diana received high praise from William Maxwell of *The New Yorker*, who wrote her that "all practicing novelists must feel as I do that if there is any help to be got from reviews it will be from yours." But Diana's greatest wish was to be published in his magazine.

Two years after publishing the book on Forster, Lionel published a short story, "The Lesson and the Secret," about a writing class full of rich women and run by a young male teacher. The story was actually a chapter in an unfinished novel. (Lionel, of course, had taught such a class.) The story was published in *Harper's Bazaar* after its literary editor praised his story "Of This Time, of That Place," about a poet-professor and two of his students, which had been published in *Partisan Review*. The editor, Mary Louise Aswell, told Lionel that "our audience isn't as select as *Partisan Review*'s, but it's larger, and I covet the quality of your writing for us." Diana, who said that she "didn't think" she "changed a word of any of the stories he wrote after we were married," liked the idea that her husband was branching out to all kinds of magazines.

In fact, a year later, in May 1946, Diana began a monthly column, "About Books," for *Junior Bazaar*, a short-lived spin-off of *Harper's Bazaar* meant to appeal to teenage girls. Just as the *PR* crowd was starting to respect Diana's reviews in the *Nation*, they turned against her (but not Lionel) for slumming by publishing in *Harper's Bazaar*. Only Diana, who said she "hated the idea of the intellectual elite and the fact that serious writing can't be available to the general public," was accused of selling out. This type of accusation would become a pattern in her life. A scapegoat in her private life, she would become one in her public life as well.

Diana's pride was always that she could write with the same seriousness for *Junior Bazaar* or *Vogue* (as she did later on) as for *Partisan Review* or *The Saturday Review of Literature*. Once when discussing with William Phillips that someone should write about third-rate movies and their attraction to serious people, he turned on her, saying "That's the kind of thing you talk about with your mother; you don't write about it for *Partisan Review*."

Diana always held that "it is not *where* you work that matters, but *how* you work," so she wrote what she wanted, and what she wanted to do for *Junior Bazaar* was the same range of books she might consider for *The Nation*. She even chastised her husband's publisher, James Laughlin of New Directions, when he was reluctant to send her books for review. She told him somewhat cryptically that while her "critical method is not very *thick*, I find a real pleasure in trying to form a style of literary criticism for such a youthful audience." Her message must have gotten through to him because New Directions books began coming to her for review.

Many of her selections were by writers who would not be heard from again but who she believed held promise: Gladys Schmitt (whose second novel sold more than a million copies, yet she never became hugely sought-after), Marianne Roane (whose work was considered too experimental), Peggy Bennett (who wrote short stories only until 1950, although she lived for several more decades), and Denton Welch, who died in 1948.

Diana's columns were often flowery ("very few literary roses are born to blush unseen these days") and sometimes too wordy, but she never spoke down to her readers. She told them to buy *The Partisan Reader*, an anthology of writers who appeared in the magazine. (Lionel wrote the introduction to the book.) "The volume is not always easy reading," Diana warned, "but it contains some of the best thinking and writing that has been done in the last decade."

She recommended Jim Corbett's *Man-Eaters of Kumaon*, a best seller about the hunting and killing of man-eating tigers in India, and she later explained in a letter why: "because such discriminating readers as Lionel and myself found it exciting." She dismissed Somerset Maugham's *Then and Now* as "junk." She recommended F. Scott Fitzgerald's notebooks, *The Crack-Up*, as "profoundly moving," pointing out to her young audience that Fitzgerald's letters to his daughter were particularly instructive. She offered political lessons when reviewing George Orwell's *Animal Farm*, "more parable than satire." She wrote at length that the book "simply reproduces the historical situation in Russia without the addition of any new moral or political insights" and concluded that it is "not, I think, a very important book." World War II preoccupied Diana in many of her reviews at this time.

Robert Penn Warren's *All the King's Men* was "swift and readable," although his "characters are finally such stock types that they quite waste his great gifts of pictorialization." Even though she was always thinking of her audience and never wrote down to them, Diana sometimes got close to doing so, as when she wrote at the end of a column, "I can promise that there is no pedagogical self-torture hidden in these recommendations." What would a teenager have thought of such a sentence?

In one of her *Nation* columns Diana worried that "work that calls itself important is often only pretentious," and such a pretentious writer "comes to feel that he has only to pamper his stylistic or thematic solemnities to achieve literary stature, while the more modest writer, rejected out of hand by the intellectual world, is encouraged to out-and-out commercialism." The point of this unusual ("self-tortuous") rant was to chastise herself for holding off reviewing a "very interesting book" (she doesn't name it) because it was a Literary Guild selection. (The Literary Guild had been founded in 1927 to compete with the Book of the Month Club, founded a year earlier.) Diana's disdain for book clubs didn't last long because in 1951 Lionel and a former student, Gilman Kraft, along with Jacques Barzun and W. H. Auden, would found The Readers' Subscription Book Club. Diana proudly gave the club its name. (In 1959, after the Readers' Subscription Book Club disbanded, Lionel Trilling, Barzun, and Auden founded the Mid-Century Book Club, which lasted until 1962.)

Diana got praise she secretly coveted when she was told by a *Nation* reader that "like the psychoanalyst, you can see the shadow behind the shadow. The result is that every review you write is at once a challenge and a warning to a would-be writer."

One of Diana's analysts once asked her, "Everything you perceive is accurate, but why do you have to see it?" She acknowledged it was "a haunting question." Her friend Bettina once reminded Diana that Lionel had some time ago told Diana that she didn't simply get mad at him; she threw him back into his infancy and psychoanalyzed him.

But Diana's way of seeing, and her seeing the shadow behind the shadow, was often at the bottom of the *PR* crowd's hostility toward her. They didn't mind psychoanalysis, but they didn't want it done by an amateur.

Diana also prized a letter she received from a US Army corporal who wrote: "Since *The Nation* is forbidden bookshelf-space in the army area in which I am stationed, I do not often see the magazine except when I buy it, and I never buy it except when it contains your criticism." Diana was part of the forbidden, and she enjoyed it.

Sometime in late 1943, Leo Lerman, a flamboyant, witty, and prolific young contributing editor at *Vogue*, interviewed Diana for his May 1, 1944, column "Before Bandwagons," which was about up-and-coming artists and writers. With the dramatic flair and mischievousness he was known for, he wrote:

Two years ago, Manhattan-born, Radcliffe-educated Diana Trilling was merely a critic's wife. Her husband, Lionel, wrote for several of the more advanced weeklies. One day his telephone rang. *The Nation* needed someone to write brief fiction notices, did Mr Trilling have any suggestions? "Why don't you suggest me?" queried wife, Diana. "Why?" questioned husband Lionel, "I hate trash." Today Diana Trilling's weekly, "Fiction in Review" in *The Nation*, has an appreciative audience. With a devastating phrase, she lampoons publishers' hortatory blurbs, pinks inflated literary reputations. The body of her work is slender, but stamped with her own strength, validity and logical good taste.

Lerman—who would also write for *Mademoiselle, Dance Magazine, Harper's Bazaar, House and Garden, The Atlantic Monthly,* and many other magazines, journals, and arts organizations—introduced both Lionel and Diana to a world beyond their academic and literary one at his famous weekly Sunday parties at his small apartment on Lexington Avenue, and then in his much larger, nine-room residence at The Osborne, on Fifty-Seventh Street, across from Carnegie Hall. The grander apartment was stuffed with art and artifacts: seashells, wings of butterflies, Victorian lamps, chairs and sofas from the stage sets of various plays, paintings of volcanoes, silver boxes, and a giant iron dragonfly. One could meet Judy Garland, Cary Grant, Marlene Dietrich, or Maria Callas there, as well as Evelyn Waugh, Truman Capote, Lillian Hellman, Rebecca West, and Anais Nin, who wrote in her journal that Lerman's conversation put one in mind of "a magician's tour de force." It was at Lerman's that the Trillings first met W. H. Auden, Tennessee Williams, Noel Coward, Christopher Isherwood, the English writer and editor John Lehmann, his sister, the novelist Rosamond Lehmann, the novelist and critic Glenway Wescott, Anais Nin, Newton Arvin (the literary critic once the lover of Truman Capote), and Pearl Kazin (the editor/ book review sister of Alfred), whom Leo called "The Cultured Pearl." Lerman had met Katherine Anne Porter and Carson McCullers when he was in residence at Yaddo the summer of 1947, and whenever they were in New York, they dropped in to his parties. Marianne Moore was there once and later praised Diana in a letter for her "sanely feminine insights."

Both Trillings became good friends of Lerman's, although Diana alone had frequent gossipy phone conversations with him ("on the blower," as Lerman called the telephone). In his journal Lionel wrote of "Leo Lerman's infallible sense of people. Strange that he should seem one of the best people in the world."

Diana continued to review also for other magazines. She reviewed *Gentleman's Agreement* by Laura Z. Hobson for *Commentary*, making a sociological point in her first paragraph that it is interesting that this novel about anti-Semitism should be published "by the same house [Simon and Schuster] that a few years ago voluntarily suppressed a book by Jerome Weidman on the grounds that its unattractive Jewish characters would increase anti-Jewish feeling in the country." She went on to say that "if it is nothing else, the novel [about a journalist who goes undercover as a Jew] is a strong appeal for Gentiles to bring the Jewish issue full into the light and fight it." And while she applauded its "purpose," in the end she said the novel is "poor—dull—non-dimensional, without atmosphere," adding "of course thesis novels usually are poor." (The film adapted from the book, directed by Elia Kazan and starring Gregory Peck and Celeste Holm, won three Oscars: Best Picture, Best Supporting Actress, and Best Director.)

Diana continued to cope with Lionel's rages, always reminding herself that "it seems to be a Trilling thing," even though Lionel's anger "was much more contained" than his father's. Still, she said, "most people couldn't know Lionel for long without being aware of something seething beneath the surface." (She once stated melodramatically that instead of his pipe being tossed into the gutter on Bank Street, "it might have been *me*.") "There was something off-base about him," Diana said. "I think he was visibly paranoid. But who could have suspected any kind of ferocity in Lionel? This thing he had with me was truly a little pocket of madness. But how it played on my guilt!" She meant her guilt over putting Lionel through all her own neurotic symptoms—her multiple phobias, fears, and extreme dependence; guilt over her own unexpressed, even unidentified, anger over the sexual assault from her father's friend that had occurred when she was just out of college; guilt over not yet conceiving a child. "I went into psychoanalysis for didactic reasons," Diana said. "It was mandatory, made necessary by intense emotional strain," she wrote in a draft of an unpublished book. She had first written "emotional *upset*," then changed it to "emotional *strain*." The strain of not being fully aware of what her body knew took its toll. The body was full of danger, she had learned from her childhood.

Lionel had a similar burden. Under certain circumstances he moved his body recklessly, not looking around him, not seeming to care where he was. During one summer in the 1930s when they had rented a house in Babylon, Long Island, Diana said that Lionel would go swimming in the canal in the late afternoon and would swim never lifting his head out of the water "right into the path of returning boats, with everybody standing on the shore screaming, 'Lookout, Lionel, lookout,' because the boats wouldn't see him; his face was buried. He would go plunk right into them." Diana said that "you could never get him to understand that it's useful to take your face out of the water once in a while. . . . He was a good, strong swimmer, but he had no sense of the reality of this at all. . . . Strangers on the beach would start screaming, 'What's the matter with him?'" Diana said that she "remembered that a graduate student at Columbia once said he had bumped heads with Lionel in the university pool" and had been sure Lionel must have seen him coming toward him. But he probably hadn't.

At one point Lionel wanted to learn how to play better tennis. "His idea about learning to play any sport was to read a book about it," Diana said. "Well, he played what I would call just below fair tennis, but with great eagerness." She went on: "He didn't know how to get to the ball! So he was running constantly, and he hopped all the time he was waiting to receive his serve. . . . His face would begin to get red, then a deeper red, almost a black red and pretty soon it was getting to be a deep purple because he had been running, running, running, sometimes for a couple of hours."

But he also had great physical grace at times, Diana insisted. He walked with elegance. As for his tennis and swimming she even contended that "he was very, very charming actually doing these things, except that it was maddeningly awful at the same time." She recalled a time Lionel was asked to referee a game during a tournament among some friends, and "he went out there and he called every shot mistakenly.

He just couldn't keep it in mind. He couldn't do it anymore than he could tell people what direction to go. . . . This brilliant man couldn't keep track of the score of a game of tennis." Lionel would get into "ugly" situations, with one player once insisting he leave the court, Diana said. She even once saw him "in a murderous rage" on the court, threatening to hit his opponent with a racket (though he never did). Diana said quite seriously that matters "got to the point where I said I wouldn't stay married to him if he didn't stop playing tennis. I knew our marriage could not sustain this because he made such a spectacle of himself on the tennis court."

And then there was Lionel's driving. Diana said that "when he drove a car, there was nothing in the world I wanted except for him to stop driving the car." She said that he took lessons and passed all his tests and at first seemed to do well. But then "it went downhill all the way. He could never learn how to park. He never learned how to back the car. He could never stay in one lane; he drifted from lane to lane, willfully; he'd say, 'That's a nicer lane.' He couldn't measure the distance between the side of the car and the shoulder of the road so that the sides of his tires were likely to graze whatever little curb there was, and you'd feel the car spinning away in a rather dangerous way since he was going faster usually than he should have [been]. He could never keep his speed down. It was exactly like his swimming into the face of those oncoming boats; he wanted to live dangerously. . . . Driving with him got to be one of the major horrors in life."

Diana said that Lionel also had a peculiarity his mother had, of "going into a daze and not receiving things." His brain seemed to just cut off certain information, not take it in, and he'd seem to be in a trance.

Both Trillings eventually took Dexamil to help with their multiple "horrors." (Diana had stopped the Luminal.) Dexamil, first marketed in the United States in 1950 for "everyday mental and emotional distress," contained both an amphetamine element to lift the patient's mood and a barbiturate component (a sedative) meant to counter the amphetamine effect of agitation, or feeling high.

In 1947 Diana edited *The Portable D. H. Lawrence*, a collection of the writer's short stories, novellas, and parts of two novels, poetry, letters, and critical writing. She received the standard fee of $1,000 for her work from her publisher, Viking Press. Her editor was Pat Covici.

Kirkus Reviews wrote of the book that "the introduction, in this newest of the Portables, is concerned more with the revolutionary note in his work and reasons for his hostility than with the events of his short life. Some emphasis is given to the relation of religion to his personal, social and political thinking. Passing comment is given to the sexual sphere, which the editor considers has been overstressed."

In the introduction Diana mentioned that there was not much interest in Lawrence anymore, and she later received a stern letter from his widow, Frieda Lawrence. Although she liked the foreword, Mrs. Lawrence asked the publisher to tell Diana that "she is mistaken that there is no interest in Lawrence." She continued, "Also she has not understood that Lawrence's writing was called forth by sheer love for his fellowmen, not sentimentality or some cheap sympathy, but a violent desire to change them, so that they would get more out of life. The people who have suffered much know that or feel it instinctively. He is read all over the world." Pat Covici told Diana not to be too bothered by the letter, so Diana never answered it.

Diana's close friends Quentin and Thelma Anderson wrote her that the book "is your first *explicitly* complementary role and hence the first that is quite completely your own." They were pleased Diana had taken on a writer who was so well suited to her very special nature in terms of versatility and earnestness.

That same year, Lionel published a novel, *The Middle of the Journey*, which he dedicated to Diana. The novel revolves around a young, wealthy couple—Arthur and Nancy Crooms—who live in the fictitious town of Crannock (think Westport), Connecticut, and are fellow travelers. The Crooms have been hosting their friend John Laskell as he recuperates from a serious illness, as well as from the death of his lover, Elizabeth Fuess. Enter a member of the Communist Underground named Gifford Maxim, who had dropped in unexpectedly on Laskell in New York City right before he had left for Connecticut. Maxim now tells Laskell he has quit the Communist Party and fears for his life. The Crooms, too, know Maxim.

There's much deception in Crannock: political disagreements, treachery, betrayal, the sudden death of a very young girl, and a love affair after Laskell meets Emily Caldwell, the wife of the Croomses' alcoholic handyman.

The dedicatee and others described the book as "a novel of ideas." Diana also said that "I think it's one of the best novels of ideas that have ever been written, but it is a category that isn't finally as satisfying as a novel that's conceived under the aspect of feeling. But within this novel of ideas, Lionel was technically extraordinarily adroit, extraordinarily fluent. . . . In a way he was a born novelist."

Diana has said that Mary McCarthy was Lionel's model for Nancy Crooms and that her fellow-traveling husband, Arthur Crooms, was based on Dwight McDonald. Gifford Maxim was modeled on Whittaker Chambers, with whom Lionel had a passing acquaintance at Columbia. The serious illness that John Laskell is recovering from was taken from Lionel's own bout with scarlet fever as a young man.

Lionel once told Diana that *The Middle of the Journey* was "only a brief interruption to some big novel that he was working on." Actually, Diana had more trouble than she admitted accepting a novel of ideas and thought Lionel could do more with the genre. For decades she worried that she might have interfered too much at times. (Indeed, decades later in a letter to Norman Mailer she wrote, "I once told Lionel to throw away the beginning, maybe some sixty or seventy pages of a novel— curiously, it was set in ancient Greece. He tore it up, and I still have worrisome moments about it. Maybe even he, who had more claim on me for courage and honesty than anyone else in the world, shouldn't have invited me to assume this much authority in his professional life.")

In her memoir, *The Beginning of the Journey*, Diana writes that not only was Lionel's novel "written without my having any knowledge of its inception; it was virtually completed before I knew what it was about." Yet in a series of taped interviews Diana revealed that she knew exactly what the novel was about and, in fact, talked a great deal to Lionel about it, further explaining that "I was reading it as chapters, although I can't say I was interfering or having much to do with it at all until the ending. . . . That is where my editing came in; otherwise, I had very little to do with the writing of that, very little, much less than I did with any of Lionel's writing." Diana also said that "it seemed easier for [Lionel] to write *The Middle of the Journey* than any critical piece." He wrote it in six to eight months, she said, while he was on sabbatical from Columbia. (In his journal he complained that people ask him, "How is the novel going? One knows what they hope. They ask, 'What is the novel about?' An unbelievable question.")

Another unbelievable question: Why would Diana not want to reveal in *The Beginning of the Journey* that not only did she know what the novel was about but that she had actually read it chapter by chapter? It is conceivable that the plot revealed too much about certain aspects of their lives for her to go public with—things that either threatened or frightened her, or both. Things like the true nature of their relationship—the rages, the depression, the disappointments, the fears. (Diana later said that Lionel's difficulties with fiction were perhaps because "he was afraid being a novelist would give away his secrets.") Or perhaps she just didn't want to acknowledge her real feelings about the book, despite proclaiming it one of the best novels of ideas that has ever been written. It is possible that Diana was actually disappointed—even embarrassed—by aspects of its structure and themes.

In fact, Diana disclosed that "after the scene [in which] Laskell and Emily Caldwell make love beside the pond where she's been swimming and washing her hair, then I think it's the next day or a few days later and Laskell is about to leave Connecticut when he meets her on the road." She went on, "Well, Lionel wrote that scene, the scene of their meeting on the road, and it was totally incomprehensible."

Diana, who would be misleading in her memoir about knowing the details of her husband's novel, actually knew a lot about the details, details that troubled her and were perhaps too close to home. Diana said Lionel "had Laskell act absolutely hateful to Emily, as if he despised her." She continued: "I read this and I said, 'But why? What had happened except that they'd made love?' I told Lionel that it just doesn't make any sense in terms of his narrative, although it makes plenty of unconscious sense to me. So Lionel went back and wrote it again and then he came back and wrote it again. And again. And again. . . . But it was never enough. . . . And each time the same thing happened. Laskell was ugly without cause."

In the end Diana told her husband, "You cannot send in that book until you get this right." She said, "It's my impression that Lionel must have done it over six or eight times before Laskell got over being nasty to Emily. But I couldn't let it stand. The whole end of the book would have been ruined. Now I'm never sure that it was right, but it was changed and finally he did it, and I said it was fine, and it went to press that way." (Diana also said that like his criticism, "all those versions of the novel seem to have disappeared. I'm sorry about that. It would have been very interesting to trace the stages of Laskell's regeneration.")

Diana added that "Lionel's hatred of women at certain moments and in certain situations" was what was going on in his writing of "that scene" with Emily and Laskell. "I think this is the male neurosis of our time. Some men are afraid of women, and I think it's because they want extraordinarily to be treated and see that lovely Edenic situation of being an infant in the mother's arms." Diana went on to say that "I think it's very, very seductive and that they are constantly fighting it. The ones who fight it cognitively get this kind of neurosis like Lionel's, and the ones who accept it become passive and put themselves totally in the hands of some women, usually their wives and take all the direction of their lives from the women they're married to. I think men are en-thralled to [sic] their infancies in a way that women cannot be because women have not been nurtured by their fathers the way men have been nurtured by their mother."

Diana reached into literature and said that "Lawrence's phrase comes to me: 'the lapsing back.' . . . [Lawrence] is always talking about lapsing back. . . . He knew it. . . . He lapsed back into the infant relation with his mother. And I think Lionel was lapsing back when he could not in fan-tasy free Laskell from the seduction of Emily. In other words, his harsh-ness to Emily was an inversion of his capitulation to her."

Quentin Anderson later told Diana that Lionel's mother, who wanted her son to be a critic and not a novelist, was not at all pleased that he had published a novel and that when Lionel presented her with a copy, Anderson said, "She never cracked a smile of appreciation." Diana later explained to Anderson that Fannie Trilling wanted Lionel "to use the non-erotic gift, the cerebral rather than the erotic, which a novelist uses."

Diana soon realized that Lionel, who had "lapsed back," was now completely dependent on her, a circumstance she had once feared would happen.

9

GLOWING

I find myself thinking I want Diana to myself.

—LIONEL TRILLING, JOURNAL ENTRY, SEPT. 1948

O n July 22, 1948, 286 days, or nine months and thirteen days, after the publication of Lionel's novel, James Lionel Trilling was born. Both parents were forty-three. Was Lionel energized into potency by the publication of *The Middle of the Journey*? Did he embrace his dependency on Diana? Did his depression lessen and his sense of self-worth heighten? Edward Mendelson, the Lionel Trilling Professor in the Humanities at Columbia, suggests that Lionel "felt like Hemingway, whom he always envied and admired for his uninhibited masculinity. Trilling associated creativity with masculinity, and to publish a novel made him feel masculine—especially a novel where his stand-in has extramarital sex on a riverbank with a beautiful woman."

Diana, by the time her son was born, had been in therapy for nearly twenty years. She wrote in a draft of a book she titled "The Education of a Woman," which was to be a childhood memoir (some of the material found its way into *The Beginning of the Journey*), that most of their friends "greeted the news of my pregnancy with such disquiet wonder as might have been warranted by the news that we were transplanting to Alaska—did we really feel this much confidence in our power of renewal and endurance? Was I prepared to give up my work, and could I do this lightly?"

The answer was yes.

Both Trillings wanted very much to become parents. Yet even their cleaning woman was suspicious. Lionel wrote in his journal that she laughed at and mocked Diana, saying, "You? How do you know? You ever had one before?" And Cecilia had some words for her sister: "I've always told you that you're very clever, Diana, but you're not fit to have a child."

In 1930 Diana had thought she was pregnant and reluctantly had considered an abortion because she and Lionel were too poor to afford a child. As it turned out, she was not pregnant, much to Fannie Trilling's relief—a baby would have interfered with her son's rise in the academic world.

Diana's thyroid problem—hyperthyroidism, or an overactive thyroid— for which she had been operated on early in their marriage, sometimes makes conception problematic; there can be a lack of ovulation, cysts on the ovaries, or irregular menstrual cycles. But it's an underactive thyroid, or hypothyroidism, that more often causes trouble. In any case Diana's weak physical condition was no doubt a factor in her childlessness, although one of her psychoanalysts believed she chose to have "panics instead of babies." A gynecologist she consulted thought that perhaps she was too old to have a child.

He was wrong.

Her pregnancy, which was announced in Walter Winchell's gossip column (via Leo Lerman), was not without its complications. At one point during her fourth month Diana began bleeding and thought she might be having a miscarriage. Her friend Bettina (now married to Charles Hartenbach, a lawyer) had arrived at the Trillings' apartment at 620 West 116th Street to celebrate New Year's Eve and reported that she saw that "all hell had broken loose." Fannie Trilling, who had been visiting, was unusually composed and "behaved magnificently," Bettina said, adding that it was a great blessing that she was there when Diana

needed just the comfort and reassurance that she was able to give."
Diana's sister-in-law, Harriet, also helped out.

Bettina later wrote Diana that Lionel said that the doctor thought it possible that Diana had not been pregnant at all. But this proved quite untrue. She was indeed pregnant, and the slight bleeding was not anything to worry about. In fact, Bettina recalled that in the following days Lionel was more concerned about a cold he had recently caught. And Diana was more concerned about Lionel and the possibility that he might miss a *Partisan Review* dinner, so she had asked Bettina if she and Charles would stay with her so Lionel could leave the apartment. Although the crisis was over, Diana wanted someone to be with her in case she had to be rushed to the hospital. Bettina and Charles obliged. But for days afterward, various dramas with the Hartenbachs developed—missed phone calls, unclear arrangements, and disorganized meals. Once again Bettina begged her friend to "please take down your shingle for the duration of this emergency." Bettina had had almost enough of Diana's anxiety and super-sensitivity, as well as her "tone of a psychiatrist talking calmly to a lunatic," yet she also said that "as friendships go, ours has been one hell of a good one." She meant it. But when Diana called her friend "rigid" during the days of the emergency, Bettina countered that she was the one who had "been as flexible as a trapeze artist." Bettina knew she had to be adaptable in order to remain Diana's confidante, and besides, she adored Diana. Theirs was an enduring bond, and the near-fracture healed.

Bettina was thrilled for her friend: "For the baby is a triumph, and perhaps the most wonderful triumph of all," she wrote in a letter. She also reminded Diana that "the focus of your pregnancy should be in the home, in you and Lionel, and not what relatives and friends thought about your pregnancy." Bettina always knew how to bring back the balance in their friendship.

James Lionel Trilling, close to six pounds, was born at French Hospital on West Thirtieth Street in the Chelsea neighborhood of Manhattan, where Diana's obstetrician was affiliated. James (soon to be called, more often than not, "Jim," although Leo Lerman persisted in always calling him "James Lionel") was both automatically baptized, because French

Hospital was a Catholic institution run by the Sisters of the Holy Cross, and medically (not ritually) circumcised. There had been much hemming and hawing over whether or not to have the circumcision at all because both Trillings believed not only that there was not quite enough Jewishness in their present life to justify it but also because it was not the right, that is ethical, position to hold.

Diana liked giving birth at a Catholic hospital because she had always secretly admired Christian ritual. She had never revealed to Polly Fadiman just how much she had relished their visit to St. Patrick's Cathedral the Christmas Eve she had been introduced to Lionel. At one point Diana had even wished she had been a Catholic and became a little obsessed with the Virgin Mary. A close friend believed it was because she wanted to find a mother figure in world history, and the Virgin Mary was the perfect, idealized mother. Diana, this friend said, blamed mothers for everything. She certainly blamed Fannie Trilling for Lionel's shortcomings.

French Hospital had some deficiencies. Diana thought that the maternity section was understaffed and not as clean as she would have wished. But, most important, she was made to feel, she later wrote, "as if the baby didn't belong to me" because Jim was brought to her bedside only three times a day and then for only twelve minutes. She said that she could always identify his cry in the nursery down the hall from her room.

Mariana Barzun offered Diana a handcrafted wooden cradle, telling her that "all the Lowells have been cradled in it." Jim was a loved and thoroughly cradled baby by both his parents and a long series of baby nurses. There were five in his first two years, ranging in age from eighteen to seventy. Sooner or later Diana found fault with all the nurses, and a few turned against Diana for what they considered her overbearing manner.

Diana often spoke of how helpful Jacques Barzun was when Jim was an infant. "In came Jacques into the midst of a squalling household," she remarked, adding that "I mean, Jim crying with gas, terrible gas pains, a very colicky first few months." Jacques was magic with Jim, especially after he told Diana that he was sure that the baby needed a "heavier" formula. And he comforted her by reminding her that she had to be in charge, that she must not always listen to the doctor. This was "a great man putting his mind to the most immediate," Diana said. She also said that after she and Lionel met E. M. Forster, she wished she could have hired him as a baby nurse "because he was so marvelous with our small child, but with grown-ups he was rather too conscious of his own virtue."

Diana said that Lionel had never liked his name and that he "longed to be Jim, a John, a Mike, Bill." Now, at last, he had a Jim. "How the boy glows for me," he wrote in his journal, later also observing, "saw my face in the mirror—it was the face my son has—smiled at it affectionately and forgivingly." Whom and what was he forgiving? He doesn't say.

Diana was overjoyed to be a mother at long last, and she was determined to try to remain a working writer as well. Her star was not going to dim. "It is very easy to use a baby as an excuse for not doing one's work: one must be very alert to one's own motives," she wrote in a letter to a friend.

In late January of 1948, when she was four months pregnant, Diana had published a review in *The Nation* of Truman Capote's *Other Voices, Other Rooms*. Although she basically praised the novel—she wrote that it had a "striking literary virtuosity" and that so "much writing skill in one so young [Capote was twenty-three] represents a kind of genius"— she faulted the author for not only being "the latest chic example of Southern gothic" but for not being sound enough in his explanation of "the source of homosexuality." (Diana believed that although there was a psychological component to homosexuality, one more complex than just having to do with the type of parenting received by the individual, something about "modern society"—she wrote this in 1987—"accounts for the vast increase in male homosexuality.")

A few months before her son's birth, Diana had reviewed Virginia Woolf's posthumous collection of essays, *The Moment*, and the republication of Woolf's *The Common Reader*, in *The New York Times Book Review*. Diana began her review in a very unusual way: by describing the well-known photograph of Woolf by Man Ray (it would accompany the review). She commented on "the long, tense face," "the large, too-precisely socketed eyes," "the aristocratic nose and the surely troublesome hair dressed in such defiance of fashion." She pointed out that Woolf was always handled carefully during her lifetime and since her death and that she generally received preferential treatment from "the literary community" because of her insistence that she not be considered a "mere woman." Still, Diana argued that Woolf "always takes ultimate refuge in her female sensibility." When writing about Woolf's previously uncollected essays on "little-known figures of the past whom she could re-create out of scraps of letters and journals," Diana scornfully pronounced them "lady's art." When Woolf wrote on major literary personalities such as Montaigne or George Eliot, Diana said, "we face the fact that Mrs. Woolf's hand lacks the strength to grip at essential truth." Every now and then words of praise were tucked in and around her review: "unique gifts of grace and appreciation," "beautifully educated imagination," and "lapidary precision of language." But generally, Diana pounced on her, later saying that Lionel "didn't care for her that much," either. "I think he held her in slight male contempt. And he didn't like sensibility; he liked the hard irony of Jane Austen very much. . . . In fact, I don't think he liked Bloomsbury very much. I don't think he liked that phenomenon. . . . I think he tried to rescue Forster from the bad influence of Bloomsbury."

There were many reactions—most were unfavorable—to Diana's words on Woolf, but none was as succinct as the letter she received from the poet May Sarton, who did not agree at all with Diana's analysis. "What shocked me in your article was that the limitations seemed entirely to overshadow the achievement," Sarton wrote, and she emphasized that Diana had overlooked Woolf's genius. Moreover, Sarton said that she had met Woolf several times in the mid-1930s and found her certainly not "in defiance of fashion." Woolf was "completely in command of any situation, where her wit overbalanced her sensitivity." In a second letter, written two weeks later (it is not known if this was a reply to one of Diana's), Sarton decided that perhaps, after all, Diana's criticism "makes us all think and for that blessings on you. . . . Stir us up again! We shall consider ourselves only your more devoted (if argumentative) readers." There was no further correspondence.

Diana continued to review for the *Book Review* for years, most of her pieces appearing on the front page. "Stir us up" effectively became her mantra and was one of the reasons she became such a sought-after reviewer. It was also one of the reasons she began to attract dissenters. She was not afraid to express her opinions, whether they were popular or not. *The Nation* had given her a platform, a longed-for one, and her psychoanalysts had helped her suitably frame her ambitions. Her experiences from childhood had reinforced her belief that honesty at any cost was the path to take.

Four months after Jim's birth, Diana received a letter from *Mademoiselle* magazine asking her to contribute to an article on freelance article writing. The magazine wanted her and a few other writers not mentioned to participate in a survey to prove its theory that "it is difficult to get started, almost impossible to make a large income by writing articles, and that anyone attempting writing as a career should be well-prepared for it." There was irony here: there was to be no payment to the contributors. Diana was beside herself. Should she be grateful she was being recognized to perform a public service for a magazine that was, as she described it, "a highly profitable commercial enterprise" and for which she was to receive no fee at all? No. Writing without any payment at all was not in the cards. She said so in a reply to the magazine but received no answer and, of course, no further assignments from the magazine, either.

She began thinking of writing about her experience with her baby nurses. According to Lionel's journal entry at the time, one of the first nurses, a Miss Nichols, seemed indifferent toward Jim in the beginning. But this soon changed: "D has seen her fondling him and lavishing the most tender language on him."

Diana was breast-feeding, but with some difficulty, and quickly discovered that Miss Nichols was sneaking bottles to Jim every so often. Outraged, Diana fired her on the spot, but Lionel rehired her. During the time when Diana was interviewing applicants, she was told by one agency that "no proper baby-nurse would dream of working for a mother who nurses her own child."

Many years later, Jim Trilling observed that "it was a little diaboli-
cal" on his father's part to rehire his baby nurse, but it was "done
secretly," he learned, because his father wanted his mother's prepreg-
nancy body back. (Lionel thought that breast-feeding would delay the
process.) Jim also remembers being told by his mother that his father
would not help with a special corset she had to wear during her pregnancy, and Jim remarked that his father "basically refused to touch her
during her pregnancy." In a draft of the unpublished book Diana called
"A Biography of a Marriage," she wrote that one of Lionel's "worst sufferings was being dragged along to the corsetiere by his mother and
aunts." Perhaps this experience contributed to his horror of corsets.
Nevertheless, Diana wrote in *The Beginning of the Journey* that she
"had an unshared pregnancy because Lionel could not let it be real for
him." She also wrote that her husband might have been trying to "conceal from himself the memory of his mother's pregnancy with Harriet:
for seven years he had been an only child, alone in his mother's affection. I suspect that he never forgave her (or any woman) the injury of
having been betrayed by his mother's having another child. Throughout his life he was prone to the kind of jealousy which a child feels at the
birth of a younger sibling."

Lionel also commented in his journal that Miss Nichols shows "deep
animosity toward Diana, possibly unconscious, [but it] suddenly
abated." He also remarked on "her expressions of admiration for my
wisdom."

Nurse Nichols believed Father Knows Best.

Diana often worked while Jim was in a playpen next to her desk. As
she wrote a friend, "I am writing very rapidly, and, I fear, not as coher-
ently as I would wish. My child is in his playpen at my elbow and
protests every time I stop to think. He loves the clatter of the typewriter." Diana tried to write three hours a day, often not meeting that
goal, because Jim "was a very demanding child." Still, she later agreed
that "I would never have traded the experience of motherhood for another book. Never. . . . There was no question in my mind that my family
came first. My responsibilities as a wife and mother came first. Before I

had a child, my responsibilities as a wife and homemaker were absolutely first."

In January of 1949, when Jim was six months old, Diana was asked
by the college department of Farrar, Straus and Company to edit "The
Selected Letters of Jane Walsh Carlyle." Mrs. Carlyle, a poet who had
once written a novel when she was just thirteen, was the wife of the essayist and historian Thomas Carlyle and was considered largely responsible for her husband's wealth and eminence. She was best known for
her legendary letters to such correspondents as her own husband, Robert
Browning, Charles Dickens, Ralph Waldo Emerson, and Alfred Tennyson.
The publishing house agreed to pay Diana an advance of $500, but she
never signed a contract, and the book was never done. Around the same
time Diana considered writing about Freud's friend and student Lou
Andreas-Salomé, one of the first female psychoanalysts, but she decided
not to pursue the idea. In 1949 motherhood came first for her.

Although the world was full of unsettling developments, Diana hadn't
participated in anything political for years. She remained on the sidelines
until the Communists seized control of power in Czechoslovakia, and
Alger Hiss was accused of being a Soviet spy by Whittaker Chambers
(and convicted of perjury in 1950). Those two events caught her eye.

Soon, the Cold War began in earnest. And in March of 1949 the Waldorf Conference (named as such because it was held at New York City's
Waldorf-Astoria hotel) convened to promote peace with Stalin at any
price; the group included well-known writers, musicians, academics,
philosophers, social scientists, doctors, and actors. Present were such
people as Thomas Mann, Lillian Hellman, Arthur Miller, Clifford Odets,
Norman Mailer, Aaron Copeland, Marlon Brando, and Charlie Chaplin.
A year later, the American Committee for Cultural Freedom, an
anti-Communist organization, was formed by Waldorf dissenters, and
Diana eventually became a major player in the group.

Being an older mother in 1948 came with its problems. Diana was
often ostracized by other mothers who were wary of her. Diana thought
it was perhaps because she had a baby nurse for Jim's first two years.
The nurse took him on walks and to the park as often as—if not more

than—Diana or Lionel did. There was also tension between the Columbia faculty mothers and the neighborhood mothers. But the strife, not ever major, was resolved when Diana decided to bring Jim to the park herself every afternoon; she would write only in the mornings.

She began working in earnest on a piece she called "The Baby-Nurses." Names were changed, personality quirks were conflated, and some of the incidents were altered, for nowhere in the twenty-seven-page piece does Diana mention that any of the baby nurses were not in favor of her breast-feeding. Furthermore, she writes that her pediatrician had, in fact, ordered supplementary bottles of formula, a common practice at the time. She even worried that the nurse, who was seventy years old, would not have enough eyesight to make the formula properly, and she worried the nurse might drop Jim. But Diana's invented "Miss Purvis" handled everything just fine, although "she was quite mad," Diana wrote.

The piece was especially long, and it was hard to figure out its point of view. Was it satire? Comedy? *The New Yorker*'s William Shawn was puzzled, too. In his rejection letter he told Diana that "mainly it was thought that your strong feelings on the subject (undoubtedly justified) would stand in the way of your making the piece objective enough, or simply 'funny' enough for our purposes." He suggested she try a magazine where "the feelings and the very personal treatment would be more acceptable." But Diana didn't try other places (she knew that Shawn meant she should try a woman's magazine, which just didn't interest her at the time.) She was determined to be published in *The New Yorker*. So she decided she needed to work harder; she wanted to learn the right approach and emphasis for long essays. She would teach and train herself. At the same time, she also realized that she was getting tired of the grind of producing her *Nation* column. She had to make certain choices, so in 1949 she resigned her position as its book reviewer. "It has become very much of a blind alley," she wrote in a letter to some friends; "space is curtailed, [and] the magazine is too dead. I think I have got as much out of this fiction subject as I now can."

She could concentrate on her own work, because at the moment Lionel "had his own prose going well," she later said. Still, she wrote in the same letter to friends that she was finishing up an editing job "to which I am committed"—without mentioning that it was for Lionel.

Although Diana's father had barely anything left in his estate when he died in 1932, six years before his death he had managed on the quiet to create insurance trust funds for his children, with the money to be delivered to them when they reached the age of thirty-five. The trust remained intact throughout the years. In 1940 Diana turned thirty-five, and she received $12,890.68 after taxes. The money was, of course, a very welcome gift, with most of it going to their general household income, which always included hefty medical bills, although some was used to rent summer houses.

By the time Jim was born, Diana's psychoanalyst was a well-known New York doctor, Marianne Kris (who treated Marilyn Monroe in the 1960s). Her husband, Ernst Kris, was also an analyst, as well as an art historian, and both were part of the New York Psychoanalytic Institute, although Ernst Kris was not a medical doctor like his wife. Lionel was in treatment with Dr. Rudolph Lowenstein, a close associate of Ernst Kris, and as Diana wrote in *The Beginning of the Journey*, Dr. Marianne Kris thought he was not the right doctor for Lionel. She recommended that Lionel switch to Dr. Grace Addabte, which he did. (Diana believed that Dr. Lowenstein did harm to their marriage by "colluding" in Lionel's ambivalence toward her. Dr. Kris agreed.)

For two months in the summer of 1949 the Trillings rented a small house—actually a cottage that had been converted from a garage—one block from the beach, in Westport, Connecticut, near where they had honeymooned. Although Jim was taken to Riverside Park every day, Diana wanted him to experience the real countryside. Westport, a coastal town on Long Island Sound, had areas of abundant woodlands full of oak, sugar maple, and elm trees. A state park was also nearby. As she wrote in a draft of an unpublished book:

> From the day of our arrival, I have been able to record the increasing ecstasy with which he has discovered the variety of outdoor life. . . . A new yellow flower has appeared at the edge of the lawn. He sees it well before either his nurse or I, stops, frowns as he studies it, delicately

probes it with his finger, cautiously puts forward his cheek against it to learn its texture, wrinkles his nose in a vast, joyous parody of savoring its odor; the flower meets his approval. The nurse complies with his demand that she capture it for him. She says, "Give the pretty flower to your mom," and he lurches across the lawn to make his presentation, his whole being suffused with the delight of his possession.

Diana then reminisced about her own childhood and how her parents always said they loved nature (although only her mother had). She continued in intense, sprawling prose (one reason the book was not ever published) that most Jews feel removed from "the world of out-doors" because they are "a people sired in ghettos." Furthermore, she wrote, "Jewish farmers, except in Palestine, will still strike most other Jews as an anomaly. . . . The Jew represents a racial choice of the mental over the physical way of living, a Puritanical preference for the domin-ion of the mind rather than of the body and senses." Despite her par-ents' efforts and her camp experiences, Diana said she "grew up with a deeply ingrained though unformulated aloofness from nature. . . . I was not only left untaught about the world of nature but made fearful of it." (Dr. Kellogg's book certainly hadn't helped when it came to the nature of sex.)

Her son would not be afraid of nature, and as a one-year-old he was already bold. If young Diana had dared to roll in the grass in view of her parents, she had sinned. "Nature is seduction to sin, temptation to aban-donment," she wrote, and then completely crossed out in a draft of her unpublished book. Diana was learning to be bold from her infant son.

When Jim was two years old, Lionel, who became a full professor at Columbia in 1948, published *The Liberal Imagination*, the collection of essays that most people would consider his most significant book. Quen-tin Anderson wrote that it "enforces the demand Trilling made in all his work that we should look at the imaginative consequences of our politics and the political consequences of our use of the imagination." The book, which was dedicated to Jacques Barzun, sold seventy thou-sand copies in hardcover and one hundred thousand in paperback.

Diana gave the sixteen essays in the book the lightest of polishing (she had already done more rigorous editing on them when they were published individually in magazines), and as she always emphasized, she never modified his ideas but, when required, only clarified them. And, as Lionel himself explained in the preface, many of the essays were written from 1940 to 1950, but the majority from 1946 on, and although he "substantially revised almost all of them, I have not changed the original intent of any."

Diana described Lionel's work as having to

do with the way he thought. And he thought with so much space around every sentence that I could not put in or take out. That was the quality of the way he thought. I always thought of it as being like the concept in painting. If I paint this room, there is space between the chair and the table. It will only be space on the canvas, but it's space into which four or five people might fit. And that used to be called negative space. There was this negative space around everything that Lionel wrote—negative in the sense that it hadn't been filled in positively. But there it was and it existed in a very positive sense, and that was where the thought was. He was thinking all those people between that chair and this table.

She said that she would look at Lionel's work and say, " 'What is it that has produced this effect of masterliness?' which is the word I would use to myself. It had nothing actually to do with how to write, because I am afraid it will become public knowledge once his manuscripts are available, that there was scarcely a sentence he ever wrote that I didn't rewrite." (Of course, at the time Diana said this, she didn't know that the drafts with her editing on them would be destroyed by her husband. Jim Trilling later said that "it's probably the only thing she kept coming back to with sorrow and anger—'How could he do this to me?' ")

Diana never had much to say about her life to the other mothers in the park because they were young enough to be her daughters. Why would they be interested in her? She was generally amused by their youth, and even by their stares, but she never tried to reach out to any of these women to ask about their lives.

In a draft of an unpublished book she says bluntly that "I blame my own belated maternity on my professional ambitions," adding that "a myriad subtle fear of life can hide behind a devotion to one's work, and must hide behind the refusal of parenthood, whether by men or women and whatever the authority the culture of one's group may give to one's rationalizations." It was certainly true that both Trillings hid their "refusal of parenthood" in socially acceptable ways that concealed their real reasons, whether it was work, lack of work, ambition, anxiety, depression, impotence, or other physical or psychological factors. Diana wasn't about to risk letting any of the mothers in the park discover the reasons for her late parenthood.

She also said that because her mother was not a very articulate person, she never heard her "state the theory that lay behind her maternal practices," except once while Diana was recuperating from her appendix operation while at Radcliffe. She and her mother overheard some young mothers arguing in favor of telling their children the truth of where babies came from as soon as they asked. Diana didn't expect what happened next. Her mother intervened and told the young women *she* didn't agree, because she believed "children should keep their illusions as long as they can."

Diana's theory behind her own "maternal practices" was clear. Her Freudian leanings structured her life and were the reason her husband and close friends often told her to take down her shingle. Freud was always next to her every step of the way. Would the young women in the park understand this?

When Jim became afraid of a picture of a mole in a children's book, Diana was concerned. What was he trying to say to her? What had she done wrong? When Jim became afraid of elevators, she knew it had to be, as she wrote, his "fear of male genitalia being lost on the endless chasm of female genitalia." (Jim later commented that because the elevators were so small, he was genuinely afraid that the cables could break. Also, the elevator was noisy; any machine that made a loud noise frightened him. This was a typical preschooler's fear. Jim said that he was told that he was also afraid of policemen, black raincoats, blimps, and giant meteors.) Lionel wrote in his journal that Jim "abhors the stethoscope." But what baby or toddler likes a (usually) cold instrument placed on his chest?

Diana told Thelma Anderson that "the paternal instinct in Lionel was extraordinary. He could wake at night if Jim let out the faintest peep. He was wide-awake. Other times I could shake him and throw cold water in his face and couldn't wake him." She said that there were certain things Lionel could do "only when Jim was small. . . . He could fix toys . . . but all that kind of mechanical genius left him the minute Jim was not making demands, just as it had arrived with Jim's arrival on earth."

After Diana read Erik Erikson's *Childhood and Society*, his innovative study of childhood (which he believed had eight stages of development), she wrote him a letter about Jim's fear of elevators. She received no answer, so she wrote again. He answered that he hadn't received her first letter and offered her an appointment. An appointment? Diana didn't want an appointment; she wanted therapy by mail. Furthermore, in his reply Erikson seemed to mock her story about elevators, and she felt snubbed when he told her that obviously *she* had a problem with mechanical conveyances because she seemed reluctant to drive to see him. There was no further correspondence.

Jim's early introduction to the countryside had encouraged his inquisitiveness. He was never afraid of snakes or worms and was always full of scientific curiosity as a toddler and young boy. He was a very bright and enthusiastic child. Lionel observed in his journal that when Jim was nine months old, while crawling around the apartment, he accidentally touched a hot pipe, which he later always avoided. "Some weeks later," Lionel noted, "I held him up to the trunk of a tree, he refused to touch it but at last he did so, tentatively, then boldly; when he came back to the house he went at once to the stream riser [pipe] saying, 'ot'" (hot). Lionel was enthralled. Touching the tree had made Jim understand and articulate something essential about the physical world.

Diana was a protective mother but also at times an unusually progressive one. When Jim, at eight, showed an interest in weapons, she encouraged a collection of knives, swords, even bayonets. This trust was especially surprising because as Jim later said, "I was unpredictable throughout my childhood, had rages, and yelled and screamed. . . . I was subject to outbursts at my parents all my life—any frustration would set me off."

When Jim was seven, he began child analysis, the use of psychoanalytic principles in play therapy or in conversations with the analyst. It was what knowing parents did with "hyperactive," "difficult" children at the time. The year before, the Trillings had bought Jim two kittens for his birthday, pets the family named "Paws" and "Lemhi" (after the Pass bordering Montana and Idaho that Lewis and Clarke explored). Many of the Trilling friends believed Jim was indulged too much—two kittens at age six?—and they "openly and subtly disapproved of Jim's rearing," Lionel wrote in his journal.

Norman Podhoretz, one of Lionel's star pupils in 1949—he took just one course with him in his senior year—became a close friend of both Trillings (and then, later, an ex-friend), along with his wife, the writer Midge Decter. (Decter once told Diana that the Trilling of whom she had been aware of before 1950 was not Lionel but Diana: "I was the literary editor of my St. Paul Minnesota high school newspaper, and for years I plagiarized your reviews.")

Podhoretz, who visited the Trillings often in the summer, and commented that he spoke to Diana "probably a million hours," has written that he always believed that she had a "skewed sense of reality," whereas Lionel "understood exactly what I was trying to say." He said that "I always found myself in a slightly false position trying to be polite in responding to things Diana said; she just seemed to be on a different wave length. . . . I had trouble communicating with her." As for Lionel, Decter said, "he was preternaturally sensitive, so if you sat in a room with him and there was a conversation, if you paid attention to him, you saw that he was seeing everything that was going on. He wouldn't necessarily comment on it but you could tell he saw everything. Diana was not like that. First of all, she was not preternaturally sensitive. She was something else. So you could tell he was seeing everything and she saw whatever she saw."

Decter also commented that Diana was a figure of sometimes nasty humor and sometimes of hostility in their literary community and was not considered a particularly good mother. "She was sneered at a lot." For years the Columbia faculty crowd mocked that she "didn't know the depth of her ignorance," and they belittled her with the title "Queen of Claremont Avenue" because she "put on airs that were tiresome," Elisabeth Sifton remembered. (Sifton, who said Lionel "never put on airs," knew the Trillings since her childhood. Her parents were Ursula and Reinhold Niebuhr.) "Diana often had court-like intrigues about social things," Sifton went on to say.

Norman Podhoretz said that he thought the Trillings "really didn't know what they were doing" as parents. Ann Fadiman, Kip's daughter with his second wife, Annalee Jacoby, thought the Trillings "were devoted but peculiar parents." Midge Decter said that "in those days having a baby at that age was very unusual. . . . They were so full of consciousness. I mean there is one thing you can't do if you have a little kid and that is to live without a sense of humor. And with this terrible focus and they [Lionel and Diana] were both Freudians, that added to it and so the boy was a mess." Both Decter and Podhoretz thought that Jim, although he was "incredibly intelligent and perceptive," was a wreck. He also had violence problems. "And," Podhoretz added, "the more of a mess he was, the less capable they seemed dealing with it, and this included Lionel."

Another former student of Lionel's said that when Jim was an infant and wasn't kicking as Diana had expected him to, "She pulled on his legs." "Oh, dear," the student recalled; "I felt so sorry for her."

For *her*.

"Happiness is nothing, achievement is everything," Diana once said to another of her husband's students. In 1948 it would become her maxim.

10

OH BE BRAVE

By most people the "sense of reality" is understood to be the submission to events and indeed illusion is often salvation.

—LIONEL TRILLING, JOURNAL ENTRY, 1951

Caring for Jim and coordinating the care of him by others, making sure the household was always in good order, managing the finances, keeping numerous doctor appointments (now including a pediatrician), and, of course, editing Lionel—all this took up much of Diana's time, but proceeding with her own writing was becoming more and more essential to her existence.

As she wrote in *The Beginning of the Journey*: "a woman writer is of course better situated than other working mothers for bringing up children. She can be home and keep an eye on things, and she has the flexibility to meet emergencies. By the same token, her working life is exposed to constant interruption." So at one point Diana rented a room in the apartment next door, but Jim made too much of a protest when she came and went, so she gave the room up. "I learned to work at my living room desk, whatever might be going on around me," she said.

After "The Baby-Nurses" was rejected by *The New Yorker*, Diana remained determined to find the right tone for such an essay. It didn't take long.

Just a year after she left *The Nation*, Diana published a lengthy essay in *Partisan Review* on the anthropologist Margaret Mead's new book on gender roles and their evolving implications, *Male and Female*. The book consisted of Mead's further exploration of the South Sea that she first wrote about in *Coming of Age in Samoa*. Mead argued that culture, not biology, was the principal drive in shaping a person's behavior. "Talking about our bodies is a complex and difficult matter," Mead wrote in *Male and Female*, explaining that "the differences between the two sexes is one of the important conditions upon which we have built the many varieties of human culture that give human beings dignity and stature." She now said, however, that women should be able to take part in more activities usually associated with men; she was evolving into what could be called a scientific-based feminist, except that Diana didn't think she really was.

She wrote that Mead's two main points are, first, to demonstrate that "the attitudes which define the adult sexual behavior of both men and women are established in their earliest instruction in their sex membership" and, second, that "apart from the single sexual difference given by biology—the difference between the male and female roles in procreation—sexual character is entirely determined by the needs of the social group." But Diana charged, despite Mead's concern "with [the] most primary of sexual material—the knowledge of our bodies in relation to their sex differentiation"—the book ("a strikingly comprehensive document") "is as remote from actual erotic activity as if our differing sexual organs had been given us merely to distinguish the different jobs we would do in society." Diana went on to write that Mead "says no word for sex as a pleasure, for sex as a physical urgency, or sex as an act or aspect of the imagination": these were matters to which Diana was beginning to give serious thought, and she emphasized, "although Mead seems to understand Freudian theory, nonetheless, she bends or discards Freudian principles at will."

As for sexual pleasure, imagined or real, Diana, at forty-five, was beginning to explore her own destiny. She concluded her review by reminding her readers that the "sexuality of *Male and Female* is the sexuality of ego, never of libido. It is directed toward achieving, not toward being." Diana did not want to live in Mead's world, "where the whole of our sexual motive would seem to be social motive." Where did pleasure lie? she asked. She was looking for answers.

Diana received a lively letter about her essay from the well-known psychiatrist Karl Menninger, who commended her for exposing Mead's "Horneyism" (referring to psychoanalyst Karen Horney, who questioned Freud's theories) and for disparaging what he called Mead's "diaperology" theories, "which also irritate me and most of our group here." After Diana wrote that she didn't understand the term, he spelled out what he meant in a second letter: "Diaperology is a disparaging word applied to the theory that you find out how the people of some country or community treat their babies for the first six months, and then you know exactly whether they are going to be Republicans, Democrats, Dixiecrats, Titocrats, or Communists." Not amused, Diana did not pursue a correspondence.

In 1950 Diana had applied for and won a $3,000 Guggenheim fellowship for a book "on certain aspects of contemporary American culture," which she never finished. (She won a second Guggenheim in 1991 for *The Beginning of the Journey*.)

She also wrote in 1950 an essay for the *Partisan Review* on Ralph de Toledano's and Victor Lasky's book, *Seeds of Treason*, about the Alger Hiss/Whittaker Chambers case. She let her readers know upfront that she believed that Chambers told the truth and that Hiss lied. She later said that Lionel "had little liking for Chambers, but he didn't believe him capable of bearing false witness; and this continued to be his judgment." She continued: "Lionel had known Chambers for some time, enough to say that he would not have accused somebody falsely—that was his opinion. He might have been wrong with that, but it was his opinion, reached seriously on the basis of some knowledge of Chambers. It is considered very damaging to feel that way about Chambers, which means that you think Hiss was innocent and Chambers guilty—it's as simple as that. It's prejudicial thinking—it's not thinking."

Diana agreed with her husband completely. Jason Epstein, the writer and publisher, recalled (a little mischievously) how he took Lionel's class on Wordsworth, but "all Trilling wanted to talk about was Hiss, so I stopped going to class."

Monroe Engel, a novelist and Harvard professor, wrote Diana that the essay on *Seeds of Treason* "is one of the few examples we have had in recent years of the 'liberal imagination' engaged in politics." Diana had used the review to explain her liberal anti-Communist beliefs, which grew out of her anti-Trotskyism, her anti-Stalinism, and her anti-McCarthyism. She wrote that "the anti-communist liberal maintains, that is, a very delicate position. He firmly opposes McCarthy. But he doesn't automatically defend anyone McCarthy attacks. He demands that there be no public accusations without proper legal evidence. And even where this evidence is presented, he calls as much attention to the political motive of the accuser as of the accused. But he does not make the mistake of believing that just because the wrong people are looking for Soviet agents in the American government, there are none."

Her political position would stir controversy in her life, and that of Lionel's, ever after. (Norman Podhoretz says that they—especially Lionel—were what years later he would call premature neoconservatives, a label that Diana repeatedly denied. Still, Podhoretz asserts that even though Lionel himself "resisted classification, . . . it didn't bother him to be called a conservative. More than once he said to me, 'I quite like being called a conservative.'")

But that didn't mean he—or she—was one. "Lionel wouldn't have called himself a radical in politics," Diana said, "but he certainly wouldn't have called himself a conservative. He was a liberal, an old-fashioned nineteenth-century liberal. Like me, just a real old-fashioned liberal. . . . There was a conserving spirit, without question, but he was not a radical in his political thought."

Years later, Diana was accused by the writer A. Alvarez of being "a disillusioned radical, or an adjusted liberal. She represents a generation that has been psychoanalyzed out of politics." But Diana's detractors often went out of their way to be outlandish and obscure at the same time. It was sometimes impossible for them to hold two (seemingly) conflicting ideas in their heads at the same time. But Diana always could.

In 1955, when Jim was seven, the Trillings moved from 620 West 116th Street to another ground-floor, dark apartment—a larger one with six rooms—which was just around the corner, on Claremont Avenue. Thirty-Five Claremont was an eleven-story building constructed in 1910 and owned by Columbia University; the Trillings would live there for the rest of their lives. The apartment faced the street, although the curtains were often closed. But when they weren't, sights and noises from the street—students walking past, chatting; people with dogs on leashes; women and men carrying groceries from the markets on Broadway— could be heard and seen.

One entered the apartment directly into the living room, which was outfitted with rugs, two rose-colored silk brocade sofas, a coffee table usually covered with books, a couple of comfortable chairs, a few lamps, and various prints and photographs on the walls. It was from the very beginning what one guest called "a ladylike apartment." Lionel was always slightly uncomfortable over there being no entrance foyer and that guests were immediately confronted with the living room.

The Trillings frequently went to parties, not only to serious *Partisan Review* gatherings but also to more glamorous parties given by Leo Lerman. Their circle of acquaintances widened. As Steven Pascal wrote in his introduction to Lerman's letters and journals, at Leo's parties "friends beget friends." It was sometimes hard to know who had met whom where, when, or why. Many years later, according to Lerman, the writer Harold Brodkey, who had met the Trillings at one of his parties, and took a dislike to Diana, once impertinently told her "she had no taste [and] lived with 'mail order' furniture and a collection of 'cheap' third-rate drawings and Japanese woodcuts typical of academe house furnishing." Understandably, no friendship ensued.

Jim had different rooms at different times on Claremont Avenue. The largest bedroom in the back, painted a dark army green because his mother thought the color "neutral but masculine," was his until he was sixteen or seventeen, when it became his parents' bedroom. Jim then moved to a smaller center room. He remembered returning from Exeter's summer school to find that his mother had painted the entire room red because she thought he'd like it, which, as a matter of fact, he said he did. Everything, everything, was red—the chair, lamps, even the design on the bedspread. He also recalled once wanting fancy wallpaper in his room on 116th Street in order to cheer things up. He asked for a big all-over pattern—but his mother said he'd get tired of anything elaborate, so she chose a simple repetitive pattern—"something very bland with sprigs of cherries." Jim said this experience—the knowing what was needed even though he didn't get his way—was the beginning of his interest in the history of ornaments, which has led to his distinguished career in the field.

When Jim was five, he spent a year at Tompkins Hall Nursery School, which had been founded in the 1930s by a group of Columbia professors. In his first quarter report a teacher told the Trillings that like all only children Jim was "experimenting with social techniques." She went on to say that "consequently, Jim, in his eagerness to draw children to him, often used physical force as an overture to friendship." But the teacher assured the Trillings that Jim was trying to find better approaches, although he "has difficulty staying with one activity for very long because his primary interest is the children and what they do." The teacher also said that Jim didn't like getting his hands messy with mixing materials, although he "never hesitates to sail boats or blow bubbles in tubs of soapy water, and he has also helped with planting seeds carefully and watching them grow." She praised his curiosity and energy.

By the time Jim was seven he had been in five different schools. "I was unpredictable throughout my childhood," he said; "I had rages and screamed."

After Tompkins he was enrolled in Dalton but left after a week "because of tantrums; I couldn't control myself at all." He then went to the Birch Wathen School (later Birch Wathen Lenox) for another two or three weeks and left once again because of his outbursts. Next was the Boardman School (later acquired by the New Lincoln School, which eventually merged with the Walden School, and was closed altogether in 1991). Jim stayed at Boardman and New Lincoln for a couple of months until he went to a special education school, the Reece School, in 1955, when he was seven.

There were several months between New Lincoln and Reece when he was not in school at all, but as Diana wrote in a May 12, 1955, letter to his pediatrician, Dr. Morris Greenberg, "both Lionel and I are deeply pleased by the progress Jim has made in the last year toward emotional maturity. His overt aggressions have surely been reduced by 75 per cent, if not more, and he has learned a great deal of self-control, although the control is naturally not yet entirely operative under conditions of strain, which is why he can't yet be in school." He was seeing his analyst regularly.

The main reason Diana put her thoughts in a letter, she told "Morris"—they were on a first-name basis—was that she could think better that way. She had two concerns: she didn't want Jim's not being in a school to be a cause for his not receiving a polio vaccination (the Salk vaccine became available in April 1955), and she was concerned that Jim had not received a thorough enough examination after she said that he had stomach pains that she believed were caused by his eating too fast and "often too much." Dr. Greenberg replied in a lengthy handwritten letter, explaining first that there was only enough vaccine available for first- and second-grade children, and even that supply was short. He suggested that Diana wait until the fall or winter term for Jim's shots. As for her second concern, he reminded Diana that "Jim is an unusually bright child. . . . Consciously or unconsciously you have been sharpening his mind. His intellectual keenness is sometimes startling. But emotionally he is still a child. He still wants continuous and exclusive attention. He gets it by asking questions, by creating scenes, by pretending to be exquisitely hurt and in a thousand other ways that little children learn to torture their parents." Dr. Greenberg went on to say that his examination of Jim (in which he used his "experienced intuition") "was sufficiently thorough to satisfy him beyond a shadow of doubt" that Jim had "exaggerated bellyaches which most children have now and then." He ended the letter by telling Diana, "You may be a bright woman but your son is bright enough to take you in. You needn't worry about his physical health." In a follow-up letter a few weeks later in reply to Diana's phoned concern that despite everything he said, she still felt he had shortchanged Jim, Dr. Greenberg countered that he had treated Jim as he would any other child, "without giving him extra comfort," which he understood Diana and "the psychiatrist" recommended he should have offered. He knew that she and Lionel read a lot in the psychoanalytic field (he even praised Lionel's essay on Freud in *The Liberal Imagination*), but *he* was still not convinced that psychiatrists "know precisely what they are doing." Although he wrote that "Freud's greatest contribution has been toward making psychoanalysis a dynamic rather than a static discipline and to encourage people to look without fear into the dark corners of individual cases," he believed that "Freud's contribution to therapy of individual cases has not yet, to my mind, been proved." Diana read the letter with skepticism, accepting, as she did, that most psychoanalysts knew what they were doing, despite her flawed early encounters with a few.

Still, in *The Beginning of the Journey* Diana revealed that her analyst, Dr. Kris, "said of my literary criticism that I must 'neutralize' it, by which she meant that in my writing as in my life, I must be more accepting, less given to the making of judgments; as a critic, I was to be less critical." Diana said that Dr. Kris reminded her that "it was a time when Freudian doctrine identified female normality with 'passivity,' a counter to the 'activity' of the male . . . but in commenting on my work in these terms," Diana wrote, "Dr. Kris was not just expressing a biased sexual view; she was moving into an area in which she had little competence—psychoanalytical training is not a preparation for literary judgment."

But it was the 1950s: a time when pediatricians functioned as parents, psychiatrists, and book critics; when psychoanalysts functioned as judges; and when most mothers and fathers were considered slightly off course, even though their children could grow up to be remarkable in spite of the obstacles. And mothers, just about all mothers everywhere, continued to know what was best, and as Diana wrote in her unpublished poem, they also continued to "Oh Be Brave":

Summon the wind with your whistle
Bend the tall tree at your touch

Much that is loud is pretending
Much that you fear is defending . . .

The year the Trillings moved to Claremont Avenue, Lionel published two books, *Freud and the Crisis of Our Culture*, a fifty-nine page volume that contained the talk he gave at the New York Psychoanalytic Institute and Society as their fifth annual Freud Anniversary Lecture, and *The Opposing Self*, a collection of nine essays on such subjects as Keats's letters, *Anna Karenina*, and *The Bostonians*. In his preface he wrote that most of the essays were written as introductions to books, "and all of them were written for occasions which were not of my own devising." The idea of self is what joins all the essays, and he noted that most of them were revised after their original publication, "but none has been radically revised." In 1956 he published *A Gathering of Fugitives*, essays about such figures as Charles Dickens, Edith Wharton, and Robert Graves; some of the essays first appeared in *The New Yorker*, *Partisan Review*, *The New York Times Book Review*, and the *London Review*. A number of them also appeared in the Reader's Subscription Book Club's monthly magazine, *The Griffin*. As with the other books, Lionel revised some of the essays, added material to others, and "corrected some infelicities of prose," as he put it.

Although Diana did little work on these essays at the actual time of their publication in book form, she once complained to Thelma Anderson that she "could work on a manuscript of [Lionel's] for hours and hours and days and days, and he would scarcely say thank you. In the most cursory way, he would say, 'Oh thanks, dear, that's awfully nice. Thanks a lot. That's wonderful.' Then he'd come in later and say, 'Marvelous job you did. Marvelous job.' And that was it."

Diana also told Thelma that every now and then Lionel would thrust at her a shirt that needed a button sewed on, and he would look with wonder at her when she said that it would only take her a second to fix it. Diana said that Lionel "went overboard in his thank yous. I was never thanked for anything I did the way I was thanked for sewing a button." Diana asked Lionel why he made so much of it, but she reported that "he never answered me. I never knew. I don't know the answer."

Diana was proud of being her husband's lifeboat, even explaining to Thelma that Lionel "didn't have the intellectual, inventive genius of a Freud certainly, and he didn't have the literary gifts of a Dickens, but his critical gifts were developed to the degree they were by the same forces that were impelling Freud—that he was the golden son who was going to do something distinguished—something special." Yet, she said, even when Lionel was on a good path with his work, he still always "had difficulties in composition."

Although Diana never changed any of Lionel's ideas, she did try now and then to influence his thoughts. "I remember how often he did say to me, 'You cannot feed an emotion into me and expect me then to make it my emotion. I cannot do that. I have to operate on my own emotions or not at all.' "

Diana said that although Lionel "lived a rather close, domestic life," he also "saw life from a grand moral and social perspective. I've never known anybody else quite like that. He didn't see himself as somebody who had a right to transcend the demands of ordinary life. "She went on to say that "he behaved like a very everyday sort of person like anybody else. . . . After Jim was born, it was a pleasure for him to walk in our neighborhood and be greeted by all the kids as Jim's daddy. 'Hello Jim's daddy.' And this tells you something about his lack of egoism. He wasn't so much retiring or recessive as genuinely modest."

But sometimes it backfired, or, more accurately, he needed to protect his real self from exposure. Diana was mystified and embarrassed after one of Lionel's former students, who at the time was on the Columbia faculty, sought advice about having a child, and Lionel refused to become engaged with him. The young professor told Lionel he himself was only "bits and pieces," while Lionel was "a whole person." The young instructor was desperate for guidance. As Diana later remembered, "Lionel just sat there quietly and let him think this way as if it were indeed an accurate description of the difference between them. . . . I got into a boiling rage. . . . Why did Lionel insist on this unbroken front of self-possession? . . . Maybe he couldn't risk that much licensing of feeling, feeling so akin to impulse. Or maybe it was a necessary condition of his work, to make the assumption that he was this kind of whole man in order to speak with authority and be rid of self-pity." Diana never knew the reason. She said that every now and then they'd argue about "letting people think that he was in such entire command of his life" and that "it was often in the air between us."

Debt continued to haunt the Trillings' lives, and they continued to borrow from friends, especially from their neighbors, Elsa and Jim Grossman. Lionel had met Elsa as a teenager when she was a mother's helper at a camp near Saranac Lake, and Jim, at the time the family lawyer, and later a lawyer for various publishing houses, was a friend from Lionel's student days at Columbia. In one of her thank you notes, Diana wrote the Grossmans, "Lionel, immersed in The Great Work Push, asks me to write on both our behalfs (behalves?) to thank you most affectionately and sincerely for your lovely prompt response to our perennial cry for help." Diana's brother often helped, too, once writing her in a note with a check for $800 that "I sort of mildly resent your instructions not to go to too much trouble to help you. I think a little trouble is in order if it is the means of assisting you."

Although Lionel's university salary was not adequate for their expenses, once, on a whim, Lionel had bought Diana an elaborate silvery brocade hostess gown as a gift. She was not pleased. "It was his extravagance that angered me," she said, "his intent on deceiving himself [about] how we lived." Diana said that such gift-buying was a legacy from his father, "who had filial love but not personal love" for Lionel. David Trilling "would always decide the pile of presents on Christmas Eve was never enough, and he would run out and buy more," in compensation for feelings he couldn't express any other way to his son.

Some of the money the Trillings borrowed went for childcare and medical expenses, and some often went toward the rent for summer houses. It was more crucial than ever to her to be away from New York City in June through August, and she said that she completely took it for granted that this would be possible, no matter what their financial circumstances.

For three straight summers the Trillings rented a large house in Fairfield, Connecticut, from Robert Penn Warren and his second wife, Eleanor Clark (who early in her career had been the first reader at Norton for Lionel's book on Arnold and who later won a National Book Award for her nonfiction book *The Oysters of Locmariaquer*). The Robert Penn Warrens were not friends, just acquaintances, although Lionel wrote an undated and enigmatic entry in his journal that "William Phillips informed D of the affairs I am supposed to have had—with Eleanor Clark—rather revoltingly I was somehow conned into that one!" There are no further—or known—explanations for the comment.

Diana had heard the house in Fairfield was often available for rent, and she wrote the Robert Penn Warrens about it. Jim Trilling remembers the house as a "daring architectural venture made from barns put together. It had a pool and an extensive rock garden." As a young boy he collected toads and recalls once deciding to place some on a large tin, which he covered with Saran Wrap, the clear food covering that came on the market several years earlier in 1949. But the toads naturally managed to escape from under the wrap and were found all over the house, even on his parents' bed. Diana was extremely upset. "I took unfair advantage of my mother's squeamishness," he admitted.

The Warren house was the most expansive and expensive one the Trillings ever rented. Diana wrote in a draft of a book she later discarded that "Lionel had to be well into middle age before he developed any sense of himself as an earner, and even then his economic identity seemed to elude him. . . . He couldn't at any moment have told you whether our bank balance was $100 or $1,000—it was my job always to keep the family ledgers and to announce to Lionel our periodic crises when we confronted a stack of unpaid bills and an overdrawn bank account."

Diana also did their income tax and "all the things that were done in private that the world didn't have to know about," she told Lionel's former student and colleague Stephen Donadio. Diana went on to tell Donadio that Lionel "couldn't keep a checkbook. Half the time he couldn't remember to write down the check . . . yet he was efficient enough with his college affairs, and he answered his mail, and he did all the things that had to be done to keep the literary life going except on a business level. On a business level he could not manage it."

By the 1950s, both Trillings were far, far away from the time when Diana's main worry was that Jack the Ripper would come to New York and strangle her. Now the couple's choking money concerns were often on her mind. Yet she always felt in control, despite their constant debt, because she knew what was or wasn't in the bank and was in charge of figuring out what to do. And Lionel, whose greatest childhood fear had been a fragment of peeling wallpaper in his bedroom, had only to worry about his flourishing literary life.

11

GUILT MAKES US HUMAN

Of sexual activity, one motive may be said to be the desire for sin—what afflicts married couples is that with time their relationship no longer has any touch of sin in it. Sin in the sense of St. Augustine's pears. The other, D says is the desire to have a new side of the personality brought into the light.

—LIONEL TRILLING, JOURNAL ENTRY, SOMETIME BETWEEN 1938 AND 1943

In November of 1954 Diana, approaching fifty, published another long essay in *Partisan Review*, which had been welcoming her as a contributor for quite a few years. Her piece was on J. Robert Oppenheimer, the celebrated physicist often called "the father of the atomic bomb," whose security clearance was canceled in 1954 because of his outspoken belief in international control of nuclear power, his opposition to the H-bomb, and his alleged association with Communist Party members. His censure was a defining moment in American security policy. Diana considered her essay a defining moment in her career.

She had torn up her initial Oppenheimer essay, or rather she told *Partisan Review* to destroy it after she submitted it. She explained that "when the Oppenheimer hearings took place, I thought I smelled guilt." She thought he somehow must have betrayed his country. "But, then," she said, "I couldn't sleep at night; I felt I had done something wrong. I'd read all the evidence. I felt very unhappy." So she read through all the testimony. "I spent weeks and weeks doing that . . . a million words." The new piece that she wrote, which didn't take the strict anti-Communist line, followed her conscience, she said. She knew some people would be outraged by her less-popular liberal anti-Communist views. Diana subsequently commented that she always "swam against the cultural tide."

Much later she wrote in a letter that "in the fifties, I diverged from the dominant *Partisan Review* political-cultural viewpoint . . . on the Oppenheimer case—in a piece which several members of the Atomic Energy Commission (Conant, Rabi) felt to be the most accurate analysis of the case that ever appeared. I recognized the role of McCarthy in creating the climate of opinion in which Oppenheimer had his security clearance taken away from him, but I did not accept the single-minded idea that *only* McCarthyism lay behind the case." James Bryant Conant, president of Harvard from 1933 to 1953, was an innovative chemist who served on the General Advisory Committee of the Atomic Energy Commission. Isidor Isaac Rabi, who won the Nobel Prize for Physics in 1944, served as a member of the Science Advisory Committee of the International Atomic Energy Commission.

She went on to say that *Partisan Review* then immediately published a stronger anti-McCarthy essay, which she suspected was meant to disassociate the magazine from her own point of view, which didn't condemn McCarthy sufficiently. (But, she later wrote, "I was against both Communism and McCarthyism. They were enemies of each other, but I was the enemy of both.")

Over the years Diana became convinced that her star had begun to descend because of the more nuanced political-cultural opinions that her critique of Oppenheimer reflected and that because of these positions, she would never achieve the full recognition she deserved, the kind of recognition that she had begun to receive in the 1940s when she was writing for *The Nation*. She also came to believe that her piece on Oppenheimer was a watershed for *Partisan Review*. "I think that was the end of its principled life. . . . It was a Cold War period and the magazine didn't want to be cold warriors. They wanted to be radicals." Diana later wrote that the magazine was anti-Stalinist in its politics but radical in its culture.

The writer Bernard Malamud happened to have published his short story "The Magic Barrel" in the same issue as Diana's essay. After she read Malamud's story, she was moved to write him a letter of praise. "It was one of the few fan letters I've ever written," she said. Malamud wrote back that her letter meant a lot to him, adding that the reception of the story gave him "confidence to continue in my vein: people first (and with mercy); the tale wrought from an idea, not biography; theme pointing out inevitabilities of plot, not vice versa; style secondary; story over author." He told her also that he was "laboring at a new novel (my first, *The Natural*, was, in a way, to test the power of my imagination and to make me not afraid of the day when I give up my 'Jewish material') and the magic, if any, comes hard. I almost wish that the barrel were not invented, because it sometimes makes my present performance seem inadequate." He added that her Oppenheimer piece was being read at Oregon State College (where he was teaching) "with a good deal of interest. First for the drama of event, and that of personality created and revealed by your discerning analysis." Later he worried that he might have offended her by saying she had "created" Oppenheimer's personality, and he wrote her that "all I meant was that through your article you had 'recreated' him as a personality for me." He emphasized that he went "along with your thesis concerning the liberals, except that I feel it was not only they who were lacking in morality and insight vis a vis the communists. That doesn't excuse them, of course, but true morality is very hard to come by. I think we have to give credit to those who, even blindly, attempt to seek it." He told her that Oppenheimer would be visiting the campus soon and that there had been controversy over the invitation. Later, Malamud wrote Diana a six-page letter describing the event, which included two formal lectures by Oppenheimer (one was moved from a site that could fill five thousand seats to a basketball stadium which held ten thousand), appearances at various classes, and meetings with select professors. He mentioned a lecture William Faulkner had given two weeks before Oppenheimer's visit, which

Malamud described as "sad" because the sound system failed and the audience of two thousand people could barely hear a word. Attempts were made to fix the problem, but nothing worked, and, as Malamud wrote, "Faulkner, controlled but uneasy, talked on, uncommunicating. Straining, I heard him speak of the loss of privacy in American life. He cited himself, Colonel Lindbergh, and J. Robert Oppenheimer."

Malamud described Oppenheimer talking to a colleague's philosophy class, "where he appeared very nervous. Later, at a smaller group of twenty people . . . he smoked nonstop, so that there was almost always a smoke haze around him. . . . His crew cut is entirely gray; he is thin, almost gaunt. His brown suits softened by something like heather hung loosely on him." Malamud continued, telling Diana that Oppenheimer told the group about a recent experiment in brainwashing at McGill University that involved "enforced solitude." After three days of seeing only light (they were wearing thick glasses), the participants forgot how to multiply and divide. Oppenheimer, Malamud wrote, "had stressed the importance of this attack against intelligence."

Malamud, a New Yorker no doubt lonely in Oregon despite the presence of his wife and two children, had picked the right correspondent and somehow knew instinctively that Diana would be a generous audience. Her keen reception of his story had told him she would be a good listener, too, and she was. Lionel's Columbia colleagues and most PR people often didn't give her a chance to be heard; they frequently spoke over her. But Diana's acute sense of logic was more and more merging with a strong intuitiveness, creating just the right degree of effectiveness in conversations.

During the spring of 1956, two years after writing her Oppenheimer essay, Diana and Lionel were asked by the Carnegie Corporation to evaluate a group of books that, as the requesting letter stated, were to be "sent abroad" in a venture called "American Shelf." Diana took the job very seriously, although sometimes her brief reviews—called blurbs by the Carnegie Corporation—were criticized, and she was told that such blurbs were "a difficult art form, at best," and that perhaps the organization was "asking too much of it."

She often compared books she was vetting to ones not on the Shelf's list, which was confusing. She was once told that she had "strained" to place Edna Ferber's *Showboat* in terms of its reputation rather than what it was, "so that you seem to be approving its popularity while disparaging its merit." (The novel, first published in 1926, was the basis for a Broadway musical, three films, and two more musicals, one in 1936 and another in 1951.)

Elmer Davis's book of essays *But We Are Born Free* was also on Diana's list. Davis, a distinguished newspaper and radio commentator, and the director of the Office of War Information during World War II, was fiercely anti-McCarthy and wrote in his book that Americans currently live in "a perilous night" and that he was convinced that the night was not yet over. He said that McCarthyism was continuing to invade the minds of all Americans, that fake patriots wanted to tear the country apart, and that Americans needed clearer thinking and more optimism. Although the book was praised by the cultural critic Gilbert Seldes as "the most concise, witty, informed, and impersonal account of recent attacks on the freedom of the mind I have yet read," Diana wanted it excluded from the American Shelf. She objected to the book because Davis made McCarthyism sound as if it was a unique political phenomenon in America, which she didn't think it was; it was just another chapter in America's political history. The country was not in a reign of terror, "a perilous night," Diana said. McCarthyism should not be treated as the end of America—that was going overboard. Furthermore, as she wrote to the Carnegie Corporation," there is nothing in Mr. Davis's volume to suggest that McCarthy's powers might shortly be curtailed." (He was censured by the Senate on December 2, 1954.)

The book remained on the list, with Diana writing a blurb that she said "made an effort to correct whatever untruthful impression I think it conveys." She strongly believed in her political position (she had joined the board of the American Committee for Cultural Freedom, an anti-Communism and antitotalitarianism group) around the time of the publication of her essay on Oppenheimer), and she wrote in a letter about the Davis book: "Undoubtedly I am particularly concerned about this kind of thing because I spend so large a part of my time, as Chairman of the Board of the American Committee for Cultural Freedom combating the attacks upon our free institutions from both the McCarthyites and the Communist side and trying to keep the American picture straight in people's minds." She went on to affirm that "no more than I feel that anti-Communism is served by the excessive emotions which speak in its name can I feel that the cause of civil liberties is served by the excessive emotions which speak in *its* name."

At the end of the letter she mentioned that she had another matter on her mind. "I have your note about the elimination of *Plainsville, U.S.A.* from the list," she said, not yet letting on what else she had to say. (This book was a study of a small midwestern rural community, by James West—a pseudonym used by Carl Withers, a poetry and folklore anthologist—that had been published in 1945 by Columbia University Press.) Diana continued, writing that "this book was my husband's job, not mine, and I am afraid he had already read [it] although he had not yet written about it. In such a circumstance I should suppose that half payment [to him] would be a sufficient compensation." Money was on her agenda, and because finances always remained a priority, Diana could mix a literary/political matter with a plea for payment.

Before Diana had joined the American Committee for Cultural Freedom board, Lionel's name was the one that appeared on the masthead as a member of the American Committee "in formation" in 1951, a year after its actual founding. One of the honorary chairmen was Bertrand Russell. Stephen Spender was a member of the executive committee. Sidney Hook was chairman of the American Committee, and others on the list were Jacques Barzun, William Phillips, Philip Rahv, W. H. Auden, and Upton Sinclair. Only two women appeared among more than one hundred names: Dorothy Canfield Fisher, the social activist and writer who brought the Montessori child-rearing method to America and also served as a member of the Book of the Month Club Selection Committee for nearly twenty-five years, and Sylvia Marlowe, the harpsichordist, also well-known for her Leo Lerman–like parties, which Lionel and Diana attended frequently. The committee's executive secretary, Pearl Kluger, was also listed. Kluger was a political activist who had once worked with the committee defending Trotsky.

A five-page draft of the committee's mandate stated that the "nonpolitical" group, while hospitable to diverse points of view, was "intractably opposed to totalitarianism of whatever kind" and that "of the many threats to cultural freedom that exist in the world today, that of Communist totalitarianism is by far the gravest." Even Communist sympathizers were to be included (as threats), the mandate said, as are "certain men and groups who represent themselves as militant opponents of Communism." Furthermore, calling anything "un-American" or "Communist-inspired," demanding loyalty oaths, or attempting to intimidate magazines and radio programs is "wholly inappropriate to democracy." Additionally, such practices "obscure the fact that a Communist conspiracy actually exists and they interfere with the devising of means to counter it."

They had a difficult task ahead, the document concluded.

Diana signed on. This was the group she had been waiting for, the one that mirrored her own nonconformist views; this was where she belonged.

Another committee directive made clear that "a prerequisite for an authentic struggle against Communist influence is scrupulous attention to fact. Reckless accusations and gross distortions are as self-defeating as they are immoral." (Not yet acknowledged publicly was that the committee's parent organization, the Congress for Cultural Freedom, was backed by the CIA. The congress had branches in more than thirty countries and had received funding from the Ford Foundation (in cooperation with the CIA).

The committee became enraged that Senator McCarthy had accused Senator William Benton of Connecticut of sending "obscene literature which followed the Communist line" to England, including Edmund Wilson's short story collection *Memoirs of Hecate County*. "The idea that this book is obscene is preposterous," the committee held. "As for the book following the Communist party line—the idea is as preposterous as it is malicious. Mr. Wilson has for the past fifteen years or more vigorously fought to expose the intellectual deceits of Communism. His book,

To the Finland Station, published in 1940, is one of the significant intellectual efforts of our age to explore the ideological roots of Stalinism."

At a planning meeting on March 1, 1952, at which Diana was not present (although she was sent the minutes), members decided that the main job in the country was to fight McCarthyism. Participants in the planning meeting said that the non-Communist Left needed to isolate the McCarthyites "at one end of the line and the Communists at the other. . . . The fellow travelers are still very well-organized and are able, by concentrating on specific issues, to spread a line quite easily." The members also believed that as Stalin's crimes (he died the following year, 1953) involving secret police raids and slave labor camps became more widespread, the influence of his Marxist-Leninist ideas on intellectuals would decline.

Most Americans did not really know how to distinguish between Communists and fellow travelers, participants said, so they suggested that the committee needed to provide lectures and pamphlets. They recommended also that the committee "discover new problems and issues." (For instance, the committee was suspicious of anti-Stalinists who continued to hope for some form of socialism.)

One particularly outspoken member had suggested that the committee needed a "greater concentration on college campuses." This was Arnold Beichman, a Columbia-educated journalist, the son of Ukrainian Jewish immigrants, who worked nationally and internationally for the *New York Herald Tribune*, *PM*, and *Newsweek*.* Beichman had suggested at the March 1, 1952, meeting that the committee support *Partisan Review*, *The New Leader*, and *Commentary*, which, he told the other members, "have an essential political sophistication." Diana had particularly perked up when reading this in the minutes; she liked his ideas very much, especially that they could be embraced by magazines she respected. Later, when she met Beichman, she found him to be an appeal-

---

* He later wrote five books, including a biography of Herman Wouk. His best-known work, *Nine Lies About America*, dismissed 1960 New Left claims that the United States was a racist, materialistic, imperialist nation. He eventually became an aggressively anti-Communist political scientist at the Hoover Institution and the conservative-leaning *Washington Times*.

ing, if often uncompromising, personality. The two took an immediate liking to each other; Beichman appreciated Diana's shrewd, quirky mind, and she liked his animated spirit. He was an enthusiastic storyteller about his days as a labor reporter and a foreign correspondent, and he always filled the room with wonderful accounts of his work and his colleagues. He and his wife, Carroll, a well-to-do Canadian aristocrat from British Columbia, became friends of both Trillings, and the couples socialized often in the 1950s and 1960s. "The Beichmans were at our house a lot," Jim Trilling recalled. Many of the parties also took place at the Beichmans' large but sparsely decorated apartment on Central Park West.

Diana usually planned their social activities. Lionel did not socialize with any of his students, and Diana preferred it that way, although occasionally there were exceptions, as with Norman Podhoretz and Midge Decter. Diana told the poet and editor Alan Kaufman in an interview in *Jewish Frontier* magazine that "we were all four of us friendly—but the major relation was theirs to Lionel, who instructed Podhoretz and his other students of the late forties in the meaning of Stalinism, both in politics and culture. He was probably the first person who alerted them to the vital connection between politics and culture." But, Diana went on, "there was also another much more subtle and persuasive influence that he seems to have exerted on these students. His rigor of thought proposed, not without logic, that they exercise a similar rigor in the realm of moral behavior; and this, in particular, made him into a father person."

In a draft of her unpublished "Biography of a Marriage" Diana wrote that "it was only the second or third time that I had met Podhoretz, he was still very young, when I remember telling him rather unkindly that I was surprised that he was studying literature instead of law because, excellent student of literature though he was, he seemed to me to be primarily interested in power."

Diana's sharp tongue was often at the ready; using it was, for her, an extension of the rigorous form of reasoning that had already enveloped her life. This gave her an edge over people that she had not had as a child and young woman. Later, an anonymous reviewer would comment that Diana "has a gangster's memory for insult, a taste for vendetta."

Diana's long friendship with her college friend Bettina Sinclair Hartenbach would not survive her lashings. Although their bond had almost been broken during Diana's pregnancy, when there was fear of a miscarriage and Diana's panic caused her to turn on Bettina, the friendship had managed to continue. But three years later, in 1951, the relationship worsened. Their letters at this time don't explain the direct cause of the rupture, although they hint at unresolved issues over Diana's refusal "to take down her shingle" with her friend. Bettina was plain tired of Diana telling her that her anger stemmed from her own weakness and that Diana will "hereby explain it" all to Bettina. She was finally weary of Diana sending the arrows right back and blaming her for their trajectories and, most important, acting as if Bettina were a madwoman. (Years later, Jim Trilling remarked that during disagreements his mother "treated people as if they were sick. She did this to everyone. . . . She was hair-trigger sensitive to anyone saying she was wrong.")

Yet the Trillings and Midge Decter and Norman Podhoretz remained friends for a long time—until politics moved them apart—Diana remaining an anti-Communist liberal and the Podhoretzes becoming anti-anti-Communists, and then neoconservatives. But at one point the couples were so close that Diana would particularly recall one raucous New Year's Eve party, when everyone was drinking heavily, and Norman made a pass at her. (He vehemently denies ever having done any such thing, recalling that "not only did I never make a pass at her, but never in a million years would I even have dreamed of doing so.") But Diana remembered it differently and said that Podhoretz even taunted her after she turned him down. "He told me I was incapable of a kind of disgusting lying—he didn't use the word 'disgusting,' he had disgust in his voice—but didn't use that word, and he said, 'You're incapable of the lying and cheating that are involved in leading this kind of free sexual life. . . . He was trying to shock me. I was Mama and he was going to shock me."

Diana told the writer Peter Manso (in his oral history of Norman Mailer) that "Lionel was Big Papa, and if you're married to the Big Father, you're the Big Mother. . . . If someone could win my friendship and respect, then he got some of the paternal blessing, if only at second-hand. That was true for so many younger people we knew." She qualified that it "wasn't true of our relation with Norman Mailer, though. For Norman, I was the primary person. . . . It was different with him." They met at a dinner given by Lillian Hellman.

Diana said that Lionel had met Hellman briefly in the 1920s—they knew people in common—and then much later they met again at lectures and meetings of the American Academy of Arts and Sciences (Lionel was elected to membership in 1952, Hellman in 1960, and Diana in 1976).

Lionel had warned his wife that their politics were in such disagreement that a friendship with Hellman couldn't work. "What he meant," Diana later explained, "was that she was a very well-known Communist fellow traveler. Nobody knew whether or not she was actually a Party member, but she was there for every Communist cause—every single one over a long period of time." But eventually Lionel changed his mind and told Diana, "What's the use? She's a very entertaining woman and it would be fun to go visit her." And they did.

Diana later commented: "Lillian makes a profession of friendship. She really works at it," adding that whenever politics came up, Lillian would tell them, "We're all just liberal democrats together." But generally they avoided talking politics, and the friendship "thrived," Diana said, not only because of "Lillian's power over people and her social position, but because she knew everybody and she gave extraordinary parties. . . . You met a great variety of people of a kind whom I wasn't likely to meet in the course of my life."

Although Diana once claimed that the playwright was always more interested in Lionel, Hellman (who often forgot the names of the wives and referred to them all as "Madam") soon focused primarily on Diana, and they became close friends. Diana had always wanted what she called "a large scale woman friend," and she believed she had found her in Hellman—the most powerful personality she had ever known, she said. "Most of the women I knew were sort of second-class citizens, even within their own marriages, and I always wanted to know somebody who lived on a larger scale than that."

172 GUILT MAKES US HUMAN

When they met, Norman Mailer was working on his third novel, *The Deer Park*, and had already become celebrated in 1948 after he published his World War II novel *The Naked and the Dead*; *Barbary Shore*, about a wounded war veteran who wants to be a novelist, followed in 1951. Diana remembered that Mailer "had been paying total attention to the grand dame lady on the other side of him. He listened to every word she said, and spoke to her very, very directly. I was terribly impressed with that. He wasn't being restless and looking for some pretty young girl he could go and talk to. . . . After all, he was a very, very good looking young man, very very good looking, slender, lively looking . . . and when the proper moment came, he turned—and I thought—now he's going to give his attention to me. And the first words he said were, "How are you, smart cunt?" And I collapsed, absolutely collapsed. I got into such giggles. I just roared at that. And that's how we got acquainted. . . . I had the reputation of being Lionel's wife and somewhat formidable. I just loved his breaking through that. Very smart of him." Later in the evening, or possibly on another evening, Diana said that Mailer

sat down next to me on the sofa and started to play that "I'll stare you out game" of his; he loved all those things. It's like arm wrestling with the eyes; it's a form of wrestling. I put up my dollar and he put up his, and another guest, Glenway Westcott, joined us; he put a dollar on me. Bet on me, very gentlemanly. And I said to Norman, "Are you allowed to smile?" And he leaned over and took my dollar and took Glenway's dollar. I said, "Hey, we hadn't started to play yet. I was asking a question about the rules." He said we had started to play. I said, "You're a cheat." I wasn't kidding. I've never been so angry about the loss of one dollar. . . . I was furious. There had been no gong. I hadn't gotten all the rules straight in my mind. I wasn't ready to play. Well, I could see Glenway Westcott was completely in accord with me and just hoped I wouldn't get myself too agitated about this, so I just sort of let it slide off, but I didn't like it. But Norman and I did become friends despite that bad beginning. . . . Lionel and Mailer got along perfectly pleasantly, but they were never friends. The friendship was between Norman and me. Lionel liked him all right. Mailer, I think, was a little frightened of Lionel, a little intimidated by him. He felt more comfortable with me.

In a draft of her unpublished "The Education of a Woman," Diana wrote, "I encouraged most of the men of my acquaintance, throughout my life, to regard me rather as if I were a member of the third world of humanity."

But it was different with Norman Mailer.

"We were really very close in some way," she said, revealing somewhat reluctantly that "he wanted to have an affair with me. His way of wanting to have an affair was not to ask you, because he would never be on record as having been refused. But he did go as far as [Diana doesn't finish this thought but then continues]—there was no missing that that's what he had in mind." She told Peter Manso, "I've often wondered what Norman is like in bed. One thing is for sure: he doesn't take any chances of rejection; he's a very wary seducer. He puts out the smallest feeler. . . . He wants the woman to take the chances." (Several years later, Mailer wrote in a letter to Diana "that what women never understand about men is that men, strong men, move in quiet fear, in some sadness, with pessimism—they succeed because they are unaware of their strength.")

Diana said that William Phillips told her that Mailer's second wife, Adele (whom he married in 1954), told him that Norman had fallen in love with an intellectual. Diana also said that Phillips later remarked to Mailer in some other context she no longer recalled that, "Well, of course, you're in love with Diana Trilling, aren't you? And Mailer said, 'No, I love her, but I'm not in love with her.'"

"The Mailer complex," Lionel later wrote in his journal, "my growing sense of the man's intellectual and ideological power—his moral energy—interesting how little respect he has from the intellectuals—my own awareness of him, comes, of course, from Diana—her sense of her having failed him, which she did—my wry sense that this was the first man she could not comprehend—encompass—understand—or in any way influence or control."

What did Lionel mean by saying his wife had failed Norman Mailer? Did he mean in a literary way? A sexual way? In another journal entry

Lionel wrote, "It was on the basis of her response to [Mailer] [at a party] that I made the observation to D that meant much to her—her physical fear of a sexual encounter, her fear that harm will be done to her."

Was Diana still concerned about the dangers that Dr. Kellogg's sex book warned her of so many decades ago? In her unpublished "Biography of a Marriage" she wrote that after she and Lionel had premarital sex, she "suffered a sense of sin, which she differentiated from guilt, with which I was also burdened." Had the sexual assault by her family's friend left haunting, indelible memories that bubbled up into her consciousness every now and then? Did any possible sexual encounter stir up not only old memories and fears but perhaps desires? Desires she might not be able to control?

Diana once confided to the Andersons her interest in the sex industry, and partly as a joke they sent her a number of advertisements for massage parlors and adult entertainment nightspots. And the one and only pornographic movie she ever saw—she described it in a letter as "a sociological evening"—had also been viewed by Mailer, who was in the audience. "We left together, with Norman lightly commenting to me that the movie should perhaps be suppressed because it was anti-sexual in its effect. I agreed," Diana wrote.

In their extensive correspondence over the decades, Diana would often pass judgment on Mailer's work and life. She became his mother confessor, of sorts, and a scolder, when required. Mailer respected her enormously.

There was never a love affair.

In the summer of 1959 Mailer sent her a copy of his sexually explicit short story "The Time of Her Time," not exactly for her literary opinion but rather for her support in averting possible censorship trouble with the US Postal Service. (The story, in which the Irish American protagonist attempts to bring his Jewish American lover to orgasm without success until he penetrates her anally and calls her "a dirty little Jew," was shocking at the time. It would eventually be published in *Advertisements for Myself* yet was still so controversial that Mailer's English publisher refused to include it in its edition of the book.)

DIANA'S FAMILY LIKED HER TO PLAY HER VIOLIN IN FRONT OF RELATIVES.

AT CAMP LENORE, DIANA (ON RIGHT) "LOVED LEAPING AROUND IN THE OPEN AIR WITH THE SUN BEAMING DOWN ON HER BODY, KNOWING HER MOTHER WOULD PROBABLY DISAPPROVE."

CANOEING ON LAKE ASHMERE AT CAMP LENORE. DIANA LATER BECAME A
COUNSELOR, TEACHING ARCHERY, BASKETBALL, AND DRAMA.

AT RADCLIFFE, 1924 (DIANA ON LEFT).
THE PURPOSE OF THEIR EDUCATION
WAS ONLY TO "INCREASE THEIR
DOMESTIC EFFICIENCY." . . .
THE PRACTICAL WAS THE GOAL.

DIANA FELT HER RADCLIFFE
EDUCATION WAS MUCH TOO
FOCUSED ON THE HISTORICAL,
INSTEAD OF THE CRITICAL.

RADCLIFFE'S BARNARD HALL, 1924.

ONE OF THE "ODD CHARACTERS" DIANA "PICKED UP" ON HER TRIP
TO SOUTH AMERICA WITH HER FATHER AND SISTER, 1928.

"WE LAUNCHED OUR MARRIAGE IN GUILT," DIANA SAID.
"EVERYONE HAD TO BE LISTENED TO, APOLOGIZED TO,
THANKED FOR GIVING US PERMISSION TO LIVE OUR LIVES."

LIONEL'S MOTHER FAINTED WHEN
SHE HEARD OF DIANA'S ENGAGEMENT
TO HER SON.

DIANA'S PARENTS, IN A PHOTO
TAKEN SHORTLY BEFORE HER
MOTHER'S DEATH IN 1926.

DIANA'S PATERNAL GRANDFATHER. HE ALWAYS
REFUSED TO SIT AT THEIR NON-KOSHER TABLE.
HE REMINDED DIANA OF MOSES.

DIANA'S SISTER, CECILIA RUBIN, 1933.

THELMA ANDERSON, CAPE COD, 1947.

Courtesy of Abraham Anderson

QUENTIN ANDERSON, NEW BRUNSWICK FISHING TRIP.

Courtesy of Abraham Anderson

LIONEL AND DIANA IN RIVERSIDE PARK.

JIM TRILLING. "HER SON WOULD NOT BE AFRAID OF NATURE, AND AS A ONE YEAR OLD HE WAS ALREADY BOLD."

DIANA IN WESTPORT, CONNECTICUT, 1950.

ARNOLD AND CARROLL BEICHMAN AT A CAFE IN PARIS, EARLY 1950S.

Courtesy of Charles Beichman

THE "VERY INTERESTING, ENTERTAINING AND AFFECTIONATE LITTLE GROUP"
AT DINNER. LEFT TO RIGHT: ARNOLD BEICHMAN, STEVEN MARCUS, CARROLL
BEICHMAN, LIONEL TRILLING, DIANA TRILLING (HIDDEN FROM VIEW, GENE MARCUS).

Courtesy of Charles Beichman

DIANA ONCE ASKED CARROLL WHY SHE LIKED TO RIDE HORSES
IN CENTRAL PARK. "FOR JOY," SHE TOLD HER. DIANA REPLIED,
"HOW WONDERFUL TO BE ABLE TO SAY IT SO SIMPLY."

Courtesy of Charles Beichman

MIDGE DECTER.

Courtesy of Midge Decter

DIANA AND LIONEL TRILLING, 1967, ON A TWO-WEEK
MISSION TO PROMOTE GERMAN-AMERICAN GOODWILL.

NORMAN PODHORETZ. IN
TIME, DIANA WOULD
BECOME AN EX-FRIEND.

Courtesy of Norman Podhoretz

DIANA, JIM, AND LIONEL TRILLING, 1971. THAT YEAR DIANA HAD PARTICIPATED
IN A PANEL HELD AT TOWN HALL IN NEW YORK ON WOMEN'S LIBERATION.
"I THINK OF FEMINISM AS BOTH FIRMER AND GENTLER, LESS COMPETITIVE
THAN WOMEN'S LIB," SHE LATER WROTE.

"WRITERS ARE WHAT THEY
WRITE, ALSO WHAT THEY FAIL
TO WRITE"—DIANA TRILLING IN
THE BEGINNING OF THE JOURNEY.

Photo by Thomas Victor

"WE WERE REALLY VERY CLOSE IN SOME WAY," DIANA TRILLING
SAID ABOUT HER FRIENDSHIP WITH NORMAN MAILER.

LILLIAN HELLMAN IN A *VOGUE*
MAGAZINE AD FOR BLACKGAMA.

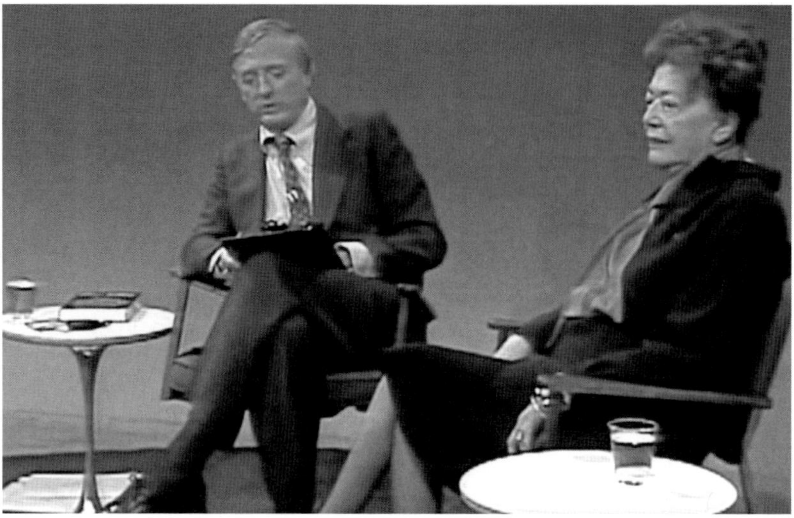

DIANA ON *FIRING LINE* WITH WILLIAM F. BUCKLEY, JR., 1981.

DIANA KEPT NOTES IN THE THIRD PERSON.

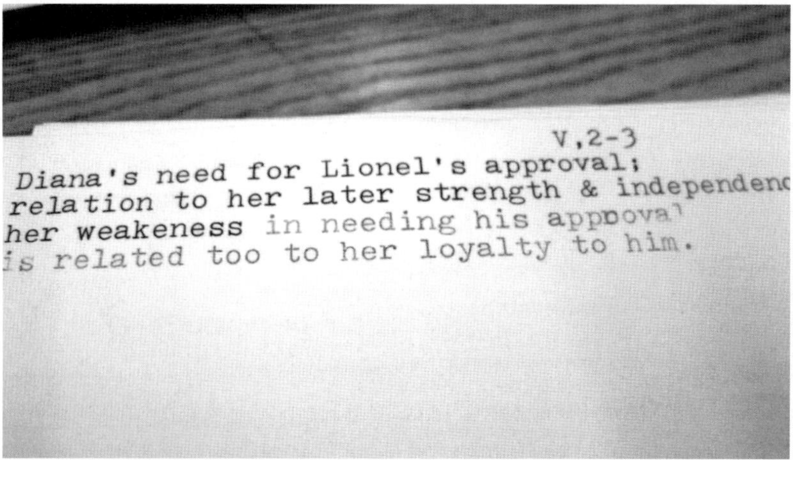

V,2-3
Diana's need for Lionel's approval;
relation to her later strength & independenc
her weakeness in needing his appoova
is related too to her loyalty to him.

"DIANA HAD MET PUBLISHER WILLIAM JOVANOVICH AT VARIOUS COLUMBIA GATHERINGS, AND THEY HIT IT OFF RIGHT AWAY. . . . HE LOVED LITERARY WOMEN."

Photo by Tom Palumbo; courtesy of Patricia Bosworth

Not able to resist being a tough, sophisticated critic, Diana started off her letter by telling him precisely why she so much disliked the story. She said that if she were the editor of a magazine, she'd reject it but not because it is pornographic. "I don't find the story pornographic," she wrote Mailer:

I find it anti-pornographic—peculiarly chilling in its sexual effect because it is so clinical. . . . I of course realize that you intended the story to express your own revulsion from this kind of clinical tyranny. But despite this intention you were somehow yourself tyrannized, in reverse. Perhaps it has something to do with the fact that nowhere in the story is there a voice to say that this mastery-submission struggle with which you are dealing, although true to life, has been made in our society an object of the wrong kind of consciousness, which is merely the same old Puritanism in new dress. Your hero is clearly the victim of this culture. But the author is, too. At least I don't see anything in the story to separate hero and author—no irony, no detachment. Thus the whole story is as anti-sexual as the situation in which the hero is involved, which is why I find it unpornographic and don't care for it.

Having made her somewhat labyrinthine feelings known, Diana said that she didn't want the Post Office to suppress the story in any way whatsoever. She would "wholly oppose" such censorship. Censorship was an important, separate matter, not connected to whether or not she liked the story. (In 1957 she had protested by telegram the banning by the Detroit police of John O'Hara's National Book Award–winning *Ten North Frederick*, which was considered obscene. The ban was eventually lifted after all the protests.)

In his reply Mailer, bypassing her literary judgments, warmly thanked her for a letter that "was more than adequate to my needs. I think there's a fair chance of getting the story printed now."

And he asked, "I wonder if Lionel could send a short paragraph, if he feels the story is not pornographic. Indeed, even if he does, by the ethic of this matter, it might be best to hear from him."

176 GUILT MAKES US HUMAN

But Lionel never responded, and it is not known if Diana told her husband about Mailer's request.

This sort of moral-intellectual sparring went on with the members of the family—that is, "the Family," as in New York Intellectual Family, of which Mailer was a young member, along with older members like Diana and Lionel, Sidney Hook, William Phillips, Philip Rahv, Alfred Kazin, Mary McCarthy, and Delmore Schwartz.

In 1953 Rahv commissioned Delmore Schwartz, the poet and short story writer, to write an essay about Lionel. The essay, "The Duchess's Red Shoes," reproached Lionel for not being sufficiently supportive of modern writers and for being too enthralled with nineteenth-century writers like Jane Austen, Henry James, and E. M. Forster. He decried Lionel's study of manners in fiction as a literary posture, as when he said that American writers have turned away from society. Schwartz wrote, "Mr. Trilling is often difficult to understand because he is so sensitive to all points of view, so conscious of others and of opposition."

Diana later said that although she thought the essay was fundamentally unfair, Lionel felt the attack was a legitimate one. She said that he also felt "there was something going on there more than what was on the page." He was right.

In a series of notes Diana made for a proposed memoir, she mentioned the sense of antagonism between Rahv and Phillips as a possible source for Rahv's having solicited and published Schwartz's criticism of Lionel. (It was well-known that Rahv and Phillips often clashed over content and strategy and that by 1953 Rahv's anti-Communism was no longer as strict as Phillips's.) Diana jotted down in her note that she and Lionel "continued to be friends with Phillips even once the antagonism became open in the mid-fifties," but she explained no further, most likely because, as she already knew, political differences are often just a smoke screen for other disagreements.

But what might have been the source of Schwartz's hostility toward Lionel? Hadn't he hoped to teach at Columbia and been thwarted? Diana told a friend that "when Schwartz came to do a sample lecture, he couldn't hold his class, couldn't lecture for an hour because he was far gone [into mental illness]. . . . Lionel would have been crazy himself to have given a job to that crazy man." Delmore Schwartz always believed that Lionel was the one and only person who prevented his appointment.

In another note to herself Diana jotted down that Rahv was "more malicious in his judgments, and would let things appear to make trouble, [to be] more sensational than Phillips." She went on to record that "William was never as given to malice and gossip as was Rahv." But, she also wrote that "the personal motivation, the hate—the malicious personal motivations—of these people were phenomenal."

Among the women, particularly, gossip was supreme. There seemed to be no sense of guilt—about anything, especially about their sex lives. This was new territory for Diana—new territory for her to talk about with Lionel, too. After all, she had confided in him about her flirtation with Mailer.

Her generation, she said, "learned late that women had the right to have sexual responses. . . . It wasn't just men. . . . In my day it sometimes took years of induction to get a woman to be sexually responsive. . . . Women came into their own after the First World War, when women went to work. . . . They wore different clothes and took off their corsets; they got the vote. . . . There was a whole new moral code. An early pre-statement of the later permissiveness. . . . I'm a post-Victorian," she said, recalling that she once had an argument with Mary McCarthy about guilt. "Mary thought she was against guilt, and I said she shouldn't be. I think guilt makes us human. And to be against guilt is to be very unimaginative."

12

WEAVING

The only good husband I have ever known was George Calingaert. He lived in the 18th century, and he created his own wife.

—LIONEL TRILLING, JOURNAL ENTRY, 1960*

Afterwards many years in analysis Diana decided that she "used a sense of reality in daily life as a defense against analytical reality." She also began to understand how "undeeply" [*sic*] she "had penetrated in all her years of treatment," even though she had made progress in keeping her phobias at bay.

Although Diana said that Lionel's view of what analysis could accomplish was different from hers—he was more interested in Freud's theoretical, historical, and cultural aspects—she "was the one who criticized the therapeutic aspect of psychoanalysis." She began to acknowledge

---

* George Calingaert was a chemist, not a writer. He died in 1960. LT, a longtime friend, gave a eulogy in which he said "George Calingaert's mind was modern, but owed its particular virtues to the vision of the 18th century." Calingaert's "real" wife, Dorothy, was a friend of Diana's from Radcliffe.

that "most of my interest in psychoanalysis is directed to where I think some of its therapeutic weaknesses may lie."

Diana became a frequent contributor to the "Letters to the Editor" sections of various publications; these letters served as both a private— and, of course, public—outlet for the multitude of ideas, especially about analysis, that swirled in her head.

In a letter to *Encounter* magazine she wrote that her "chief quarrel with present-day psychoanalysis derives from the fact that its clinical investigations exist in total isolation from cultural speculation," and she went on to write that when mentioning this to analysts of her acquaintance, she received either "bewildered looks or grimaces of irritation." But she was deeply concerned that psychoanalysis was failing to understand that it "was working in a period of radical cultural change"—she meant on college campuses—and that it needed to accept this new reality of upheaval if it expected "to attract the best minds of a new student generation." Diana wanted these students to be encouraged to use the "changing culture" to better the medical profession. She said that an eminent doctor, whom she does not name, told her, "We are not interested in cultural speculation; we are interested in doctors." She agreed, she wrote in her letter, but also said, "I believe the analytical profession can no more be built on doctors alone than a university can be built on men and women whose sole commitment is to teaching." Psychoanalysis must "take into account" cultural change "if it is to maintain its own authority in the intellectual community."

Diana believed that "child analysis was more successful because the analyst sees his patient in the context of the family, which is the total context of the child's life, or the most important part of the child's life, and one can therefore gauge the truthfulness of the child's report on reality. With an adult patient, the analyst has no way of making this kind of check. . . . An analyst is like a loving spouse, believing it all." Overall, she thought of analysis "in terms of conquering illness, conquering handicaps, making people better."

When she and Lionel would talk about these issues, and she would ask probing questions such as if he thought an analyst could ever be "enough analyzed" out of his or her own problems, "Lionel would sit there," she remembered. "I could see his mind was wandering. I don't know what he was thinking." She explained that when a psychoanalytic conversation got "too immediate, too human in a personal way, he backs away from it . . . yet far less than most literary intellectuals," she also admitted.

She said that "if problems came up in relation to me or later in relation to Jim that required some understanding of the role that the unconscious might be playing in producing a certain attitude or behavior, you could get very little help from Lionel. I used to be furious because for all his intelligence and knowledge he was of so little help, especially in trying to figure out what was upsetting Jim."

And, as always, Lionel's rages at her (never at their son or anyone else), while intermittent, continued. Brom Anderson, the son of Thelma and Quentin (he is six years younger than Jim Trilling) remembers Diana coming to his mother weeping and saying that Lionel had told her she was a monster. Jim, at ten, remembered a time when his father would pick a fight with his mother every single day. "He would sit down with a drink, and would find a pretext to rail at her; then we would all sit down at dinner and very ostentatiously pick at the food; sometime[s] my mother would leave the table, and then later things got better."

Jim recalled that around this time, he wanted Jacques Barzun to be his guardian in case of his parents' death, "because he sees things the way my father does." Jim naturally favored his father, despite Lionel's behavior toward Diana, but he also must have observed Barzun's quiet defense of his mother in certain situations. In fact, Jim said that he never had any flare-ups in front of Barzun because, he believes, he "represented an ideal of control and dignity." Barzun's very presence allowed Jim to remain composed.

As Jim got older, the Trillings vowed to curtail what Lionel called in his journal a "violence beyond what anybody might guess." The journal describes the nature of Diana and Lionel's parenting style, which could be described as remotely enlightened, with more than a touch of self-absorption. They decided, Lionel wrote, to "discipline ourselves to express no anger toward Jim and also that he should see no anger between us, the domesticated habitual anger especially. In this conversation there were expectable [*sic*], some notes of bitterness and recrimination as [*sic*] between us, but not many, all things considered. . . . I was therefore able to speak simply about the old feeling, that resentment so central to our marriage, against being judged and blamed." In the same entry, written between 1952 and 1955 (probably closer to 1955), Lionel commented that Jim had not bought an anniversary gift for his parents. He was also concerned that Jim would be "troubled" if he didn't see his parents giving each other a gift. In 1955 Jim was only seven years old. What child of that age is expected to buy his parents a gift? But the Trillings sent Jim out with a babysitter to get one, and Lionel wrote that

> through that day and the next I found myself able to deal with J's troubles with extraordinary ease—it was as if pride had been excised from all parts of my feeling—I did not feel affronted or humiliated by his bad conduct. On the morning of the 12th he woke us at six in order to give us his present—was wonderfully sweet and charming about it (a double cruet, salad forks and spoon, funnel, rack, Japanese version of French peasant ware). He went back to bed and allowed us to sleep or rather D, for I got up. He had found 2 "read-it yourself" books and undertook to read the first, which he did without difficulty, thus proving what I knew, though his teachers did not, that he could read. He was very proud of his achievement in a nice, strong way. In the evening a terrible tantrum, the result of his injured pride because D had told him a story of the Greeks and Romans; she knew so much and "on the day I read my first book and was so proud." The tantrum went on for one and a half hours and was extremely violent and yet I was never moved to anger—I felt only pity for his trouble and what I later realized was a profound admiration of his passion and innocence.

Diana kept in touch with Jim's psychoanalyst, Dr. Marjorie Harley, with frequent phone calls and letters and once asked how she should explain certain of his behaviors to her son. Dr. Harley said that it would not be helpful for her to try to do this because Jim "knows that you took him to me so that he could have an analyst and because mothers are mothers and not analysts; therefore, I feel that comforting and reassurance is the most appropriate and ultimately the best method for you to employ." But just offering reassurance was sometimes difficult for Diana—and Lionel; they longed for a more prescribed plan.

Lionel wrote in his journal that they left for the country the day after their anniversary and that Jim "was in an especially ugly mood. . . . After arrival, in the course of the afternoon he drenched me with the hose because I had told him not to cut up the lawn with the stream. But with momentary near-lapses I kept my equanimity. . . . Dexamyl perhaps helped, was needed at any rate." (Both Trillings continued to use this drug daily.)

Earlier in his journal, Lionel had written of his "feeling of disgust with my public 'noble' character," and now he brought this characterization up again in an entry about Diana calling him an "angel" for the way he was behaving with her and Jim. Lionel believed that what "was operating was the repudiation of the public character, the character of prestige that must not be assailed and questioned."

Diana told Patricia Bosworth that Lionel did not like any of the qualities in himself for which he was most admired. "He did not want to be thought of as that moderate, sweet-tempered, well-mannered person. He felt that part of his character was what had kept him from being a novelist." Yet at certain times when he was free to be "himself" and not some "public 'noble' character," he could let his indignations evaporate in a less pressured manner that allowed him be thought of as an "angel."

A former babysitter, Lina Vlavianos, remembered that Diana always thought she needed to support Lionel and never resented having to do so. Vlavianos also recalled that the reverse was true, as well, and vividly remembered a time when Lionel helped Diana with one of her essays. "It dealt with love and I heard him tell her 'this needs to be corrected.'" Shortly afterward, Diana told Lina that she was going to have to rewrite the whole article.

"The Case for the American Woman" appeared in *Look* magazine, which had solicited the article from Diana and paid her $3,000 for it. The article was at times personal, as when she wrote that "the modern woman is made to fend for herself emotionally and is even required to sustain her mate. In such circumstances it should be no surprise that female pride has become tinged with self-pity and bitterness. What else except acerbity is ever the response of a group or individual that feels unloved?" She also explained that the modern woman wanted "private reassurance that despite her new 'masculine' skills, she has not lost her womanly grace and charm." But her main point was that she wanted society to stop telling women they are destroying men, and while she asked for women's "freedom," it was not to be had at the expense of putting men in bondage, and, she stated bluntly, "The male sex is as guilty as the female." Diana later reported that Viking, Lionel's publisher at the time, protested that she was demeaning his stature.

Nonetheless, the essay marked the beginning of Diana's becoming what could be coined "a family feminist," that is, a woman who believed that women in concert with men and their families will transform modern life. She became a pioneering feminist, although she was rarely acknowledged as such.

Motherhood, while at times demanding, had led her to a new independence and boldness, yet Jim Trilling said that his mother "believed that the desire for women to be equal in the workplace would cause hopeless conflict in families. . . . She always refused to take an actual feminist stance." Still, he said it was "fair" to call her a family feminist. Diana was not going to go where others necessarily went before her. Indeed, the book editor Elisabeth Sifton once remarked that Diana "was a freelance soul."

On October 3, 1956, in her role as chair of the Board of Directors of the American Committee for Cultural Freedom, Diana had written a letter to novelist James T. Farrell, of *Studs Lonigan* fame, which chastised him for the way he had resigned from the committee, when he was its national chairman. As well as she could, Diana refuted his many charges against the committee, ranging from cultural elitism to the neglect of fighting for civil liberties, including not sufficiently combating censorship. She also admonished Farrell for the way he resigned—too quickly, almost secretly, and most important, drunkenly. She was clear and persuasive in her letter—showing not a sign of timidity. Diana reveled in writing such letters.

Matters were so complicated in the committee that Diana often had a hard time describing them—from the intricacies of the various political strategies to the details of the personalities involved in suggesting the strategies. She tried to explain to the sociologist David Riesman—he had published the best-selling and landmark book *The Lonely Crowd* in 1950, and he and his wife, Evey, were good friends of both Trillings for many years—that the committee was so full of "tangles" she could write a book. But, she went on, "it would be the kind of book one would feel one had to revise virtually every time the phone rang with a new report or a new point of view announcing itself." Diana was filling Riesman in about the committee's inner workings because his name had been proposed as a possible member of the National Advisory Council, along with nearly sixty others, among them Lionel, Jacques Barzun, Katherine Anne Porter, Robert Penn Warren, Bruno Bettelheim, J. Robert Oppenheimer, and Whitaker Chambers.

Diana often turned to the Riesmans—especially David—for advice about personal matters involving her career and motherhood. Diana had been an enthusiastic reader of Evey Riesman's novel-in-progress and offered sound encouragement, even though ultimately the book never found a publisher.

Diana appreciated that the Riesmans were nonjudgmental and particularly sensitive to her worries. After a dinner in New York, when Jim was still an infant, Diana had written that their advice was always so sound but that she "felt rather guilty having absorbed so much of the conversation with my personal problems. Except, of course, that—as it turned out—problems like these are so much more general than we are likely to recognize." She was referring to society's making women feel as if their professional work was finished after they had a baby. David Riesman reminded her in his reply that "before James arrived, you made yourself into an interesting woman" and that "this 'capital' will not depreciate." Those were words Diana needed to hear, for bringing up a child, while joyous, had also begun to leave her with an unfamiliar instability. Jim was an assertive, precocious toddler. She hardly ever doubted herself when it came to handling political matters, writing book reviews, articles, and letters to the editor, or revising and reworking Lionel's writing. She instinctively knew when she was on the right track. But mothering was different. Was she doing everything right? Lionel wrote in his journal that at a party one of the guests asked him if Diana was "still being ruled by Jim." Yet Diana never shied away from asking the right people for guidance, even though over time she preferred to be the one dispensing advice. And as David Riesman also wrote her, "You are very sure of yourself and you admire others who are sure of themselves (even if you disagree with them)."

When Diana shared a work-in-progress with Riesman—a journal on motherhood—he was very supportive. He wrote her, "The very format is inventive, a challenge and stimulation to others—a statement that fleeting thoughts, reactions, and so on need only the courage of one's free association to become literature and amateur sociology." He continued: "Reflecting on the journal, my memory of it is of a sunny piece, full of wit and esprit, even when it touched on the most serious concerns of a mother and citizen. To read it, as I did in bits, meant having to put down something which lured me on; I was as sorry when it stopped as a child whose mother ends a fairy tale. I couldn't wait for Evey to read it. . . . Diana, dear, for Heaven's sake, do go on."

The journal was published in *Partisan Review* to much disapproval, even from Jacques Barzun (He was "J" in the journal), who objected to Diana's saying she played "Berlioz which is my favorite sexual music" after a visit from him. People asked whose marriage Diana was complaining about in the journal, a few of the letter writers thought readers would think it was *their* marriage.

On March 20, 1955, Diana had reviewed Rebecca West's *A Train of Powder* for *The New York Times Book Review*. The book, she wrote, "is about trials. Or to put it more precisely, each of the pieces finds the occasion in a moment when moral society calls immoral man to account for grievous infringement of its laws." West reported on four trials— an unsolved murder, a spy case, a lynching in North Carolina, and the Nuremberg Trials. The review was essentially praising, although Diana faulted West's "endemic ascendancy of her intellection over her feelings."

But the review caused friction between Diana and the *Book Review*. As she wrote Francis Brown, the editor, she had been accused by "some people" of being "high-handed" and "arrogant" in the review, and why? It was because Brown had broken their agreement that no changes would be made in her work without first consulting her, and in the West review "disturbing" changes and "drastic cuts" had been made without contacting her. Brown replied politely two days later that he knew of no such agreement between them and that he had asked for eight hundred words, but she had turned in more than thirteen hundred, and he had compromised by printing a review of a thousand words. He ended his letter by saying, "It may be ungallant to say so, but I'm afraid I feel that the cutting improved the review, but that may be because I've always suspected that everything except the Lord's Prayer would be improved by judicious pruning." A week later Diana wrote another letter saying that she strongly disagreed with him about the alterations made. "Apart from the relatively minor fact that you removed the one explicit compliment which appeared in my opening sentence, there is the very significant fact that you excised the quotation from Miss West on which I based my analysis of her motives in devoting herself to trials." She went on to mention that in the past, when asked, she had been allowed to shorten the reviews on her own. She also couldn't resist telling Brown that she might be considered arrogant, but that many writers, including her own husband, lack the ability to edit themselves or others, but she "is very good at it." And she ended the letter, "I should certainly want to further our connection rather than put this barrier of editorial controversy between us." Brown agreed in his deferential reply and promised to "be in touch whenever the [editorial] problem is more than minor."

In any case, a year later, Rebecca West wrote Diana "in a state of nervous humility" to thank her for the review. It was the sort of chatty letter one might write to a dear friend, full of asides on her recent travels that had caused such a long delay in writing. West also chastised Diana for not being "sufficiently interested in the facts about Germany she had presented" and said that she "only seemed interested in the book as a manifestation of my moral nature." Still, she told Diana that she and her husband, Henry Andrews, would be coming to New York soon, and they'd like to meet Diana and Lionel "for I admire you both so much, and I've had my curiosity aroused by your review of my book."

Candor on both sides prevailed, and the two spirited writers met. Diana later said that "of all the people I know, Rebecca West is the largest size mind I've known in a woman—the best intellect I've ever known, but I don't think she had the largest possible spirit."

Diana was always on West's side regarding the trials and tribulations in her tumultuous relationship with her son, Anthony, by her lover H. G. Wells. In March 1959 Diana chastised Anthony West in a letter to *The New Yorker* for his insensitive review of Harry Moore's biography of D. H. Lawrence. (Diana's friendship with Rebecca West lasted until West's death in 1983. However, Diana's friendship with Lillian Hellman, "the most powerful personality I have ever known," as she once said, would not last.)

In 1958 Diana edited and published *The Selected Letters of D. H. Lawrence*. All of the letters in Diana's compilation had been previously published elsewhere, and as she wrote in her preface, she made "no effort to investigate the still-unpublished material in libraries and private collections."

In an introduction, which she called "Letter to a Young Critic," Diana wrote in an elaborate opening paragraph:

> Although you have never written about Lawrence, we have often talked about him and I know how large a figure he is in your experience of literature. But am I mistaken in believing that while he is so much there for you, he is also the one major writer of our century whom you and your whole critical generation—all of you who came out of college in these last ten or twelve years—can't finally settle with, who exists not as a fixed point in the recent literary past but as a continuing disturbance, rather like a contemporary whose genius you wouldn't wish to deny but to whose ultimate disposition you are not ready to commit yourselves?

The young addressee was none other than Lionel's former student Norman Podhoretz, who later observed that Diana's "writing often suffered

from the same fault as her conversation, and the problem was exacer-
bated by the tendency of her prose to grow clotted and twisted in making its points."

But such clots and twists in language were not why his name was removed at his request in later editions of the book. Although Podhoretz
acknowledged that her use of his name was "a loving gesture," he later
explained:

> What caused the trouble was the merciless teasing to which I was sub-
> jected by other friends of mine, and even some of hers, who thought
> Diana was announcing that I was her "baby," and what made things
> worse was that so public an identification with her, even on a literary
> issue that did not directly impinge on politics, created the impression
> that I was still clinging to the hard anti-Communist position of which
> in those days she was one of the most uninhibited spokesmen. In fact,
> however, I was already moving away from it and toward the ant-anti-
> Communist camp, whose members while retaining their high regard
> for Lionel considered Diana a fanatic and ragged me endlessly for al-
> lowing her to make free with my name. Deeply humiliated, I decided,
> young fool that I was, that I was honor bound to tell Diana that she had
> embarrassed me, and of course she felt hurt and betrayed.

His name was removed from all future editions.

Two years later, in 1960, Podhoretz became the editor of *Commentary*, turning it, Diana said, into an anti-anti-Communist magazine.

Diana soon resigned from the Executive Committee of the American
Committee for Cultural Freedom, which had taken over sponsorship of
Partisan Review. "There developed," Diana said, "a very great rift in the
intellectual and literary community with [the magazine] really falling,
essentially, into the anti-anti-communist camp." She explained that "the
committee had broken up" and didn't have any funds, and to keep its
tax exemption, "it provided a tax shelter for the magazine. . . . It was really just a pro forma thing."

But she was also enraged that in the early 1960s, *Partisan Review* published a piece called "An End to Anti-Communism." In her lengthy

letter of resignation she said, "I don't see why I should help publish a magazine which opposes my political point of view and dislikes my feelings." The committee ultimately voted that the magazine should find a new sponsor, but Diana did not budge on her position or withdraw her resignation, telling the board that "not a single ideological issue was raised in support of their action." Her strong sense of logic once again came into play. "Apparently," she said, "I gave you a wide skirt behind which to hide your criticism of a magazine which none of you has criticized but of which you nevertheless moved to be rid."

Later, Diana said that Sidney Hook, after encouraging her "to destroy" *Partisan Review*, and she refused, then went behind her back and accused her of destroying the magazine. (They stopped speaking for a long while. Hook told Diana, "You never did have any political sense," to which she replied, "You never did have any literary sensibility.")

"The story [about *PR*] spread not only to America but to England, and I heard the story from all sides for a very long time, when I had undertaken to do nothing but to slip away [from the committee] quietly." But, in saying in her resignation that she didn't "see why [she] should help publish a magazine which opposes [her] political point of view and dislikes [her] feelings," she *was* basically participating in a call for the magazine's end.

Still, in a letter Diana told Arnold Beichman (with whom she always remained on warm terms, despite his eventual swing to the right of her politics, and who took over her leadership role on the committee) that she hoped the magazine would continue to exist, "whatever my present differences with it, and even hope that I will again be able to appear in its pages."

There were always big differences between Diana and Beichman concerning the CIA's involvement in the committee—Beichman had been opposed to taking the money, "not so much for moral reasons as because I felt that someday the whole tawdry business would be exposed," while Diana said, "I did not believe that to take the support of my government was a dishonorable act. . . . I never liked the secrecy but was willing to live with it because I thought we [the committee] were doing useful work."

Beichman and Diana wrote frequent letters to each other, and he often addressed her as "My Dear Provincial Lady from Morningside Heights." He was always respectful of her morning writing schedule, once beginning a letter, "I write timidly after reading your plea with friends to stop phoning you during your morning hours of work and study. After all, this letter might be such an intrusion but, at least, you can read it a paragraph a day."

They enjoyed debating and gossiping about such familiar but endlessly fascinating things as "the sharpness of the rift between the anti-anti-Communists and the anti-anti-McCarthities [sic]," which, Diana wrote, left her "lonely in my own central position. . . . I consider both camps worthy of having a mild plague visited upon them. In my view, there is only one decent position a liberal can take and that is plumb in the middle shooting in both directions." But finally Diana told Beichman that "debate by letter, private or public, is not very satisfactory," although the letters kept coming, some addressed to both Diana and Lionel.

When Diana liked the company of a person, she usually let politics slide. But with Sidney Hook it was different. Earlier, in 1955, he had responded to an Indonesian resolution by committee member Sol Stein in a manner that Diana could not forgive. Stein, a writer, editor, and publisher, had wanted the committee to intervene in Indonesia against the Communist-backed president Sukarno, but Hook believed it would be "an open foray into politics" that was outside the purview of the committee. Diana said that Hook's reaction was "one of the most shocking experiences of my intellectual career." In a letter she told him his stance was "intimidation," and "terrorization."

Two decades later she again berated him for writing in a memoir that Lionel had "instituted" a luncheon party between Hook and Whittaker Chambers (she insisted Hook had confused Lionel with someone else) and for saying that this supposed lunch took place in a vegetarian restaurant. "Lionel loathed vegetarian restaurants," she wrote. Hook stuck to his story.

Diana remained on good—if feisty—terms with William Phillips throughout the *Partisan Review* episode and beyond. (After all, he had agreed to publish her journal, even if somewhat reluctantly.) She wrote him in a letter that "old relationships have a life of their own which is impervious to disruption; one fights, one makes up; one attacks and is forgiven; one is attacked and forgives; one criticizes, one wounds, but there is always a reservoir of faith and affection." He later wrote in a memoir that Diana "seemed more interested in people's lives and was usually available for help or advice." High praise in her estimation.

So she continued to write for *Partisan Review* and in 1958 published a piece there called "The Other Night at Columbia: A Report from the Academy," an account of a poetry reading by Allen Ginsberg and two other Beat poets—his longtime lover Peter Orlovsky and Gregory Corso.

All hell broke loose—on Claremont Avenue—on the campus—in Columbia's English department—even at *Partisan Review*. Diana, who never really liked being a faculty wife, was, of course, accused of being condescending to everyone, and worse, being too wordy about it.

"All the fellow travelers rallied around the Beats," she said, "and said I was being snobby to them." Jason Epstein, Lionel's former student, said that the students were always in awe of both Trillings, although he, personally "considered Diana too judgmental."

In a letter Diana wrote that "in many conversations with William [Phillips] about why *Partisan Review* did not like my piece about the beat poets, William has spoken about its wrong tone. . . . I think that what he means is that he dislikes the literary expression of my personal, emotional and cultural attitudes. Someone writing to me recently about my beat piece," she went on, "said of it that 'its judgments are its feelings.' . . . The judgments I express in my writing are inseparable from the feelings I express; the judgments *are* the feelings—and *Partisan Review* recognizes this integral relation. When the editors speak of my wrong tone, what they are actually saying is that the quality of feeling in my work is alien to them, and that the ideas which generate, or are generated by, this quality of feeling are also alien to them."

Complaints about Diana the Writer and Diana the Faculty Wife were no longer just whispered. Diana! Diana! What had she done or said that was so horrible? Had she threatened Western civilization? Some faculty members and their spouses were always made nervous in her presence, fearing they'd say the wrong thing. One former student of Lionel's said (only half-jokingly) that "if you weren't on her wave length, she thought you were a Communist."

The *Partisan Review* piece had been considered contentious because of Diana's snobbish views on the Beats in general ("It was of some note that the auditorium smelled fresh. . . . I took one look at the crowd and was certain it would smell bad, but I was mistaken.") and on Ginsberg, himself (he was "clean and Corso was clean and Orlovsky was clean"). Diana had attended the reading with two other faculty wives, Mrs. F. W. Dupee, whose husband was the evening's moderator, and one other woman she doesn't mention by name.

Diana had a history with Ginsberg, she explained in her piece, going back to his being a student in one of Lionel's classes in the mid-1940s and then much later, when Lionel and Mark Van Doren helped him avoid jail (he was sent to a psychiatric hospital instead) after getting arrested for, as it turned out, being a passenger in a car that held stolen goods. (Ginsberg had also been suspended—and then reinstated—from Columbia his senior year after he wrote "Fuck the Jews" and "Butler [Columbia president Nicholas Murray Butler] has no balls" in the dust and grime of his dormitory window.)

Diana wove history and more into her piece: a description of several visits Ginsberg made to Thirty-Five Claremont Avenue, references to the range of literary traditions, comments on differences in style in America, references to middle-class life, life in the 1930s, emotions (especially pity), children's cries, the personalities of poets, the nature of fathers and mothers. She created a tapestry that could both enrage and enrich her readers. This approach would eventually become her trademark and attract not only devoted followers but also critics, including Columbia faculty and spouses. But not her own spouse. Lionel thought "The Other Night at Columbia" was one of her very best essays and often reread it, she said.

In the essay Diana related that when she got home, a meeting of the Readers' Subscription Book Club was taking place in the living room. She announced to the assembled and her husband in particular: "Allen

Ginsberg read a love poem to you, Lionel. I liked it very much." W. H. Auden, who had been at the meeting, later "chided" her, Diana said, telling her that "I'm ashamed of you."

Ginsberg had told the audience that a poem called "Lion in the Room" was addressed to and dedicated to Lionel. "It was about a lion in the room with the poet, a lion who was hungry but refused to eat him," Diana wrote. "I heard it as a passionate love poem. I can't say whether it was a good or bad poem, but I was much moved by it. It was also a decent poem, and I am willing to admit this surprised me; there were no obscenities in it as there had been in much of the poetry the 'beats' read."

Ginsberg later told writer Lis Harris that it was not a poem about Lionel. "The poem I read that night was one I'd written in Paris about a mystical vision I had about a lion in my living room. It's called 'The Lion for Real,' and begins with a quote from the nineteenth-century French poet Tristan Corbiere: 'Soyez muette pour moi, Idole contemplative.' I guess she misheard it. I visited them for years afterward, but I never brought it up; I thought it was better to just let it go."

Diana's reaction to Harris when told about the poem was to "shrug" and say "dryly" to her, "Ah was I wrong? He should have told me I was wrong. But in any case, the fact is that that night I was trying to throw a bombshell into the respectability of my home. I was writing from the point of view of somebody who was trying to live in two different worlds—the imaginative world of bad children and the ruling world of good, ordinary grownups."

All the same, Ginsberg's father, Louis, also a poet, who was in the audience the night of the reading, wrote Diana that her piece "reveals a wise woman" and that the poem his son read "was indeed a sort of love poem to your husband, whose sympathy and understanding Allen really desires." He also wrote that "Lionel Trilling and Mark Van Doren have been household words with Allen and me."

At a later date, in conversation with her friend Thelma Anderson, Diana talked about Ginsberg's visit after her piece on the reading was published in *Partisan Review*. Lionel was either not home or working in a back room, she told Thelma, and as she let Ginsberg into the living room, he said very sweetly, "I've come to talk to you about the piece you wrote about me in *Partisan Review*. It hurt my feelings." And I thought this was very endearing, and I said, "I didn't want to hurt your feelings. In what way did I hurt your feelings?" He said, "Well, you said we were in jeans and that we were dirty." I said, "Oh, no, no, no, no, I said you were in blue jeans, but I didn't say you were dirty. I said you were very clean. I said you were absolutely clean despite the fact that Orlovsky had read a poem about 'if I shave, the bugs will fly out of my beard.' Do you remember? I said, 'Despite this, you were all as clean as you could be and very well-behaved and obviously very happy to be in the academy.'" So he said, "I couldn't afford any clothes but jeans. I had bought these in an army and navy store." It was as he said that—the talk must have gone on before that maybe ten or fifteen minutes—that Lionel came into the room, greeted him and said, "Oh come off it, Allen. You know that you could afford to buy a suit in Brooks and why don't you?" And poor Allen was terribly disconcerted, because he knew he had stolen suits from Brooks.

And then, speaking of her essay, Diana told Thelma, "I had written that [jeans] were standard nursery school attire and they had appeared in proper costume. I got letters and all kinds of attacks: how dared I condescend from my middle-class life to these poets? That was the whole point: that I lived this great upper-middle-class, millionaire middle-class life, and that here I was condescending to Bohemians." Irony refused. It often became the case with Diana Trilling.

She received several letters from people who had been at the reading and had also read her report on it. One correspondent said that although he was "against" her, and "for" Allen, he "felt that [she] had, in some way, 'gone naked' as Allen has challenged people to do. . . . I was touched by your self-exposure . . . even taking us to your house after [the reading]."

In a speech called "The Self as Subject," which she would deliver decades later, Diana reminisced that the mid-1950s were a time when personal and social facts would have been admired for their truth "if only it had been presented as fiction." After all, she told her audience, "wasn't society itself a fiction?" Diana sometimes wished it were. She received a letter of praise from Byron Dobell, another of Lionel's former students, and an editor at *Esquire*. He wanted her to write something for the magazine. Diana answered promptly that she wondered if he'd be interested in a regular monthly column about politics, books, even television. "And the tone would always be informal—light but yet serious in intention," she wrote Dobell, offering some ideas that just "popped into my head": writing about "a gallery opening in which the guests were given guns with which to shoot at balloons full of different colored paints, by which method they were to produce their own abstractions, . . . or if you could permit the sacrilege, I'd like to write about the total unreality of Mrs. Roosevelt's autobiographical volumes." She explained no further.

No column was ever offered to her.

13

SUBVERSIVE SEX

*D's anger at my "betrayal" of our past—"For you it's research."
The next morning she speaks bitterly of my "depersonalization"
of her, of myself.*

—LIONEL TRILLING, JOURNAL ENTRY, OCT. 19, 1958

The years leading up to 1958, and a few years afterward, were exceptionally transforming ones for the Trillings. What Diana Trilling once suggested to her husband as a motive for adultery— "the desire to have a new side of the personality brought into the light"— would generate mystery and intrigue for them, and their lives would become more and more *complicated*.

Diana, more than ever, began to voice her displeasures (really frustrations, whether sexual or not) everywhere she turned, even at a food market on Broadway around the corner from Claremont Avenue. In time the owner would bar her from even entering because of her "demeaning" and "imperious" behavior toward him.

Jim remembers that at times his mother indeed did have "a temper and a temperament." Gray Foy, Leo Lerman's companion for over fifty years, called Diana "fierce and not elegant at all." Still, he and Leo were always "very cozy with Diana and Lionel," mentioning affectionately that "if she liked you, she liked you forever." In fact, if a so-called sworn enemy of hers was a friend of someone she loved, she usually found a way to forgive such a transgression. People with difficult mothers (more often it was women) were drawn to Diana because her sharpness never ran deep enough to pierce a devotion born of a mutual admiration.

Diana's dissatisfaction was over the lack of focus in her own writing, as well as over her marriage, specifically Lionel's rages. Even though Thelma Anderson often comforted her friend, without knowing the full extent of Diana's grievances, she also felt Diana "didn't respect her enough later in life," according to her youngest son, Brom, who, from an early age, "was always part of the conversations." When the Andersons moved to Twenty-Nine Claremont Avenue, they chose a fourth-floor apartment so Diana would be able to visit, instead of a higher-up apartment around the corner on Riverside Drive, which had a wonderful view. Thelma was always "the understanding one" when it came to Diana. The families remained very close, and Brom saw a lot of the Trillings, both in New York and in his parents' Rockland County house. He said that he was one of the few people who recognized and enjoyed Diana's sense of humor. He also said, however, that she "could be extremely egocentric," remembering as an example a time when his father was ill and couldn't go to the Trillings' for dinner; Diana later wrote his mother a letter about feeling "betrayed" by his absence. Indeed, it was murmured by others that in many ways she acted like a three-year-old, with unconcealed egotism and a sense of helplessness, and, moreover, that she took it for granted that anything that happened in her orbit was the result of people acting to help or hinder her.

Diana even felt betrayed that the owner of the grocery store from which she was banned considered her "high handed." After all, when it came to food, Diana knew what went with what, and why, and how to cook it properly. (For instance, corn was put in a pot with cold water, heated to boiling, then the flame or heat was turned off immediately, and the corn was done. There were to be no seasonings in her carrot soup—just four or five "sizable" carrots, a stalk of celery—four cents a pound at the off-limits market—and chicken broth.)

Diana once said, "I really can't tell you which gives me more pleasure, cooking something people like to eat or writing something which someone may enjoy reading. I need both like mad, and that really is too much to ask of oneself. I suppose it derives from an uncertainty about myself as a female person. The cook is the feminine side and the critic, the masculine, and I don't know which one to turn to." But she always embraced one or the other without trepidation. She soon found a new market a short distance away.

"Di" and "Li" were now in their early fifties and had been married almost thirty years. Lionel was a renowned public intellectual; students packed his classes, and Diana, despite her growing reputation for haughtiness—words remained her bullets—was emerging from his shadow once again (as she had in the 1940s) with new essays and reviews. But it wasn't enough for her growing ambition.

Still, in the spring of 1959 she enjoyed being honored at the Harvard Club as a "Distinguished New York Alumna of Radcliffe College," along with thirty-two other women, including historian Barbara Tuchman, novelist Rona Jaffee, and Margaret Kahn Gresser, "the best woman chess player in the U.S." But there was no book by Diana on the horizon, no full-length original book of her own. An article called "Whatever Became of Romantic Love," which she wrote for *Look* magazine, elicited a letter from Evan Thomas of Norton to expand it into a short book. But Diana wasn't interested. The truth was there was no time because Lionel's work continued to be Diana's main work, even though she had managed to find the time to edit *The Selected Letters of D. H. Lawrence.*

Lionel had his own troublesome issues; even the very fabric of his marriage to Diana seemed at one point ready to fray. In a notation in his journal, written in 1961, Lionel recorded that "it is four years since the summer of the Great Instauration and its collapse—that was the summer of the threat of cancer—of the birthday letter that did not come from S."

The summer he was referring to in his entry was 1957, two years after he published *Freud and the Crisis of Our Culture* and *The Opposing Self,* and the year after he published *A Gathering of Fugitives.* In 1958 he published his essay about *Lolita*—concluding that the story "was not about sex, but about love" and also deciding that in general, "marital infidelity is not thought of as necessarily destructive of marriage, and indeed, the word 'unfaithful,' which once had so terrible a charge of meaning, begins to sound quaint, seeming to be inappropriate to our modern code." Diana, when guiding that prose into greater clarity and balance, surely, if somewhat bitterly, now agreed with him. Years later she would tell the writer Kathleen Hill that "fidelity in marriage was not easily defined, that she thought it a strenuous and lifelong enterprise—but that she considered it dirty-minded . . . to make fidelity a matter of whether you slept with someone other than your spouse."

"The Great Instauration" was Sir Francis Bacon's term for his proposal to revitalize the world to its original energy and force. But Lionel used the phrase in his journal in a more personal way; he intended to revive his potency that summer of 1957. (Jim Trilling later commented that he had never heard anyone use the word *instauration* before and says he thinks it was his father "being profound and deliberately using obscure language because he doesn't want anyone to know what he is saying.")

There is no evidence that either Diana or Lionel had cancer symptoms in 1957. It's possible that Diana, approaching or already into menopause, was experiencing spotting from irregular menstrual periods brought about by hormonal changes, and she was concerned that this might be a precursor of cancer. Erratic cycles are common right before menopause, and periods can skip altogether, followed by ones with heavy flow, until finally, after a year, the process ends, and the fertile phase of a woman's life is over.

The mysterious "S" in Lionel's journal entry apparently refers to Steven Marcus.*

Marcus had graduated from Columbia in 1948 and began teaching there in 1956, after a three-year stint in the army. (He had received his master's degree in 1949, then taught for a year in Indiana and two years

---

* This assumption is supported by a notation in Diana Trilling's handwriting. After Lionel's death she went over many of his journal entries, adding and deleting names. Much earlier, some journal pages were removed by Lionel himself.

at City College in New York, studied under F. R. Leavis at Cambridge, remained in England from 1952 to 1954, and received his PhD from Columbia in 1961.)

A course with Lionel in 1947 had convinced him he had a chance at a career in literature, and he abandoned a plan to attend medical school. Marcus described Trilling's teaching style as a "planned improvisation. . . . He was ironic, he was reticent. If he used the word 'virtue,' he would refer to the Greek sense, which meant manliness and power." Marcus was hooked.

Diana said that Steven Marcus and Norman Podhoretz spoke of Lionel "as someone who had taught them repression. The diminution of impulses and the suppression of pleasure in favor of beauty." Indeed, they were all—the students and their professor—dealing with matters that might—or might not—require repression.

Diana went on to say that Lionel was " a super-ego person essentially. He believed that one gave up commitment. . . . This was very deeply a part of Lionel. . . . I'm a super-ego person, too."[†]

Marcus became so close to his teacher that when he went out to Indiana in 1949, Lionel felt comfortable enough to tell his student to "look out for your accent. You have too strong a New York accent." Marcus later told Diana it was "a hard piece of advice" and that he had never told anyone about the remark before. He also asked his teacher if he thought he would succeed, and Lionel told him, " 'I've given up predicting on my students a long time ago.'. . . He wasn't going to butter up my ego," Marcus recalled.

But that summer of 1957—"The Great Instauration"—Lionel had expected the usual birthday letter from the person everyone on campus considered his protégé, and he was disappointed enough that none had arrived from Marcus to mention it in his journal.

Steve Marcus had married in 1950 (to Algene Ballif, known as "Gene"), and only Lionel, not Diana, was invited to the wedding, although he had

---

†   Freud claimed that there were three components to a person's psyche: the id, ego, and super-ego. The id follows instinct; the ego is the realistic mediator between the id and the super-ego, that part which acts as a conscience and moralizer.

been unable to attend. But the couples soon became so close that they often vacationed together. "Steve Marcus was always around," Jim Trilling said. "He was the younger older man I idolized. He played a big role in my life at the time." Indeed, Gene and Steve Marcus, the Trillings, and the Beichmans—Arnold and Carroll—became what Carroll Beichman referred to as "a very interesting, entertaining and affectionate little group," and "we saw a lot of each other." And as Diana later said, "Lionel and I began to recreate a youth which we hadn't had, doing youthful things like picnics."

After many decades of silence, Carroll Beichman decided to speak about the "little group." It was time, she said. At first she talked about her husband and Diana. "Arnold and Diana were on the same wavelength. . . . Both were very direct. Neither took prisoners. She and my husband had wonderful battles—intellectual squabbles—about the American Committee for Cultural Affairs and student revolutions, although they didn't differ a whole lot." And then she spoke of Lionel, who she loved talking to at parties. "We took great pleasure in one another's company. . . . I was an intellectual groupie of some kind—he was more than twenty years older than me, and I thought he was the most intelligent thing that crossed my path. Our minds worked along the same lines."

As for Diana, Carroll said that "she was a very impressive woman and she over-awed me. She was a difficult woman to be a friend of, somewhat domineering, so it would have been a strenuous relationship, although we were always polite when we met in groups. But she wasn't a woman friend of mine, and we never had lunch or anything like that together." Still, Diana once gave her a man's sweater she had bought and thought would suit Carroll, and as Lionel remarked in his journal about it: "How well it looked on her."

Carroll particularly remembered one evening at Thirty-Five Claremont Avenue "when Diana asked why I liked to ride horses in Central Park. 'For joy,' I told her. 'How wonderful to be able to say it so simply,' Diana said to me." Carroll remarked that "Diana and Lionel were an amazing pair, although it was a slightly mixed-up marriage."

In a journal entry written on October 19, 1959, Lionel noted "C's glances" and said that after experiencing them, he had the "the sense that I wanted nothing but gravity and impersonality." Carroll Beichman recalled that he always had "a detached way of looking at things, in contrast to the shrill things going on around him. He wanted to detach himself."

Right after mentioning Carroll's glances, glances he had been aware of and enjoyed for several years, Lionel wrote in his journal about "the ugliness of adultery (or at least adultery allowed to be publicly attempted)."

It was his strong feelings for "C" that Lionel was attempting to dismiss and hide. (He later noted obliquely that "a feeling for C and a feeling for politics have the same root.")

His analyst had warned him that his feelings for Carroll, while they brought him "pleasure, also caused annoyance and defiance—an ensuing sense of bondage—depression."

"He was much attached to me," Carroll Beichman said. "For him, it sort of hit him, as it does men of certain years. . . . In many ways it was a courtly love thing. . . . He always said he was a nineteenth-century man, and I was sort of a nineteenth-century woman. . . . Also, my background was not New York Intellectual. It was one of the things he liked." Lionel also liked that Carroll didn't think of him as a professor and that she was enthusiastic about his wish to eventually leave university life.

And, she added softly, "I loved him very much. It bent my marriage to Arnold."

Lionel Trilling, conscience-stricken but revitalized, had fallen in love also.

Carroll Beichman (she was born Harriet Childe Atkins but, not seeing herself as a "Harriet," changed her name to Carroll, her father's given name) was just thirty when she met Lionel Trilling in the mid-1950s. She had interests ranging from horseback riding to arduous ranch work and was a teacher at the Brearley School, in Manhattan, for many years, as well as at Milton Academy in Massachusetts. "She was flamboyant in a Beryl Markham way," Jim Trilling remembered. (Markham, a British-born

Kenyan writer and adventurer, was part of the imposing and often scandalous "Happy Valley set" in Africa.)

"I was the anti-Diana," Carroll Beichman said, although she also said that she probably represented youth to Lionel. She had been just twenty-one when she met Arnold Beichman, who was thirty-six and recently divorced, and they married soon after, dividing their time between New York, Boston, and Naramata, British Columbia, where she was born and raised. Her father served on the Supreme Court of Canada. She had met Arnold at a party at the British Information Service in New York, where she worked when she first came to America in 1950.

An entry in Lionel's journal dated July 27, 1957, records a visit to Claremont Avenue by Arnold Beichman. Lionel remarks on "my new disturbed sense of him. D's new disturbed sense of him. Sex. D's (unspecified) shocking experience with him. What this says about C—the unhappiness in her life with him—but what made her marry him in the first place? D speaking of this. Speaks of the danger of my missionary zeal for a proud and delicate girl in that situation."

Certainly, Arnold Beichman and Diana were close friends, but was their relationship a sexual one also? Diana might have wished for it, yet she rebuffed Beichman's advance in 1957. What was the nature of its "shocking" component, as Lionel mentioned in his journal? Had Arnold requested a rough, crude form of sex that Diana found revolting? After learning of Lionel's journal entry, Carroll Beichman would only comment obliquely, saying that both Arnold and Lionel "could explode, although [she] never witnessed Lionel losing his temper."

Lionel's journal does make one thing very clear: Diana knew that her husband was involved with Carroll, that she didn't seem to mind, and that, in fact, she was concerned her husband really didn't understand what he was getting into with this mission.

Two summers later, in 1959, Lionel recorded in his journal:

At the time that A had some attraction for D, he was much in love with C and spoke of her with great tenderness and delicacy. But as his feelings for D grew, he began to speak harshly of C and to behave with his curious brutality. At this, D lost any interest in him she had had. The situation was worsened by his response to my involvement with C, which led him to want to talk in a vulgar "conspiratorial" way with D about C and me. In that strange little flurry of emotion in his life— flurry of deep emotion, it should be said—he contrived to lose 2 women.

"There's a fair amount of truth in that entry," Carroll said, acknowledging that her husband's feelings for Diana included sexual ones and perhaps even an affair that didn't end well. "There's always a strain of truth in this stuff," she added. She said she didn't want to elaborate, except to comment that "Lionel did not find Arnold likeable," and, she said, "Lionel was fastidious. But not Arnold. He was an outspoken man."

Had Diana been turned on and then off by a blunt ("shocking," "brutal") request for sex? Had she had enough of men with short tempers?

According to a journal entry written by Lionel a few months later, on December 3, 1959, Diana told her husband: "'In the last 3 years you have become for me so much more an object of Romantic interest when you walk into a room,' etc. I ask why this is so and she replies that perhaps it is because I ceased to regard her in a symbolic way and treat her as a person."

Carroll had apparently enabled Lionel to begin to see and appreciate women in a new and honest way, and Diana was grateful. Maybe her husband's lifelong anger at all women would be curbed. Maybe he could begin to look at himself in a less calculating manner that would transform into what they once had had when they first met in the Speakeasy. But, she added, even though her marriage wasn't ever really "a romantic" one, perhaps now it had a chance to become that if Lionel's sexual problems could be abated and his libido revived. Still, she had once said that she could never understand what a marriage built out of a love affair could be like.

For years she had endured her husband's "aggression against women." And while she herself had perhaps not "betrayed their past," the notion was occasionally on her mind. She certainly questioned whether she had made the right choice in marrying him. She later said that it took more than twenty years of analysis before she was ready to express her own form of aggression against her husband, and she admitted, "when it did come out it was stupendous."

Carroll said that Lionel never talked about his marriage at their "odd lunches and walks in the park, except to say that he owed an enormous debt to Diana in terms of his work." She went on:

> I'm sure Diana was angry, but I think she gave him some rope. It's possible she went along with it to help his creativity. She might have thought that my relationship with him was therapy for her. I thought she'd just ride it through. I don't know if he ever wanted to leave Diana, he may have wanted to. Yet he also made it clear his marriage could not break up. . . . He told me there was no moment of the day that Diana didn't know where he was. . . . I knew he was attached to me but not enough to write about it in his journal. I'm extremely flattered. Actually it's stunning the degree he was obsessed with me. . . . He was a bit of a novelist.

Then she added quietly, "Up to a certain point we were meant for one another."

But as with Diana, Lionel was impotent with Carroll the two times they went to a hotel. "It didn't work," she said. "I thought he was in analysis because of it. . . . His analysis went on forever." She continued, "I don't think it was a permanent condition. . . . Lionel might have been embarrassed but actually I think he was relieved. He did say he was worried about affecting his relationship with Diana; he couldn't succeed with either of us." Carroll remarked that "it was very frustrating and he kept quoting Montaigne . . . 'There are some defeats more triumphant than victories' or perhaps it was 'in all things pleasure is increased by the very danger which ought to make us flee from them.'"

At some point in 1959, Lionel had written in his journal about William Phillips telling Diana of Lionel's supposed affair not only with Eleanor Clark but also "with Gene Marcus—whether or not D gave me a full account I do not know."

William Phillips particularly loved to gossip, and Diana told her husband that when they had had drinks, he had "pleasure" in learning about her "youthful homosexual experience." (Lionel's journal is the only place where mention is made of this. Diana never wrote or spoke about such an encounter.)

Other members of the family were also gossiping, picking up signals that all was not as it seemed in the Trilling marriage. "Lionel once told me he had an encounter that worked," Carroll Beichman said. "I have no clue who or what it was, but it wasn't with a prostitute." She said also that sometimes she wondered if Lionel "had a proclivity for picking up women like me."

After a party at Edna and William Phillips's that Diana had attended alone because Lionel had gone trout fishing that weekend, Lionel wrote in his journal about his wife's physical fear of a sexual encounter. He had also once noted in his journal that Diana tended to become "horny" when she was ill, which was often. In such entries, was Lionel thinking about past incidents involving his wife? Their discussions about her flirting with Norman Mailer? Or was he musing about current circumstances she had overcome? Perhaps with Arnold Beichman? Had Diana also had a "Great Instauration"—some sort of revitalization?

During that period of time, Diana also developed an intense friendship with Steven Marcus despite the nearly thirty years between them—perhaps born of Diana's initial resentment of Marcus's claim on Lionel's time. Lina Vlavianos, Jim's babysitter, remembers the three summers in Westport beginning in 1957 and particularly the summer of 1960, when Lionel Trilling and Steven Marcus were working on the abridged volume of Ernest Jones's *The Life and Work of Sigmund Freud*. "I was with Jim morning, noon and night," she said. "Diana worked from 9:30 a.m. until lunchtime." Marcus told Diana that he and Lionel "would work together for months, steadily and easily. We came to structural agreements about changes with no difficulty at all. The work proceeded literally without a hitch. Lionel would write sometimes transitional sentences, I would write sometimes transitional sentences. . . . So the working relationship was all that anybody could desire, and I'm sure that we were both surprised that it went with such ease."

Vlavianos said that Diana "was a difficult person, but we never got into any quarrels. I looked up to both Lionel and Diana." And she recalled

that Diana and Steve Marcus "would disappear by the pool," where
they could talk in confidence. "I knew they were talking about Diana's
problems or Steve's problems. . . . Diana had difficulty with his wife." Diana later told a friend that Gene "wouldn't entertain anybody, so I would
say to Steve, 'If you'd like I'll make sandwiches. If you have people in I'll
make the sandwiches for you and send them over.' Steven felt bad he
couldn't have people in his house because Gene wouldn't entertain them."
(Despite everything, Diana remained friends with Gene throughout
her life.)

Vlavianos went on to recall that "Steve was a partner in writing with
Lionel, and there was no question he looked up to Lionel, but he somehow felt more comfortable with Diana. She was more approachable."

Many years later, Diana said that "an intimate friend, a man," told her
he had "made the wrong choice in marrying his wife." He said, "I could
have done better if I had married a more intellectual woman. This was
a way of flirting with me because I was more intellectual, but it was
serious, too."

Was this intimate friend Arnold Beichman? Or perhaps Steven Marcus? Someone else? And what kind of closeness was Diana referring
to? Carroll Beichman would not comment on her husband but said, of
Marcus, that it "was entirely possible no one knew of an affair, but it
was unlikely. For heaven's sake she could be his mother!" Jim Trilling
said that "if there were an affair between Steven and my mother, it would
be truly bizarre." "Yet," he added, "it would be reciprocal—my father
and Carroll and Steve and my mother—in a mathematical sense." Gray
Foy recalled that he had always heard there was "*somebody*" Diana was
interested in, and that she had "a girlish quality about men, and was
coquettish." There is no explicit evidence, however, that Diana ever had
an affair with anyone.

Marcus told Diana that the summer of Freud "had a bad influence
on me. It raised my expectations," and Diana replied that it had "lowered hers for the rest of her life. I knew I could expect to be nothing but
a drudge." In addition to her own writing—she was working on a long
essay about Norman Mailer—she was responsible for preparing three

meals a day, keeping Jim content with friends and activities, and was being paid to tutor a young neighborhood boy in reading and writing.

Working with Lionel had no doubt made Marcus, still a graduate student, feel as if he and his former teacher were equals and that he had reached literary heights he could only dream about, and he had done it faster and easier than he had ever expected.. Lionel would write in his journal:

> As I walked to my office it occurred to me that S's relation to me made the most primitive situation of my mature life—that this young man, who so much wishes for power and eminence, wanted especially my power and eminence . . . that a way of getting them was by his willing me to have them, and that this was efficacious—that my knowing this diminished my sense of power and eminence, meant realizing and immobilizing me. . . . In this [theory I thought of] Midge's [Decter] speech to me of two years ago, that she was sick of hearing about S's talents etc., and how long was I going to put up with this man who felt it necessary to want my mind, my style, my job, my reputation, my wife, my son!

Jim Trilling said that his father "would have seen everything in as complex a way as possible. If it could be complex and tormented, all the better!" (Decades later Diana wrote in a letter to the historian Gertrude Himmelfarb that "Steve has long been in the business of patricide." In response, Jim Trilling speculated that "Steve's induction [as Jim's father's heir] could have extended into the personal as well. You don't have to be a Freudian about this—you kill the King and you get to be King, and the Queen comes with the deal. My mother could have been lured into a Folie a deux.")

Diana sometimes saw Steven Marcus as a rival for her husband's attention—in both their private and public life. She, not Steve Marcus, was her husband's editor. She was the person who knew what her husband could and could not do. And certainly she felt she was a better writer than both men. But she knew Marcus was important to Lionel, and she did not want to make her husband's disciple her rival, her enemy. So she sought to make him an indispensable friend, whatever the cost, one aspect of which would be her husband feeling threatened by their devoted relationship. After all, Lionel had admitted that after Jim's birth he worried that he'd never have Diana to himself again. Perhaps close friendship or even a flirtation with Steven Marcus could bring a frisson to her marriage.

Diana soon became so attached to Marcus that she could ask him with ease to do even the most mundane of favors. Carroll Beichman recalls that the relationship was an "intense friendship—there was *enormous* intensity there. An intense affection." One time during the summer, when Lionel had to return to New York for a funeral, Diana asked Marcus, who came for four or five days at a time, to arrive earlier than usual so she wouldn't be stranded without a car. Marcus told her that Gene had to do laundry and they couldn't arrive any earlier. "I had worse than a conniption fit," Diana later admitted. She was furious and let Marcus know how angry she was. After all, she had been working hard over the summer, and she was only asking for a small thing. A small thing to make her feel less trapped, less isolated, less alone. A small thing that any dear friend would do for another.

"Yesterday after my conversation with D, after her grieved letter from S," Lionel wrote in his journal,

> I begin to feel more as I would wish to be than ever before. The infantile and passive state—very bland it was in its hopelessness and helplessness . . . seemed suddenly to have gone and with no particular sense of heroism. I felt free and poised. Some show of jealousy there was but chiefly that D—and I!—had to be protected from her impulse to negation—I do not want to go into details about this but I do want to note the part played in these feelings by D's expressed awareness of the difficulty of my situation (at the same time she spoke of the diminution of her love for S in the degree that his for her had grown). . . . It was as if this rescued me from the humiliating sense that I was dealing with fantasies. At the same time it gave me a clear and simple awareness of the intensity of d's feeling for me.

The summer of the Great Instauration made Lionel "feel more as he would wish to be." He felt free. Diana understood his love and need for Carroll.

Diana had told her husband that "S" loved her even more than ever, although her feelings for him were less. Diana's willingness and need for Steve had seemingly not only lessened Lionel's guilt and worry over his inadequacy but had made him understand how deep her love was for him. And that Diana could be so honest about her feelings—no matter how unexpected they were—made Lionel feel more loved than ever by her. It was, of course, complex, especially since she had once told him that "no one is in love with a person, only with a moral situation."

Several years later, Lionel wrote in his journal:

> Today it came over me with fuller force than on the previous occasion how bad an effect on me the relation with S has had, how it has diminished my sense of myself, very pleasurably to be sure, how it has led me to think of myself as being quieter and with less force, how it has lessened tension in myself and in relation to D (even though at times it seemed to make tension in her, it did not). Lobotomized was the word I used. And after thinking this, I had occasion to read some of the essays in *The Liberal Imagination* and thought what genius I had then! And how I had submerged my sense of my own powers won at such cost to put myself on a happy equality with S—

Edward Mendelson, Lionel Trilling Professor in the Humanities at Columbia, suspects that Lionel Trilling took pleasure in fantasizing about Steven Marcus and Diana together, that it "pleasurably" diminished his sense of himself. Jim Trilling, thinking of his father's snake story, written years earlier during his parents' honeymoon, quoted what his father noted in a journal entry that "perhaps men cannot hate—but rather love—the lovers of their wives." In an introduction to that story, when it was later published in the *Kenyon Review*, Jim wrote, "What is a man to do when he realizes that he is forever excluded from some aspect of his wife's sexuality? My father seems to equate the exclusion with a fundamental lack of masculine force for which the palliative is masochistic pleasure with overtones of homosexual submission." Diana told Patricia Bosworth, when they were discussing a story about Walker Evans making love to James Agee's wife, that "if you ask your friend to make love to your wife that is not a simple act. It's not an innocent request. . . . There's a great homosexual incentive to making love to your best friend's wife."

Lionel Trilling possibly had some homoerotic feeling for Steven Marcus, or perhaps he was just experiencing his own complicated sexual psychology, while Diana felt "depersonalized" by all the dramas. Around this time Lionel, who believed that if sex wasn't subversive, it wasn't fun, noted in his journal his "growing interest in the idea of orgy." He didn't elaborate.

After working on the Freud with Lionel, and then a book about Charles Dickens, Steve Marcus began a study of sexuality and pornography in mid-nineteenth-century England. In his acknowledgments (*The Other Victorians* was published in 1966) he included "a special note of thanks" to the Trillings, saying that "discussions with them during the earliest phase of my research were of great value to me." Both Trillings no doubt had many insights to offer.

In Lionel's snake story, which Diana called "brilliant" but "morbid to a pathological degree"—adding that "it worried her for their future together"—Lionel wrote of his female protagonist "that she held to a strict logic of emotion. . . . There was a division between their love and sensuality, which made it possible to find sensuality elsewhere without danger. One might have several loves at once; their own love was so great that nothing, not even another, could touch it." The story was written nearly thirty years before his "Great Instauration."

Diana once referred to her husband's nature as "mysterious." She herself had a mysterious side: she was never openly jealous of Carroll Beichman. Lionel had remarked in his journal that his wife and Thelma Anderson "with unobtrusive tact" once gave him a moment alone with Carroll after a party when they were all in the bedroom together collecting their coats, and indeed at that party he noted not only that he and Carroll had a kiss in the kitchen (later changing it in his notebook to read that they had simply "touched") but that Diana also gave

Carroll the man's sweater she had bought last year. In previous years Diana had been unduly concerned over the attention other women paid her husband at parties. She was sure Hannah Arendt wanted to seduce Lionel, and she was concerned that Muriel Spark did, too. But Diana "never had any resentment against Carroll," Jim Trilling said, "possibly because she was so terrific." He went on to say that his mother knew that his father "was always dissatisfied—not sexually—he craved adventure—to be an artist like Hemingway.... If it would take an affair to make him happy my mother would put up with it she said many times—my mother minded less than some wives in comparable circumstances—but it doesn't mean she wouldn't have felt pain." Diana herself wrote in *The Beginning of the Journey* that she "could have wished [Lionel] to have a thousand mistresses were this to have released him from the constraints upon him as a writer of fiction." And, Jim said, his father "wanted things to be complicated because intense feelings would happen and he would feel he was living life a little more aggressively. My father liked drama." Diana later said that she "always thought that monogamy was against nature. I don't see how you can go to bed with the same person and not want to change after a while."

In 1958, a year after the summer of the Great Instauration, Lionel wrote a mystifying entry in his journal: "D, S, and Victor Rosen—S puts off his visit because he cannot bring himself to speak of D. D's speculation about this is the same as mine—that S is ambiguous [i.e., ambivalent]—that he wants to tell, to shock, to brag. Bad effects of this."

Jim Trilling said that Rosen, a psychoanalyst connected to the New York Psychoanalytic Institute who was also once president of the American Psychoanalytic Association, was a family friend from their summers in Westport and that neither of his parents were ever his patient. "But he was someone who my parents trusted. He had been at the house when my [paternal] grandmother had a mild heart attack, and he kept my mother reassured until the ambulance came. He displayed great calm and authority." (In her later years Diana made peace with her mother-in-law. Diana said that she always believed that Lionel's "unadmitted early love for his mother was a stronger factor in his dealings with women than his reasonable complaint against her.")

Jim called a purported visit with Dr. Rosen "truly strange" and wonders if what was going on was simply "psychic games—mind games." What could Steven Marcus "brag" about to Dr. Rosen that would also shock him? It is not even known if such a meeting actually took place. Jim went on to say that his parents "wanted badly to be bad because not being bad was being bourgeois. They wanted to be interesting—mind games, seduction, being jealous and enjoying it." (Dr. Rosen himself was considered a bad boy in psychoanalytic circles—he caused a scandal by falling in love with a patient, later marrying her.)

Diana's complicated friendship with Steven Marcus hobbled along, although in Diana's last years they were no longer close. Michael Rosenthal, a writer, a former dean of Columbia, and a professor in the English department, said that Marcus and Diana had "a terrible parting of the ways" after Lionel's death, explaining that at a Lionel Trilling seminar where Diana was not an invited speaker, she, nonetheless got up to speak, and Marcus sharply told her, "Mrs. Trilling, will you please sit down." Rosenthal said that Lionel "was abusive to Steve Marcus and that he was the only person who Lionel thought less of as a person."

Brom Anderson reminisced that a poet friend once saw his parents, the Trillings, and Steve Marcus and Gertrud Lenzer (his second wife) together in the country. "She looked at the three couples and said she felt something between the Trillings—a relationship that was very delicate but real—and between his parents something very solid," he said; "but between the Marcuses she didn't really see anything." (Decades later, Anderson remarked that Steve and Gertrud certainly stuck together, despite that impression.)

Lionel's affair with Carroll Beichman ended by the summer of 1961. "I told him I wasn't going to see him again. He took me to tea somewhere. I said I wasn't going to be part of his therapy. We occasionally saw one another that winter, it might even have been on and off, and we all continued to be perfectly civil. . . . *Civil* was our middle name."

Diana and Arnold kept up whatever it was they had together.

After the Beichmans moved to Boston, Carroll and Lionel had dinner in the area two times, and once the four of them had a picnic at Bronson Alcott Farm. "Lionel walked me to the car and said he thought of me every day of his life. He said that people change but some things are permanent. He meant his feelings for me."

"Last terrible party of the year at the Beichmans," Lionel had noted in his journal in 1960—"only D, S and I find anything wrong. Quarrel with D on way home—over what—my sense, which has controlled all my summer, that I did not ever again want to see people in groups of more than 4!"

By 1961 the threesome Lionel indicated—Diana, Steven Marcus, and himself—could once again—assuming they needed to—hide any so-called antibourgeois wickedness of their lives. Fifty years later, Carroll Beichman, long away from the "very interesting, entertaining, and affectionate little group," stressed that any earlier affair between Diana and Steve Marcus was "improbable" and that one should "stay clear of the Marcus angle with Diana." As for those earlier years in her own life, she said, "Arnold and I survived this. My marriage settled down and lasted close to sixty years."

"I am one of the last living witnesses," she said wistfully, adding that she "sometimes felt as if I was in an Edith Wharton novel."

Carroll Beichman died on January 8, 2013, in Palm Springs, California, when a van struck her as she was crossing a darkly lit street.

14

A LIMITED KIND OF CELEBRITY

*Should the Oxford possibility again begin to seem attractive,
[the Trillings had been at Balliol College, Oxford, for a year
beginning in 1964] one thing must make against it—that in
England D is much more insecure than in America. During
the summer in London, the Athenaeum and the London Library were the only 2 places where I could go without her
being anxious.*

—LIONEL TRILLING, JOURNAL ENTRY, C. 1967

n 1962 Diana published the piece she had been writing in Westport
the summer Lionel and Steve Marcus worked together. "The Moral
Radicalism of Norman Mailer" appeared in *Encounter,* a magazine
she would later learn had definitely received CIA funding, as had been
rumored for several years. "If I could honorably write for *Encounter*
when I suspected it had CIA funds, I cannot consider it less honorable
to write for it now that my suspicions are confirmed," she wrote in a letter to its editor, Melvin Lasky. (*The New York Times* later reported that
Lionel stopped writing for the magazine after the disclosures.) But very
early on, Diana had a hunch about the CIA, and she had once written

Arnold Beichman that she didn't think accepting the support of the government in the cause of Cold War anticommunism was a "dishonorable act."

Diana continued to be on courteous but edgy terms with *Partisan Review* (which also had received CIA funding). She said that William Phillips once told her that it was "her literary judgment that made her work unwanted, not her political views." He was, of course, thinking of her essay on Ginsberg, which had caused such a ruckus. But Diana chose not to take his criticism too seriously—deciding William was just being mischievous. For his part, Phillips wanted mainly to remain on cordial terms with Lionel. He mattered more than Diana. Some members of the *PR* "family" speculated that pleasing Lionel was the real reason *Partisan Review* had published her peculiar journal in the first place.

Diana felt that of all the *PR* "Girls," she was the only one "in the shadow of her husband," as she put it, despite the fact she was often criticized as "a very dominating woman," dominating because at parties and other gatherings she often openly argued with Lionel. "I interrupted him, I contradicted him . . . [and] this upset people," she said. They would never understand the importance she placed on her razor-sharp tongue.

Jacques Barzun always came to her defense (having long since forgiven her for the reference to him in her published journal), and Diana said that he once told a group of Columbia professors, "There's only one faculty wife I've ever known whose advice you could listen to," and, she added, "everybody knew it was me." She said that "Jacques would always be asking my advice as Lionel was always asking my advice. I received a kind of regard and respect that most women did not have, and yet I was still the wife whom you discuss in a negative way." She decided later that perhaps envy was behind it all, envy of her "good fortune in being married to someone as attractive and agreeable and distinguished as Lionel."

Diana usually let such unpleasant matters rest, saying that if she "had made more of an issue with this," she and Lionel "would have had a very, very bad time." So she lived with it. Still, it rankled when a reviewer once pointed out that she was "first of all, the wife of Lionel Trilling, and secondly, a matron of feminism, embroidering samplers for liberalism." Another reviewer once said her style was one "associated in America with faculty wives' clubs." She would even be compared to a clerk, someone who worked for a powerful person pushing pencils and shuffling papers. (In response to an essay she would write in 1969 about the student uprisings at Columbia, Robert Lowell would offer "his ultimate courtly insult," Diana said, by calling her "a housekeeping goddess of reason.")

Diana went on to live her "double life as a wife and a writer," and it made her "very vulnerable," she admitted. She sometimes wished she had continued to use her birth name, but Lionel liked her using Trilling. "They'll think I'm your daughter," she used to tease him, and he'd retort, "No, they'll think you are my mother." She later said that there really was a rumor going around literary and academic circles that she was his daughter.

Lionel also experienced a dual perception of their marriage, although of a different sort, telling Diana that after every party they attended together, he "looked across the room and said, 'Hey I want to go and talk to that woman,' and it turned out to be you." Diana treasured this declaration, which carried a great deal of truth even in the face of his love for Carroll Beichman.

Someone who did not patronize her was Norman Mailer. Diana's essay on Mailer, whom she knew well by the time the piece appeared, stressed *his* duality. She wrote that he has "so much moral affirmation coupled with so much moral anarchism; so much innocence yet so much guile; so much defensive caution but such headlong recklessness; so much despair together with so imperious a demand for salvation; so strong a charismatic charge but also so much that offends, even repels; so much intellection but such a frequency of unsound thinking; such a grand and manly impulse to heroism but so inadequate a capacity for self-discipline; so much sensitiveness and so little sensibility; so much imagination and such insufficient art."

She told Peter Manso that she didn't discuss her essay with Mailer when she was writing it, although he knew she was writing about him, but he knew nothing about her approach or framework. At one point

Mailer said she should talk to his father if she wanted any biographical material (she didn't), and when she was finished, she asked Mailer if he wanted to see it. "He came to the house to read it," Diana told Manso,

> and I could feel something strange was happening. He finished reading and then sort of made a move as if he'd had a lot of air stored in his lungs. He asked me if I would mind if he went for a walk, so I told him to go ahead. I was troubled too. Before he went out he said, "I didn't expect such a formal piece." I acknowledged that it was formal literary criticism. But what had he expected—some kind of "My friend Norman piece"? He said, "No, I don't know what I thought, but I wasn't prepared for this." It was obvious that he was disconcerted, and while he was gone I thought, I've treated him the way I would treat a major writer, he ought to love the piece. If he's not smart enough to know what I'm doing with it, then that's too bad. I'm not going to let myself be upset. So when he came back I wasn't all a flutter: "Oh, dear Norman, have I not written a good piece? Do you not like it?" Precisely what he said I don't remember. If it had been memorable I'd have remembered it. He never mentioned it to me again. His word about it was "formal." I suppose by that he meant I had written a masculine essay— probably that wasn't the part of me he cottoned to. On the other hand, it should have been nice for him to feel that I was putting my best force of intelligence so largely on his side. Not that at the time I was aware that he particularly needed legitimization. Thank God I didn't think about that one way or another or I could never have written the essay to begin with.

(Robert Silvers, then an editor at *Harper's*, had heard through the grapevine about the essay and had written Diana about publishing it, but by then it had already been promised to *Encounter*.)

Diana and Mailer always exchanged letters more than they saw each other socially, and he often used Diana as a sounding board for his ideas. The summer after her *Encounter* piece was published, he did write her about it (or at least her impressions of his talents) in a letter that she obviously forgot about when talking to Peter Manso. Mailer said that

Diana basically thought he was a very good and talented writer but that he could be a great writer if only he would stop posturing. (She had written that he has "obstructed the development that might once have followed the early flowering of so much talent" and that "increasingly, he has offered the public the myth of the man rather than the work of the writer.") Mailer told Diana that for years *he* was "aghast at the peculiar vision of the critic. You, all of you, are forever ascribing powers to us we don't have, and misreading our strengths as our cripplings. Faulkner's long breath, Hemingway's command of the short sentence, Proust's cocoon. . . . Faulkner writes his long sentences because he never really touches what he is about to say and so he keeps chasing it; Hemingway writes short because he strangles in a dependent clause. . . . Proust spins his wrappings because a fag gets slapped if he says what he thinks. . . . These men . . . became great writers because of their infirmities." And then Mailer wrote emphatically that he "was able to write *The Naked and the Dead* because I was one of the first who could dispense comfortably with roots; my infirmity was my strength. . . . The answer is not for me to go back to an earlier, simpler, healthier and less self-conscious way of working, but to learn how to strip the fats of unliterary indulgence, save myself for the work (which may still involve certain kinds of stunts) and let the work take care of itself." On and on he vented to Diana in a four-page single spaced letter.

Diana sometimes vented to *him*. She wanted to write about Hemingway, but Lionel was discouraging her from doing so. "I think you should write about him," Mailer told her; "I was certainly struck by the similarities and differences you saw in his way of going at it and mine."

Diana continued also to vent in "Letters to the Editor" and to well-known people. In 1961 she had proposed to Edward R. Morrow, the broadcaster/journalist who had become the head of the United States Information Service earlier that year, that the government should create a new agency to deal with "significant errors in American public sentiment." She had been "dramatically struck," she wrote in her letter, by the similarity of Fidel Castro's offering in 1961 to trade a thousand prisoners for five hundred bulldozers to Hitler's offer in 1944 to trade Jews for trucks, and she believed "this parallel could be put to use in combating the kind of public opinion which has never faltered in its opposition to Hitlerism but which can see no similar offense to its humanitarian principles in Castroism." She was not suggesting to do away with free discussion, but she felt many such ideas now "weakened the democratic effort." The letter was signed "Diana Trilling (Mrs. Lionel Trilling) formerly Chairman, The American Committee for Cultural Freedom." She invoked Lionel's name, as she seldom did in correspondence, but there was still no known response from Mr. Morrow.

In 1962 Diana published a long essay in *Redbook* on the death of Marilyn Monroe, an essay that one critic called "so perceptive as to be a masterpiece of analysis." However, the *Kirkus Review* later reported (when the piece was in Diana's first collection, *Claremont Essays*) that it was full of "unchic ideas," and another review called it "over-important for the occasion."

Diana was generally faulted for her style of combining personal observations with meticulous facts about whatever it was she was discussing. But she was, in truth, an unacknowledged member of the "new journalism"—a term for an unconventional form of news reporting that began to be used in the mid-1960s and was applied to such writers as Tom Wolfe, Gay Talese, and, of course, Truman Capote and Norman Mailer. These writers—as well as Diana Trilling—wanted to make nonfiction as creative and imaginative in style and scope as the novel.

Sometimes Diana got to her point in a somewhat convoluted, yet always engaging, manner, and the rationale of her approach was not always immediately clear, but the result was more often than not a well-designed essay that showed her subject's significance to American culture, whether she highlighted Allen Ginsberg, Norman Mailer, Alger Hiss, or Marilyn Monroe. It had taken her until late middle age to find her destination, but at fifty-seven she was sure she had found her voice at last.

That same year, Diana was asked by Collier Books to write an introduction to its edition of *Tom Sawyer*. She did write one, later reprinted in her first collection of essays, but its publication was not without drama. She complained to the editor that "extraordinary changes were made without [her] knowledge or permission" and that in her twenty-year writing career her copy had never been altered so "arrogantly" and "illiterately." Her rhythms and "turns of speech which define an individual style" had been distorted, and "extreme violence was done to the English language!" She threatened to stop the distribution of the book unless her essay was printed exactly as she wrote it. She also let the editor know that Steven Marcus had also had his copy "mishandled" by Collier Books and was ashamed of the final result but was so busy he hadn't had time to complain but "authorizes" Diana to speak in his name.

Diana's introduction was printed as she wrote it.

By 1962, the Trillings had achieved such prominence that they were invited to the White House for President John F. Kennedy's dinner in honor of the Nobel Prize winners from the Western Hemisphere. On the day of the dinner Dr. Oppenheimer was on the same train to Washington as the Trillings, and Diana reported that as he walked by them, he stopped briefly to greet Lionel, whom he had met before, "but just stared, stared, stared very hard at me for just that moment." She added that the dinner was really an occasion for the president "to reinstate Oppenheimer officially. . . . It was very clever of him."

The writers present, besides Diana and Lionel, included Katherine Anne Porter, Robert Frost, John Dos Passos, Rose and William Styron, and James Farrell. Thirty-four years later, Diana would write an exquisitely detailed essay about the event that *The New Yorker* would publish eight months after her death in 1996.

She wrote about all the ceremonials surrounding the dinner before, during, and after—her search for the correct dress, which involved buying two since she later found out the first, a short one, was not appropriate because a long gown was required; a handbag she borrowed; Lionel drinking six martinis ("I'd been counting," she commented); their sitting at separate tables; and Katherine Ann Porter's "annoying" fidgeting during the after-dinner reading from the works of three Nobel Prize winners. She wrote also that "actually I've never been a less important feature in our shared social life. I had nothing to do with this occasion except as Lionel's wife. . . . Neither Kennedy had ever heard of me."

In the receiving line, when the Trillings were first introduced to the president and Mrs. Kennedy, Lionel, after some brief banter, had told

Mrs. Kennedy, according to Diana, "'Wait till I tell you what they said about you at Vassar!'" Jackie Kennedy laughed and then asked, "What?" and Lionel said mischievously, "Later I'll tell you." The president then joined the conversation and asked what they had said and Lionel repeated "later." There actually *was* a later, and the Trillings were asked to the residence after the formal dinner was over. Lionel then had a chance to say to both Kennedys, about Jackie: "They said that you were a serious student. A very devoted student. And quite shy." Diana then wrote that "Jackie repeated after him. 'Shy. Yes. I am shy.' Lionel said, 'I'm shy, too.' She looked at him and they both burst out laughing. She knew that he was teasing her, and she liked it."

Diana's lengthy notes before she wrote the piece, notes that she taped, are full of tedious and rambling facts that she didn't, wouldn't, or couldn't use in the published piece. She begins: "I want to do this terribly, terribly much in detail, some of which may be boring about clothes and stuff like that." Not a rousing beginning, even for notes. Yet notes are just that, and in this case they offer a glimpse into the way Diana thought about her subject and her research; she took *everything* down so she could later decide what were the most relevant and useful facts.

In the finished article she mentions succinctly, "One morning when the mail arrived, Lionel asked me to come out to the hall." In her notes she goes into great detail: mentioning that "Lionel always breaks his neck to get to the door first to get the mail," that their accountant was in the living room doing their income tax, and that at the moment she and Lionel became aware that they were holding an invitation to the White House, she said to their accountant: "'We've just gotten an invitation to the White House that will cost us a million dollars, is that a tax deduction?' And he said it was. So I felt better about the whole thing. It's a professional expense."

The notes reveal her thought process and how she eventually created a frame that lifted the chosen details into an essay of broad significance and also how she applied what she learned about narrative skills.

Many of the notes, especially the lengthy ones about the dresses, stores, and the salespeople, are entertaining in themselves and might have made separate essays. At one point she takes Lionel to see one of the dresses: "And Lionel looked at [it] and said, 'Oh, it's much too theatrical with those long tight sleeves. I don't think that's the right thing at all.'"

There's also a long reference to a phone call from her sister, who told her that she heard that Lionel was picketing the White House, and Diana's description in her note reads like slapstick. She told Cecilia they were not yet in Washington but still in New York, but Cecilia was certain of what she heard on the radio. Diana finally called the station to protest and was told that what they reported was not that Lionel Trilling was picketing but Linus Pauling.

The notes also make many references to Diana's "little pink pillbox." She needs it because on the train to Washington she begins to get a migraine, wonders if she should take a pill that an English friend gave her, checks with her doctor in New York who knows what the pill is by its description, says to take two, and the migraine soon begins to fade. The pillbox does not make an appearance in the finished article.

Diana goes on in awkward detail in her notes to say that Jackie Kennedy's behind "sticks out a little bit like a shelf" and that "in evening clothes you don't notice the bow legs," but in the published piece she writes only that Jackie Kennedy has "a charming figure rather than a perfect one."

Commenting on the after-dinner reading from one of Hemingway's works, Diana noted, "I saw the President do the one human thing I saw him do the entire evening." But in the published piece she wrote not that the president had done only "one human thing" but that she simply saw him "do something so nice. He squeezed [Mrs. Hemingway's] arm comfortingly." Many of her narrative decisions were intuitive and didn't follow any obvious sense of reasoning, but it is clear that in the case of the president of the United States she was not going to be derogatory.

In 1964 Lionel received one of the world's most esteemed visiting professorships—he became the George Eastman Visiting Professor of Balliol College, the oldest of Oxford's colleges. It was a one-year appointment. The professorship was established in 1929 from an endowment created by George Eastman of the Eastman Kodak Company in New York and New Jersey.

The Trillings were welcomed in England with flowers and a reception and assigned a "comfortable and familiar—but more luxurious than Claremont Avenue" house in Jowett Walk, which was in the central part of the city, "a town that didn't charm me as I had expected," Diana wrote Elinor Hays. Other things about Oxford didn't charm her either. "We haven't any of us stopped shaking with cold since arrival," she wrote to Elsa Grossman, later commenting in another letter to Elinor Hays that the house "was over decorated—out of *House and Garden*." But the women were decidedly not, "dressed in boring tweeds and shapeless knits. . . . They have very poor figures—wide seats and bow legs."

Diana the cook was also not happy about the food situation. She complained to Elsa that "the simplest things taste absolutely awful and cook even worse." Exasperated, Diana explained, "for instance I boiled a tongue—inedible, and the potatoes falling apart on the outside were hard as brick inside. As for the vegetables, of fresh there are almost none except the cabbage family, of canned, familiarity ends with the brand names." She soon begged Elsa to help her and asked for a care package of Vita herring snacks, Vita red caviar, eggplant appetizer, two cans of smoked oysters or mussels, two packages of Wild's light sliced pumpernickel, and some Anacin. Perhaps to distribute the burden more equally, she turned to Elinor to send her Jell-O, commenting that "I have a desperate need of easy desserts—one can easily buy, inexpensively, dark pitted cherries." A few weeks later Diana asked Elinor for eight more packages of Jell-O, saying two of the earlier packets had broken in transit. She even suggested that Elinor add additional cardboard to the package in the future. Diana felt secure in asking for these favors, telling Elinor (who had recently asked Diana to be her literary executor) that she "and the Grossmans are my sole dependables." It never occurred to Diana that she might be overstepping the boundaries of friendship with these mundane requests. After several months, Diana asked Elinor even to buy her some new bras and girdles at a special shop in New York because the water in England seemed to be rotting the elastic on the ones she had brought. When Diana realized that Elinor's knee might be bothering her for this kind of errand (the Jell-O jaunt seemed to be within limits), she went so far as to ask her to see if Gertrude

Himmelfarb could get the items, although she was embarrassed to ask her herself because Gertrude, a working historian, also had small children and "a very taxing mother." Himmelfarb agreed to do the task, later writing Diana she "was happy to oblige," adding that when she and Irving (Kristol) were in England, "it was not bras that were a problem but shoes." She explained no further.

Eventually, one of the college wives drove Diana to a shopping center where there was, as she wrote Elinor, "a true supermarket—what a boon!" Diana could browse, and pick and choose, and buy what she needed.

Meanwhile, the Grossmans continued to help Diana and Lionel financially, and midway through their stay in England Diana asked Elsa to deposit $1,000 in their New York bank account, which she would pay back on their return to New York. Diana needed the sense of security the loan would give her, and she hoped the request wasn't "an embarrassment." One time the Grossman's even paid a bill for the Trillings that Diana was mystified about when Elsa brought it up, but the Grossmans always seemed to understand the Trillings' confusing money woes.

They sublet their Claremont Avenue apartment to save money on rent while in Oxford. This was hard for Diana because she was meticulous about her belongings and did not like the idea of other people in her house. But she disliked money woes even more. As it turned out, at the end of the year in England Diana was not pleased with the way the renters left the apartment and wrote them a detailed, point-by-point letter, accusing them of breaking or chipping many of her dishes and glasses, damaging some lighting fixtures, staining the furniture, bleaching the color out of her Saks Fifth Avenue deep beige towels and bathmats, removing all the contact paper in her cabinet, and damaging her seventeenth-century desk by somehow taking a chunk out of it. The renters, a doctor and his wife from San Francisco, were so outraged by Diana's accusations—especially her charge that they had gossiped about the "filth" they found in the apartment—that the doctor resorted to an undignified attack in response: "We are proud of the way we took care of your place. We are outraged at your attitude. . . . As to the gossip

I am amazed that you would bring it up again, and if you want gossip I can tell you plenty that was said about you by your help, your friends, in the building and out. I am ashamed to have to write this last but you went too far."

Nonetheless, Diana may have been justified. Jim Trilling remembers them as "the sub-tenants from Hell" who went through his mother's "private stuff," and he thinks even one of the Trillings' cats died under their care.

Other than the purchasing of food, Diana and Lionel had no other considerable expenses in Oxford. Balliol College provided two caretakers—a husband and wife—for the house, but because they were seventy-five years old, Diana was asked not to overburden them with work but also not to make them feel useless. They agreed on light house-keeping duties for the pair, and the college would also hire someone for an hour or two each day to do heavier work. The college would also bring in waiters whenever the Trillings entertained at home. When Diana asked about table linens, she was told there were some, but in the three years the house had been in use none of the other occupants ever had guests to dinner. Diana, of course, liked to entertain, and when things were difficult around her, cooking always helped make things seem better, especially after she figured out the British food shopping situation.

Of course, her biggest issue was her role at Oxford. "For a very long time I had resisted going to England because I had been told that the life in English university towns was very difficult for women. They were excluded; it was a man's world, and the women were not welcome," Diana said. But what a surprise, she admitted, "Far from being unwelcome, I've never been so warmly received and never had a better time anywhere under any circumstance." She was even told that "no American visitor had ever adapted to Oxford as I did." The single unpleasantness was a visit from her brother and his wife. She wrote Elinor that Sam greeted her "with the expectable remark that Li looked great but I was fat," and said that neither Sam nor his wife, Bettye, asked one question about their life in England." A few months later she wrote Elsa that Bettye had proudly written "the biggest most important news "that Sam had been made a deacon of their church." What an "improbable" development, she told Elsa, and so worthy of a "marvelous transatlantic giggle." Sam, who never liked being a Jew, was finally no longer one.

Diana had a chance to share some of her feminist views when she and Lionel entertained or were entertained. Sometime in the spring before they had left for England, she had been asked by the Inter-University Committee on the Superior Student, a group funded by the Carnegie Corporation consisting primarily of college deans, to address their conference on "Talented Women and the American College," which was going to be held at Columbia; they were offering a $500 honorarium. Diana accepted and suggested she speak about the image of women in contemporary literature. (Besides a woman from CBS television, she was the only nonacademic participant.) Her talk gave her an opportunity to dig into the roots of her "family feminist" views, which she had begun to talk about in her 1959 article in *Look* magazine. She told her audience that

> the woman in advanced present day fiction, in short, is no longer recognizably related to the "ball and chain" of American folklore, a goddess knocked off the pedestal of romantic courtship to become that most dismal of folk figures, a wife who saddles her poor husband with a home whose mortgage he cannot meet, with children who squabble and brawl, with a furnace to stoke and a lawn to mow. Feminism and technology have transformed the harassed shrew of a few decades ago [in]to someone who is man's equal, even his superior, in the ability to meet the requirements of daily living.*

As for Lionel's experience at Oxford, Diana said that Fannie Trilling had always wanted Lionel to get a PhD at Oxford, so his year in England "was a sort of fulfillment of his childhood upbringing and rearing. . . . I think that probably one of the major disappointments of Lionel's life was the fact that he was not given an honorary degree by Oxford.

---

* The speech was later published in *The Woman in America*, edited by Robert J. Lifton and published by Houghton Mifflin.

I suppose I'm the only person in the world who knew this; he wouldn't have let anybody know that he wanted it."

Lionel's mother died while Diana and Lionel were in Oxford. Fannie had been living with Lionel's sister, Harriet, and her husband under what Diana called "very, very peculiar circumstances" that involved staying in her room whenever Harriet's husband was home. Lionel received word of her death by a telegram on November 25 that arrived seven hours before the funeral, which meant he had no time to return to America. Diana believes that Lionel's descent into illness a few months later—double pneumonia and pleurisy—began with his not being able to properly mourn his mother, even though some Orthodox Jewish students came to the house to pray for her. "It was all very unsatisfactory because they spoke perfect Hebrew and Lionel was barely able to stumble through the prayers; . . . he was humiliated," she said.

In the beginning of their Oxford year Diana complained to both Elsa and Elinor of homesickness, going so far as to enumerate the people who had or had not written her and Lionel; Edna Phillips and Gertrude Himmelfarb had written only once, as had Arnold Beichman "incoherently," Diana added wickedly. Jacques Barzun and Steve Marcus had not written at all. Yet as the weeks went by, there were many lunches and dinners to fill up her calendar—lunch, tea, or dinner with Elizabeth Bowen; John Bayley and Iris Murdoch; Goronwy and Margaret Rees; Pamela Hansford Johnson Snow and C. P. Snow; John Osborne and his wife at the time, actor Mary Ure; Isaiah and Aline Berlin. After listening to a series of lectures Isaiah Berlin had given at Columbia, and getting to know him and his wife well, Diana said that "he is, without question, personally, the most successful human being I have ever known." But, she added, in her customarily blunt way, "he has never really done good original work by his standards or by the standards of the people he most admires. . . . He's a fine historian of ideas, but he isn't an original thinker at all, and nobody can say he is. . . . He's a wonderful explicator of other people's work and a marvelous teacher."

Diana did her own work while in England, though she complained to Elinor that she had no typewriter table and that "the British have never heard of them!" She soon improvised and told Elinor that she was typing on "a very wobbly antique table of almost suitable height."

A year or so before leaving for Oxford, she had completed a short story she decided to submit to Byron Dobell at *Esquire*, who forwarded it to his managing editor, who wrote that "the story has a tendency to ramble along pretty slowly at times and could probably be tightened . . . but that it is surely smooth and competent enough for her to try some slicks—by slicks I mean of course, the ladies magazines, not us." Dobell suggested that Diana send other things to him, and he ended his letter by saying, "If I'm not being presumptuous, I would certainly welcome any suggestions from Mr. Trilling." None came from his former professor, and Diana eventually also abandoned the story, as well as any further submissions to Dobell. Two rejections were enough for her.

At her makeshift typing table in Oxford, Diana was working on an essay commemorating the first anniversary of President Kennedy's death, a piece that would remain unpublished until she made it the opening essay of *Claremont Essays*, published in New York by Harcourt, Brace and World in 1964, and in England by Secker and Warburg the following year, 1965. Both editions came out while the Trillings were in Oxford.

In 1963 Diana had been selecting the essays to be printed in the anthology, one she was pleased to be putting together, although it didn't wholly satisfy her need for an original book. A decade earlier Lionel had been under contract to Harcourt for a book to be called "Memorable Essays," so the publishing house was familiar and homey to Diana (even though Harcourt wouldn't become Lionel's publisher until after his death, when it published uniform editions of his work). But Diana had met publisher William Jovanovich at various Columbia gatherings, and they had hit it off right away, and he thought that a collection of her essays was a terrific idea. He loved literary women.

In America *Claremont Essays* was received as "a welcome event. . . . We are in her debt for a moving and often profound book." The reviews were generally favorable, calling her prose "faultless" and saying she was "a superb arguer." But some critics used the opportunity to attack her politics, calling her "a rather hysterical anti-communist." Another said she had borrowed all her ideas on liberalism from her husband and that whereas his interests were always on the highest level of artistry, hers were "concretely . . . the embarrassments of recent history." Diana, who was reading these reviews while in Oxford, was reassured by C. P. Snow, who told her, "We suffer from a great deal of this. . . . Some people suggest that I am the Svengali behind Pamela's books." He told Diana that he was "always astonished that people can be so insensitive . . . [but] obviously in your marriage and ours we can laugh these things off."

Another reviewer said that male critics are always more sure of their ground and can safely toss out ideas, while the females, "like Mrs. Trilling," need to build an "elaborate framework" that is so academic it leaves no room for humor or playfulness. She is "over-anxious" another reviewer announced. The appraisal in *National Review* was especially nasty, the reviewer wondering if Lionel accepted the book's dedication to him just to keep "the family harmony." Diana wrote Elsa that Lionel considered the remarks concerning him "actionable," although a lawyer was never engaged.

Ever loyal and devoted Arnold Beichman raved about the book in the *Christian Science Monitor*: "To read Mrs. Trilling's essays is to feel oneself in the presence of George Orwell. Not that she derives from Orwell. Rather both derive from the society and the politics which engaged them." Stanley Edgar Hyman's review in *The New York Review of Books* was positive but so confusing that a letter to the editor in the next issue asked "if it was intended to be a parody, either an intentional parody, definitely *not* a parody, or an *unconscious* parody." Several months earlier, *The New York Review of Books* had asked Diana to review *High School English Textbooks*, by James J. Lynch and Bertrand Evans, but her "excellent" review (the only one she would write for the publication) was postponed because Robert Silvers, the editor, told her the next issue was running a review of *Claremont Essays*. In general, Diana was not happy with *The New York Review of Books* over her essay about Timothy Leary's use of LSD, which it had rejected (but was subsequently published by *Encounter*). Diana wrote a seething letter to Robert Silvers, telling him, among many other things, that he should not have interpreted a previous letter from her as "kind and forbearing," because "in the first place this is not at all my style."

The review of her book that bothered Diana the most was the one by G. S. Fraser, which appeared in *Partisan Review*. Diana first learned about the review from Steven Marcus, who was on the magazine's editorial board. Marcus wrote her that Fraser "tried to be fair to you and your work but didn't succeed, in my opinion." Marcus explained that "he deals with you harshly for being harsh to others. There did not, however, appear to be grounds for turning the review down. . . . William did the most he could; he wrote Fraser a note saying something general about the quality of the review. Fraser replied by writing an additional last paragraph, which has the intention of mollifying what he has said before. I am not at all certain that he succeeds in this intention." (Fraser added to his review: "I should certainly have said two things which I omitted to say: what an excellent 'straight' literary critic Mrs. Trilling is, when she devotes herself, too rarely in this volume, to that discipline: and what clear, plain, and vigorous prose she writes, a model for any writer attempting the genre.") Marcus concluded, "As your friends, both William and I felt in impossible positions, and I can speak for myself when I say that such incidents are the worst part of being an editor."

Diana wrote Quentin Anderson that she was not at all pleased with Steve's "conduct," and she faulted what she called his belief that "he is the purest of spirits and one's loyal friend." She added, "There was a time when I tried to make him see that he was working both sides of the street, but I had, finally, to give up the effort as hopeless." She had been disappointed in his reaction to her essay on Ginsberg (first admiring it and then remaining silent over the storm) and said that, ever since, their relationship had been "precarious and necessarily attenuated." Anderson had been harsh with Marcus, telling him to put up or shut up—resign from *Partisan Review* or "take a stand in print." Marcus replied "that no intellectual issue of gravity was involved." (Several years later, when Marcus asked Lionel for his opinion of an article he had written, one Lionel thought was "very pretentious," Lionel, in a vindictive tone, wrote in his journal that he had lied about his judgment of the article and noted how Marcus had "leaped for the lie.")

William Phillips wrote Diana, stalling with four paragraphs of gossip and news before he could tell her: "I had to walk a tightrope when I wrote to Fraser. I told him that of course we could not censor his review . . . but that I personally felt it was quite harsh." Phillips told Diana, "I've also asked a couple of people to write letters. I should add that not all the editors know that I've done this."

Diana, who now, more than ever, enjoyed throwing her weight around, did not want to appear vulnerable to Phillips and told him she was not really upset with Fraser's review. It was important to her to remain tough in his mind, although she told him it was "sweet" of him to have worried on her behalf—and that she was grateful for the added paragraph, which she found "soothing."

After much back-and-forthing Diana decided not to reply to the review, and she wanted also to stop Elinor Hays from writing a letter of protest. Elinor was beside herself for such statements as "Mrs. Trilling's own concept of civilization is, it seems to me, not only Freudian, but typically both Jewish and Puritan" and for Fraser's blunt name calling: Diana was "smug, ungracious, contemptuous, condescending, judgmental, incoherent." Additionally, Fraser wrote that Diana (in her essay on the Hiss case) "did not consider what seems to me the most interesting possibility, that Hiss really was a fellow-traveller, and that Chambers knew it (and a new fanaticism being just as unscrupulous as an old one) had no hesitation in framing him."

But in the end Diana decided that, after all, she absolutely needed to write a letter (as did Elinor, although her letter was never printed), so Diana asked Phillips to give her "a good bit of space" in the next issue, and she told Phillips she could not promise to be "impersonal." Indeed, Diana said that on rereading the review, she thought it was beneath *PR*'s standards to print it and that the magazine would have been "entirely" justified in refusing to print it. In addition, before it was determined that Elinor's letter would not be printed, Diana did a little fine-tuning of it— she changed "pomposity" to "complacency," as when Elinor wrote, "Literary malice can have its charm, but when, as here, it is combined with a lack of critical perception which mistakes self-irony for 'complacency,' it hardly deserves to be in your pages." Diana told Elinor that "nobody (yet) has used the word 'pomposity" of my Ginsberg essay . . . so your use of the word would be adding to the vocabulary of invective."

Diana eventually composed a detailed ten-page letter addressing each and every one of Fraser's criticisms. Fraser replied to each of her points, and name-calling went on. He wrote that he was not, as she said of him, "a sort of improvising existentialist. In fact, I am very much of a traditionalist," adding that "like Arnold," I believe in the "free play of mind." He further wrote that he had no "covert motives as a spokesman of some political or literary group for my attitude to your book. Have you never met anybody who—without any 'material interests'—in Conrad's sense, being involved—disliked you freely, spontaneously, and disinterestedly?" And, he concluded, Diana Trilling just would not—could not—take any responsibility for what *he*—Fraser!—was saying.

Putting aside her disappointment with many of her reviews in America, Diana wrote Elsa from her Oxford typing table that "the highlight of our current life is that Lionel got off the ms. of a new volume of essays," and she asked Elsa if she liked the title. (She did.) Lionel's book, *Beyond Culture*, would be published in 1965 by Viking. Diana was more excited about his publication than hers.

She wrote Elsa that "at the moment he struggles to revise and strengthen the last essay which is the lecture he gave . . . at Cambridge, and he still must do a tiny preface." Although Lionel still grappled with his writing, Diana said, she did just moderate editing on that book, a great deal of it before they actually left for Oxford. The rest she completed at Oxford. Some sensitive critics of Lionel's work believe that a certain "sludginess" exists in a number of the essays. This is most likely attributable to Diana's not helping him enough; after all, she was working on her own collection. "He needed me in his criticism," Diana said firmly, "and he knew he had problems." Analysis had "taken the edge off his writing difficulties" and had helped somewhat with his depression, "but not enough."

The New York Review of Books attacked *Beyond Culture* in what was considered by many a patronizing review. In a reply to several letters to the editor, the reviewer, Robert Mazzocco, a poet, said that Lionel Trilling is a splendid literary critic and literary historian, but as a "thinker"

Mazzocco had his doubts. Diana was told that as a personal favor to Lionel, one letter in his defense was printed without asking for the reviewer to respond.

Diana would do much more extensive editing on the book Lionel would publish seven years later, *Sincerity and Authenticity*, his six Norton lectures, delivered while he was the Charles Eliot Norton Professor of Poetry at Harvard. However, she said that during their year in Oxford Lionel "lectured vaguely on the themes of sincerity and authenticity, playing with this book in some way, but he hadn't really written the lectures at all; he had to do this while he was in residence at Harvard [1969–70]."

Diana understood that in England she was a celebrity "of a very limited kind," doing her "quiet, serious work," and she was pleased that she was rarely excluded from events. "I was invited with Lionel all the time." Thelma gushed in a letter that "we love the clear sound of your lives." Diana wrote Elinor that when Lionel was toasted at a male-only event, the master of ceremonies "talked all about his distinguished wife, whom they were glad to have in Oxford with him." She had also earlier confessed to Elinor that he "went to his first do on Saturday night and came home two hours later than he had said, *reeling* drunk. I hope my response to that Initiation will protect me against repetition!!! He had another [party] tonite."

A newspaper in Edinburgh asked Diana to write an essay comparing Oxford and Columbia cultures. She was also asked by the Oxford Critical Society to give a talk on Edward Albee, and she used a lecture on Albee's *Who's Afraid of Virginia Woolf?* she had first delivered to the Radcliffe Club of Princeton in the spring of 1963. She told her audience she was not an expert in the theater but would talk about the play "as a document of contemporary society" and that she was certain that playgoers said what they thought of any given performance right off the bat, while readers of novels waited for critics to help them decide what they thought. She argued that "the message of Mr. Albee's play couldn't be more terrible: life is nothing, and we must have the courage to face our emptiness without fear. Yet his play is a spectacular success. . . . Why?" She said that Albee's view of the world confirms the audience's sense of victimization and that Albee tells us we have nothing to be ashamed of in terms of our transgressions. Diana went straight to the point: "It is not our fault."

She wrote Elsa that her talk "was successful in the sense of my having held my respectable own against their concerted wish to preserve Albee against attack. It was a hot question period, but you would have been satisfied with my performance." Later, under the auspices of the State Department, she was invited to give the same lecture in Amsterdam, and she wrote Elinor that "Holland's leading literary critic [Diana does not name the person] addressed not a word to me, only to Lionel—I felt I was back in America!"

Diana wrote Elinor that the women of Oxford "don't rebel against the male supremacy," as they do in America, and under certain circumstances neither did Diana. Because in England she felt secure about her literary position, she liked the after-dinner tradition of the women departing upstairs for the hostess's bedroom and the men departing to drink their port. This ritual did not offend her as it often did in New York because she said she got to know the other women and then later got to talk to the men whom she hadn't met at dinner, a dinner where her partners on either side "had the responsibility to entertain her throughout the dinner." She told Elinor that "all the men at these gatherings pay far more attention to me than I ever was used to in New York." England had some sort of sorcerer's charm for her. (She later told Elsa that she thought "there was a kind of polarization of sexual feeling in the [American] community as a result of women's liberation.")

Diana was particularly impressed that the husbands helped during the dinner. At one very fancy party hosted by a headmaster, the husband and his grown son did all the serving. "That made me laugh," Diana said, "because they thought they were following the American pattern, and I was trying to remember when I had ever seen a husband get up from a table in America." She said that Lionel helped more than other husbands, but he did so "behind the scenes until the company came. He would help me clean the vegetables, clean the house and set the table, polish the silver," but once the guests arrived, he sat, not wanting his friends to see him helping in any way. And despite her father seeming to be forward-thinking about his daughters always being self-sufficient, she eventually admitted that he "would have thought it the most humiliating thing in the world to get himself a glass of water; and he didn't know how to make himself a cup of tea." But Diana later told Elsa that while they were in Oxford Lionel did not help her as he used to, even behind the scenes, and that from the time they returned to New York from Oxford "there was a steady diminution of any participation in the household. It was as if he felt that he had to conserve his energies for work as he got older."

Diana once asked Iris Murdoch why she had been told to expect nothing but rejection while they were in England. Surprisingly, Murdoch answered that Oxford "is a wonderful place for women like us, women who are professionally established in their own right." The English had heard of Diana's work, that was the main thing, and she later concluded that it "was absolutely a wonderful year for me. I think I enjoyed it more than Lionel did." There was mischief, too, as when one of the Fellows from another college asked her to dinner alone." Diana wrote Elinor that he told her "that'll show 'em how to treat women!" At another dinner she met the only female Fellow, who also asked her to dinner, telling Diana that "the rule is that a woman can be invited only if she is asked 'in her own professional right.' Therefore if she asked Lionel there might be the question whether I was there in my own right or as his wife."

Jim, now sixteen, had come to England with his parents. While the family was still in New York, C. P. Snow had advised Diana on all the suitable schools and said he thought Westminster was his personal preference, especially since Jim "would be within easy taxi reach of us and other friends, which might be useful. Westminster 'boys' are often free for a couple of hours around tea time." As it turned out, Jim loved Westminster, but the school was in London, and an hour and a half from Oxford, so not an easy taxi ride.

After Diana's lecture in Holland, when Jim was on a school break, the three Trillings traveled to Paris, where, Diana wrote Elinor, "Li and Jim were strangely resistant, and a nuisance in the early days. . . . I'm afraid we are not as a family very avid travelers. Lionel, especially, is very restless and muted, sort of turned inward on himself in strange surroundings." Diana said that both Jim and Lionel were "overwhelmed with anxiety," and all they wanted to do was read in the hotel room.

A few years earlier, Jim, an avid cello player, had given up playing it, to his mother's great disappointment, because although he played well, he couldn't seem to tune the instrument himself. Diana later discussed the situation with Leo Lerman in one of their almost daily phone chats. Lerman recorded in his diary that Diana told him that Jim "could have had a brilliant musical career, not as a soloist, but as a member of a quartet," and that this never happened because Jim found it "unbearable" to have his mother, "with her perfect pitch," tune it for him. Lerman also noted that Diana told him that Jim refused to give the cello away and then wrote, "So the instrument remains a permanent monument of this son's hatred of his mother. 'There's something in me he really loathes,' Di told me months ago; 'we're friends, but he hates me.'" (Jim Trilling later commented that this statement is an example of why he began to be at odds with his mother. "I hated practicing; part of it was I wasn't given pieces I liked. And how could I explain I had talent but didn't have an ear? The problem was impatience and frustration. But why did my mother have to make it personal? '*He hates me*'? She often did that.")

Jim was doing well at Westminster, away from his parents, although Diana often wrote her friends that there remained much pushing and pulling between them. Still, she said, Jim was beginning to grow out of his difficult, sometimes out-of-control, behavior. Lionel noted in his journal that he thought his and Diana's sometimes "joint derogatory remarks about their closest friends," as well as years of "expressed exasperation" toward his [Lionel's] mother had had a bad effect on Jim, "leading him to disrespect."

In the spring of 1965 Norman and Adele Mailer (his second wife) were scheduled to visit the Trillings in Oxford, and Diana wanted to impress him with a lavish dinner at the faculty dining room. But Norman wrote her: "Oh, Diana, I know you. You're such a devil, fully aware of my wild British reputation, you will say, 'Norman Mailer is coming to tea on April 20th,' and your Oxford friends will say, 'Are you out of your mind, Diana?'" Mailer requested a small party, and Diana agreed. One of the guests was Iris Murdoch, and Diana said Mailer wanted to discuss how to dramatize novels with her, but Murdoch found his questioning of her offensive. Diana said Mailer was completely confused by her attitude and was hurt by it. "She was really being very unpleasant with him, I had never seen her that way—she was always very pleasant with me."

Still, on the whole the party was a big success, and Diana wrote Mailer afterward that the guests "adored" him. She told him also she had felt slightly jealous that they had taken to him, and Mailer replied, "Bless you for your jealousy when they said nice things. How human you are, the very last one." (But Diana was all too human; she later wrote Elinor that she hadn't liked *An American Dream*—published in 1965—and thought it was the book of "an insane man.")

Diana awaited the English publication of *Claremont Essays* with some trepidation. As it would turn out, the reviews there also had an edge that was painful to her: she lacked originality. She was too romantic. She saw things "smudgily." She used "too many manufactured portmanteau Americanisms," one reviewer wrote, meaning words like *self-reference*, *self-evaluation, self-discipline, self-delusion, self-definition, self-mythologizing*, or *self-pity*. A reviewer for *The Guardian* called her vocabulary "too permissive," saying it would "baffle British readers."

But the review that incensed her the most was one by the novelist, poet, and critic A. Alvarez, in *The Observer*, which stated up front that in comparison with Hannah Arendt, Elizabeth Hardwick, and Mary McCarthy, "Diana Trilling is less original." Furthermore, he said, "she is a victim of cultural circumstances" in which "her writing is now settled into a comfortable, established, psychoanalyzed maturity." This was certainly not flattery; Alvarez, whose parents tried to kill themselves when he was a child, never saw psychoanalysis as a harbinger of everlasting wisdom.

Diana wrote a letter published in the paper a week later, saying that Alvarez had not only distorted her work but vulgarized it. That was the end of that—what else could she do? After all, "psychoanalyzed maturity" was what she had always wished for! Still, she wrote Elsa Grossman that she was certain "people are embarrassed seeing me—they hadn't known I was such a monster. . . . If only, like Hannah Arendt, I had influential friends to protest on my behalf. But maybe here, as at home, when *my* friends protest, they'd not be printed."

She looked inside her own family and decided, as she wrote in *The Beginning of the Journey*, that she had a "simpler explanation of why my marriage may have detracted from my literary recognition." She concluded that "people will celebrate one member of a household but not two."

Lionel didn't leave enough room for Diana to be lionized.

Decades later, Alfred Kazin would describe Diana in a memoir cruelly as "a dogged woman and looked it," and he would go on to attack her frequent letters to the editor, saying that "sometimes she wrote in to criticize an unfavorable review of a book for not being unfavorable enough." He continued that with this seething sense of her "intellectual political righteousness," Diana "always seemed more alert to the wrongdoings of other intellectuals than to the beauty of the creative art." Diana said that Kazin's dislike of her enraged Lionel, who almost punched him when Kazin said that Lionel should disassociate himself "from that wife of yours." But Diana had to learn to live with such denigrations. In his book *Ex-Friends* Norman Podhoretz quoted from a letter Mary McCarthy wrote to Hannah Arendt about Diana, in which she called Diana a "fool" whose recent letter to the editor should have been thrown into the wastebasket, but it wasn't—only because of her marriage to Lionel.

Diana was almost sixty and had pretty much accepted life's disappointments and obstructions. She had a good year in England but was glad to be back on American soil again. Fortunately, the only debilitating phobia that lingered was her fear of heights, which had not been a problem for her while she was in Oxford. Writer Stephen Koch remembers going to a party held on the ninth floor of a building in New York, and Diana was present "because the windows were covered with blankets so it was like a padded cell—but that's how you got Diana to come up above the second floor."

New physical ailments—migraine headaches and a gall bladder problem—began to plague her. Diana explained that the headaches "would begin sometime around six or seven in the evening. By between seven and nine it would start to get more and more acute and with nausea. By nine I was gritting my teeth to keep from throwing up and by then I had to go to bed. . . . Eventually around midnight I would be so exhausted and fall asleep and wake up newborn the next morning, never felt better, I never felt better in my life than I did the mornings after these migraine attacks."

Toward the end of the 1960s she complained of "fuzziness" in her eyes, a symptom that would be the beginning of serious eye problems.

And there was Lionel to deal with. He continued to blame Diana for everything that went wrong, and she said "his charges against me for being neurotic long outlasted most of my neurosis. . . . My undue dependency on him was all but cured." Yet she strongly maintained that his rages did not carry over into the rest of his relationship with her. His rages "were just crazy talk that passed each time the words erupted," she said resolutely. She concluded that it would take most of her life to realize that "it was a pretty even balance between us emotionally as in every other way. Our neuroses meshed. Yes, sure, Lionel suffered from my neurotic symptoms, but it didn't ruin his life; in fact his life wasn't ruined. And he similarly inflicted his neurotic symptoms on me. In the long run it evened out. Obviously if it hadn't we wouldn't have stayed together the way we did."

"We were a ritualistic pair, and as long as Lionel lived, we celebrated our wedding anniversary," she wrote. "We did this even in years when we were little in the mood for celebration of any kind." She believed that marriage "was the greatest invention of civilized man . . . but, to give up sexual experience, adventure, for the sake of your marriage is very sad. It's a very big deprivation. I think very few people manage keeping a serious marriage going while being unfaithful. You have to be an awfully good liar and you have to have a husband who's not home all the time the way mine was. You can't be married to a writer or a teacher; you at least have to be married to a traveling salesman."

The last line of a letter Lionel wrote his wife when he was giving a lecture out of town speaks volumes about the complexity of their life together: "Do be happy, Sweet. I love being away from you to think about you. Lionel."

Diana never found the perfect man (as she had fantasized at Radcliffe) who tea-danced (or remained faithful), but as she wrote in an unpublished book, "Lionel would have been willing to dance had I encouraged him, but he danced badly. Even for a literary man he danced badly. But how could he not have liked to tea-dance at the Plaza? It would have been field work in F. Scott Fitzgerald." But the Trillings did go to concerts and operas together, "always in the top balcony," as Diana had envisioned while at college.

In 1966 the Trillings were invited to Truman Capote's Black and White masquerade Ball at the Plaza Hotel. They had met Capote in the early 1940s at one of Leo Lerman's soirees. A few years later, Newton Arvin, who also knew the Trillings from Lerman's parties, wrote Diana to ask if he could bring his new lover—Capote—to her dinner party. Gerald Clarke, Capote's biographer, writes that Diana gave Arvin "a firm no," adding that she "indignantly answered" that "when I want anybody to come to my house to dinner, I invite them." Clarke goes on to write that "Newton angrily showed her reply to Truman who tore it up. 'Of course you have to go anyway,' Truman told him, and Newton did."

Lionel, at sixty-one, "discovered [at the Ball] there was another way of dancing rather than just holding a woman and guiding," Diana told Thelma Anderson. He could basically dance by himself. "You could do something by yourself, which was very free and relaxed," Diana wrote Thelma, adding that the partner "just moved back and forth while a woman spun around or didn't or did things with her hands in the air or didn't, and that all a man had to do was shuffle his feet a little bit. And Lionel was dancing perfectly adequately."

He did not stop dancing that night at the Plaza. "He danced with everyone in sight," Diana told Thelma, and he later announced that because "I didn't teach him the right kind of dancing . . . it was all my fault." Once again, Diana was the wrongdoer. Diana was to blame. Even at the Plaza. Even after Lionel learned to dance on his own.

15

AT A TABLE

Perhaps this was the act of courage he was facing all his life, and
Diana replied: "Perhaps the act of courage he was facing all his
life was to stay alive."

—LIONEL TRILLING, JOURNAL ENTRY, 1961 (RE: HEMINGWAY'S SUICIDE)

I n 1967 the Trillings, under the auspices of the Ford Foundation and
a German organization called Atlantik-Brucke [Atlantic-Bridge],
went on a two-week mission to promote German-American good-
will. The delegation was made up of Irving Kristol (who was in charge);
Midge Decter; her husband, Norman Podhoretz; Dwight MacDonald;
Stanley Kauffman, then the film critic of *The New Republic*; Richard
Rovere, a critic for *The New Yorker*; his wife, Eleanor; the writer Harvey
Swados; the writer and critic George P. Elliott; and Daniel Patrick
Moynihan, who would become a US senator for New York a decade
later. (Gertrude Himmelfarb, Kristol's wife, was not on the trip.)

Although Decter, along with her husband, Norman Podhoretz, was
part of the group, as was Eleanor Rovere, Diana wrote Elsa Grossman
that she was the only female member. She wondered if she'd be regarded
as a writer or a wife and told Elsa that "the American officials are in a

tizzy trying to resolve the dilemma." (Diana later said that Decter and Eleanor Rovere, who, she said, "was totally self-effacing and expected to be paid no attention to whatsoever," came along at their own expense and were not official members of the delegation.)

Diana was not prone to out-and-out lying, only to the occasional dramatic exaggeration to make a point. What point was she making to Elsa about the trip, that she needed to say she was the only woman? Did she mean the only *official* one? Did it galvanize her to appear to be the lone woman in a sea of men? Was she anxious to be counted equal to the men? After all, she once said that "most of the men I know in the intellectual community are much better read, much better informed," than she was and that she "was brought up to be deferential to men and to think that men knew all kinds of things that women couldn't possibly know, and that their minds worked better."

Was she challenging her sense of self-worth? Was she simply expressing how alone she felt despite having Lionel by her side? Or was there a veiled agenda?

At the time, the Trillings and the Podhoretzes were "very, very close," Podhoretz later said, and there was no reason for Diana to feel abandoned or left out. Decter said that despite Diana's intelligence and sensitivity she "always stood at an odd angle" to the literary community. "She was not given a fair shake," Decter pointed out, "and at the same time she responded by not giving a fair shake to many people who no doubt deserved it. But it put a funny color on her relations with the world in which she lived."

Diana once explained: "When I talk, I talk very sharply and very decisively. I don't mumble around. I come to the point. And rather fast. That is my manner. And since I'm already usually irritated because the men in the room aren't getting to the point fast enough, I will sound even faster, and a little fiercer than I actually am." She was always trying to push away her instinctive submissiveness.

Decter concluded that Diana was "too complicated for me to ever be sure I understood what she was up to—or that *she* ever did." She added that "ultimately I joined the ever-growing army of people with whom Diana had a falling-out (in my case, in defense of my husband)."

Diana had once told Podhoretz he wasn't interested in literature; that what interested him the most was power. "This could not have endeared me to him," she admitted. "I have a way of saying things like that and expecting people to never think about it again." She also remembered "this was at the height of Norman Podhoretz's radical days, and it was right after he had sent *Making It** to Lionel, and Lionel had told him to put it aside. Now here we were traveling together, and this was sort of hanging over us, not to be referred to." On the goodwill mission, Diana would find it hard to consider Podhoretz's wife an official delegate, although she really was, so Diana, at least in her correspondence, excluded her.

The group started out in Hamburg, staying in one of that city's most attractive hotels. ("A dream of old-fashioned elegance," Diana said.) They then traveled to Berlin, Düsseldorf, Bonn, and Munich. "We're always on the go," Diana wrote Elsa, "meeting with the Mayors, big shot publishers, and bankers." The group was given tickets to the opera, theater, movies, and concerts. They visited many museums, and even a Night Club in Berlin.

Diana later described the trip as "one of the most sexually invidious experiences of my life where I was simply excluded from what was my professional right to be involved in. I never saw anything like that in Oxford." She complained that at a dinner with an industrialist from the Ruhr region, she was kept away from the after-dinner discussion, with the host telling her, "But Madam, we do it this way in Germany. We keep the wives away from our business." Diana was hurt and frustrated that "no male member of the company protested my exclusion," not even her husband. "He was upset for me but his public behavior was no different than the others. . . . I guess I've never had any situation as a Jew which equals this for humiliation. I've never had any anti-Semitism directed

---

* Published in 1967, this was Norman Podhoretz's frank, controversial autobiography of ambition and opportunity. Although not asked to read the manuscript, Diana did (with Lionel's consent) and agreed with her husband that Norman's "central polemical point, that success was the dirty secret in our society, not sex, was a perfectly sound point . . . [but] for this point to be properly presented it shouldn't be couched in journalism. Lionel just realized this as an inferior kind of literary work and he felt that it would be harmful to Norman's career."

to me which is the equivalent of the anti-femalism [*sic*] that was directed to me on that occasion, and throughout the trip but especially on that occasion. It is the most painful experience of being discriminated against that I've ever had in my life." She later said even though she always "deferred a great deal to the men around me, she came to wonder whether any of them are quite as smart as I am," despite their being better informed.

After the dinner with the industrialist, when Diana was excluded, she, Midge Decter, and Eleanor Rovere were eventually allowed to sit in a balcony overlooking the library where the men were congregated. She noticed that Lionel was not sitting at the table with the men but on the steps. "This was his way of trying to show that he was trying to make a bridge between us," she said. "But it wasn't a very effective means of action." Eventually, the host looked up at the balcony and asked the women if perhaps they had any "childcare" or "health" questions. Diana, wanting revenge, decided to ask a tough question about trade unions, "which threw the whole place into a commotion." The host ("a Nazi at heart whatever he was politically") blushed and stammered and finally said, "I'm afraid I can't answer that at the moment." Diana later wrote, "It was the most politically indiscreet thing I could have asked, and I did it purposely. It was a very quiet revenge; half the people didn't know what was going on." But Diana's "quiet" rebellious conduct did bring about a small change when the group had an interview in Bonn with the chancellor, Kurt Georg Kiesinger. Before the meeting, while the group was waiting in an anteroom, an aide walked up to Diana and told her that because of her age—she was sixty-two—she would be asked to sit at the right of the chancellor. Even though Diana realized that the government used her age as an excuse to place a woman nearby, she was pleased that the person she considered the only legitimate female delegate—herself— was placed at the table.

Diana grumbled to Elsa about the amount of food they had to eat out of politeness everywhere they went. "Each of us in turn had now been violently ill, but manfully, and womanfully, we continue doing our duty. And when we are not eating, we have to talk, talk, talk." She wrote about the student demonstrations against the "recrudescence of Nazism" they saw in Berlin and about how the arrival of their group "meant a great deal, and in fact, we seem to have had a considerable political influence" in terms of newspaper coverage. The group understood a new Nazism *could* be forming, and demonstrations like those in Berlin were necessary to stop any possibility of its reemergence. She added in a postscript that she thought Berlin was a "terribly ugly city. As for the wall, it must be seen to be believed—no pictures can give you any sense of its actual horror."

In the essay she wrote on the mission for *The Atlantic*'s April 1967 cover story, Diana said that "however disparate our temperaments or our political emphases, we were plainly a group made coherent by our shared suspicions of Germany's capacity for political health. . . . We had not forgotten, nor could we forget, that we were in the country which had been able to devise, and implement, Nazism." She described the German personality as "a kind of layer cake—plausibility on top of denial (in the psychoanalytical meaning) on top of guilt on top of carefully masked anger." She said the cities she visited seemed "not to breathe." The modern architecture "rises, in my view, like a monument to extinction: denying the past, it already memorializes the future." She underlined that only in Bonn was she "able to re-create for myself any sense of a pre-Hitler Germany." She later said that the whole time she was in Germany, she felt she was in "an alien world," and the country looked nothing like the one she had visited with her parents and siblings when she was a child.

In Midge Decter's essay in *The Atlantic* she said that she found the Germans "obsessed with Nazism," and when the subject came up, which was often, they responded with "extreme irritation, self-pity, claims of innocence, attacks on the sins of others, references to their sufferings during the war, and the young, of course, by announcing the year of their birth." Decter also described in moving detail a visit to Dachau concentration camp. "My rage at the Germans was now direct," she wrote, "and in an answering way, of human proportion."

Decter later said that she couldn't "remember whether the Trillings were with us or not on the trip to Dachau; everybody else in the group was." Diana never mentioned Dachau anywhere. Her essay made only one reference to a concentration camp. When describing a Catholic church she visited in Berlin, she wrote that "its courtyard reproduces the approach to a concentration camp; its interior is stark and terrible in its modernity, the eternal Church symbolized to a single piece of traditional sculpture, a fourteenth century wooden Virgin standing quietly at peace near the bare altar." Diana was trying desperately to accept a reality she could not fully comprehend. She concluded: "Here, because there was no attempt to disguise, only the wish to confront, the full awful truth of the recent past, one might indeed feel fortified for the future." Diana relied on her secret desire to be a Catholic (as well as her fascination with the Virgin Mary) to help her understand—as well as to conceal—the horror she was confronting on the trip, and a visit to Dachau would have been more than she could bear of "the full awful truth of the recent past."

Diana had once written a letter to *The New York Times* criticizing an editorial about the death of Dorothy Thompson, the celebrated journalist who had been expelled from Germany in 1934. Diana felt that the newspaper "failed to memorialize her as she deserves." She said that Thompson "did more than any other individual, or group of individuals, in this country to alert the public to the menace of Nazism in a period when isolationism and inertia might otherwise have had their way with us." The savagery of the Nazis was often on Diana's mind, and she wrote about it in her own special manner and form, even though her letter was never published.

Midge Decter said that "the whole journey to Germany was a very special thing for Diana, who up to that point had hardly been able to venture above the ground floor of a New York apartment building, let alone fly in the sky, and thus we were all both encouraging of and attentive to her." But evidently not encouraging enough, or attentive enough. Diana felt forlorn on the trip, disheartened. The fib to Elsa Grossman served to take the edge off what was really troubling her. It was not necessarily being in Germany—although that was hard enough for her—or being in the company of so many distinguished men. Despite her attempt to be always outspoken, inwardly she was still the girl who was warned not to be a smarty-pants. During the trip to Germany she felt her debating skills had diminished somewhat even though she could continue to see "the logical flaws in the positions that people are taking."

The real reason Diana was troubled during the trip—the hidden agenda—was that she was basically jealous. "In no time at all Midge had established herself as one of the prominent members of the group and had edged me out," Diana said. She tried to get used to the situation but said that "she had found no way to cope with it. . . . When we sat at long tables I discovered that of course Midge was sitting near all the important people, and I was virtually sitting by myself." The important exception had been the meeting with the chancellor, and Diana had been more than pleased that she had edged Midge out on that one, even if it took her age to do the job.

Another thing rankled her: one of the literary people the group met (she doesn't say who) had only heard of Norman Podhoretz, and was thrilled to meet him, but "had never heard of Lionel or me. . . . Norman Podhoretz was the big cultural news." How could this be? Diana wondered. Who were these people that had suddenly sidelined her and Lionel? What did this say about their reputations, *their* reputations?

She wouldn't allow herself to dwell on it. She'd remember the best of times in Oxford, feelings that had sustained her after their return to New York in late 1965.

After her own book publication in America and then in England, and after Lionel's publication of *Beyond Culture*, she worked on and off on an article comparing British and American television. It was published in *The Atlantic* in 1967, the same year as the reports on the trip to Germany. Her ideas mattered.

The Trillings had bought their first television set in the mid-1950s, and Diana said that she "would watch television with Jim in the late afternoon and also over the weekends." She would "watch all sorts of things: cowboy movies and baseball games. . . . There was a period in which I knew quite a lot about baseball because I used to watch." As Jim got older, she "began to watch things she wanted to see, like *Hawaii Five-O*. . . . And Lionel would come into the room and sit down and watch, sometimes for five minutes sometimes for fifteen, but he would never feel the need to watch out a full film the way I did. He would then get up and go to his room and do whatever he was doing."

She wrote in a letter that she eventually became "a TV addict"—and her favorite shows were detective and medical dramas, from *The Nurses*, a series that ended in 1967, to *Starsky and Hutch*, which began in 1972, and *Hill Street Blues*, which began in 1981.

Diana began her TV article by saying that "it always comes as startling news to the British that an American visitor can find their television so vastly superior to our own." That opening contained the whole premise of her twenty-six-page appraisal, although British TV didn't score all the points—America had more channels, and more technical virtuosity. But British TV had very few commercials, since it was primarily government-owned, and Diana was particularly impressed that "there is no British TV aimed at the bored housewife—no soap operas, no shopping quizzes." She also praised British TV for instilling a feeling of intimacy in its programming, especially in its political news, which "is reported on the air as if it were an immediate family matter." Certain programs dispensed with objectivity, and Diana liked that the broadcaster of a story about a brutal headmaster did not hide his feelings of revulsion. It was the same about programs dealing with sexual matters, which were treated with "unsensational frankness." American TV evades reality, she said, while British TV never did. The series she enjoyed the most during her stay in Oxford was Galsworthy's *Forsyte Saga*, which was so popular that "all classes" clamored to it. "Everywhere I went in England the latest episode was the topic of talk, as how could it not be—the series represented a new high in the adaptation of fiction to the popular screen."

Diana also praised the "concreteness" of British television—in fact, of all of England, from its shops to its buses, lanes, and streets.

Writing about British television emboldened Diana. In February of 1968 she wrote a letter to Bill Beutel of WABC-TV News castigating the station for an appearance the journalist Jimmy Breslin made on the eleven o'clock news in which he commented on the ongoing New York City sanitation strike and did so in a way that she believed showed contempt for the audience. Breslin sometimes used language that was offensive to just about everyone. It was considered by many his trademark, in fact. His presentation was "grotesque," Diana said, and insulting to the audience. She wanted her letter passed on to the executives in charge. Mr. Beutel took three months to reply and then told Diana he had indeed passed along her letter but knew of no action taken "one way or another." But he, himself, he wrote her, was moving to London in ten days to become the London correspondent for ABC News and was planning to read her article on British TV in preparation for his new job. Jimmy Breslin, as far as it is known of the incident, just went on being Jimmy Breslin, never evading the reality that Diana in fact thought American TV should show more of.

Diana wanted to continue writing at length about issues and events that had social significance. She had not paid much attention to the 1960s counterculture—the social pressures involving authority, warfare, women's rights, and the unfolding of the New Left. Antiestablishment events were widespread in the United States and Britain, with much of the dissent centered in London, New York, and Berkeley, California, where the Free Speech Movement was conceived.

Diana decided to look in her own backyard, especially after her return from Oxford. The Columbia University protests of 1968, in which students occupied five buildings to protest the Vietnam War—specifically the university's affiliation with an armaments research think tank—were ripe for Trilling's pen. The students also opposed the university's plans for a new gymnasium that they argued would be segregated by limiting its access to Harlem's African American residents, even though it was to be built on public land.

The *Columbia Spectator*'s editorial page announced on the second day of the student demonstrations, "The bedraggled and apparently bewildered administrators seem to make a wrong decision every time an opportunity presents itself." The student paper reported that there was not even "a glimmer of intelligent action." Diana was appalled by the events. By day three, the paper reported, plainclothes police hiding billy clubs under their clothing charged a line of faculty members, but by the following day a preliminary panel of faculty members had been formed to help deal with the growing crisis.

Lionel, at the time the George Edward Woodberry Professor of Literature and Criticism (in 1970 he would become a University Professor,

Columbia's highest honor), was one of twelve faculty members hoping to find a basis for a speedy settlement with the students. Diana remembered that "nobody looked to anybody on this committee as a moral leader except for one person: Lionel." No faculty member could walk through the streets without a police escort. "Lionel resented being brought home by the police," Diana said, adding that "I've never seen Lionel so exhilarated as he was—that's from the very first morning after he came home after being up all night. . . . He slept for two hours, got up and went back and was up for the next twenty-four hours. And he wasn't the least bit tired." She commented that "everybody was having a good time if you want to put it uglily. I mean a university was being destroyed; many careers were destroyed in those weeks. . . . Even someone as serious as Lionel was having a good time. It was exciting. It was like being on the barricades. . . . It was like being in the army. . . . And Lionel admitted this to me all the time. He never used the words 'having a good time,' but he really got a kick out of it. . . . They had a sense of living intensely and of living in a critical situation in which important decisions had to be made on the spot." But the mildly conciliatory solutions of his—and another larger—committee were not accepted by the administration, and a thousand police were called in to oust the students by force.

It was treacherous and violent. Blood had been shed. There was a faculty strike. Classes were cancelled. But within days the president of Columbia, Grayson Kirk, ordered all police off the campus, and over time, the university began to consider restructuring. A university Senate—one including faculty, administrators, and students—was created. Some of the student demands were met—the gym was never built—and the students were promised better communication with the administration. The relationship between the university and Harlem improved. The university severed all ties to the military. Peace, of a sort, prevailed, although the university's reputation (and fund-raising efforts) plummeted for a long while afterward.

Did the university become too liberal as a result of the highly publicized student disturbances? Did it lose its center as a place of intellectual debate? These were two of the questions that Diana decided to tackle in an essay about the Columbia protests. She cited John Dewey's definition of manners as "small morals" and went on to say that "a significant part of my opposition to the uprising derives from my translation of its manners into morals." She said that her goal was "to generate some serious discussion on the problem of the future of liberalism in democracies."

She wanted *The New Yorker* to be her publisher, although she admitted to editor William Shawn that she had an arrangement with *The Atlantic*, but they wanted a piece drastically shorter than the one she had in mind. But Shawn passed, even though the essay was not yet finished. She hoped then that the completed piece could be published in *Harper's*, but Midge Decter, an editor there, told her that as "splendid and full of spine and care" as it was, the magazine would not be able to use it. And despite her telling Diana that she didn't think *Commentary* would be able to use it either, because they had already commissioned such an article, the magazine (edited by her husband, Norman Podhoretz) did indeed publish Diana's essay.

Diana began her essay, which she titled "On the Steps of Low Library," by explaining why she borrowed Norman Mailer's title for his piece in *Harper's* called "The Steps of the Pentagon" (later published in book form as *The Armies of the Night*). Diana said that "the two events, Mailer's and the university's, were continuous with each other in political and moral style." She concluded that the revolution at Columbia "was no more a liberal than a Marxist revolution and that, indeed, it was a revolution *against* liberalism, which in actual effect polarized the University between the radical position . . . and a conservative position." She wondered whether liberalism still mattered or had gone as far as it could. She explained no further.

Norman Mailer's name is a leitmotif throughout Trilling's sweeping, detailed examination of the uprising. Very few people found fault with the essay, except for its exceptional length, and one person, she said, criticized her for never joining the March on the Pentagon in the fall of 1967. In a letter she explained that although she was against the war, "I cannot make a united front with the anti-Americanism which provides the overarching principle of all 'active' protest of our Vietnam engagement, nor adopt its strategies. . . . Most important of all, I will not march under the flag of the Viet Cong."

Her essay elicited several harsh letters from Robert Lowell, who thought Diana was "not too much on target" and that "all's twisted in the current of ignorant, unseeing didacticism, in the rattled sentences." In a follow-up letter he told her that her article was "haunted with apprehension," as well as "bristling with the professional logic of prosecution." He ended by telling Diana that "controversy is bad for the mind and worse for the heart." Naturally, she did not agree.

In a letter she wrote to *The New York Review of Books*, about an essay by F. W. Dupee on the uprisings, she faulted Dupee for not announcing in his "first person account" that "he had decided to leave the campus and the city at that time because of his disgust with the behavior of the revolutionary students." She knew this because he had phoned her to tell her that he was leaving town for a few days. She said that anyone reading the piece would not have guessed its author had any doubts about the conduct of the students. He should have included his reservations in his essay and mentioned that he was so disgusted by what was happening at Columbia that he left the city for a while. But in the end, she decided not to send the letter.

In 1969 Diana and Lionel moved to Cambridge, Massachusetts, for a year when Lionel became the Charles Eliot Norton Professor of Poetry at Harvard, which required that he deliver a series of lectures. Once again, as in Oxford five years earlier, they had excellent housing, staying in one of the three or four oldest houses in Cambridge. Their residence the first semester belonged to Mason Hammond, a well-known Harvard professor of Latin and the history of Rome. Diana loved the house, especially that every room had a fireplace, and she did her best to keep the rooms filled with guests and comforting fires. "To have a fireplace in New York demanded either more bohemianism or more wealth than Lionel and I could ever attain," she wrote in an unpublished book. On trips out of Manhattan she always liked looking at houses in the country and often secretly remodeled them in her mind. She knew that she and Lionel would never be homeowners. Lionel noted in his journal, "My first sense of being poor came the year I spent at Harvard—so many instances of inherited wealth. At Columbia this is very rare."

Lionel delivered his six Norton lectures, which were published in 1972 as *Sincerity and Authenticity*. He noted in his journal that "not one of my friends showed the least interest in my Norton lectures to which the response of strangers was so strong."

Diana said, "The composition of that book was different from anything else Lionel wrote. . . . He didn't write them in advance. He was under awful pressure on the deadlines." She explained how they collaborated:

> On the last one he still didn't have the pages finished, and he got very overwrought and I had to tell him to put the paper in the typewriter and we'd work out the rest of the lecture together. He'd sit next to me and I'd say, "Now what would you want to say about that?" Then he'd say something, and I'd go on: "And what would you say about *that*?" He'd look desperate and he'd say, "Nothing." But I'd keep nagging—"You have to say something," and eventually something would come out which I'd elaborate, with his amending or correcting my suggestions. . . . He'd say, "No, that isn't what I'm saying," and I'd say, "Well, what's wrong with it?" Then he'd say it, and I'd say, "Well, right, why don't you say just that?" It was a tortuous procedure, but the lecture got done.

Jim Trilling commented that his mother "had the ability to turn messes into brilliant prose."

Lionel, who was reluctant to hand out credit, wrote in his journal that "the work situation was, of course, most deplorable. All that resulted from daily repair to my study in the college was not one lecture—sheer hell to bring a semblance of creation with D's help."

Their very close collaboration was far from an isolated instance. Diana had done the same thing with his *Prefaces to the Experience of Literature*, which had been published in 1967. "Lionel had the worst time with them," Diana said. "He didn't really want to do the book; he put it off, lied to himself, lied to me about what he had to do. It was ten years late, and he would have made money if the book had been published on time. The essays were badly written. I virtually wrote the preface."

Perhaps not paradoxically, she was having trouble with her own work. She wanted to have a new book of her own. She submitted a chapter of a book-in-progress about her Radcliffe days (which she eventually titled "The Education of a Woman") to Harcourt, which had been her publisher for *Claremont Essays*. But William Goodman, the executive editor, told her in a blunt letter that it was his "sad duty to return your extraordinary preliminary draft chapter," and the reason given was one often told to writers—there was not a sufficient market for such a book.

Diana was devastated, especially since she was under contract to Harcourt, and both Goodman and William Jovanovich, a friend as well as her publisher, had encouraged her and had liked the early pages she had shown them. She decided it was about money and that they thought she was going to demand more than a minimal advance. So she assured them she did not want a lot of money. The situation was further complicated by the fact that Lionel wanted Harcourt to be *his* publisher. He thought he could extricate himself from Viking, but it turned out not to be possible at the time. A further complication was, as Diana learned, that Jovanovich hadn't ever authorized the rejection of her chapter. In a complete turnaround William Goodman wrote Diana on October 16, 1972, that "Mr. Jovanovich would like to see your book," but because he, himself, had thought that Diana "felt the book had strong commercial possibilities and wanted the ultimate advance to reflect that view," he had rejected the proposal. Diana told Elinor Hays that Harcourt's renewed interest in her had made a "fantastic difference in her ability to work." Nonetheless, the book was rejected again. Two years later Diana asked for a formal release from her contractual obligations in order to find a new publisher. Even though Diana felt betrayed by Jovanovich, she wanted to remain on some sort of cordial terms with him in case she thought of ever returning to him. Whatever the true explanation—business or friendship—his hold on her was enduring.

In 1972 Lionel decided to accept a second invitation to become a Visiting Fellow at Oxford, and the Trillings happily returned, this time to All Souls College. They stayed not in a house but in a comfortable apartment on Crick Road in North Oxford. Diana wrote Elinor Hays that her household routine was similar to the one at Claremont Avenue. Lionel again helped out occasionally, cleaning up the breakfast dishes and shopping for groceries when needed.

Diana felt at home in England right away and told Elinor that she was working well. She was writing a review of a biography of Frieda Lawrence for the *New Statesman*. She was now fully aware that her start at *The Nation* three decades earlier had made her not an "accidental" (her term) writer but a sought-after reviewer whose strength was an ability to interpret literature in three distinct ways—psychologically, socially, and politically—all realized in a single essay.

"Have I told you how satisfying I find Oxford a place to live in this time?" she wrote Elsa Grossman. "And we're not being given the Visiting Fireman treatment like the last time, but perhaps for that very reason I'm liking it even better." She also liked the setting—"just the joy I feel at being able to see sky, grass, trees from every window here on the ground floor and my pleasure in walking around those pretty streets to shop." She told Elinor she'd been the only woman in a short dress at dinner parties, so she went out and bought "a long black and white print dress and a bold black and white wool skirt and two cashmere sweaters." Lionel did some shopping, too, and Diana wrote Elinor that he bought a "stunning" topcoat and rain hat—"he looks beautiful." He bought some shirts and sweaters at Marks and Spencer's department store. "He loved great bargains," Diana told Thelma Anderson, adding the detail that "he loved cotton and wool, and hated synthetics."

Diana felt so content in Oxford that she decided to cut her hair and to let it go gray. The English atmosphere encouraged a new free spirit in her. She liked the openness of the English about certain aspects of child-rearing, writing in a note that "the English talk about education and discuss their anxieties about their growing children even more, and far more openly, less self-protectingly, than we do. They never keep it a secret if their children are having psychiatric help as we do in America. Yet of course there is so much less Freudian 'currency' in conversation than at home. It may be that an English mother, while indeed feeling guilty for the inadequacies of her offspring, is not *as* guilty as an American mother." She even liked the English use of the word *Oh* in conversations, that it was a way "of winning time to think of an answer, covering embarrassment, implying disapproval."

About finances (which were always on her mind) she said that Oxford was "perhaps the only place I've ever known where you can live on what to an American is no money," adding that she had "allotted $600 a month of Li's salary to cover living cost in England—but that she finds it covers much more—certain household equipment plus 'jaunts' to London." Nonetheless, she told Elinor, who handled many chores for the Trillings at their apartment on Claremont Avenue, that they would have to cut the cleaning woman down to just three mornings a week because "this will be the last year of full salary for Lionel, and I must begin to pull in on all fronts." Despite such worries, Diana confessed to Elinor, they were seriously thinking of retiring in Oxford. "To be old is inevitably to be lonely but I do think it better being lonely in pretty rather than sordid surroundings. I read here, hungrily, which I never do in New York, though I know not why not." But the pull of Columbia, New York, and America was stronger than England's, and they returned home for good after their second stay at Oxford.

Not everything had been agreeable in England; one person the Trillings did not revisit was E. M Forster. After a warm visit from him in New York when Jim was an infant, they had gone to see him in Cambridge when they were in Oxford in 1965 because Diana thought Forster would enjoy seeing Jim as a young student. "Well, it wasn't the way one had dreamed such a visit would be. Forster didn't really cotton very much to Jim . . . anyway; he begrudgingly gave us our tea . . . and some fruitcake. And he cut a very, very small piece for each of us, including this hulking sixteen year old, Jim, in a state of acute starvation all the time. Whenever he came down to Oxford, he ate his way through Oxford. . . . Forster didn't offer any more cake, and Jim said, 'Could I take another piece of cake?' very polite—and Jim had really good manners, everyone commented on them—and Forster said 'You'll have it when I offer it to you,' like that in a very unpleasant voice. Lionel and I were revolted by that. It soured the end of the relationship."

At home the cultural wars continued: in May 1973 Arnold Beichman wrote both Trillings that he was going to take their names out of his acknowledgments in his book, *Nine Lies About America,* to spare them embarrassment, and he said he remembered how Diana had removed Norman Podhoretz's name in her D. H. Lawrence letters when it appeared in paperback. There is no record of Diana—or Lionel's—reply. But their names did not appear in the book.

With their *affaires de cœur* behind them, or perhaps still beside them, Diana and Lionel resumed what she called their usual life of closeness. Lionel's life was always the connective tissue of her life, even when she was working on her own. She said that despite everything, "it was the most natural thing in the world for us to take hands. We would walk swinging hands. It wasn't a gesture of people in love but rather of people who loved each other and had lived their lives in that kind of intimacy." They had walked around Oxford and held hands. "It was automatic," she said, even though "I often thought how can I stay married to this man—he's a monster, because we fought all the time. . . . He was still angry at me all the time . . . but the marriage was bigger than both of us." And it remained that until the end.

But the "usual life of closeness" did not have the same significance for Lionel. He noted in his journal a few years later, "it has come to me how little I enjoyed the Oxford year 1972–1973. I was not conscious of this at the time or for as much as a year later."

Diana said that Lionel rarely mentioned writing fiction anymore. She repeated what she said often now: "It's silly to say he could have been or should have been. . . . If a person doesn't do it, then he hasn't done it, that's all. It's silly to sit around saying that Lionel's friend Henry Rosenthal could have been our American Joyce. . . . And it was the same with Lionel: He didn't do it. He told me he just couldn't be as much of a lunatic as Hemingway was."

Diana tried to keep up with her salty letter writing. She told an editor of *The Harvard Advocate* she could not contribute to a publication that used such phrases in a letter as "in the last jot" or "'cliffe loyalty." What was happening to language?! She would not stand for such expressions, ever. Except perhaps, for the English *Oh.*

16

JUST CLOSE YOUR EYES

Going to be so nice to be dead.

—LIONEL TRILLING, JOURNAL ENTRY, C. 1971–1974

S ometime in the early 1970s, Diana told Thelma Anderson that before women's liberation she was not conscious that her helping Lionel "behind-the-scenes" and his occasionally doing the same for her, especially with household tasks, could be considered a problem. But Diana was learning that men and women needed to consider sharing all responsibilities and said that Lionel didn't want to give in to the pressures that society was now putting on him to do his share. "This," she said proudly, "is exactly the opposite of Jim, who insists that men take their full share and is really doctrinaire about it." But Lionel, old-fashioned and set in his ways, would not fall into step with the second wave of the women's movement, which had begun in the early 1960s. (First-wave feminism had been mainly concerned with giving women the right to vote.)

On April 30, 1971, Diana had participated in a panel held at Town Hall in New York on women's liberation, in which Norman Mailer, who had recently published *The Prisoner of Sex*, faced four outspoken women—along with Diana Trilling were Germaine Greer, author of *The Female Eunuch* (according to Diana, Greer had announced earlier it was her wish to sleep with Mailer); Jill Johnston, a journalist and lesbian spokesperson (who later disrupted the proceedings, Diana said, when two female friends came onstage, and they "rolled on the floor, hugging and kissing"); and Jacqueline Ceballos, the president of the National Organization of Women. Mailer's *The Prisoner of Sex* closely examined feminism and was greatly concerned about man's loss of power as women acquired control over reproduction, and he concluded that the second wave had turned into "scientific vanity, destroying every act of nature."

In a lecture later in the year, Diana described the Town Hall event as raucous and disorderly, not only because of the irate audience participants but because of the harsh attacks on her friend Mailer. Lionel was not in attendance but would have been pleased with the critics of the evening, who said Diana had held an "aggressively anti-feminist" position. As Diana later said about Mailer: "from the moment the curtain went up he was under the most intemperate assault from the women in the audience. He gave, of course, as good as he got in the way of insult, and I found myself glad he was able to: when I had consented to join the panel I had not contracted to be present at the ritual slaughter of an exemplary male." It was the "family feminist" speaking up, receiving no applause for her unconventional position that year or any other. ("I think of feminism as both firmer and gentler, less competitive than women's lib," she would tell an interviewer a decade later, adding that "doing the best I could had nothing to do with being competitive with men.")

At some point during the evening Mailer had referred to Diana either as a "lady writer" or " a lady critic." She said she hadn't noticed. During a question period a member of the audience asked her if she objected to what Mailer had called her. "I replied that perhaps I ought to object," Diana said, "but actually I did not." She went on to say that her answer "was off the top of my head, in the mood of the moment, in *my* mood of the moment." She explained that

at a meeting in which all sexual differences were being dismissed out of hand, not only on behalf of equality for women under law and in the

world of work but for all purposes of life itself; in the context of an evening in which one half of the human race, man, was being treated as
expendable, I felt the need to separate my position from that of the
other women panelists and much of the audience and put myself on
the side of sexual duality—in writing as in life there were two sexes—
there were men writers and there were lady writers, and I was a lady
writer; the denomination did not trouble me.

But it made trouble for her with the other women, even though she said
that "throughout my adult life I have thought of myself as a feminist,
alert to discriminations against my sex," and by 1972 had decided that
Freud was dead wrong about women. Diana, like many other intellectuals, scholars, and writers, began to understand that he was mistaken
about women having penis envy or being sexually passive and that he
had in essence collaborated with the wide-ranging sexism of his time.

Diana deeply understood that just as "no man is a man writer—
Mailer is not a male writer, he is *a* writer," and of course no woman is a
woman writer, so she was "*a* writer," plain and simple. Some of her views
were expressed in an unpublished essay she wrote sometime in the early
1970s. "America has long been able to afford the luxury of letting its
women be women," she said. "Even in pioneer days, when the American
wife and mother moved alongside her man in the heroic conquest of
new territories, she was never propagandized into denying her femi-
ninity. On the contrary, her special virtues lay in the fact that, despite
her competence and courage, she remained first and always a female.
And this was the tradition into which feminism arrived in America—a
tradition of great competence plus great womanliness." She concluded:
"It was the purpose of feminism to increase the range of female competence and give women a more secure legal and economic base from
which to develop their large capacities—*but* without sacrifice of their
distinctively female emotions and preoccupations."

Diana hoped to summarize once and for all her family feminist position, but she was unable to find a publisher for the essay. Undeterred,
she decided to expand on the subject and write a series of articles on
the American female. She drafted an exhaustive eight-page "tentative

outline," as she called it, and planned to analyze "the various myths of American womanhood created by advertising, merchandising, and the popular arts." She posed such questions as "What is the advertising image of the American male? How does it relate to the female image?" She noted as particularly important that "good wifehood and motherhood" are "the basis of good family life, and good marketing [is] proof of good wifehood and motherhood." She spread her wings beyond her main subject to discuss "democratic progressivism as an approximation of aristocracy," because she had decided that the American middle class borrowed the old aristocratic images, and it was now easy for everyone to be an aristocrat "by following certain laws for living, regardless of birth." What exactly were these "laws"? Diana said they had to do with "appearance, attitudes toward age, leisure, luxuries (with an emphasis on outdoor living), taste (everyone's duty), and social responsibility (noblesse oblige)."

Diana had seemingly slipped into a rabbit's hole, and she fell deeper and deeper into it with another section called "Man, Women and Sex." Despite trying to either lead the reader down her rabbit hole or pull herself out of it, she could do neither. She buried herself in too many concepts. She was in overdrive. She itemized: "Sex in the service of society—mental health—'adjustment'—as the first criterion of sound character," she suggested. "Adjustment as a social goal. One's social duty to be well-adjusted sexually; sexual adjustment as evidence of one's good citizenship." She created an unintended pool of tears for her readers by overwhelming them. It was far from vaporous fantasy because so many of her ideas were concretely intriguing: "The goal of a 'good' sexuality is happy family life, not personal pleasure," she wrote. She discussed "the small part actually played by sex in the choice of a husband or wife and in our expectation of marriage" and "the disappearance of the concept of feminine 'charm.'" But it was, in the end, too much of a "Mad Tea-Party," and she left no breathing room for the reader to absorb her thoughts. She herself hadn't absorbed the lesson pointed out to her by an editor after the rejection of a novella in 1940 that "there's too much in it that you have put in to clarify things for yourself, but which in the end obscures it for the reader."

Diana eventually decided to stay only with those ideas connected to a literary theme, and she wrote a long piece called "The Liberated Heroine," in which she held forth that "our response to the heroine, unlike our response to the hero, is subjective, involved with our feelings of personal affection and identification." She pointed to Tolstoy's Natasha in *War and Peace*, and Henry James's Isabel Archer in *Portrait of a Lady*, as what she called "spirited heroines." (She commented that Jo in *Little Women* "represented my own first encounter with a heroine of spirit.")

The New Yorker's William Shawn passed on the new essay, writing Diana a frustrating letter: "This is a fine, original piece. I don't think anyone else has said what you are saying. However, we do not think that this falls within our range." Many of Diana's ideas were worth exploring and were indeed original, as when she wrote that "heroic action has always been associated with war, which has excluded women. Of the many social changes that had contributed to the disappearance of the hero from the literature of recent decades and his replacement with the non- or un-hero of our present advanced literary culture, probably the most crucial are the closing of the frontier and the growth of the anti-war sentiment. And these are central as well in the development of our fiction of female liberation." But Shawn did not suggest working with her on the essay to tighten it or strengthen its sometimes disjointed approach, which made her conclusions hard to follow. Still, the piece was eventually published in *Partisan Review* and, in England, in *The Times Literary Supplement.*

Diana needed a tenacious editor. She was still mourning the loss of William Jovanovich of Harcourt as the editor she thought would make a difference in her life. She could not make herself erase him from her life altogether, despite her profound disappointment over the rejection of what she now referred to as "the education-of-Diana-Trilling book"— the one about her years at Radcliffe.

But after she wrote Harcourt in December 1974 and asked for a formal release from "further contractual obligations," Bill Jovanovich would not let her go easily. He blamed what he called "the series of errors" and "mistaken zeal . . . to protect him from too much detail" that caused Harcourt "to lose you as a distinguished author." He invited both Trillings (it was Lionel he really wanted to publish) to join him and Bill Goodman for a dinner at Lutèce in February of that year. Diana replied that she now had plans with another publisher; at the suggestion of Richard Poirier, then an editor of *Partisan Review*, Little, Brown had signed her for a book of essays to be titled *We Must March My Darlings*. Diana wrote Jovanovich that she would like to hold his dinner invitation "in abeyance. . . . Perhaps it will turn out that I shall be signing a contract with HBJ all over again one of these days, and that, it seems to me, would make a splendidly celebrative occasion for all of us." She meant possibly contracts for both herself and Lionel.

Diana told Thelma Anderson that from the time she and Lionel had returned to New York from Oxford in 1974, she felt he was conserving his energy and that "she often wondered whether he was responding to something deeper in his own body." Jim, who had been in the Middle East while his parents were at Oxford, told his mother he saw a great change in his father.

Diana told Thelma also that Lionel, who had lost weight and was having back pain, "kept complaining about his chair being wrong, his desk chair, and I said, 'Well why don't you have the people come and see if they can readjust it,' and he'd reply, 'No that's all right.' " She "asked him to try other chairs. 'No no, no,' none of them was right. He wasn't feeling well, but he'd walk the street briskly and hold himself well." Diana added that he fought hard against the undue fatigue he was experiencing and also the fact that his stomach didn't feel quite right.

At first the doctors could find nothing physically wrong with Lionel and suggested that perhaps he was suffering from depression. Diana insisted more diagnostic tests be made. Lionel was not merely depressed; there was much more going on.

Diana agreed with what Steven Marcus had once told her years earlier, that "Lionel had a secret—again, a small bit of secret perversity. Against all empirical evidence he agreed with Freud about the death instinct. He said, 'I believe it exists.' And he would say that with a smile on his face, but he believed that it exists. And I think he believed that it exists because he felt it in himself. He felt deathward forces in himself, as any honest man I think at one point has to admit that he does feel in himself."

Two days after the last of the tests, Lionel was informed, Diana said, that he had "a pancreatic disorder and that there would be an exploratory operation to see what it was. It never entered his head that this was a cancer of the pancreas." But both she and Jim knew at once that it was cancer. The doctor told them, Diana said, that he supposed Lionel "was the kind of person who would want to be told." But Diana cautioned the doctor to tell Lionel only if he asked about his condition.

Lionel did not ask, Diana said, and he "went through the operation in very good spirits." And she said, "I already knew that he was going to die. Perhaps on the operating table or very shortly afterwards."

The doctor had said to expect either a very long operation or a very short one, in which the surgeon would take a look and then close the patient up right away. Lionel had a short operation, one in which, Diana said, "there had been no traumatization of his body." In fact, the very next morning Lionel got himself out of bed before the nurse even knew what he was doing, which was shaving in the bathroom. Lionel was "as pleased as punch with himself," Diana said, that he could move around like that after abdominal surgery.

But still he asked no questions. No questions about whether or not he had cancer. Diana, who had recently recovered from a bout of bronchitis, wore a surgical mask, not because of any germs she might pass on to her husband but to hide any facial expression that might give away the diagnosis that he had pancreatic cancer and probably had only weeks to live. The mask-wearing went on for three days, until Diana said, Lionel looked at her and said, "I know now, and you can take off the mask."

Lionel had been told he would have a year or more, which Diana knew was not the case. She was sorry that the doctor had not been more honest with Lionel, yet she said that he faced his impending death "with absolute dignity, with absolute quiet, and with great fortitude." Still, Diana said that Lionel, thinking he had at least a year, "wanted to get a year's work done. He wanted to write a memoir."

The doctors agreed with Diana and Jim's wish that Lionel be allowed to die at home. Lionel, she said, thought he would "get stronger each day." She didn't tell him, she said, "I'm now taking you home to die in your own home," but she did say to him at one point, " 'Think how much you've done in life,' and he said, 'What have I done?' which was terribly sad to me."

Contrary to his hope, Lionel "felt weaker every day," Diana said, "and he would try to sit up and he couldn't sit up any better than the day before. Or he'd try to come into the living room, and he couldn't sit up, and he'd have to be [helped] back to bed . . . and you could see this puzzlement that was overcoming him." Eventually Lionel told Diana that he had stowed away in his Columbia office all the sleeping pills that she had once cleaned out of their medicine cabinet and thought had been thrown out. He said he was saving them for a time he might need them. Diana told Lionel she wouldn't get the pills or allow anyone else to get them. "But," she told him," I will promise you that you will not be allowed to suffer. You have my word for this."

But Lionel did not have an easy death.

"He wasn't allowed to die as he would have wanted to die," Diana said, "and I was absolutely unable to control the medical situation, try as I would." She expected that he would "be dying unconscious, but it never happened that way. He was very conscious to the very, very last moment. He was psychotic but he was conscious." Diana later wrote to one of his doctors that Lionel's "last ten or twelve days were an agony of psychosis, terrible beyond belief not only for him but for us who loved him so dearly. His mind by which he lived was destroyed." The letter was not a scolding of the doctor, who, Diana said, took exceptionally good care of Lionel, but rather it was meant to "raise the intellectual, though emotionally highly charged question about the use of psychological drugs at all until more is known of their possible effects."

She recalled "one of his last decent days, when he wasn't yet doped up but was in pain. He reached out his hand and he took Jim's hand and mine and just held on and squeezed very hard, keeping his full consciousness but squeezing very hard because the pain was so great. And I think that either he should have been killed right away or should have been allowed to commit suicide right away or he should have been allowed to die that way with great courage."

Diana wrote to her friends Evey and David Riesman that right before he became crazed from the cocktail of drugs he was given, Lionel was still able to talk about his memoir: "It was going to be such a good book," he told Diana.

A year later, Diana reminisced with Steven Marcus when interviewing him for a book she was planning to write:

Lionel's father had died in 1943, and his mother and father were very alienated from each other for long long years. . . . But when his mother went to the funeral and looked into the coffin, she said very quietly, "He doesn't have to be afraid anymore." Lionel's father was afraid of death all the time and didn't live his life because of it. And I think that if Lionel had lived to write his memoir, he would have had to say a great deal about why he was so concerned with death as he was throughout his work. What he was trying to do is say that there is no life without the acceptance of death because my father was always staying alive just in order not to be dead. That was no life.

And Diana added, "Lionel wasn't at all a morbid person. What he was talking about was the tragedy of life in the life." Steve Marcus replied that one of Lionel's favorite quotations from Montaigne was "to philosophize is to learn how to die."

Toward the end, Diana said, Lionel wouldn't close his eyes. "All the last day I lay on the bed next to him saying, 'Close your eyes and rest,' and I could not get him to. I said, 'Don't be afraid—just close your eyes and rest.' And he didn't close his eyes."

Lionel died on November 5, 1975, just a few months after his diagnosis. The funeral was held five days later at St. Paul's Chapel of Columbia University. A mixture of Italian Renaissance and Byzantine styles, it was built between 1904 and 1907 as a nondenominational religious space and was a gift to the university from Olivia Egleston Phelps Stokes and Caroline Phelps Stokes, the daughters of a very wealthy, ardently religious New York family.

Lionel's funeral "was very quiet, very beautiful," Diana wrote in a letter to a woman who had once worked for the family. "The prayers and psalms were of our own choice; the Cantor sang like an angel, there was no eulogy. Everything was as Lionel would have wished." Diana told Leo

Lerman that "Li and I wrote that service out a year ago. He found the texts; I wrote it."

Diana reported to another correspondent unable to attend the funeral that "the service consisted wholly of prayers from *The Book of Common Prayer*, some Psalms, a long passage from Ecclesiastes, and a prayer of thanksgiving, which was especially written by the chaplain of the university, who read the prayers both in Hebrew and in English."

Jim remembered that he said Kaddish at Ferncliff Cemetery in Hartsdale, New York, where his father was cremated. Nonetheless, Norman Podhoretz wrote in his book *Ex-Friends* that Diana, after asking him to teach Kaddish to Jim, "changed her mind about giving Lionel even a watered-down Jewish funeral," adding that there was no Kaddish either at "the Christian building" or the "crematorium" and that he was "positively offended" by Diana's decision to omit even a eulogy from the funeral service. Midge Decter recalled that "it was not only not a Jewish funeral, but it was like a high church funeral."

Memory can be a strange thing. In fact, Jim Trilling recalled, Norman Podhoretz had actually written out a phonetic version of Kaddish for him, and had coached him in reciting it. Jim stated further that Podhoretz "was most obliging and helpful, and the recitation went well enough given the circumstances." He added:

> Kaddish aside, Midge Decter is probably more right than not. I don't know if it's quite fair to say that my mother wrote the service herself, the way young couples do their own weddings (a practice she detested, by the way), but she certainly edited and recombined to her heart's content. And [she] shopped around for a rabbi who would accommodate these interventions. The Columbia rabbi, I remember, was rejected over some point of religious observance. . . . My mother was a functional atheist with a strong aesthetic attraction to Roman Catholicism, and my father, though far more serious about his Jewish heritage, was never (in my lifetime at least) anything but a secular Jew.

In a letter to Diana written more than a decade after Lionel's funeral, the literary critic (and professor emeritus of English at Columbia)

Robert Gorham Davis said he "had always thought of Lionel as a humanist, whose views were consistent with his use of Freud as a cultural critic. I was surprised at the dominantly religious character of his memorial service. As I remember it, both a rabbi and a protestant clergyman took part, and the substance was largely biblical."

Diana replied at great length. "About the religious nature of Lionel's funeral service: you mustn't read too much about his own religious character into it, perhaps only something about the connection between the religious emotions and the aesthetic emotions in certain personal circumstances." She continued: "Both Lionel and I, perhaps I even more than Lionel, have always been appalled by the lack of dignity in the funeral services of atheists and agnostics. The speeches that are made by loving friends are inadequate. Whatever the degree of praise, they are bound to seem reductive because what one is looking for is something that will transcend the immediately pressing fact of personal loss." She then related a particular story: "My brother died a few months before Lionel. He had been converted to Presbyterianism, and his funeral took place at the Brick Presbyterian Church. It was wholly religious in character; I don't think his name was even mentioned. I freshly realized that day that religion, as an undertaking in transcendence, was the only thing that met the 'aesthetic' requirements of a death ceremony, and I went home and quickly wrote a 'service' that could be used for Lionel's funeral and my own." Diana noted to Davis:

Because we are Jews, the readings that I chose make no mention of Jesus. I also wanted them read by a rabbi. Because I love a good cantor and good music also has its part in transcending the moment, I decided we should use one if a good one was available—it turned out that one of the best was at Temple Emmanuel in New York. When I had got this amount of instruction on paper, I showed it to Lionel, who shrugged his shoulders as his way of saying it was okay with him, no more, no less, than that. It was in deference to the university that, at Lionel's funeral, I asked the Protestant chaplain to say a prayer.

And then she ended her long reply to Davis with a reprimand: "By the way, you refer to it as Lionel's 'memorial service.' It was not a memorial but a funeral service. The coffin was there, the plain wooden box that Lionel had always hoped he would be buried—or cremated—in."

Diana later revealed more details to her friends Jack and Susan Thompson; Jack was a poet who taught English at Stony Brook, and Susan taught at Columbia's School of Library Service after working briefly for the CIA. Jack was also often part of the Lionel–Quentin Anderson trout-fishing trips. Diana told the Thompsons that she "could control the service at the Chapel" but that "it never occurred to me that there was going to be anything but a Kaddish said out at the cemetery, so it didn't occur to me to try to control what the rabbi would do or say there. And so he stood up and he talked a lot of poetic stuff, which I found awful. . . . Later I said to Jim, 'If I had known he wanted to say a poem, I would have asked him to say 'Dover Beach.' And Jim said, 'Oh, thank God he didn't or we would have all collapsed.' He said, 'We could not have sustained that.' And I suppose that's true. But that's my favorite poem in the world."

Diana was able to control the seating at the funeral and made a list of thirty-eight friends (individuals and couples) who would be given reserved seating in the chapel. She noted in ink at the top of the typed list that the "English department will be seated, with wives or husbands, in a separate section." There was nothing surprising about the friends list—the Barzuns; Elinor Hays and her husband, Paul; Mrs. Eliot Cohen; Leo Lerman (who recorded in his journal that "much of the service [was] in Hebrew, a cantor singing beautifully . . ."); Gray Foy; the Kristols; the Podhoretzes; her psychiatrist, Dr. Marianne Kris; and Carroll and Arnold Beichman. (Diana would later give Carroll Lionel's copy of Wordsworth's and Coleridge's *Lyrical Ballads*.)

Diana wrote her friend Goronwy Rees several months after Lionel's death that she "still wakes up each morning with something she must say to [Lionel] unable to believe that I won't see his head there on the pillow next to mine, and just in these last few days it is as if all the resistance I had built up to shield myself against his loss has broken down: he seems so active a presence—that his death seems to me to be an hallucination, not a reality." She continued: "I go out, I see people, I have my hair done, I make jokes, I buy new clothes, and no one need be reminded of what is constantly on my own mind. Work is of course the most important thing. I don't know what I would have done without it."

And she meant not only her own work.

"The desire to do an autobiographical but essentially impersonal memoir, an education, had, I think been with Lionel for some while," Diana said. In an unpublished book she wrote that Lionel's memoir was to be "an intellectual memoir. It was in these terms that he always referred to it: it was an intellectual memoir, never an autobiography. I took his emphasis on the word *intellectual* to mean that walking in the broad footpath of Henry Adams, he intended to bypass his private life, not dwell upon it in details or delve into it deeply but concentrate on the development of his thought as this might throw light on the history of his intellectual times." She also said that she hoped someone would one day write about Lionel as a figure in the twentieth century as Lionel had written about Arnold as a figure in the nineteenth century. "Lionel always saw Arnold as a figure in his time," she said; "it was always a huge canvas he planned, which is why it was such a mad project for him to have undertaken as a doctoral dissertation. . . . Lionel's sense of history was acute: it's an important endowment for a critic."

It was this belief in what Lionel wanted as his legacy—an impersonal memoir—that partially fueled Diana's near obsession with getting all his books published in uniform editions. But the most crucial reason for her obsession and eventual need to control his work was a far simpler one: she considered his work all but her work. She had molded it, made it what it became.

William Jovanovich had always wanted to publish Lionel, and because Diana had kept the door open for a possible future relationship, he now felt secure in proposing that he be the one to publish a uniform edition of all of Lionel's work. A former editor at HBJ said that Jovanovich, who was "movie star handsome," liked especially to give advice to his select group of "glamorous and intellectual" widows and "would advise them of everything." He had a knack for making these women (Hannah Arendt, Mary McCarthy, and later, Anne Morrow Lindbergh and the actor Paulette Goddard) feel important. "He always had to have a glamorous or intellectual woman to be the savior of," the former editor commented. Jim Trilling said that his mother's "professional relationship with Bill Jovanovich was stormy, not the least because she had an intense and lasting crush on him."

Finances remained a concern. Diana said that Lionel was still worrying about money when he died and that they only paid off the last of their loans in 1970. At one point, years earlier, Diana and Lionel had loaned money to her brother, although it is not clear why Sam needed it or where the money came from that Diana and Lionel gave him. But a year after Lionel's death, Diana wrote her sister-in-law that there was still $2,500 due on the loan, also acknowledging that her sister-in-law had been "thoughtful enough to send me a $500 payment after Lionel's death when you rightfully guessed that I was under pressure of large expenses."

Diana had applied for a National Endowment/Rockefeller Foundation joint grant to write an intellectual history of the past five decades, but she told Bill Jovanovich that, although she was given one, "It was so lousy I refused it." She had asked for $160,000 over two years, then "had pared it down" to $130,000, but finally was offered only $50,000, which she told Jovanovich was not enough for a secretary and a salary for herself over two years.

But many different projects were brewing in the year or two after Lionel's death. There was, of course, the long and exacting preparation of what would be a twelve-volume set of all of Lionel's books. Diana was involved in every aspect and demanded absolute control, although she asked for an "Edited by Diana Trilling in the smallest possible type."

Drenka Willen, a longtime editor at HBJ (in her distinguished career she has edited four Nobel Prize winners), said that Jovanovich "could be very very charming, and of course he took Diana to restaurants, a car was available to bring her to the office and take her home—she didn't come to the office because I don't think she ever stepped into an elevator." This was, of course, because of her fear of heights. (During the time when Diana was working on Lionel's books, a problem occurred with his gravesite, and Diana felt comfortable enough to ask Bill Jovanovich to intervene with the cemetery officials, which he did. Her *savior*.)

Willen first met Diana when she accompanied a book designer to Princeton the summer of 1977 to show Diana sample designs for Lionel's books. "Drenka is all that you promised me," Diana gushed in a letter to Jovanovich. "I can't begin to tell you what a relief it is to deal with someone this conscientious who is also this respectful of books that may not sell a million copies! And she's so charming, too! I'm sure it will be the greatest pleasure to work with her; we're off to a great start." Diana told Jovanovich she had a suggestion for a new title for Lionel's books—she thought that "The Uniform Edition of the Works of Lionel Trilling" should be changed to "The Works of Lionel Trilling Uniform Edition."

The uniform editions caused some friction with Jacques Barzun, who, Diana said, wanted to be involved with the publication, but Diana didn't like the way he was planning to organize the essays by subject matter, and so she broke with him. "Jacques and I have never been the same," Diana said, "never been as close as we were as a result, but I know that I was right."

In 1976 Columbia University initiated "The Lionel Trilling Seminars." One of the first speakers, despite everything, was Jacques Barzun, who spoke on the death of modernism. "It was a sweet and dignified and well-attended occasion," Diana wrote in a letter, adding that "Jim and I felt good about it."

Around this time she managed to hire a professional archivist to help her organize all of Lionel's papers, and she wrote in a letter to a friend that she was also beginning "to put the first bit of order into her own papers." Diana's future archive mattered, too.

Diana was involved in some bitter feuds in the decade of Lionel's death, starting with Lillian Hellman. Diana and Lionel had continued to see the playwright over the years, and Hellman remained, in many ways, Diana's best "large-scale friend." They spoke on the telephone often, wrote letters, and shared dinners and parties together, usually at Hellman's apartment.

"We're all just liberal democrats together," Hellman had once told Diana. Indeed, Diana had written Hellman a long and strong letter after Hellman's testimony in 1952 before the House Un-American Activities Committee, where she had delivered her well-known line: "I cannot and will not cut my conscience to fit this year's fashions." Diana had written her friend:

> As I told you on the phone, Lionel and I had great respect for the position you took in Washington, the willingness to answer all queries about yourself but not to incriminate your friends. The copy of your statement, however, gives us pause on several points. The most important is arriving at one's decision to speak or not to speak against this one or that one. It is your blanket whitewash of all your political associates on the ground that they were *all* loyal citizens, which makes—I believe— your position an unsound one. By your statement, you would feel it your duty to report anyone whom you thought disloyal. The whole weight, then, of your position rests on the soundness of your political intelligence . . . and here, frankly, I do not concede your competence.

Although their correspondence, phoning, and socializing would go on for two more decades, including the swapping of recipes ("I think Lionel would like this: it's a famous New Orleans dish," Hellman scribbled on one for cassoulet with duck), she never forgot what Diana had once written her: *I do not concede your competence.* She did reply to Diana's letter, telling her, "I like you, I respect you and I have a good time with you. That is almost always enough for me. I did think that time between us would, or could, take care of things. But I can't offer to discuss myself. I had a long analysis and I know the difficulty in telling, and in listening to, the truth. Anything else is now for me rather unpleasant comedy."

Little, Brown was also Lillian Hellman's publisher, and her new book, *Scoundrel Time*, was being published in 1976, the year before Diana's book of essays, *We Must March My Darlings.* When Diana learned that Hellman was going to use as "the springboard for an assessment of Lionel," as Diana phrased it, the new introduction that he had written to *The Middle of the Journey*, in which he referred to Chambers as "a man of honor," she asked Roger Donald, her editor at Little, Brown if she could add some material about Hellmann's new book to an essay in her collection. It was agreed that she could.

In Diana's essay, "Liberal Anti-Communism Revisited," she said that she had "written a very, very few sentences about Lillian and *Scoundrel Time*. (Actually she wrote four detailed "passages," as she called them in the paperback edition, where she also added a very long footnote.) As *The New York Times* later reported, one of the passages appears at the beginning of "an expanded version of an article [written in 1967] about a symposium by Mrs. Trilling in 1976." The newspaper quoted Diana: "The issues . . . have continued to divide the intellectual community with ever-increasing acuteness, albeit with always-diminishing intellectual force. The most recent document of this division is . . . *Scoundrel Time*." The paper went on to report that "Mrs. Trilling says the words Little, Brown wanted deleted were 'albeit with always-diminishing intellectual force'" and went on to quote Roger Donald as saying that he "objected to the fact that Lillian Hellman is an example of 'diminishing intellectual force.'"

Diana felt that Hellman had implied—actually more than implied— that she and Lionel were among the "scoundrels" of her title because the three of them differed politically, specifically about Whittaker Chambers. Diana went on to say that Hellman had completely missed Lionel's point in calling Chambers "a man of honor" and that her old friend "knew precisely what she was doing" and that she "intended to tar Lionel with the brush of McCarthyism." She said that if he were still alive, there would have been grounds for a suit.

Hellman wrote, "Facts are facts—and one of them is that a pumpkin, in which Chambers claimed to have hidden the damaging evidence against Hiss, deteriorates—and there had never been a chance that, as [*Lionel*] Trilling continues to claim, Chambers was a man of honor." What Hellman appears to have meant in a somewhat confusing statement is that pumpkins decompose over time and that if Chambers had placed the papers in one, they also would have decomposed, so this indicates that he never had any intention of producing evidence to back up his accusations—thus, Chambers was in no way a man of honor. In answer to Hellman's statement, Diana wrote that "facts are indeed facts—and the papers which helped to convict Hiss were never near the pumpkin. There were *no* pumpkins among the so-called pumpkin papers, and no one acquainted with the facts had ever, as Lillian Hellman's report in *Scoundrel Time* might be taken to suggest, proposed that there were. There was a handful of microfilms, some undeveloped, and even uncapped, which Chambers hurriedly took from documents he had hidden elsewhere. And these microfilms stayed in the pumpkin *only a single day*, outdoors, before being turned over to the authorities." (In *The Beginning of the Journey* Diana returned to the controversy, making clear that Hellman always thought the so-called "pumpkin papers" were literally composed of paper and were not microfilms, and thus would have rotted along with the pumpkins.)

Diana's passages—thoughts, opinions, ideas, sentences, whatever one wishes to call them—about Hellman had caused Little, Brown to ask Diana to remove them, but Diana had refused, and her contract was terminated. She wrote a friend that it took three martinis for her editor, Roger Donald, to give her the news. Jim Trilling said his mother felt a "terrible betrayal that he chose Lillian Hellman over her, all the more so because she found him terribly attractive."

Diana had also written that Hellman's book, an autobiography, "is being read as a political revelation innocent of bias," and Diana, in essence, damned Hellman's lack of objectivity, which Hellman later told *The New York Times* was actually "a hysterical personal attack on me."

Diana wrote in a letter to Aline and Isaiah Berlin that "from then on life became a kind of gleeful hell [*The New York Times* ran several news stories on the quarrel] in which the telephone never stopped ringing and in which Little, Brown cum L. H. never stopped acting stupider and stupider." Diana had hoped Hellman would object to the censorship and ask for Little, Brown to continue to publish Diana, but Hellman did no such thing. Diana didn't understand that Hellman was never going to forget "I do not concede your competence," despite immediately writing several letters that Diana described as "wild alternations between seduction and threats of legal action," and in fact even continuing with the semblance of a relationship for decades. The clash highlighted Diana's conviction that, as she later wrote, Lillian Hellman "was one of the most ardent of fellow travelers. She never had a position that disagreed with them [the Communist Party] and they knew her as one of their best, most trustworthy friends, of very very great service to them."

Lionel had once written in his journal about Hellman: "She is an impossible person, stupid and disloyal, but she has the great and curious virtue of making life seem interesting, ordered, valuable, like life represented in some plays." He also once quipped in his journal that she was "a greatly underdepreciated woman."

The drama went on for weeks. It was also full of mystery. Diana wrote the Berlins that a snake—nonpoisonous, she was told—was put next to the front door to her apartment, and that the snake disappeared "under my floor where it lived for five weeks until it was caught and decapitated."

Friendships were put on the block: a person was either for Hellman or for Trilling. "Lillian began to get busy on both the professional and social fronts," Diana wrote in a letter. Diana said she invited Richard Poirier to dinner, and he declined, saying that Lillian "was nervous, and he didn't want to upset her." Diana also said that at a dinner party in New York where she was present, a close friend of Hellman's "retreated to the bathroom and didn't again emerge until there was no risk that he would have to speak to me."

And then there was the blurb.

Norman Mailer had promised one to Diana for *We Must March My Darlings*, and confusion about it arose on several fronts. After a friend of Diana's told her it was "undignified" for someone as established as she was to have blurbs, she told HBJ to cancel any blurbs. But Mailer had already sent in his and had, in fact, even sent in a revision of it, one that Diana described as "disheartening" and "very, very *down*" from the original version. When Diana saw the new version, she was sure that Hellman had made him change it to a less enthusiastic one, even though the original one had been, according to Diana, also quite "unusable" because of its "ambiguousness" about Mailer's "political sympathy" with the Trillings. Diana told Mailer that the new blurb, "while better written than its predecessor, is an even firmer disclaimer of approval of me." She said that she had heard from "many sources" that he had altered the blurb at Hellman's "insistence."

Mailer replied to Diana that when he saw in the newspaper that Little, Brown had broken Diana's contract, he said to his secretary, "I'm going to lose the friendship of both women." He couldn't believe, he told Diana, that she listened to idle gossip over his word. He then documented how "Lillian and I went into the back room at her place and had it out." He continued, "I can assure you a rough ten minutes with Lillian back and forth is not, to my mind, a terrifying experience to endure, and you ought to know I'd lose anyone's friendship before I would alter a quote at 'their insistence.'" Peter Manso, who became "a late in life good friend" of Diana's, and who credited her with displaying a "directness and healthiness" toward the literary scene so that it "no longer [became] an unreachable mantle" for him, says emphatically, "That's a lie," adding that Mailer told him that he was "intellectually compelled to change the quote."

Manso quotes Lillian Hellman in his biography of Mailer as saying to Mailer that she was "shocked that you would endorse a book that attacked me." Hellman said that Mailer replied that he had "read half of it and liked it. But I shouldn't have endorsed that book or any book that is against you." She went on to say that Mailer confessed that he "didn't write very much of a blurb in any case, but I will certainly take care of it. And I wish to apologize."

Whatever the truth, Diana hung on with Mailer and wrote him that his letter was "a sweet and loving intention, and it quite transcends any detail of how we do or do not, did or did not, understand each other. Politics did not divide [the two of] them, as it did so many other friends." Still, Diana said that a lot of friendships do disappear, and she told Mailer, "I read about the great poems to friendship of the 19th century and I think, 'What has happened to friendship?'" Diana and Mailer managed to make theirs a lasting one and in the ensuing years met often at the homes of mutual friends.

17

NOT GIVING A DAMN

*The biggest challenge of my widowhood is whether I'll manage
to read John's journal without desecrating his memory: will I
be able to keep him intact? Not make him a symbol of scarred
love? I pray for that. . . . Anything that was bad was part of
everything that was wonderful and good—is this not true in
any important relationship? The marriage of the good and the
bad: this is what I must work to preserve in the memory of our
life together.*

—DIANA TRILLING, EXCERPT FROM "I WAS IN ACADIA TOO"
(UNPUBLISHED NOVEL)

Widowhood prompted Diana, now seventy, to think hard
about all her friendships. She could always count on Thelma
Anderson, Elinor Hays, and Elsa Grossman, of course, and
she had other friends and acquaintances, too, but in Lionel, she had lost
her best friend—"anything that was bad was part of everything that
was wonderful and good."

In the aftermath of Lionel's death Diana had dozens and dozens of
condolence letters to answer, and she sometimes used the occasion to

branch out beyond speaking of Lionel and say a variety of things she couldn't reveal to Thelma, Elinor, or Elsa. She told one correspondent that most of her friendships had seldom been an experience of love and that instead she found them filled with envy and a layer of ill will.

For instance, Diana said that her ever-devoted Arnold Beichman showed some animus toward her in the fallout with Little, Brown, even though he had written a review of *Scoundrel Time* that, as she had told him, she considered very well done and effective. But in a casual letter to Diana—not a condolence letter—he expressed worry that historians would look upon Hellman's book as the truth, and he cautioned his friend that "history is being rewritten right under our noses." Diana chose to see his reasonable qualms as a murderous indictment of herself. She wrote back with all the pent-up feelings she could muster, that how dare he call her "to moral account," and tell her that she had "a defective relation to history." She told him she knew what she was doing, and he must stop lecturing her. After all, she wrote, "I am already launched on a great big study of these last decades of our common political experience—I shall give, no doubt, the remainder of my working life to it." (She finally accepted a small $7,500 grant from The National Endowment for the Humanities to help pay for her taping equipment.)

"I have no apologies to make for myself on the score of my political record, ever," Diana wrote Beichman. "I know no one [other than myself] whose politics have been more on the open record and more consistent. I also have no apologies to make for the standards on which I have constructed my particular brand of liberalism, of which I am proud." (But Diana chose not to send the letter, perhaps because she detected a whisper of paranoia in her response.) The contentiousness between them went on in future correspondence, with one or the other being accused of writing an "ugly" or "sick" letter. Yet Beichman kept writing his friend, and he often included news of Carroll's doings— "Carroll, wonderful as ever. She's bored with teaching." Beichman had by that time made peace with his wife's affair with Lionel, but perhaps Diana had not yet done so to the same degree.

Diana created a major fuss over a letter Beichman wrote to *Commentary*—"a totally innocent letter that was not about Lionel,"

Beichman said, "but really about Nicholas Murray Butler." But Diana felt the letter was so full of biographical errors about Lionel that it needed to be suppressed. For instance, President Butler did not know of Lionel until *after* his Arnold book, Diana told Beichman; "You were making him out to be already celebrated many years earlier." And Beichman had said that Lionel taught the colloquium in 1934 with Kip Fadiman, not Jacques Barzun. "Don't put that one on the record, Arnold," Diana snapped at him. "It's one of the sorrows of Fadiman's life that he *never* taught at Columbia." She accused Beichman of trying to make her own writing about Lionel seem false and wanting to put her "in the wrong, to undermine my point, or was this merely an accident of ineptness?" (Beichman's letter to *Commentary* was never published, and Diana later told him that she had no part in its censoring, which he subsequently learned was actually the truth.)

In one letter Diana berated Beichman for trying to read correspondence that was left open on her living-room desk during his visit for tea on Claremont Avenue. He denied ever doing such a thing, and she countered that when he went to use the bathroom in the back of the apartment, she was sure he had also tried to poke around papers left on Lionel's desk, which he would have had to walk past en route to the bathroom.

On a more serious note she accused him of being an active CIA agent when he worked with the International Confederation of Free Trade Unions (ICFTU), which Diana said was a CIA "operation." How could he have kept this a secret from her? Beichman admitted that he had recently learned that he had "once been used by them" when he unknowingly passed on phony quotes from a Soviet defector diplomat. But Diana's accusation was absurd, he told her; "What in heavens name would I have been doing? Spying on fellow Board members on the American Committee for Cultural Freedom?" Beichman wondered who in the world had told Diana he had been a real spy—"whoever he/she [is] is a villain, an assassin of reputations."

He was more forlorn than angry. "It now seems obvious that whatever we were to each other, we were not friends," he wrote Diana, adding, "It's also sad, so long ago and so dusty." She replied that he simply doesn't seem to understand that she is able to "hold two different judgments . . . in my mind at the same time," and this is why she will always continue to think of him as a friend. Perhaps, she added, he should "read me more as you might read about a character in a novel." Beichman, ever a literalist, replied that she was decidedly *not* a character in a novel, and that he still found it difficult "to understand how you can say the most awful things about someone to me on the phone or over a teacup and then be at that person's house for dinner or cocktails." He went on: "I never understood how you could remain friends with, say, [William] Phillips after telling me some of the awful things about him, his rumors about you, stabs-in-the-back criticisms and how *PR* did awful things." But most important, how in the world did she live with "a cloud over our friendship?" (meaning the CIA agent accusation). "You must be, after all, a most extraordinary person to accept a 'shadowed' relationship," Beichman told her, acknowledging that the politics of the 1950s and 1960s "were a lot dirtier than he had suspected."

The CIA charge had deeply wounded Beichman, and he brooded about its ramifications for years, writing Diana in 1982 that he knew there was no proof of his innocence that would change her mind, since his "simple word of honor that he had never worked for the CIA" made no difference to her. Even a letter to him from Arthur Goldberg, the former Supreme Court justice and US ambassador to the United Nations and one of the founders of the ICFTU, did not strike her as important proof of his innocence.

Beichman wrote Diana also that what really seemed to worry her most was that *she* was being accused of spreading rumors and that she resented being implicated like that. But, Diana countered, "It is you who are spreading this rumor about yourself, and in doing so, maliciously impugning me. I now call on you to stop involving me in this fashion in your efforts. Do what you will to clear yourself of whatever charges against you but leave me out of this enterprise which continues to absorb you."

Diana seemed to be using the full force of a free-floating anger against everyone who had ever angered her in her life; it was an unpleasant outburst and an assault Beichman could not forgive. He knew their correspondence needed to end. But he also knew that his memories would not be so easily terminated—"my sweet and warm memories that I have about the Trillings and about you, particularly."

"Goodbye, Diana," he ended his final letter to her.

But another old friendship did not end. HBJ's publication of *We Must March My Darlings*, and later, in 1978, a collection of some of her *Nation* reviews, gave Diana the opportunity to stay in constant touch with Bill Jovanovich. She wrote him dozens and dozens of letters about everything, including such minutiae as her purchase of a fur hat. She wrote him about her travails with her sister, telling him in great detail "that there's no one to take care of her but me." Cecilia, who was living in a nursing home in Riverdale in the Bronx, had recently married a fellow patient, and Diana mentioned that a Channel 7 news team, along with the residence, "had secretly contrived to put the ceremony on television to elicit popular support in their fight for more Medicaid funds." Diana managed to stop the filming from ever happening, without spelling out exactly how she did this, although she did tell Jovanovich that "I myself hid in a closet." She later learned that the nursing home would be closing, and she would have to find a home for *two* people, she said, "which makes it that much harder."

HBJ celebrated *We Must March My Darlings* in what Diana considered a regal manner. She thanked Jovanovich profusely, not only for the publication dinner but for "the lovely flowers and beautiful necklace," and she said, "I have no place to hang my necklace to look at it all the time, but I keep taking it out of its splendid box to try it on with various dresses."

In the same letter as her effusive "thank you" she included some editorial notes he had asked for on his novel-in-progress. "I hope you are happy with what you have wrought. You should be," she noted at the end of her comments. (In his memoir, *The Temper of the West*, Jovanovich praised her editorial advice, especially about titles. It's best to use "literary ones," Diana had told him.)

She wrote Jovanovich also about her trepidation over reviews, some already out ("some ambiguous, some scurrilous") and some still to come. She wrote Jacques Barzun that the "strange" reviews she got "have put her quite high on the dung heap." Yet she was not going to give up and told him, "Let's form a club: Workaholics self-proclaimed!" (She wrote Norman Podhoretz that "the criticism is to me as interesting as the praise.")

Publisher's Weekly had been cheeky, she commented; her interpretation of what they said was "she write a good English." *Time* magazine's review, she noted, was "smashing," so was *The New Leader's*, and she guessed *The New Republic* would have a favorable one, given that Irving Howe was writing it. Still, she accused HBJ of sabotaging her for not "promoting me in its own voice" (an advertisement, of course). She even wondered if the advertising department "harbors Lillian's friends," or else, she suggested, the department had "a lack of respect for my work" because of her "small sales potential."

In actuality, she was genuinely respected—to the point of being given editorial control of ads—that is, she could veto those she did not like. She would eventually gain almost total control over all publication details and point out everything that was wrong, even that the crease in one of her stockings in an author photo needed to be retouched. Still, in her letter to Jovanovich she threw in: "If I'm going to have to go through this same mumbo-jumbo about the publication of Lionel's work, I['d] just as soon call the whole thing off."

And then there was *The New York Times*. She decided to focus all her grievances into a battle plan with that newspaper. She told Jovanovich that the people at the *Book Review* "don't love me; what guides their conduct is not the wish to do me harm but the desire to protect Lillian." She suspected that Richard Locke, the deputy editor, was "the engineer of this defense system, and that the editor, Harvey Shapiro, was his willing comrade. Locke later commented, "I'm sorry to learn that Diana thought that, but she was mistaken."

Diana said that whatever approach HBJ takes with the *Book Review*, it must be "innocent—its point that both my book and I are eminently suited to the kind of exploitation that they go in for—I am good interview material, the book has excellent possibilities for excerpting . . . and they need to keep entirely off the subject of politics." She wanted the Radcliffe section of the book emphasized (especially the section on sex) to entice young readers. Diana was getting more and more sure of herself as she progressed with her plan.

She let her near obsession with Lillian Hellman enter the picture. Another approach she had in mind with her publisher involved the bringing up of "the censorship issue," and she suggested in a letter that someone should say that "Mr. Jovanovich (mentioning you by name) dislikes any kind of censorship, overt or covert, and that he plans to promote my book in such a way as to counter the unfair treatment I received from Lillian's publishers." Diana was discovering a new kind of inner voice that she used to promote herself.

At the end of her letter to Jovanovich she reminded him that she, herself, was working on a piece for the *Book Review* on *The Auden Generation*, by Samuel Hynes, a review she was told would appear on the front page. She needed to tread carefully to avoid losing the weekly as an outlet for her own criticism. (Still, so sensitive was she about Hellman, she later wondered if the *Book Review*'s asking her to do the Hynes book was a way "to get my own book off the front page.")

A year later, when Alfred Kazin published *A New York Jew*, which she said contained "malice and envy" toward Lionel, Diana once again put on battle gear with *The New York Times*. She wrote her friend David Riesman that "the reviewer was chosen as one who could be hoped to praise the book and confirm the malice just as, in the instance of *We Must March My Darlings*, the reviewer was chosen to line up on the side of Lillian against me." She stormed again against deputy editor Richard Locke for not making the reviewer, Mordecai Richler, revise his appraisal so he was not "a conduit for Kazin's malice," although she never talked directly to Locke about it. Still, she felt that something had to be done, so she lined up her good friend Quentin Anderson to write a protest letter to the *Book Review*, and, as she wrote Riesman, "twenty diverse persons of high standing in the intellectual community from Leslie Fiedler to Howard Mumford have now put *The New York Times* on notice that its *Book Review* editors are in certain instances not making even a primary effort of disinterestedness." She concluded somewhat cockily, "What fruit this will bear we don't know, but it seems to me that the protest can only be useful and that indeed it was mandatory."

Diana wrote David Riesman: "There has already been one sizable return on Quentin's investment of time and energy: Kazin was interviewed by Dick Cavett the other night and *not a single word* was said about a single individual mentioned in the book. It is hard to suppose that Cavett wasn't told by Kazin that they would have to stay off personalities, personalities being Cavett's chief stock in trade." But Cavett, unlike most other talk-show hosts, did read his interviewees' books, and no doubt shrewdly "stayed off personalities" in order to present a more balanced—and even more stimulating—show.

In an outrageous moment Diana told Leo Lerman that "the real truth is that Alfred had deep homosexual feelings for Lionel. Anybody who reads the book should be able to feel that, but who will?" Lerman, enjoying the moment, said that Diana told him all this "unhysterically, with plateaus of laughter, scaling successfully whole ranges of emotion."

Diana was invited to appear on William F. Buckley Jr.'s *Firing Line* television program to discuss *We Must March My Darlings*. She told an interviewer for *The Saturday Review* she agreed to appear if the questions were given to her in advance. But ultimately she declined the invitation, telling Bill Jovanovich that she was offended by the magazine's publishing on its cover a photo of Lillian Hellman in the black mink coat she famously wore for a Blackglama fur advertisement. (Others who had posed included Judy Garland, Marlene Dietrich, Elizabeth Taylor, and Ray Charles.) The cover line had been "& Who Is the Ugliest of Them All?," the headline for Buckley's review of *Scoundrel Time* in the issue. Diana wrote Jovanovich: "It's the first time I've ever known Buckley to be ungentlemanly: he's been all courtesy to me even when I've attacked him in the most direct way." (She told *The Saturday Review* that "Mr. Buckley had reduced political polemic to personal insult.") But the photo excuse turned out to be a smoke screen. She later confessed to Buckley, whom she liked and trusted (she kept a photograph of the two of them in her dining room), that the real reason was that she sometimes had stage fright. "Actually, I've never been on television," she admitted, also revealing that she was afraid he would "rattle" her.

As she put it somewhat over-flatteringly, "Just because I'm capable of thought, why should I have to stand up to the challenge of your mind?" Diana knew when to surrender. (Nonetheless, in 1981 she agreed to stand up to Buckley, appearing on *Firing Line* to promote her book *Mrs. Harris: The Death of the Scarsdale Diet Doctor.*)

National Review's treatment of *We Must March My Darlings* "couldn't have been sounder," she wrote Buckley, also reminding him that her new book, to be called *Reviewing the Forties*, would be coming out soon.

On the new book Diana had been working more with Drenka Willen than Jovanovich, and she managed to convey her grave disappointment over this in a way that was insulting to Willen. Diana told people that she had *no editor at all*, since that's how she felt without Jovanovich at her side all the time. Willen recognized that Diana was unhappy, and she eventually asked to be relieved of her duties on the book. Diana took no responsibility for her part in the situation. She had also been upset that *The New York Times* had been on strike, so her book was not going to be reviewed; she blamed Willen for not being aggressive enough. Ultimately, Diana made a mistake in complaining about Willen to Jovanovich; he admired Willen's talents enormously and was convinced she could do no wrong. "Diana was her own worst enemy," Willen commented later, adding that "there was also something sweet about her." But Diana was truly frightened that Willen might "put her in a bad light" with Jovanovich. In fact, Diana appeared just plain jealous that Jovanovich respected Drenka as much as he did. Diana felt under siege and eventually wrote Jovanovich that she "could no longer really sustain the kind of attacks that were being directed at her." Somehow, as always, he managed to calm her down.

Publicity—and all its trappings—was now on Diana's mind a great deal of the time. She even asked acquaintances to help her reach the fame she thought she deserved. She felt at liberty to tell Jovanovich that HBJ was selling her new collection short. "It has a cultural-historical interest beyond my expectations for it," she lectured him.

Lionel's death had given her a new freedom to say more than ever what was on her mind. It translated in many ways to an arrogance that

some of her husband's colleagues—and her own—said was destructive—
to his reputation. She was becoming flinty.

She told Jacques Barzun that she was criticized "because I am elitist
(usually from my lofty perch on Morningside). I am absolutist, I am
humorless, I lack compassion for the young."

In another letter to Jovanovich, Diana announced that "I guess you
realized I can't really afford many more bad things done by people
around me. I don't know if it has anything to do with widowhood in
general, or my widowhood in particular, but it's been so increasingly so
since Li died that it frightens me. Sure, Kazin is a shit and Lillian is a
she-shit. But I'm thinking of people I've deeply cared about and looked
up to: Why am I suddenly a target for them?" She decided the answer
was that she "simultaneously asserts too much power and not enough,"
she told Jovanovich. "That's dangerous," she added, because "it leaves
space to set up quite a shooting field. It also has to do with my being
a woman, my kind—I mean—very smart, all too smart, but always de-
ferring to Lionel—not in any immediate way, but always finally—and
because my family always came first; I thought of myself as only accidentally a writer though I did my work professionally."

Surely and substantially, she had found one answer for why she had
become a target. Her family would always come first. Jim made her so
proud she wrote an acquaintance. "He's a born literary critic—Lionel
and I saw that very early," she asserted. "That he had to move into a different field [he became an art historian, specializing in Byzantine art
and the history of ornaments], one in which his father and I weren't
even acquainted with, is understandable." Diana and Jim's relationship,
while difficult during his early years, was, in his adulthood, a devoted
one.

"I have always adored letter writing," Diana wrote Jovanovich in the
summer of 1977. She told him, "They roll from my fingers." She enjoyed
entertaining through her correspondence, and wrote at length about an
encounter she had had with Henry Kissinger at the Morgan Library's
award ceremony in honor of Joseph Lash and his Churchill-Roosevelt
book:

ME. Who's your publisher, Mr. Kissinger?

K. Little-Brown.

ME, *reprovingly.* Uh-uh.

BYSTANDER. Don't you remember they broke Diana's contract because she wrote four sentences in criticism of *Scoundrel Time?*

K., *wide blue-eyed.* Oh, I remembered the incident but not the publisher.

ME, *all graciousness.* It's a big firm and you have a different editor. There's no reason for you to have it in mind.

(Pause of maybe five seconds while my unconscious rallies)

ME. Just before you came over we were wondering what Morgan would have thought about this ceremony taking place in his beautiful house.

K. He'd have loved it, wouldn't he?

ME. No, I don't think so. I think he'd have hated it.

K. Why?

ME. A Jew presenting an award to another Jew? In his library?

K. King Faisal said I was neither a Jew nor a non-Jew, but a diplomat.

ME, *in my dearest sweetest voice.* But you see, Mr. Kissinger, I'm not King Faisal. To me you're always a Jew.

End of Scene

Sometime during that summer of 1977 Diana got a new idea, which she proposed to Bill Jovanovich. "I think I want to write a novel. . . . It will be a book about Sex, Power, and Fantasy. . . . Here's what I have in mind, a whole book done by means of letters . . . and I don't mean that I want to do a novel in which a character is obsessed with letter writing." She went on, "fictional letter writing, though it presents its own technical problems, would take care of what I told you were my reasons for always backing away from doing a novel: my inability to get people in and out of rooms, in and out of chairs, streets, station wagons. . . . I'm thinking of a whole book done by means of letters. . . . I haven't yet worked out

the whole line of action but the main line is beginning to take shape."
She decided also the letters would alternate with excerpts from her female protagonist's journals.

Diana would be that protagonist. Jovanovich would be the male
protagonist.

She told Jovanovich she still had to figure out "how to protect myself
from over-exposure—maybe I'll have to use a pseudonym. Or maybe
just learn not to give a damn: that takes a little longer."

She said she hoped to write the novel in six to eight weeks, although
she worried that she might be "flipping onto a manic side." But while she
was "going crazy," she might as well say this: she'd outdo even *Herzog*
and *Mr. Sammler's Planet*—and "do what they together should have
been."

Saul Bellow, an acquaintance, had written a warmhearted condolence
note, telling Diana that he hoped that Lionel "understood that I was a
friendly nuisance, not a hostile one." Diana replied that Lionel "found it
astonishing that someone like yourself could have misread him to such
an extent . . . but that this did not create any hostility." But it had. Lionel
had, in fact, ended communication between them after he strongly objected to the way Bellow had characterized him in a 1974 essay in *Harper's*
magazine. Diana also recalled that in the 1960s Bellow had once taken
Lionel to an unsavory part of Chicago just to shake him up, and even
earlier, in the 1950s, she had accused Bellow of imitating Lionel's voice
in a crank phone call. Bellow, who enjoyed mocking Diana (he did not
like any literary critics) had written to a friend about Diana's sleuthing
that she "will never replace Agatha Christie." Still, Diana ended her reply to Bellow's condolence letter on a poignant note: "It's hell without
him. I keep enormously busy like a mechanical woman, which is the
only way I know how to manage."

As for her novel, Diana decided "not to give a damn," so she subli-
mated all her romantic feelings about Jovanovich in the book. She told
Jovanovich she was always cannibalizing their conversations "for the
sake of literature" and doing so "day and night." She told him that instead of writing certain feelings in her letters to him she put them aside
in her notes to add to the novel. Jim Trilling said that his mother seemed

to be writing the novel "as she was living it. . . . I think she understood that she was writing a journal of her relationship with Bill Jovanovich." In fact, after Jovanovich sent Diana flowers on her birthday, she enthusiastically told him, "You'll be amused. My book starts with my protagonist's birthday and a gift of flowers."

She named "herself" Deborah Wagnell, a widow of sixty-seven, and made her an admired, but not best-selling, novelist. Bill Jovanovich became Stuart Winton, who was in charge of a publishing empire's many television stations, although some of Jovanovich was also in the character of the publisher, Mike Brennan. Deborah's late husband, John Wagnell, was a poet, classicist, and an expert in cryptography, who worked with the OSS during World War II. He kept a journal.

"Deborah," or "Deb," was in love with, and had a long affair with, "Stuart," who broke it off when he fell in love with a younger employee. "I went to Stuart but came home to John," Diana wrote, and she later had Deb wondering if she went to Stuart after she found out that John had had an affair, which he wrote about extensively in his journal. "I don't mind the friendship, I don't mind the affair," Diana wrote in her book, "but why did he have to go on and on *in writing* . . . his filling up his notebooks with her. . . . That's what diminishes me in the eyes of posterity; certainly everybody I know is going to think of it as a diminution of me." Deborah also worries that Stuart loves her only for her relationship to John, a poet he admires and envies. "He hadn't the ability to write John's poetry, only the ability to make a billion dollars," Deb writes in *her* journal. "Wasn't there triumph for you in getting John's wife away from him if only by the hour?" she exclaims to Stuart in a letter she marked as never sent. She adds in that letter that "fidelity or infidelity means very little to me. I think monogamy is against nature, but loyalty means a great deal, and if I indeed helped you feel triumphant over John, that's a disloyalty of which I shall always feel guilty as I shall never feel guilty because I am unfaithful." Deb's journal notes that "I never kidded myself that John's literary prestige wasn't central to our relationship."

Diana eventually wrote Jovanovich that she was a little embarrassed by "the emotional truth and seriousness" of what she was writing in her novel. Her fictional John had left behind thirty-five notebooks, and Diana said that "giving Deborah the decision of whether or not to publish them added considerable 'plot' and texture to the book." Yet at the same time, Diana was "troubled by the Stuart-Deborah relation, which seems to be contrived, emotionally inadequate, untrue to Deborah's character." Diana added, "After all, she is the vehicle of my best ideas. I don't like her to be involved in a relationship which is somehow unsuited to the ideas and feelings with which I entrust her." Jovanovich told Diana that she "has created a truly interesting woman who is trying to be fair to herself but isn't sure she will be. She's intricate and she's likeable."

Diana often used the letters in her novel as she had used them in real life, to let off steam and get across her protagonist's ideas in a direct and public manner. Deb believes that "the existence of fiction is what leads us to believe in the existence of its opposite, truth, but fiction is in a curious way *more* truthful." Deb thinks that "maybe the only people who can feel they have wholly accomplished their lives are actors and actresses—with every performance they give, they complete the life they were meant to portray and thus fully discharge its burdens and their own."

Deb believes that "only with widowhood has she begun to address herself strenuously in her career" and says that "no biography is to be trusted as anything except an interesting speculation." Deb keeps every scrap of paper of her drafts in case one could contain something lost but necessary to her story—"our poorest scraps are treasure." As a widow, Deb "loathed coming home by herself. . . . Neighbors are the only solution for a widow—neighbors who are also friends, people who are there for you." Of Stu's new love interest, a woman named Celeste, Deb writes that perhaps she, Deb, envies Celeste because "she dared make such a male [independent] life for herself." Deb says that she herself is secretly "full of frustration at the choices she has made . . . but it's not that we hate men because we envy them, the way so many women do who turn to women's liberation. It's both better and worse than that, more hopeless: we want to be men." At the same time Deb declares herself a committed Freudian and writes that "nothing on earth could

convince me I don't want to be the sex I am. Maybe I just want everything, both worlds, the androgynous best of both sexes."

Jovanovich sometimes worried that Diana would never get the novel
written or that it would, as *she* put it in a letter, "assault you with all the
embarrassments." She wrote an acquaintance that she was "inundated
by doubt and fear" and that she planned "to cop out any minute." She
said that writing a novel was the "most unsettling enterprise she had
ever embarked on" and that she had no sense of command, as she did
when writing criticism.

Diana told Jovanovich that "I cling to the reassurances you give me
that our friendship is forever" and that she hopes nothing she writes will
hurt him. Later she told him that "nothing is so revealing as the nature
of our fantasies. I find myself depressingly shy about such self-exposure.
I'd a thousand times rather tell the world what actually was or is in my
life than where my imagination leads me."

Although her novel went through several drafts, Diana finally abandoned it. Jim Trilling said that his mother had been "very very pleased
with it until she saw it wasn't working as a novel." He also said that his
mother decided that "people were not going to take much interest in
it . . . and that the image she created of her stand-in wasn't sufficiently
varied—rich—for people to overcome their shrug of boredom." No
doubt Diana was also extremely self-conscious about her fantasies becoming so public.

In the winter of 1977 Diana wrote a friend that her eyes "are kicking
up." It had been a little over seven years since she had complained to an
eye doctor in New York that she had a feeling of discomfort and "fuzziness" in her eyes. She was told that eventually she would need cataract
surgery and that, meanwhile, she would receive a prescription for new
glasses, ones that would be "a little different" from her current ones. But
the new glasses seemed wrong to Diana; in fact, she was told by her
doctor that the optician must have used the wrong prescription. But as
it turned out, that wasn't what had happened. The doctor had made a
mistake and had given Diana the wrong glasses—twice. Diana let him
have it, writing him that "I have a great tolerance for human error but
I draw the line at being held responsible for serious errors made by

someone else for which I have to suffer." And as livid as she was, her curiosity got the best of her, and she wanted to understand what had caused the confusion. But she never heard from the doctor again.

Over the next decade Diana continued to have eye problems, first enduring two retinal hemorrhages in her left eye, for which she received laser therapy, and then a cataract operation on her right eye, which improved her vision somewhat. She would eventually be diagnosed with low-pressure glaucoma, which was accompanied by some vision loss, and then with traditional glaucoma, a more serious condition that can cause optic nerve damage and macular degeneration, or the loss of sight.

After 1977 she would describe her circumstances to Bill Jovanovich: "I can't read except through one or another form of illuminated magnification. Using magnification to read makes me seasick, so I no longer read a whole book." Over time she would have friends and acquaintances read to her, and she would eventually write by dictation. In the winter of 1977 Diana wrote a friend that she "managed to forget my troublesome eyes" and was able to attend an evening session of the Modern Language Association devoted to Lionel's achievements. She said that all of the papers, except for Quentin Anderson's, "were fairly thoroughly off the mark, and all sounded to me as if ultimately motivated by the desire to kill off the father so that the sons would thereby flourish." As if to fight back, she added, "but no son lives by killing off the father, blood or cultural, and how extraordinary that grown people should not know this." She often thought of the letter Howard Mumford Jones had written her, telling her how Lionel always seemed to him "an institution like the Washington Monument or the Presidency of the United States. . . . He had a kind of agelessness, a vast serenity . . . a kind of communion with the gods."

Despite such a tribute, Diana felt it was time for her to step in once again, although it would take two more years for her to write and publish in *Commentary* an encomium, "Lionel Trilling: A Jew at Columbia." She described Lionel's early life with great tenderness and sincerity, writing that "unlike others of his intellectual generation, Lionel had no need to make for himself the strategic leap into the American middle class, with what this so often involves in defensiveness. Also, unlike many first-generation Jewish intellectuals, he had not been taught to think of himself as 'smart.' It was not his sense that life was a contest of minds or that intellect was a weapon; it was more an instrument of conscience." She went on to comment that "his parents had made him feel unusually valuable, or certainly much valued by them. While he had no belief that he possessed outstanding skills—on the contrary, throughout his life he thought that virtually everyone with whom he associated had read more than he had, had a better memory, and was better trained in the use of the basic tools of the intellectual trade—he had grown up with an undefined feeling of personal worth, some secret quality of being to which he could give no name but on which he could ultimately rely."

She detailed his troubles at Columbia: "How much, then, had anti-Semitism actually been a factor in Lionel's dismissal in 1936? Who can say? Certainly it was by [President] Butler's intervention, by fiat of the top authority of the University, that a Jew was first given a post teaching English at Columbia, which in those days implied permanence." She continued, "Everyone was easy with him; Lionel felt no hidden tensions. Indeed, the generosity that he met from this point forward in his Columbia career has, for me, a legendary quality—his departmental colleagues could not have taken more pleasure in his academic or critical successes if they had been their own." She included surprising facts, such as the following incident:

One day, . . . very soon after his promotion, Lionel had a call from Emery Neff [his thesis adviser]: he wished to come to the house and he hoped that I would be at home too. Although we were mildly on visiting terms with Neff and his wife, a call of this kind was unprecedented. What Emery Neff came to say was that now that Lionel was a member of the department, he hoped that he would not use it as a wedge to open the English department to more Jews. He made his statement economically and straightforwardly, ungarnished; it must have taken some courage. And he seemed to be speaking for himself alone; he cited no other departmental opinion. Lionel and I just sat and stared. Neither of us spoke. Emery turned to other subjects and soon left.

Diana had triumphed. She wrote Bill Jovanovich that "everybody seems to love [the new essay]. I've never had such unanimous praise for anything I've written . . . and people stress their admiration for the way it's composed, its simplicity of style. And this was so easy for me to write; it went so fast." She told a friend that she considered it "unmotivated" memoir.

Kip Fadiman had written Diana in a condolence note that Lionel was his "hero and life-model." He later wrote again to praise her new essay, and Diana told him that "*Commentary* wanted to print it or, more precisely, they didn't want to give it up, but they felt that they owed it to me to tell me that they really didn't like it very much. Why didn't it deal with Lionel's *ideas* about being a Jew?" In a letter to Fadiman years later, Diana said people are concerned about Lionel's "conduct as a Jew" because of their feelings of envy that he "did not look or talk like a Jew."

In an unpublished book Diana wrote that "one's world as a Jew had more points of reference and connection than the world of gentiles. It was cozier, more family-like. This warming emotion of Jewishness required no support of religion or ritual; it was essentially a domestic sentiment." She and Lionel had always agreed on this.

In late 1977 Diana confessed to Bill Jovanovich that she saw getting all of Lionel's books ready for publication as a "distraction from her own projects." She was now thinking of a book that was "not conventional autobiography" although it would be "wholly autobiographical." She thought it would take up two volumes. "It is episodic and speculative in a way that eludes easy classification," she told Jovanovich; "you'll have to trust me that it is more than conventionally interesting."

Meanwhile, *Reviewing the Forties* garnered some excellent reviews, despite *The New York Times*' nearly four-month multiunion strike. Drenka Willen recalled how angry Diana was over the book's not getting reviewed because of the enormous backlog resulting from the shutdown. Willen also said that Diana had unrealistic expectations for the book: "to expect essays from the forties to sell better than something less historical was not realistic, but you know when you work hard on something it should just sell."

Still, Diana got impressive praise. Elizabeth Janeway wrote in *The Los Angeles Times Book Review* that "to the extent that America has an intellectual conscience, Diana Trilling is it." Janeway went on to write that Diana knew that "literature can't be understood apart from its context in social, cultural and political life. [Diana Trilling] has been disagreed with, but no one has ever thought her opinions shabby, easily come by or uninteresting." *The Nation*'s reviewer, Emile Capouya, began his review by mentioning an essay he remembered from her tenure at the magazine but which was not in the collection. The essay in question had announced that Diana "had not come across a new novel that was worth reading." Capouya commented that "for me, that announcement killed literary journalism as I had known it, the unpaid arm of book publishers' advertising and promotion efforts." He went on to call *Reviewing the Forties* "remarkable" and wrote that Diana "understands that literature is a dramatization of values, and that all its other attractions are at the service of that central preoccupation."

18

HER OWN PLACE

Writers are what they write, also what they fail to write.

—DIANA TRILLING

At one point after Lionel's death, Diana had thought of trying to write the memoir he himself had had in mind to write. For background she decided to ask various people such as Jacques Barzun, Eric Bentley, Kip Fadiman, and Lewis Mumford, as well as some of Lionel's former students, for their recollections. She would record their responses on tape. Some candidates turned her down. Norman Mailer was one, telling her the strain of preparing for such an interview was too much, later explaining that the amount of time such interviews would take was too costly in his own economic terms. But Mailer felt bad about not fulfilling Diana's "needs," as he put it, and finally agreed "to come in toward the end" in one three-hour session. "Remember, I talk twice as fast as anyone else," he reminded his friend. (But this interview never took place.)

As Diana told Morris Dickstein, who was also reluctant to participate, "I have been trying very hard, and succeeding a little better each day, to persuade those who record their recollections of Lionel to think of this project not as anecdotal or celebrative—how Lionel would have hated the latter!—but as an effort to re-create by whatever means, including the anecdotal, the social and political atmosphere in which he was doing his writing." Dickstein said: "As I recall, Diana asked me more than once but I put her off. I guessed she might disagree strongly with what I had to say, not so much about Lionel as about the '50s and '60s in general, and I hesitated to get into the ring with her. Later, I got to know and like her more, and when I read some of her interviews (with Virgil Thomson, for example), I was mildly sorry I hadn't taken her up on it, since the interviews were very good." (Dickstein wrote Diana a letter in 1981 congratulating her on the success of a new book, *Mrs. Harris*, and reminded her that he owed her an interview, but Diana replied that she hadn't worked on the project because of a lack of funding.)

Jules Feiffer recalls being interviewed by Diana about the 1960s, and as he was explaining his point of view, Diana began arguing with him. "In the guise of finding out what I thought," Feiffer said, "she was telling me everything I thought was wrong!" Diana's aggressiveness was front and center. It did not win her new friends.

She wrote in a letter that "it began to be apparent that I was engaged more in an act of mourning than in a work of generally useful historical reconstruction," so she decided to expand her project beyond Lionel and his time and to focus on their joint cultural histories and more. In fact, this expanded project was the very one that won for her and caused her to turn down a Rockefeller Foundation grant because she felt not enough money had been offered for such an important undertaking. Nonetheless, she continued making tapes into the mid-1980s and deposited them with Columbia University's Oral History office (which had offered to transcribe them).

In the winter of 1980 Diana went on the warpath with Midge Decter and Norman Podhoretz. Diana said that in his book *Making It*, "Norman had a very, very personally motivated attack on Lionel, saying that his career had been a falling away after his *The Liberal Imagination*." She raged, "He accuses Lionel of dishonesty. He accuses Lionel of a lack of character. He accuses him of things that [amount to] very dirty talk for somebody who was treated as he was treated by Lionel." That same winter, Midge Decter asked to have her oral history interview withdrawn. (Decades later Diana and Lionel would be two examples in Norman Podhoretz's 1999 book *Ex-Friends*.) But in that winter of 1980 Decter wrote Diana that "in a community where people speak seriously to one another about serious matters, there are no censors, no gauleiters, and hopefully no preadolescents lining up gangs in the neighborhood. In my opinion you have made yourself an outcast from that community. And I shudder to imagine what sort of 'history' will be put into the archives." (Despite this letter, Decter's interview was never removed from the archives.)

Diana wanted to find a lasting memorial for Lionel. A year after his death, a series of seminars had been inaugurated in his name. Columbia University subsidized the early seminars, which included talks by Jacques Barzun, Isaiah Berlin, and Gertrude Himmelfarb. Eventually outside funding was sought, and Diana helped draft the letter to potential benefactors, which over time would include The Heyman Center for Humanities at Columbia; Professor William Theodore de Bary (provost emeritus at Columbia and an award-winning professor) and his wife, Fanny; Daniel and Joanna Rose (prominent philanthropists); and William H. Janeway (an economist and venture capitalist), who, along with his wife, Weslie R. Janeway, began the Cambridge Endowment for Research in Finance.

Diana remained "the powerhouse" (as one participant described her) behind the seminars for years. "She was so powerful because she had qualities that frightened her colleagues," this person said. Elisabeth Sifton said that Diana "seemed to take advantage of [Lionel's] position and she began to throw her weight around." Sifton further remarked that her father (Reinhold Niebuhr) was often "exasperated" by Diana and found some of her behavior "embarrassingly funny." Another editor who knew both Trillings said that "I love Diana and want her to live a long life . . . but fast." Even Bill Jovanovich had misgivings. He told one of his editors that "Diana's always gaveling people out of society."

During the spring of 1978 Diana had given a lecture at Columbia based on her essay "The Liberated Heroine," the one in which she gave birth to the idea of a "spirited heroine . . . whose first concern is the exploration and realization of female selfhood." She received a long "burst of enthusiasm" fan letter from a graduate student in English at Columbia. This student had already published book reviews in *Commentary*, *The New Leader*, *The New Republic*, and *The New York Times Book Review*. She told Diana that she was impressed "by the vigor and adherence to what I can only call classical premises with which you examined the hysteria-inducing subject of selfhood." She went on: "it seems to me that it is a subject increasingly and unfortunately treated as though it existed in a void, suspended from consideration of history and imperatives of history, and that your refusal to do so indicated greater respect for its potentialities than the rantings of so-called radical feminists."

Diana took notice.

The student, Daphne Merkin, would become one of the first of several young women writers Diana would mentor, a role she fashioned for herself after Lionel's death. These writers could benefit from her editing skills. Once again she would have a worthy person that could profit from her expertise. She would feel useful and fulfilled again in a way that only such a symbiotic interaction could achieve. Diana particularly respected Brom Anderson, son of Quentin and Thelma, and offered him advice and once even a job as a copy editor on the uniform edition of Lionel's books.

Diana would eventually write Bill Jovanovich that Daphne Merkin "was one of the most intelligent people I have ever known," and their friendship would be long and complicated, until it wasn't anymore. Merkin later remarked that Diana "was in general comfortable with people who obeyed."

When Diana and Lionel had been at Oxford in 1965, she had briefly met and enjoyed the company of a young writer and editor, John Gross, who was working at *The Times Literary Supplement*. Diana's relationship with Gross soon became a chummy one—she enjoyed gossiping with him—and she admired his subdued expression of ambition. They corresponded often. Diana liked being attached to smart people, even more so after she became a widow. She communicated her good feelings to the lucky few (more that she was lucky to know *them*) and was richly

rewarded with devotion, companionship, and sometimes disappointment. Once or twice she felt "stabbed in the back" by a budding friendship that took an unexpected downward turn, often the result of a
demand not satisfactorily met.

Diana wrote Bill Jovanovich in May 1978 that John Gross, "at 43, is, of
course, the best editor in the world—in the world, that is, of serious literature." She added, "He is also a man of unimpeachable honor and integrity, tough but wholly civilized and gentle." At the time Diana wrote
this she was trying to convince Gross to leave London, and Diana desperately wanted him to become an HBJ editor. "No matchmaker ever
prayed so hard that her match would take," Diana wrote Jovanovich. Diana felt as if she were offering a treasure to her dearly loved publisher.

Diana had managed to get John Gross to believe that it was all Jovanovich's idea, and that she was "merely lending her services as a kind of
intermediary." Gross told Diana that he would consider coming to New
York if the salary met his requirements, and, in time, he and Bill Jovanovich had a warm and easy interview. Everything was looking good.
They saw eye to eye. Jovanovich was impressed. So was John Gross.

Before the meeting, Diana mentioned to Gross, who had been staying with her on Claremont Avenue, that "any public knowledge that I
had been involved in the arrangements would be good for none of us."
It's not clear why she thought she had to say this because although she
didn't want to blast forth the news of her seeming to be John's agent, she
actually wouldn't have minded whispers of it. She liked being in the position of helping people she admired, and just knowing she had put two
brilliant souls together was enough for her.

But her attitude changed significantly after she learned that at the successful HBJ meeting both men had decided that Diana's name "must
never be mentioned as having a part in [the job offer]." *Never* be mentioned? Was she some sort of villain? She wondered.

It was just too, too much for Diana, who knew only too well, that
despite everything, the literary community would put two and two
together—after all, she had just given John Gross a large cocktail party.
It was one thing for *her* to decide to stay silent, but it was completely
unacceptable to have the men conspiring, and why would they?

She wrote Jovanovich "how hurtful it is to be informed that, however affectionately, the two of you decided on my elimination. I'm not even sure it quite meets my definition of affectionateness." She wondered if a man had played the same role as she, would he have been eliminated? She doubted it. "I have been left feeling bleak and heavy-hearted where I should have hoped to be only happy," she wrote Jovanovich. "I asked nothing of either of you except my own private pleasure of accomplishment."

Diana "felt ill," she wrote in her letter to Jovanovich. Speaking of Gross, she asked, "How can one be friends with someone for whom the connection is a public embarrassment? . . . What a big price to pay for allowing myself to be concerned with the well-being of HBJ: I ask myself if I'll never learn," she wrote in sorrow to Jovanovich. How had she so misjudged John Gross?

But she would eventually forgive him; in fact, by the following year, 1979, she was writing him once again as "Dearest John." Although he didn't accept a job at HBJ, he did move to New York in 1983 to become an editor on *The New York Times Book Review* and then to serve as one of the newspaper's daily book reviewers. (He also wrote a column, "About the Arts," for the paper before he left New York five years later, in 1989, to return to London, where he became the drama critic for *The Sunday Telegraph*.)

Diana sought Gross's help when she wanted to sell Lionel's archives— he was a friend of Charles Ryskamp, the director of the Pierpont Morgan Library. But she soon realized, she wrote Gross, that "the T's are wrong" for the Morgan, and she told him she had offered the archive to Columbia "at an appraised price, low that I take that to be, but I have warned [Columbia] that my own papers, which they seem to want as a companion property, will cost them more for reasons quite extrinsic to literary value.*

Although Diana didn't bring Jovanovich the prize from England she had hoped to, several years later she would successfully bring him

---

*   The Columbia University Rare Book and Manuscript Library eventually bought the papers of both Trillings for $127,000.

Daphne Merkin. "Introducing me to Jovanovich was unusual for her and very unbelievably generous," Merkin said. She eventually became the associate publisher of HBJ. So successful was her relationship with Jovanovich, Merkin added, that over the years Diana became very jealous.

At one point Diana decided to act informally as an acquiring editor, and she sent Jovanovich a series of book ideas she thought might interest him. She suggested that Brian Urquhart, the undersecretary general of the United Nations, should write a history of various UN officials he worked with. In 1972 he had written a book about Dag Hammarskjold and would later write six other books concerning the UN, as well as a biography of the 1950 Nobel Peace Prize winner Ralph Bunche. He didn't need Diana to urge him on to even more projects. But it turns out that what Diana was really interested in hearing about from Urquhart, and was embarrassed to say so at first to Jovanovich, was his experience in the early 1960s as a captive of some cannibals in the Congo who were threatening to eat him. But she was sure he would never write such a book, she wrote Jovanovich; still, she enticed her friend and publisher with the idea. She also suggested a book to be called "Those Good Old Days at the Met," which would be an anecdotal reconstruction of great days and great stars. She said that the ideal person beside herself to do such a book would be the theater critic of *The New Republic*, Stanley Kauffmann, "but I fear he has too many other projects." Diana told Jovanovich someone should write a biography of Isaac Rosenfeld, who "was infinitely more gifted than Delmore Schwartz, not as crazy but wild enough."[†]

Diana included several more ideas in her letter, adding at the end a personal, handwritten postscript: "Isn't the jacket for *Reviewing the Forties* smashing? I'm mad for it."

She was also "mad" for finding a new book idea for herself. In the meantime, until she had one, Diana continued to review books whenever she was asked. In June of 1979 Emily Hancock of *Harvard*

[†] A biography by Steven J. Zipperstein, a professor of history at Stanford, would eventually be written in 2009, published by Yale University Press.

Educational Review "invited " her to review *Reinventing Womanhood*, by Carolyn G. Heilbrun. Diana was given specific instructions on the number and form of the pages to be submitted and was even told exactly what details to include in her review. Additionally, her review would have to be approved by the entire editorial board. Furthermore, there would be no commitment to publish the review, and no fee would be paid. The letter ended by acknowledging that "our solicitation is a statement of strong interest in your review of the book, and of our commitment to try to work with you to bring it into print."

Diana went to work, but not on the book review. Starting with an announcement that "I have never been addressed . . . as if I were a beginning student in a correspondence course in book-reviewing"; her reply went on to remind Miss Hancock that "no established writer is invited to review on a speculative basis." Diana ended by noting that since there was no mention of a fee, she assumed that the invitation alone was supposed to be "enough compensation for a week or two of difficult work! That would indeed account for the lack of professional regard in your letter." Emily Hancock had been hit with a brick and could only manage a weak response: "Like all academic journals, we do not offer a fee to our authors. The letter we sent you was entirely consistent with all of our book review solicitations. We deeply regret that its contents felt personal to you in ways that were distressing."

In the same spirit of indignation, Diana couldn't resist correcting errors in an already published essay about her husband that had appeared in *The Jewish Week* in the spring of 1977. How she wished she had been contacted before publication, to correct such errors, as she noted in her letter: "Trilling did not, I think, take on the style of the 'tweedy gentleman scholars' of England." She said that "Freud was not so much 'pessimistic' as tragic. At any rate, it was the tragic element in Freud that my husband so much admired." She berated the essayist for using the word *critiques*. "It's unprofessional," she said bluntly. And finally, she told the writer that "there is no such thing as a 'Jewish-American aristocracy.' Here again there intrudes into your statement some kind of class-inspired defensive aggressiveness. I am particularly alert to this unwarranted but frequent intrusion of class feeling into criticism of my

husband's work. . . . For my husband, as for me, class and its consequences are a reality not to be denied, and especially not in the name of
political social virtues, announced or hidden." There was one bit of
praise from Diana. "'Strained mobile face' and 'intriguing inner demons' [both about Lionel] is [sic] good and accurate," she commented.

Ever the guardian of her husband, in the fall of 1976, after the writer
Phillip Lopate published an essay about Lionel in *American Review*,
Diana wrote Ted Solotaroff, the editor of the magazine, that she found
the piece "vile and disgusting." Lopate later published a slightly revised
version of the essay in his book *Bachelorhood*, and he called Trilling "the
protector of my youth." But he also described his classroom presence as
reminding him "of someone who had suffered a stroke, and whose
struggle to employ his full vocabulary was painful to watch." Diana told
Lopate he was showing "unconscious masked hostility" toward her
husband, but she nonetheless granted him permission to quote from
Lionel's letters. Lopate wrote Diana that given her views on the essay,
he found her "granting of permission all the more gracious and large-
souled."

Between such diatribes and other work, Diana needed diversion—
relief from her demons—so she continued to enjoy watching television,
even with her vision problems, and especially liked detective and medical
shows like *Starsky and Hutch*, *M.A.S.H*, and later, in 1986, *L.A. Law*. She
also played a lot of Solitaire, using cards with large-print numbers on
them.

More and more Diana required help with many of the basic things in
her life, and she sought it from Christopher Zinn, a graduate student
who had first worked for Diana shortly after Lionel's death as a secretary
and research assistant (and would remain of assistance into the mid-
1980s). She wrote Zinn that "now that I can't read it's like having sin li-
censed by the top authority—from 7 pm until midnight every night I sit
mesmerized before that foolish box, which, incidentally grows dimmer
and dimmer as my 'good' eye fails to conquer my most recent hemor-
rhage." In later years she would be mesmerized by *Court TV* and be delighted when a friend introduced her to Beth Karas, a correspondent
there. They became close friends and Karas even did some research for

Diana when Diana became interested in an attempted murder in 1924 in which a businessman tried to poison his wife with arsenic.

Diana had many assistants over the years, and she complained bitterly about most of them, although sometimes exaggerated her objections. But she had a hard time giving up her need for control and often took her frustrations out on her helpers. She told the writer Stephen Koch, "It's hard enough to be the controlled person that I am, so much controlled, I mean by logic and reason, without an addition of having a free flow of feeling and idea impeded by the cold presence of another person." Koch had met Diana in the early 1980s (and later married Franny Cohen, a psychoanalyst who was the daughter of Lionel's cousin, the prominent physicist I. Bernard Cohen.) He remembers when first meeting Diana that he praised her review of Capote's *In Cold Blood* and even quoted the last two sentences of the review to her. But, Koch said, "She told me I was misquoting her. I was quite wrong. So my little tribute flopped." But a friendship developed, especially after his marriage. He was working on his first book, *Double Lives*, "a study of the Soviet Secret services and the larger intellectual life of the West," and he shared ideas about it with Diana. "She adored it," he said, "and so we started meeting quite regularly," despite, he said "her crazy corrections of grammar. Mispronunciation was intolerable to her," Koch said. "'Prestigious' mispronounced was intolerable to her. She'd say, why do you use words you can't even pronounce?"

Patricia Bosworth, whom Diana would mentor and become a close friend of, said that several students she knew became Diana's assistants, and she would tell Diana she was so glad they were "working with you," and Diana would correct her and say, "'They are working *for* me.' Diana really believed in various levels of society, so to speak." She even once told a young friend that her nanny should not eat at the same table as the family. Diana, "who was like a task master," told Bosworth that one particular assistant wasn't working hard enough. But Diana was very encouraging and supportive when Bosworth wrote the memoir of her father, Bartley Crum, of which she read parts to Diana. Crum was an influential lawyer who defended many targets of the House Un-American Activities Committee, and Diana particularly criticized him for defending Paul Robeson. "Diana questioned everything my father did," Bosworth said. "Of course Robson was a Communist, but that didn't mean my father was a communist." She and Diana finally decided not to talk politics—it was Diana's suggestion—because, Bosworth said, "she was afraid our friendship would be destroyed. . . . She said I don't want this to happen. I care about you. It's happened too many times to me that friendships have been destroyed over politics."

Like Bosworth, Koch, a former head of the creative writing program at Columbia, also found students to help Diana. "They always worked out to her great satisfaction," Koch said. "When they weren't from my class they were sociopaths," he explained; "when she saw something a bit wrong, she turned it into something more than it should have been."

Christopher Zinn, who went on to live and teach in Oregon, was probably one of the most successful of Diana's helpers, along with Jerome Gentes, a young writer who worked for Diana for three summers. Gentes had a strong food connection with Diana and had worked in the food industry throughout college. They always shopped together, although Diana did most of the cooking. Diana also had a strong attachment to Catherine Park, another helper, who knew just how to handle matters when Diana "often went berserk." Park was a calming influence.

Zinn not only edited some excerpts of Lionel's journals in 1986 (agreeing with Diana that "Lionel's endemic pessimism" should be edited out), but he also conducted an extensive series of taped interviews with Diana in 1983, for which he was paid $10,000 out of her advance from HBJ for a book to be called "Biography of a Marriage." (This book was never published, although much of the material found its way into *The Beginning of the Journey*.)

Zinn and Diana grew very close, and she eventually made him the Trilling literary executor, until he failed to turn in a book review! In 1986, University of Chicago professor Mark Krupnick published *Lionel Trilling and the Fate of Cultural Criticism*. Zinn was scheduled to review it (at Diana's suggestion) for *Partisan Review*. But the review never appeared. Diana wrote Zinn: "I am removing your name as a literary executor . . . as a response to your recent actions or lack of action, as most dramatically demonstrated in your conduct about the Krupnick review for *PR*." She concluded, "For one reason or another, you were unable to produce that review; let's put it that you were blocked. Everyone knows that writers get into trouble but you made no explanation of your delays."

Four years earlier, in 1982, after Krupnick had published an essay about Lionel, Diana had been quick to write him a letter pointing out his multiple errors, ranging from Lionel's position on the Columbia student uprising to his attitude toward Judaism. Basically, Diana didn't like acknowledging anyone not sharing her precise views on her late husband. In any case Krupnick was planning an "intellectual" biography, not a personal one, mostly because Diana had already refused him access to Lionel's papers. "Krupnick is an indefatigable researcher; this must be said for him," she wrote to Lionel's cousin Bernard Cohen. She went on: "He will do not merely an unperceptive biography of Lionel's mind but a slanted one, slanted to his own long-standing hostility to Li's kind of thought." (Diana considered Krupnick a "hatchet man" for Philip Rahv's magazine *Modern Occasions*, which she reminded Cohen had done a "character assassination on Li.") "Trilling's career is an object lesson in the glories and difficulties of being an intellectual in America," Krupnick later wrote in his book. (A decade later he would review Diana's memoir, *The Beginning of the Journey*, saying it was her "best book" even though it was "self-serving" about her husband.)

Lionel's death changed Diana's approach not only to friendship but also to her extended family. The book by Krupnick caused a permanent rift between Lionel's sister, Harriet, and Diana. Things had been fine enough between them until Lionel's death—and the Krupnick biography. Harriet had given Krupnick information about Lionel's early life, and Diana was angry that she hadn't first checked with her about whether to do this. Diana wrote a scathing letter accusing Harriet of a longtime hostility toward her, to which Harriet replied in a letter to her sister-in-law that Diana's "self-righteousness is monumental. . . . I think I've had enough castigation and pain for a lifetime." Behind Harriet's indignation was not really the Krupnick book but rather the fact that Diana did not "press" Harriet to come to Lionel's hospital room, "as we agreed." Harriet continued, "I waited for a sign to come. It never came. I knew then and now accept that our family was truly destroyed. Goodbye."

Diana initiated another good-bye—and meant it—to Lillian Hellman. In January of 1980 Mary McCarthy said on the Dick Cavett Show that Hellman was "a dishonest writer. . . . Every word she writes is a lie, including 'and,' and 'the.'" Naturally, Diana was asked to comment on the controversy that soon developed—Hellman wanting to sue McCarthy and Hellman refusing to acknowledge her own public-figure status. Was their feud based on an ancient jealousy between the two women, or was it a continuation of the political battle between the anti-Stalinists (McCarthy) and the Stalinists (Hellman)? It is not clear what Diana was asked about the controversy to elicit this answer: "Anyone who entertains me on Martha's Vineyard is never again invited to Lillian Hellman's house," Diana told a reporter. The comment appeared in an article in *The New York Times* and a mention in *The New York Post*'s "Page Six." Still, Diana did not want to enter "a cat fight," which she emphatically said is named as such "because we are all women—nothing is given any substance, nothing is given any intellectual content that any serious person need respect. It's just made out to be bad-tempered shrewishness. I resent it profoundly." Later she added, "Actually I did less provocation than Mary McCarthy did. Mary McCarthy took the first step against Lillian; I never took any first step." (Hellman died before her lawsuit with McCarthy had its day in court, and the matter was dropped by Hellman's executors.)

With legal proceedings on her mind, Diana told Patricia Bosworth, "I've always been interested in covering trials. As you may know, I wrote at some length about Hiss-Chambers, as well as the Robert Oppenheimer security hearing." In 1971 Diana had been asked by Sargent Shriver of The Joseph P. Kennedy Jr. Foundation to participate in a panel to discuss a medical case at Johns Hopkins Hospital in which the parents of a premature baby with Down syndrome decided not to correct their infant's congenital intestinal obstruction; the infant died after eleven days. Diana at first accepted the invitation to be on the panel, then changed her mind, seeing the issues involved as too complicated because it was "more than the general problem of biological technology." She was not ready to parse medical morality. (The ethical questions the case raised continued to be debated for many years.)

Diana was slightly embarrassed about leaving her novel behind, and she wrote John Gross that she had merely "broken it off" to do another book. This book, she wrote him, was going to be titled *A Respectable Murder* (the title would change two more times—*Love, Here Is My Heart*, from a First World War song with the refrain "Something to kiss or kill"—to the final, *Mrs. Harris: The Death of the Scarsdale Diet Doctor*). Diana enthusiastically wrote Gross that the book would be about "our famous author of the Scarsdale diet [who] was recently shot by his longtime mistress, head of the exclusive Madeira School for Girls in Virginia. . . . The upcoming trial commands great interest here and so I'm afraid does the prospect of my writing about it."

Diana had found a story—a story that stirred her: Jean Harris, a proper headmistress of a fancy southern private school, discovers that Herman Tarnower, her longtime famous doctor lover, author of the bestseller *The Complete Scarsdale Medical Diet*, has a new and much younger love. Harris confronts him about it on the evening of March 10, 1980, and ends up killing him with a .32 caliber revolver she said she meant to use on herself; only the gun went off accidentally as her lover grabbed for it. The riveting story could evolve into a full-length book—unlike her novel, which was full-length but with no narrative to speak of.

Diana's years of editing her own essays, reviews, and collections of both her and others' letters and/or writings, and of editing Lionel—more than just editing him—were about to be over. She was free now as she had never been before to become what she always had wanted to become. All the energy behind her frustrations, angers, resentments, boredoms—even haughtinesses—would at long last find an appropriate outlet. She would later tell Patricia Bosworth, "Finally, in the long run, my emphasis on the moral aspect of life may well be the result of the pull in the opposite direction. Otherwise, why did I write as frequently as I did about people who were adversaries to our society?"

Even with the aid of analysis, it would take Diana until the middle of her seventies to attempt what she wished she had undertaken decades earlier. As Peter Pouncey, a former Columbia dean and former president of Amherst College, remarked, "You could see hunger in the poor woman to get her own place," and with Lionel alive "she could only get half a place."

On May 4, 1980, the *Washington Post Book World* announced that Harcourt Brace Jovanovich had signed Diana on April 17 to write a book about a murder that had captured headlines across America. "Everyone is interested in crime stories, but they're usually located on the edge of life as we're familiar with it," Diana wrote in a note to herself, "whereas the Harris case exploded in the center of the respectable middle class." Diana was pleased the announcement came soon after the contract was signed because, as she told Bill Jovanovich, "I'm scared someone will steal my title." (She meant *A Respectable Murder*.) Two other writers would also write about the murder: Lally Weymouth, an editor and journalist (Summit Books) and Shana Alexander, also a journalist and the first woman to write a column for *Life* magazine (Little, Brown). Diana, whose book would be published first, would tell a reporter that she " was not doing a reportorial book at all. I want to write about the society in which this took place. . . . Facts aren't truth. They approximate truth." She told another reporter that she was "free-associating" about the case.

Diana received a substantial advance, $67,500, from HBJ. (Bill Jovanovich, in a spirit of hubris, told *Time* magazine she received a solid $125,000.) The industrialist and philanthropist Norton Simon and his second wife, actor Jennifer Jones, bought the dramatic rights for $1 million, with $50,000 on signing, and after six months, there was to be $100,000 more, with further hefty payments in the months to come. Diana almost couldn't believe her good fortune. It had come late in life, but it had come—and, moreover, her book would soon be a major Hollywood film starring Jennifer Jones as Jean Harris. Diana worried she might need Jean Harris's agreement, and she was also worried that the Simon-Jones team would not like her book after reading it in its entirety (they had only seen sections of it). In any case, several months later Jones decided she didn't want the role after all, and her husband dropped the option (although Diana did get to keep the $50,000 she received on signing).

Hamish Hamilton Limited bought the book for publication in England. ("I have long admired your husband's writing," the editor told her in the second sentence of his introductory letter.) The Book of The Month Club bought syndication rights, as did the Quality Paperback Book Club. Penguin Books bought the soft-cover rights. Second serial rights were sold to *New Woman* magazine and *US Magazine*. On her own Diana had contacted *The New York Times Magazine* to offer first serial rights, and she said it was "settled" almost immediately. Her two excerpts were rejected, however, because, as she wrote in a letter," The book as written is indeed different from the book I first planned to write." She insisted on a $2,000 kill fee, which she received.

Despite the promise of success with *Mrs. Harris*, Diana managed to find some faults with HBJ early in the publishing process. Although Penguin Books ultimately published the paperback edition, she had thought she had an agreement with Bantam Books, and she accused HBJ of undermining this arrangement behind her back. "I can't begin to understand how this could have been done to me," she wailed, and then insisted she be "apprised of everything of which I am by contract supposed to be informed." She felt abused, just as, she later told a reporter, Jean Harris had been; "she needed to be abused," Diana exclaimed. "Now we can all understand that can't we? Haven't we all some touch of this *somewhere* in us? I think we do." Later, more than one of her readers would be struck by the thought that the book was Diana's unconscious fantasy of murdering Lionel, a fantasy that Jean Harris had had the nerve and anger to make real.

In fact, Diana said that from the very beginning of her interest and early research into the case, she "came to the shooting of Dr. Tarnower with a bias in Mrs. Harris's favor, which meant prejudice against the man who was now dead; indeed, I could put it that before I had ever heard of Mrs. Harris, I was prepared to be on the other side from the Scarsdale doctor's." Thus, at first it was "a respectable murder" in her mind. (Lawyers changed her mind quickly about that notion being expressed in a book title.) But in another note to herself, Diana wrote, "I keep thinking of these two—Jean Harris and Dr. Herman Tarnower, and they seem so extraordinarily well-matched: both ugly, mean-tempered, selfish, dutiful, compulsive people." Still another note stated, "Mrs. Harris is the first public victim of women's liberation. It gave her the foundation for her self-pity which in turn gave her the foundation for vengeance against the mistreatment from Tarnower. It also promised her freedom from punishment."

Before the trial began, on November 21, 1980, Diana had written a draft of the book in complete sympathy with Jean Harris. During the trial—Diana hired an assistant to attend the trial with her and take extensive notes—she completely changed her mind and tore up what she had already written. She told *The New York Times* that "until the Harris book, I had worked off in another world, venturing out only to check a fact in the library, but now I know how difficult it is to report on what's happening in the real world."

Many things changed Diana's mind, she noted, even acknowledging that facts can hold the truth. First on her list was that Jean Harris had brought fifty rounds of ammunition with her in the car, and had brought ten rounds into Tarnower's house, and also that upon her arrival she had the presence of mind to ask one of his two live-in housekeepers what guests had been at dinner that night. Diana was also struck by the fact—which she learned in the courtroom—that Harris "had stopped to look at her mouth in the mirror" before facing Tarnower ("with his dry strivings and worldly salvations," as Diana wrote of him), who was in the bedroom they had so often shared. Diana, who disliked just about everything about the diet doctor (a face "more reptilian than foxy") was struck over and over again by Jean Harris's tone of superiority and emotional detachment. Tarnower, Diana wrote, was "cruelly self-engrossed."

After a trial that lasted sixty-four days, on February 24, 1981, Jean Harris was found guilty of second-degree murder, that is, according to the first two of five New York State statutes: "(1) with the intent to cause the death of another person, he or she causes the death of such person or a third person; (2) under circumstances demonstrating a 'depraved indifference to human life,' the defendant 'recklessly engages in conduct which creates a grave risk of death to another person, and thereby causes the death of another person.'" She was sentenced to a minimum of fifteen years (and a maximum of life) in prison. Diana said that Jean

Harris bore a murderous rage but not premeditation and that she did not consciously lie about wanting to kill her lover—it was just that this truth was locked away in her subconscious.

Diana put all her strength and intelligence into the writing of a book that would become a best seller. Kip Fadiman told her the book was surely a classic, and he praised the use of her "own" voice "and what it reveals of the magnificent use you are making of your own life of thought and experience." He had in mind such determined paragraphs as "The role of witness on her own behalf suits Jean Harris the way ecstasy suited St. Theresa. I've never seen aggression so thoroughly transformed into moral superiority: it combines an eagerness to speak, eagerness to shine and contemptuous anger at the process which has ensnared her. She's so queenly in her scorn, you'd think the law was trampling on the royal preserves. Does it not enter this woman's mind that we are all of us here in this court because Dr. Tarnower is dead and that she's on trial for his murder?"

Norman Mailer wrote Diana that he "loved your instinctive analysis of the situation" and thought "no one could have done it better." Jacques Barzun told Diana that she has written "one of the great trial accounts of our time." Diana heard that the book was going to be nominated for a Pulitzer, but she later told Brom Anderson that someone at *The Wall Street Journal* undermined her chances for winning. "The public doesn't know what goes on in book reviewing," she said. The *WSJ*'s review was exceptionally brutal, but Michael Sovern, president of Columbia, later wrote her that she was "among the [Pulitzer] jury's nominees [for General Nonfiction], a rare distinction. I offer my warm congratulations on your achievement" (meaning the nomination).

In an unusual marketing move, Penguin had used two different jackets. As *Publishers Weekly* reported, "a purple-beige and white cover is aimed at those who view the murder case in terms of social history and commentary; a grey-silver one is for those interested in the case's more sensational aspects." A sales manager commented, "There are Trilling fans who want to read her observations on *anything*, and then there are those who are dying to know about the case but have no idea who Diana Trilling is."

Diana wrote in a note to herself that she didn't know what Lionel's reaction to the book would have been and that she found herself continuing
to dwell on his "discouraging behavior" in response to her play *Snitkin*,
written with Bettina Sinclair so long ago. It was a hurt she somehow could
not let go of—especially that he had thrown his very favorite pipe out
the window in disgust over the play. And with every negative review she
received for *Mrs. Harris*, she couldn't help but see Lionel's "ungener-
ousness reflected now in the intellectual culture's reaction." Dorothy
Rabinowitz, of *The Wall Street Journal*, had said *Mrs. Harris* "echoes the
sensibility of the 'Me Decade'" and that Diana's "assumptions about the
middle class are extraordinarily coarse." Calling Diana "tone deaf" and
the book "tedious," the reviewer decided that Diana's conclusions were
invented "to accord with a programmed sociological vision."

The Rabinowitz review would not be the most savage one—that distinction would belong to the assessment in *Commentary*. Diana said
that it ran "the most vulgar and ugly review of any book other than Norman's [Podhoretz] own *Making It*. She went on to say that the review
"was a made to order [negative] review." The reviewer, Joseph Adelson,
a professor of psychology at the University of Michigan, said Diana
lacked spirit in a book that was full of "cultural arrogance," that she was
"too self-absorbed" and that "she has little use for anyone. There is
scarcely a kind word for another human being to be found in this book."
She was accused of doing no investigation: "what Mrs. Trilling does not
know, she imagines or invents. The book is finally vulgar, without generosity of spirit, and pretentious."

Diana said that *Partisan Review* never reviewed it because William
Phillips was "really afraid that a popular subject can't be treated" in his
magazine. She later learned that the scholar Peter Shaw (he wrote a biography of John Adams, among other books) had written a review for
the magazine dissecting the trial more than the book, but had asked that
it be returned to him unpublished. His final paragraph had summed up
the book as follows: "And yet in the final analysis the dynamic of this
book has to do with ideas—chiefly those of contemporary feminism. Its
literary contribution is to the wide ranging cultural essay—a form at
least as much in need of rejuvenation as the novel."

The National Public Radio's *All Things Considered* called Diana arrogant for titling her book *Mrs. Harris* and damned her for daring to "catch the literary tone . . . of *Mrs. Dalloway*, and even *Madame Bovary.*" Later, the commentator said that if you "push aside arrogance, which Mrs. Trilling has accumulated after many decades of practice . . . she has plenty to say," even though the book seemed rushed into print to beat the competition. *New York* magazine called Diana "Lady Di" and faulted her for "accepting a great deal of money to do something that she had never done before, and should not have attempted." The reviewer, George V. Higgins, the popular crime novelist, went on to say that since the book was just a report on Diana's reactions to the trial, the book's title should have been "Mrs. Trilling, because all she knows about is Diana, and Diana isn't very interesting."

Even the *Columbia* magazine had mean things to say, beginning with a first paragraph stating that it would be embarrassing for anyone to be seen in public with a copy of the book. Michael Sovern was pained by the review and told Diana he found her book "to be simply splendid."

The Nation's reviewer, Elizabeth Pochoda, expressed admiration for Diana's "mellow wisdom," but there ended her easygoing praise. Pochoda decided that Diana was not only attacking the diet doctor for his style and taste but for his Jewishness. Pochoda wrote, "One senses her [Diana's] disapproval of his having become the wrong sort of Jew with the right sort of money, doctor's money. The Trillings, both Diana and her late husband, Lionel, have set rigorously Jamesian standards for Jewishness in our time." It is an "affront" to Diana, the review concludes, "that Herman Tarnower . . . fails so publicly to be a Matthew Arnold."

Anatole Broyard, one of *The New York Times* daily book reviewers, mentioned Diana favorably in one of the occasional personal essays he wrote for *The Sunday Book Review*, and she wrote him a fan letter, despite revealing to him that she "used to hate it when authors wrote to thank me for something I'd said about a book—it made the situation too personal and interested, like a bribe after the fact, and I'd almost feel guilty." She had met Broyard socially a few times and felt free to gossip with him, asking him, "Do you remember when we met last summer and I was worried about [Christopher] Lehmann-Haupt [the other daily book reviewer] reviewing my book? Thus do we misread our fates: his review and the one in *Time* were the best I got."

R. Z. Sheppard wrote in *Time* that *Mrs. Harris* not only has "resonance—the rich tone that even a tabloid subject causes when drawn across a perceptive and deeply cultured intelligence" but that "in the court of literature, Trilling's Jean Harris is a great portrait of an American aberration."

The New York Times's Christopher Lehmann-Haupt understood the book's structure and force, and why Diana tackled a subject "off her usual line," as she had put it. He told his readers that with "sharp analysis" she conveyed "precisely the atmospheric details of the trial," and what impressed him the most was her "multi-shaded treatment of the case" and the degree to which she made it seem significant to American culture. Lehmann-Haupt concluded that the book moved seamlessly "from psychology to sociology and back again."

The New York Times Book Review had not been as laudatory, and Diana, ever conspiratorial, wrote a friend that it was because "the top ownership of the *Times* . . . were Tarnower's closest friends."

In England, Diana's friend Rebecca West, in a somewhat rambling review focusing on the meaning of "taste," nonetheless, called the book "heartening" and "brilliant." Anita Brookner noted in *The London Review of Books* that Diana seemed "the only enlightened witness" at the trial, yet Brookner bemoaned the fact that Diana "enshrines her observations in a genre which has been turned to sensational advantage by Truman Capote and Norman Mailer. . . . As a specimen of that genre it is superb, but it has to be said that it is an unsatisfactory, even a morally dubious genre."

Diana indeed had succeeded in making her book read like a novel, despite the reviews that disputed this idea. Some people now considered her a "crime writer," a distinction she could not accept, although she told an interviewer that "it's up to you if you want to give me this label . . . although it's *cases* I am notably concerned with."

She told another person who wrote her that she agreed that Jean Harris "had star quality" and the story contained "all the ingredient[s] of a suspense story in the movies" but that her book "never even attempted properly to explain this phenomenon—star quality." Diana went on to recommend that her correspondent read her essay on Marilyn Monroe, which had been published in *Redbook* in 1962. "It bears on *Mrs. Harris*," Diana wrote her correspondent, "if only in my statement that when I heard of Marilyn Monroe's death and how lonely she had been, I desperately wished that I had been able to offer her friendship."

Travel to and from the trial had exhausted Diana, even though Bill Jovanovich lent her his car, which her assistant drove from Manhattan to Westchester every day. (During the trial the car was stolen, and although it must have been insured, Diana insisted on sending Jovanovich a check for $3,500 to cover "the theft of the car.")

In an interview in *The New York Times* Diana said that many people asked her "how is it that I have to have had my husband die to do this much work—they don't ask in that rude way, but that indeed is what they are asking—and the answer is quite simple. I am of a generation and of a temperament in which my work was secondary to my home. That doesn't mean I wasn't very serious about my work." But once again, she doesn't say quite yet—she dare not say—that Lionel's work was her work throughout his life. There simply was no time for her own.

"Growing old is hard," Diana told Martin Amis in an interview about *Mrs. Harris* that appeared in *The Observer*. She continued: "Growing old alone is harder. You become more sensitive with your friends. You wonder if you are being asked out because of pity. There is an increased dependence on routine. I won't leave the bed unmade in the morning. . . . I won't stand by the refrigerator and eat a boiled egg. I *want* to, but I don't." In speaking of Lionel, she told Amis in a dramatic flourish: "I feel the usual things. . . . I wish now I had worshipped him a bit more."

19

RE-CREATION AND IMAGINATION

I never realized how much I wrote with my eyes.

—DIANA TRILLING TO STEPHEN KOCH, 1989

Diana continued to need more and more helpers as she aged—in 1990 she was eighty-five—and she continued to grumble about them. "They're what James meant when he spoke of Americans (I think it was Americans) failing to rise to the level of appearance," she wrote Bill Jovanovich. Paradoxically, her eyesight was now "almost non-existent," she also told him.

Jerome Gentes remained a helper she always got along with. "I really loved Diana," he said. "I told her so." Diana shared his feelings, telling him, "I love you, too." They had only two "relatively minor" quarrels over the summers Gentes was in her employ. Once he had lingered too long saying good-bye to someone, and Diana had been annoyed by what she considered a too-lengthy absence, and another time she became angry after overhearing him talking about her health to someone. But he said, "I always appreciated Diana's directness." Catherine Park did, too. "I learned discipline from her," Park said. "She worked very hard every day, and I learned about stepping back and then going over things. It

326 RE-CREATION AND IMAGINATION

was a layering process." Park also said that Diana was "easy to set off" because she was so "intense," adding that she often yelled on the phone to people who had sent her what she considered incorrect bills. She said that Diana had a very strict routine when they read the newspaper together. "She needed to [first] hear the headlines, so it was always the front page, the book review, and the obituaries."

Diana had left Martha's Vineyard and Lillian Hellman behind and had begun to spend her summers in Wellfleet on the lower Cape. Jim, who had married in 1980, visited her there with his wife, Dore Levy, whenever they could—especially on Diana's birthday, July 27. The celebration often included "an enormous blueberry pie," Levy remembered; "she did enjoy my baking, and regaled us with [stories of] meals from her past, and how fruit tasted."

The young couple lived in Providence, Rhode Island, where Dore Levy was teaching at Brown. (Before moving to Providence, Jim had commuted as often as he could from Washington, DC, where he had been the curator of old world textiles at the Textile Museum.) Catherine Park said that it seemed to her that Diana "didn't get along with Dore" or, for that matter, with Jim, either. "They had a volatile, difficult and complicated relationship," she recalled.

Dore Levy, a professor of comparative literature and East Asian studies, comments that Diana "was not an easy mother-in-law, and while I did my very best to please her, there were certain lines that Diana could not be allowed to cross." She went on: "Diana took umbrage at my career, and mocked anything to do with my work on China—except when I cooked a Chinese banquet for her guests, and then she remarked how satisfactory it was to have the kitchen properly staffed by Jim and me." She added about Diana that "China did her more good than she knew, because Jim and I early decided that we would follow Confucian principles in our relations with her, honor the parent, and try to stay just out of reach."

Diana entertained friends often in Wellfleet, "one person at a time," Jerome Gentes said. She didn't always put people together during the summer, so from time to time visitors were unaware of a number of her friendships and were taken aback that she knew certain people well enough to invite them to lunch or dinner.

Diana arranged for her helpers to drive her to the Cape, not only because it was a fairly easy trip but also because after Lionel's death, she was afraid to fly. She wasn't sure why this new phobia arose but speculated that despite everything, Lionel made her feel safe. "It had to be a very symbolic role that he played," she decided, "and not the reality."

Diana described her quarters in Wellfleet—a group of Bauhaus-style cottages called The Colony—as "a kind of elevated motel: I have a little cottage of two rooms, two baths, some terraces, a kitchenette." Edmund Wilson and Mary McCarthy stayed on the property in the 1940s, as did Bernard and Ann Malamud later on. Diana always stayed in Number 6, and a sign reading "Diana Trilling Cottage" was put up whenever she was in residence. She was the only guest allowed her own telephone line; all others had to use a pay phone.

The Colony was situated in the woods, and as Dore Levy recalled, "there were ticks. Everywhere. Crawling madly to find fresh blood." The young Trillings spent a lot of time "checking, picking, and drowning in alcohol," and Levy remembers, "Diana was at first convinced that they were fleas," but finally Levy had to tell her they were really ticks, not fleas. "Why did you bring them here?" was her rejoinder to her daughter-in-law.

Diana did a lot of work in Wellfleet on a book that was first called "Biography of a Marriage" but was later changed to *The Beginning of the Journey*. "This book is beginning to wear heavily on me," she confessed. "I wish I was through with it and could go back to writing about my childhood. Maybe I could manage that by dictation better than I manage the grown-up memoir." She wrote Bill Jovanovich that "dictation requires endlessly readings-back to me. It's very tiring." Words just didn't come to her as rapidly as they had when she was decades younger. Daphne Merkin worried about more than just her memory. "If there ever was someone who was literal about psychoanalytic concepts, it was Diana," she said. "She would literalize everything psychoanalytic. Metaphor would get lost. I always thought she was in some way an unreachable

328 RE-CREATION AND IMAGINATION

psychoanalytic patient—because she had the defenses of a walrus." Merkin said that in *The Beginning of the Journey*, which she read in early drafts, "there was some aberration—some resentment" when talking about Lionel. "She told Diana even "that it was as if she was describing someone who was castrated." Such frankness marked their friendship, and Merkin, deeply devoted for a long while, dedicated her first novel to Diana. "I don't think most people spoke to her so openly," Merkin observed; "there was a lot of sort of hierarchy in dealing with Diana."

With the help of a secretary Diana managed to continue her correspondences, especially with Bill Jovanovich. Diana couldn't get over, however, that Jovanovich never invited her to his retreat in Canada— after all, Daphne Merkin went there often. Why hadn't she been invited? "Diana was very hurt by that," Merkin said, adding that Jovanovich was an "incredible caretaker" but "also mercurial." Still, Diana continued to take pleasure in her correspondence with him. "I'm not so blind that I can't live alone," she wrote him, "but someone has to find the spices for me on the shelf, and I fear to venture out of the house alone." She wrote Kip Fadiman that she still managed to cook for herself, "although badly. I burn things because I can't see if there is liquid in the pot; that sort of dilemma."

Diana was no longer able to read, although a large magnifying glass sometimes seemed to help (she could "puzzle out an inch or two of print" she wrote Fadiman), but she said using the magnifier made her feel "seasick." She soon assembled a group of people who were happy to spend time with her and become her readers, although she told Jovanovich that "the great trouble with being read aloud to is that it's so *slow*. Also, you can't skim, which is an enormous handicap—do you realize how [time-]consuming it is to have to hear every word on the page or, if not, perhaps the wrong words?" she wrote. Later she told him more jocularly that her "worst deprivation is being unable to read in bed. I am seldom tempted to curl up in bed with a good tape recorder."

The poet Richard Howard had met her briefly when he was a student at Columbia, although his strongest tie was to Lionel, as part of "the band of people that cared for him," he recalled. Lionel was interested in him, Howard said, "as a kind of midwestern Jew of a certain class and circumstance, and I was something that he understood perfectly . . . and he was very proud of talking to me about that." Long after Lionel's death Howard spotted Diana at a restaurant, and they chatted, and after she told him her eyesight was failing, he offered to read to her. "I enjoyed her writing," Howard said. "I was very taken with her and surprised some people weren't, because I think she had just the right temperament and tone." He said that they "read some William Dean Howells and other books. . . . She liked to read books that would have interested Lionel, too. But we didn't ever get through anything easily because we would stop and talk about things that were sort of suggested by the material. . . . But on the whole the reading material was just an excuse to begin chattering, and she really loved to talk and she liked to talk to me. . . . We gossiped about everyone we knew."

Oliver Conant, an actor, director, and dramaturge who had known both the Trillings, as well as Quentin and Thelma Anderson since his teenage years, often read to Diana. "I read things I liked—Kingsley Amis's *Lucky Jim*, and Dickens's *The Pickwick Papers*." Diana also listened to Bob Dylan music with Conant, which, he said, she came to enjoy, especially after he defended Dylan as a poet.

The writer Kathleen Hill was another reader, and she wrote a poignant essay about her experience doing so. The two talked as much as they read together—particularly *In Search of Lost Time*. Hill wrote that "when we reached [the chapter called] 'Swann in Love,' *Diana* confessed she had never been subject to obsessive love, the kind Swann felt for Odette, what she supposed was called romantic love. It was not part of her makeup and she never quite understood what people meant when they talked about it."

Another writer, Patricia O'Toole, also read to Diana from time to time. Diana particularly wanted to hear the biography of Proust by George Painter, and O'Toole also made tapes of books, including her own much admired portrait of Henry Adams and his circle of friends, *Five of Hearts*. Diana sometimes asked O'Toole to read various drafts of *The Beginning of the Journey* "so she could listen to what she had written." Diana wrote Kip Fadiman that "continuing my work is what has

made this limited life which I now live endurable, no, better than that—
and perhaps as useful as it would have been had I kept my eyesight."

In 1991 Diana won her second Guggenheim fellowship for *The Beginning of the Journey*. (Her first grant had been in 1950.) She received
$30,000 and used most of the money for secretarial services. She did not
attend the welcoming party for the winners, writing in a letter to the
foundation that her "bad vision prohibits [her] moving in large groups:
I usually end up failing to greet my best friend." (Among other writers
who won a grant that year were Lorrie Moore, Madison Smart Bell, and
Francine Prose.)

Two years before she won her second Guggenheim, Stephen Koch interviewed Diana for a profile that appeared in the arts section of *The
New York Times*. She told Koch that "the beginning of our lives are likely
to be the most interesting part," so she had decided to end her memoir
in the year 1950. She also confessed that at her age "language is not at
one's service as it once was. . . . One can be neither as inventive nor as
precise as one would wish." She told him also that she was "finding it
extraordinarily difficult" to sound like herself. "It's paralyzing to have
to formulate each sentence out loud. It's so public and official," she continued. "How do you brood your way into a sentence that you have to
spell out for someone else?"

Many friends had encouraged Diana to write about her failing eyesight, and she did so in a piece entitled "Reading by Ear," which appeared in the magazine *Civilization*. Thoughtful and literary, Diana
noted that she "was at first puzzled that it is so much more time-
consuming to be read to than to read to oneself," so she asked, "Is the
voice, then, so much slower than the eye?" Her answer was yes. What's
more, she understood that "it is impossible to guess what might suddenly
catch another person's eye and fire his imagination." Was her reader
emphasizing his or her own word preferences? Was he or she skipping?
If so, did that alter the listener's critical judgment of what was being
read?

One of Diana's major complaints about being read to was how often
words were mispronounced. Her readers, she said, not naming any of
them, "have varied between mispronouncing one word in every hun-

dred and one word in every ten!" She called out a "young woman who pronounced "Iago" as if it were spelled "Ee-ajo," noting unbelievably that the reader (unnamed) "had a master's degree from a major eastern university and planned a career in college teaching. She had not heard of Othello. She had never read a play of Shakespeare."

In the early 1990s Diana had been given a computer by Catherine Park, but as Diana wrote in a letter, "I am careful not to come near it because I am a mechanical idiot, and I am afraid that I would destroy all my work of the last year if I so much as touched a button." "Actually," she added, "I haven't enough vision to be able to use it." Park used it though—it was a Dell word processor that she and Diana called "Della"—and it sped up their work together.

Diana's health was worsening. As she wrote Bill Jovanovich, she now had emphysema and had had a pacemaker installed because of atrial fibrillation.

But she continued her work, and contributed to *Newsweek*'s January 11, 1993, special series called *So Long, Soldier: The World War II Generation and How It Changed America*. Diana's essay, "How McCarthy Gave Anti-Communism a Bad Name," was an excerpt from *The Beginning of the Journey*, which HBJ was to publish in November of 1993.

Jonathan Alter, a columnist and senior editor, and Alexis Gelber, also an editor, who, at the time, specialized in politics and social issues and eventually became the managing editor of *Newsweek International*, both worked with Diana on the piece. Gelber remembers it was "very disorganized" and "all over the place." Because of Diana's failing eyesight, Gelber edited the piece with Diana in person, at Claremont Avenue. Although Diana had been "quite crotchety" on the phone, once they were together, Diana complimented Gelber on how well she had reorganized the essay. Jonathan Alter remarked that Diana "would mix stubbornness with compliments."

In 1992 Alter had commissioned a piece from Diana on the 1950s. "It was a really good piece," he says, and he recalls that Diana later asked for a column in *Newsweek*, telling him, "I don't know why I spent all these years writing for magazines people don't read." Alter couldn't believe "that at the end of her life she wanted a column!" Like Gelber, he had edited the 1950s essay in person. "Her stamina impressed me," he said, adding that Diana "made scorching assessments" of people, "basically about how they didn't treat her well."

Diana was not happy with the way HBJ published *The Beginning of the Journey*, although she was pleased with a piece about her life and work in *The New Yorker* that created a lot of prepublication interest. The book, for the most part, was reviewed favorably, but Diana was not happy at all. She even wished that she had left HBJ. She said that her "supposed editor, Cork [Corlies] Smith, never liked the book—or perhaps it is me he has never liked." There was no imminent paperback sale. There was no movie sale. In desperation she approached an agent, Georges Borchardt, to help her, but he wrote that although he thought her book was "marvelous," it was too late for him to step in. (She had approached Borchardt a year or two earlier, and he had agreed to represent her, but Diana never signed a formal agreement.) Both Trillings had unpleasant feelings about agents, although in her late eighties Diana would sign on with Andrew Wylie. But many years earlier Lionel had approached an agent, Lynn Nesbit, who, according to Diana, was disrespectful and made her husband feel like an inconsequential person. He decided then and there not to have anything to do with any agent ever again, and he didn't.

The profile of Diana in *The New Yorker* was written by the journalist Lis Harris. It was a wise and enlightening essay, and it included an exchange between Harris and Jim Trilling, in which Jim said, "I was aware most of all that my parents talked constantly to each other and they were always on the same wavelength. Very rarely have I had the impression from another couple that the whole strength of their marriage was right there in the way they talked."

Harris dug deep into the poem Diana thought Allen Ginsberg wrote for her husband in the 1960s and discovered it was not so. The profile was accompanied by a Richard Avedon photograph, and Diana wrote a friend that she was "ambivalent" about the picture, although she agreed that "it definitely captures something in my expression but I don't like the general effect of this much unbounded splash of face." However,

Avedon, an artist known for his unforgiving pictures of old age, had gone out of his way—shooting Diana through a window at The Colony in Wellfleet—to soften her image.

During Harris's final interview with Diana, her subject was celebrating her eighty-eighth birthday. She was far from finished with her work, Diana told Harris, and she had, in fact, started a new book of "recollections of people and places." Harris ended her profile: "A mighty warrior does not tarry in her tent." The writer James Atlas commented in his profile in *The New York Times* celebrating the publication of *The Beginning of the Journey* that Diana "doesn't seem frail, doesn't even seem old."

The review in *Partisan Review* began with acclaim for Diana's "commanding memory and intelligence" and went on to applaud her strong prose and "tonal variety." In the third paragraph the reviewer, Frank Kermode, said that "of all the autobiographies I know, it is the one that can accurately be described as comic." Still, he said, it "is a quite exceptional book." He went on to say that "she is by nature, and among other things, a comedian. I also know that even in her own city and among her more casual acquaintances this characterization might be greeted with astonishment." He cited Diana's story about her wedding as "a masterpiece of comic detail." Kermode ended his review by saying the book "is a tribute to the power and integrity with which [Diana] remade herself in middle life, and triumphantly, in old age."

Old age, it seems, had brought a new kind of light into Diana's life, even though her eyes were no longer processing it.

Although in *Newsweek* Richard Eder called Diana "a ferocious lasherback," and said that "she can verge on McCarthyism herself," he conceded that her portrait of her marriage "with a power of loyalty and endurance . . . elevates her final pages into a purely moving lyricism." *The Wall Street Journal* called the book "a remarkable blend of cultural criticism and private reminiscences."

Christopher Lehmann-Haupt, in the daily *New York Times*, referred to the book as an "utterly absorbing memoir" and said that Diana was "seamless in her political outlook." She was, he concluded, also "a long way from the end of the road." Indeed, in a short profile Patricia Bosworth later wrote in that paper, she recalled how Diana "would grow irritated if I arrived too early. 'I'm not finished yet!' she'd cry," reminding Bosworth she hadn't written her first book until she was in her seventies, "so I'm a bit frantic about time." Although Diana had long ago become a rarity among critics, and had learned to use both her logic and intuition to create an original and enduring voice, it wasn't enough. She wanted more. She thought of a follow-up to *The Beginning of the Journey* but knew she needed help. She asked the writer Peter Manso to work with her, telling him, "I know my time is limited," and she suggested that they work together on a question-and-answer format, insisting that "it would have to be my book. I would direct the book." But such a book never happened.

One of the reactions to *The Beginning of the Journey* that meant the most to Diana came from Jacques Barzun, who because of his health problems had to read the book in "small doses." He wrote Diana that he "savored its remarkable qualities all the more" and "relished the prose like a gourmet who takes the smallest bites to make the pleasure last longer. . . . It is a virtuoso feat." He also mentioned that there were some details about Lionel's character he wished he had never learned. "But, I can see that as you defined your task you could not leave those facts untold." He also disagreed with Diana's reason for why the joint seminar with Lionel ended: "I do not remember resisting the idea of using modern works for the readings. What I do remember is our common weariness with the old list and especially with the chore of editing the term papers."

Diana had written that Lionel taught her how to think and she taught him how to write. It was the closest she came to declaring publicly her major role in his writing life. Fritz Stern, University Professor Emeritus of History at Columbia, as well as the university provost from 1980 to 1983, later commented that he "couldn't quite accept that Diana taught Lionel how to write. It didn't ring true."

In *The Beginning of the Journey* Diana wrote that Bea (Gertrude Himmelfarb) and Irving Kristol were involved in "the politics of self-interest," that they had become "right-wing Republicans" who wanted

Diana and Lionel to sign a petition for Richard Nixon. Himmelfarb wrote Diana that she never asked Diana or Lionel to sign such a petition, and furthermore, her characterization of their politics was "personal and demeaning." "In fact," she continued in her letter, "your quarrel . . . was far more with the Podhoretzes." Diana replied that she understood Himmelfarb's "surprise that I focus the whole of my criticism of neo-conservatism on the two of you [the Kristols] rather than the Podhoretzes who have been so untruthful and ugly about Lionel and so vicious about me." She said that she has now begun to wonder "whether it was a sound decision to ignore them in my memoir. The source of this decision was my contempt for both Midge and Norman."

Decter seems to have gotten in the last word by means of a review of Diana's book in *Commentary*. She faulted Diana for a multitude of sins: stopping her memoir in 1950, saying that a future biographer might find that writing about Diana and Lionel together would be more interesting, denying that being Jewish "had any significance for either of them," employing "spin control," creating out-and-out "obtuseness," and being "revisionist."

It was the end of any sliver of a relationship between Diana and Midge Decter and Norman Podhoretz.

A few years later Diana wrote in a letter to a professor of English at Michigan State University that "Gertrude Himmelfarb was and is a great admirer of Lionel Trilling's work and that, purposively or not, she has made him out to be the father of present-day neo-conservatism." She went on to say that Himmelfarb's "present-day politics and those of my husband have in common only their opposition to a general soft-mindedness in dealing with the affairs of the world."

In the winter of 1993 Diana was the subject of a *Paris Review* interview, conducted by Patricia Bosworth. It was clear-sighted, covering many topics, from the quality of chocolate (Diana told Bosworth that "Hershey's Kisses are the best") to love, marriage, writing, book reviewing, politics, justice, feminism, celebrity, fame. "Are there certain things that you do not want to talk about in your book [*The Beginning of the Journey*]?" Bosworth asks Diana at one point. "Oh, surely," Diana answers. "Like what?" Bosworth asks. Diana replies, "How can I say if they are so private that I don't want to talk about them?" But then Diana goes on to admit that "I would not want to be graphic about my sexual life." Later in the interview, speaking about friendship, Diana tells Bosworth that "by and large the worst things that have happened to me have been done to me by women. . . . It was some kind of jealousy or envy," she explained. "It may be that they wanted to sleep with Lionel, or it might have something to do with prestige, social situation or something of that kind. Women do this to each other all the time. They make up stories. And they are very clever about it. They destroy other women. I mean what is this nonsense about sisterhood? There's much more brotherhood than there is sisterhood." She also tells Bosworth she worried about men being "emasculated" or frequently being accused of sexual harassment. "I think that a large number of men are going to become impotent if this keeps up."

Diana continued wanting to bring accolades to Lionel. In addition to the Lionel Trilling Seminars, which Fritz Stern recalled as "fun, good occasions," the Columbia undergraduates had started an annual book award in Lionel's honor. Edward Said, the Palestinian American cultural critic, had won the first book award for his book *Beginnings*. (Stern won the book award the following year, in 1977, for his study of Germany through the lives of Otto von Bismarck and Gerson Bleichröder, *Gold and Iron*.)

Three years after Said won, Diana gossiped about him in a letter to Bill Jovanovich. She was sure he wasn't going "to Europe" for a trip, as he had told her guests at a recent dinner party, but was actually going to be present at a secret meeting in Beirut between Yasser Arafat and Saddam Hussein. "I ask myself what goes on with me," she told Jovanovich. "What kind of friends have I got? What in my education makes me associate with terrorists, for God's sake?" Seven years later, she accused Said of anti-Semitism in an article he wrote, and they had a heated exchange of letters. "While my primary instinct as a Jew is to be concerned with the safety of Israel," she wrote him, "and your primary instinct as an Arab is to seek safety and justice for the Arabs, we are yet supposed to be intellectuals capable of transcending these natural partisanships at least to the extent of listening to the case for the other side and using our individual capacities, large or small, to reconcile our differences rather than to prolong or exacerbate them." After Said was diagnosed with leukemia, Diana wrote him a warm note, and he replied in kind. Diana told Gene Marcus that "it pains me greatly to hear of his deteriorating health—it touches some deep chord of affection in me. It also greatly pains me to hear of his continuing attack upon the peace process in Israel. I don't really understand the part of him which wants to keep that battle going!"

In 1994 Diana won the Lionel Trilling Book Award for her memoir, an honor that was characterized in the program as a "Special Award." Edward Said won the regular award—his second—for his book *Culture and Imperialism*. Diana wrote Bill Jovanovich that the presentation speech for her book was supposed to be about her, but the person "spoke entirely about Lionel." Still, she said, "it was the sweetest possible occasion."

That same year, 1994, Diana, at eighty-nine, found the time and energy to compose a letter in solidarity with the residents of Claremont Avenue protesting the Transit Authority's decision to reroute its M60 bus to pass right by Thirty-Five Claremont Avenue. Diana was outraged. "I feel now that our neighborhood is suffering a profound violation. We are no longer a treasured retreat from the noise of the city—we have become *part* of the noise of the city," she wrote in her letter of support to have the route changed. "If my windows are open so much as a crack, it is impossible to hear my readers," she added. (In due course the campaign was successful.)

Diana watched (or listened) to the O. J. Simpson trial (1994–95) with enormous fascination, telling Patricia Bosworth she wished she was strong enough to cover it in person in Los Angeles. (Simpson, the charismatic black athlete accused of murdering his ex-wife, Nicole Brown Simpson, and a waiter, Ronald Goldman—who were both white—was ultimately acquitted.) Diana decided to write an article about the trial for *The New Yorker*, but Tina Brown, the editor at the time, wanted it cut radically. Diana refused and eventually sold her piece to *The New Republic*, which printed it on October 30, 1995. Like most of the country, Diana was appalled at the verdict yet not really surprised. "Alert as we might be to the problems of race in present-day America, we failed to realize that our racial discord has reached the point where it could announce itself this baldly and boldly," she wrote, declaring the decision to be one that "sneered at our legal system." She was appalled that students at the primarily black institution Howard University had jumped for joy at the verdict. With exacting detail Diana dissected the trial, asking questions, describing testimony, analyzing witnesses, providing historical details. (She wondered why no one had mentioned the Dreyfus case—the Jewish captain in the French army accused in 1894 of spying for the Germans—a trial that became an international cause célèbre.) Diana held that O. J. Simpson was in "the deepest denial" about his guilt and was thus "able to convince those who are close to him of his guiltlessness." She said that "all of us employ this phenomenon of denial in our lives. . . . The mechanism comes into use without our conscious dictate." As she watched Simpson smile when he tried on the gloves soaked with his wife's blood, Diana thought of Jean Harris unhesitatingly, even casually, handling Tarnower's bloody sheets. Psychiatrists label such "inappropriate emotional detachment" as "representing lack of affect," Diana concluded in an essay that brought her many complimentary letters. She herself even wrote one to the magazine, but it was not commendatory. She complained that more than fifty changes were made without her permission, "most of them changes which were apparently intended to improve my prose." She said it seemed that editors had a great need to tamper with their writers, and all her writer friends agreed with this assessment. She concluded her letter: "To our present-day concern for the rights of blacks, women, homosexuals, and furry animals must we now add a concern for a writer's right to his—or her—own words?"

Around this time, Diana got the idea for a new magazine to be called "Op-Ed." In a proposal she said that she was offering it "as a new vehicle of opinion for the educated American public . . . a magazine which will be entirely written by the people who read it." But, she warned, "the world is full of would-be 'writers' and people who, though they have nothing useful to say, want nothing in the world so much as to see themselves in print. *Op-Ed* cannot be allowed to become a refuge of cranks." For more than half her life Diana had waged near war against those who did not, could not, would not pay contributors, yet for her proposed magazine she decided it would be better if contributors were not paid, although she said it would be "a matter for editorial determination."

Diana was working also on two new essays. One was about her friend Goronwy Rees, and the period in the early 1930s when he "was in the service of the Soviet Union," and the other was about the summer camp she had attended as a teenager. Diana hoped that both pieces could eventually be part of a volume of recollections, later saying that "this late in life, I begin to explore a kind of writing which I can best describe as semi-fictionalized reminiscence." She said she would devote herself to remembrances of people and events she had known, "sometimes with, sometimes without fictional elaboration." Her model was Harold Nicholson's *Some People*, first published in 1927. (Virginia Woolf had said that Nicholson "has devised a method of writing about people and about himself as though they were at once real and imaginary . . . and he has succeeded remarkably, if not entirely, in making the best of both worlds.") Diana wrote a short essay arguing that she no longer "perceived life critically, as a canvas of issues, but as narrative. This constitutes a profound alteration in my approach to both my experience and my profession, and it astonishes me," she said. "How is it that this has happened at this late point in my career? Throughout my writing life, the chief tools of my trade have been reason and argument. Today, they are re-creation and imagination."

She had actually begun using "re-creation and imagination" a decade earlier, in the 1980s. She wrote an essay about a crazy neighbor who lived next door to her family in Larchmont, New York. "Bobolinka's Neighbor" was published in the May 1983 issue of *Vanity Fair*. The piece begins: "The emotion I remember best from childhood is fear," and the last line reads, "We count on our children to confirm us in our illusions of progress." She was making the point that her father "could not have been more American in his premise that the mistakes and weaknesses of the past would be wiped away by a new generation." Diana, in the park one afternoon with young Jim, noticed that the mothers "looked for far more self-control and certainly a more delicate socialization" in their toddlers than they "required of themselves or their husbands or their grown children." But this was only an illusion of progress, a point Diana was pleased to be making at long last.

At ninety, Diana had changed her mind about many things she had once believed in regarding literature, but the years had not changed her image of old age. In the fall of 1995 Sally Jacobs of *The Boston Globe* had written a profile of Diana that sent shock waves through each and every one of Diana's years. "Yes, Sally," Diana wrote in a letter to her, "I am old as you will one day also be. Old age brings much pain and humiliation. Our bodies fail us and our pride is available to constant hurt. Did you need to add to a situation which I must inevitably suffer through the very passage of the years?"

Diana, "thoroughly dismayed," pointed out that her eyes "were far from being 'so clouded'" and that, in fact, they appear to be so normal that people can't quite believe she is almost blind. She hated that her ankles had been described as "bloated pink and painful over the straps of black sandals." But, worst of all she lashed out, "You speak of my 'tongue sharp as a torn tin can.' In a long life in which I have been frequently interviewed and written about, I can think of nothing that has been as ugly as that image!"

Diana's essay on Goronwy Rees was set to be published in *The New Yorker*, and, in fact, an editor there wrote Diana that the magazine had put it in galleys as "a way of finding whether you think our proposed edit would work."

It did not, and Diana, who said that the editor wanted the piece cut in half, asked for it to be returned to her. She then offered it to the *Partisan Review*, which published it in the winter of 1996. (Diana wrote Gene Marcus that *Harper's* and *The Atlantic* had refused it.) Diana wrote Gene also that the essay was "pretty generally approved and even admired by its American readers," although various English readers did not like it very much. Rees had denounced Guy Burgess of the group of spies at Cambridge University in a series of articles, as well as denouncing him to MI5, and Rees was seen more as a spy out to save himself than his country. Diana wrote that Jenny Rees determined that her father had been a Soviet agent but not "a fully fledged agent in the sense in which his Cambridge associates had been spies." Diana later wrote an introduction to Jenny Rees's memoir of her father, of which John Gross wrote in *The Sunday Telegraph* that the book "deserves nothing but praise."

In early April 1996 Diana was diagnosed with breast cancer and underwent a lumpectomy and then a series of radiation treatments. She wrote a former helper that "I find myself in a bad temper most of the time, annoyed at this sudden interference with the accustomed pattern of my days, worried by the interruption of my work." She requested also that her cancer not be mentioned in publishing circles. She asked her oncologist to give her two more years so she could finish a book, and he told her he could give her more. "I don't want more," she answered.

In May of that year her summer camp story was bought by *The New Yorker*, and once again cuts were requested; this time, however, Diana asked if she could do the editing herself, and it was agreed that she could. Diana wrote Gene Marcus that "probably it was only because Tina Brown was startled out of her mind by my request that she yielded to it." The self-edited essay was published in the August 12, 1996, issue but not without a letter of complaint from its author, who objected to its "new and inappropriate title, 'The Girls of Camp Lenore.'" Diana had called her story "A Camp in the Berkshires." (At one point she had named it "Auntie Ella Go to Hell," but that bewildering title didn't last long.) Diana wrote Tina Brown, asking, "Is not the title of a story as important as a comma? If I could be called so repeatedly for alterations in punctuation, and you now wanted a change in the title, why could I not have been called one more time? The title of a story is an important part of a writer's intention." Indeed, Diana explained that "in the middle of my recollection comes an intense almost melodramatic narrative dealing with life—presumably the 'normal' sexual life—of one of the senior counselors, and the reader suddenly realizes that this is essentially a sexual story, a story of many kinds of sexual hazards. Why was this ignored?" Diana went on: "Why was the change made behind my back when I was so easily reachable? As to the cover flap in which the public is asked 'what did I do at camp?' it becomes almost obscene in this sexual context."

Despite her letter (it is not known if it was ever actually sent) Diana's essay appeared in the magazine with the new title and the cover flap asking, "What did I do at camp?"

The publication of "The Girls of Camp Lenore" coincided with depressing health news. Diana had been diagnosed a few weeks earlier with a new cancer, non-Hodgkin's lymphoma, in her case, an aggressive form of the lymph system cancer. Once again she would undergo radiation treatments. But this time she was treated rudely, she said, and ignored when she told the technicians that the bun and hairpins in her hair were causing her discomfort because of the position of her body on the table. But she carried on, of course, because she said, radiation "gives her a fighting chance. I don't like taking death without fighting a little." She decided not to tell her son and daughter-in-law of the new diagnosis.

She wrote her longtime internist, Dr. Arnold Lisio, that "it has been a very bad time for me, close to unendurable. . . . I am no longer able to rise from bed but have to be lifted. My legs have lost so much strength that they can't lift by themselves over the rim of the bathtub; I must lift them across. My body is so off-balance that I virtually fall across the room and have to hang on to anything I can reach. When I try to stand up from bed or from my shower I am so breathless that I can't talk." She concluded to "her devoted, wonderful doctor": "I have had days in which I ached in almost every inch of my body and in which I was certain that I had to have been invaded by my lymphoma." But when Lionel's cousin, Dr. Franny Cohen, married to Stephen Koch, came for a visit, she wrote Dr. Lisio, and said Diana "was a classical example of someone who was being taken off Prednisone too quickly." Dr. Lisio had prescribed the medication. The dosage was raised, and Diana wrote, "At this moment I feel okay and am up at my desk. The one thing that seems still normal in my life is my ability to work. Once I get to my desk I am able to work better than ever before in my life—I've never produced more, or more to my satisfaction in such a brief period. Work is my great distraction from pain." Diana was working on a piece about the dinner at the White House she and Lionel had attended in 1962.

Diana requested that Dr. Lisio ("I love and honor you," she told him) find someone who could guide him about the correct use of prednisone. She had been "in the grip of what was surely a psychotic nightmare," she said.

HBJ, despite her admiration for Bill Jovanovich, also continued to bring on nightmares, although not of a psychotic nature. The previous January, she had written the marketing director of Harvest Books that in a brochure advertising the paperback edition of *The Beginning of the Journey* she was "dismayed" by "the discriminatory terms in which you describe my husband and myself, referring to him as a critic and to me as a reviewer." How could her own publisher who had published several volumes of her criticism deal with her so "pejoratively"? Diana added that "I cannot but wonder, however, whether it would have occurred to you to make this invidious distinction in reverse; that is, to describe the male partner in a literary marriage as the reviewer and the female partner as the critic?"

Feisty to the end. Nine months later, at 7 p.m. on October 23, 1996, Diana Trilling died.

She had worried, she once told Stephen Koch, that her obituary was going to read: "Diana Trilling dies at 150. Widow of distinguished professor and literary critic Lionel Trilling. Engaged in Controversy with Lillian Hellman."

But, in fact, the first line of her obituary in *The New York Times* reads: "Diana Trilling, an uncompromising cultural and social critic and a member of the circle of writers, thinkers, and polemicists of the 1930s, 40s, and 50s, known as the New York Intellectuals, died Wednesday at Columbia Presbyterian Hospital."

She was no longer, as she had once feared, at the borders of the literary community.

EPILOGUE

ARCADIA

At Diana's funeral, held on October 29, 1996, in St. Paul's Chapel on the Columbia University campus, a one-line entry in the program read, "At Mrs. Trilling's request, there will be no reception after the service." There were also no eulogies.

In a document entitled "Dreary Details About My Funeral" Diana had left for her son, she had emphasized not only no speeches but "*no* social gathering after my funeral! And no thanking people for attending. They can sign a book."

Daphne Merkin, in a reminiscence she wrote a month later about her friend, suggested whimsically that "perhaps [Diana] preferred not to be the subject of a conversation she could not preside over," adding in a more serious note that "the evident sorrow of her two granddaughters was a testament to the warmth and charm she exuded when she knew she was loved." Diana had dedicated *The Beginning of the Journey* to them. She adored being a grandmother and cherished her granddaughters, Gabriel and Julian. They had, in fact, brought to the funeral from their home in Princeton, where the family was living, two white bouquets they placed on her plain pine coffin. Jim was a Visitor at Princeton's Institute for Advanced Study, and Dore Levy—on sabbatical from Brown— was the first sinologist elected as a Member of the School of Historical Studies at the Institute.

A rabbi, a cantor, and the university's Protestant chaplain read psalms and Bible passages. In her "Dreary Details" document Diana had noted that "if the Rabbi wants the paid notice in *The Times* [she requested one in addition to 'any extended one *The Times* would run'] to refer to the 'Columbia University Chapel' instead of 'St. Paul's Chapel,' this wish should be deferred to. Also, I loathe chapels in the round. I want the pews at St. Paul's to be straight across."

Mostly Bach and (one) Mendelssohn melody filled the chapel. Guests left wet-eyed but frustrated. They needed more. But of what? The service felt unfinished, incomplete as some attendees murmured as they made their way to the university's main gates on Broadway. But there was nothing left to do but to go home and mourn Diana in private.

Jim Trilling and Dore Levy and their two daughters did not go right home. They had felt humiliated that Diana did not want a reception. "Who will believe that they come from far and away and we can't even give them a sandwich," Dore said. "Where I come from—Galveston, Texas—the funeral baked meats are a serious matter, although they tend toward crayfish and whiskey rather than small sandwiches and cold wine. And there has to be plenty! People in grief need to be fed! How could we face her friends, how could we explain?"

The family stayed at the door of the chapel shaking hands and tried to comfort the guests. "After the last one departed," Dore recalled, "we stood there, the girls exhausted with weeping, the day grey and the Columbia Campus completely drained of color. Jim said, 'Come on. We are going to have a wonderful lunch at the Plaza.'" Dore continued:

Diana loved to go to lunch at the Plaza. She would have chicken salad and many cups of tea. Once when Jim was traveling and I went to New York for the weekend and took her to the Plaza, we had a ball, with Diana telling stories and arguing about films—*Chinatown* and *Entre nous*. If we couldn't have a party in her honor, we could go to lunch at her favorite place. We tumbled into a cab and headed downtown. The girls ate macaroni and cheese and duck with lentils and ran around like Eloise. Jim and I ate I don't remember what and went through two bottles of wine. We rode the bus home, snuggled up, finally somewhat comforted.

Eight months after her death, "A Visit to Camelot" was published in the June 2, 1997, issue of *The New Yorker*. Although Diana was bedridden the summer before her death, she had insisted on going on living until the end, and that meant continuing to have people read to her—from her own work-in-progress and from books, articles, and reviews by others. She knew she was dying, but she also knew she had time to complete some important work. She would "give her ideas their full day." She was going to get her Washington story finished and published, and she did.

"A Visit to Camelot" was called "wildly entertaining"—not by a literary magazine—but by *U.S. News and World Report*. Another nonliterary publication noted that Diana observed "with grace and understatement the complex dynamics of the Kennedy marriage. Particularly endearing is her willingness to confess how even the literati are not immune to becoming star struck." Diana's essay was also one of twenty-five entries (the longest one, in fact) included in *The Best American Essays 1998*, guest-edited by Cynthia Ozick. (The anthology also had selections by Saul Bellow, Jamaica Kincaid, William Maxwell, Mary Oliver, and John McPhee.)

Diana's legacy continued to flourish. Decades later her 1962 essay on Marilyn Monroe was still remembered. In 2006 Gloria Steinem wrote in an article about the movie star's death that "just after Monroe's death, one of the few women to write with empathy was Diana Trilling, an author confident enough not to worry about being trivialized by association—and respected enough to get published. Trilling regretted the public's 'mockery of [Marilyn's] wish to be educated,' and her dependence on sexual artifice that must have left 'a great emptiness where a true sexuality would have supplied her with a sense of herself as a person,'" Steinem wrote. She went on to say that Diana "mourned Marilyn's lack of friends, 'especially women, to whose protectiveness her extreme vulnerability spoke so directly. But we were the friends,' as Trilling said sadly, 'of whom she knew nothing.'"

In 1999 startling information about Lionel was brought to light, information that Diana had known nothing about. It was kept a secret from her. That year, her son published a detailed twenty-five-page article in

The American Scholar called "My Father and the Weak-Eyed Devils." (The reference is from Conrad's *Heart of Darkness* and two kinds of devils he describes. One is "the flabby, pretending weak-eyed devil of a rapacious and pitiless folly." This devil is so subtle it hides its nightmarish, foolish qualities and is quite unaware of what it is doing. The other devil is a strong, lusty, greedy one—a "red-eyed devil.") The article, which had first been accepted by *The New Yorker* (which requested cuts Jim was unwilling to make), contained both contemporary and historical information that might have changed the course of Diana's life—or certainly have lightened her burdens—had she been aware of what her son so carefully revealed. "My father's worst problem was not neurosis," Jim wrote; "it was a neurological condition, attention deficit disorder," or ADD. (The term is considered out-of-date, and ADHD or Attention Deficit Hyperactivity Disorder is the new description, but ADD is a subtype of the condition.)

Jim went on to explain: "With hindsight, I can see that the failure to recognize medical problems was a recurring theme in my parents' lives. Disorders of the mind cast a shadow over both of them, skewing their vision. . . . Above all, it was their allegiance to Freud that discouraged them from seeking medical answers when psychological ones, however tortuous, would serve. . . . They disliked the idea that mental states can have physical causes: it took individual behavior out of the control of the individual." Jim further made clear that his parents did not reject neurology—but thought of it as a "last resort."

ADD runs in families, Jim discovered; "I have it, my father almost certainly had it and in all likelihood his father had it, too." One expert in the field says that "it isn't the kind of disease where you can test your blood and say, 'Oh you have it, like cancer or diabetes'; it's something that is based on a person's history, both family history and personal history and something that is based on behavior. So there's a collection of gestalts."

Jim never told his mother about his own ADD (diagnosed when he was in his late thirties) because he is not sure she would have understood. "It was a very difficult decision not to tell her," he said. "I was afraid she would be furious that I was reducing the whole drama to a chemical imbalance," and "I would have had to tell her about my father, which is more than she could have accepted." In his article he added that telling her "would have made me as alien and degraded in her eyes as if I had joined a cult."

The American Psychiatric Association's "DSM-IV," or Diagnostic and Statistical Manual of Mental Disorders, lists a multitude of symptoms for ADHD, ranging from difficulty sustaining attention and difficulty organizing tasks to acting as if "driven by a motor" and often losing one's temper, while blaming others for one's own mistakes or misbehaviors. "The symptoms are almost as diverse as the demands of life itself," Jim Trilling remarked in his article, "and it is easy to see why many people see the individual symptoms as no more than weaknesses of character, and 'attention deficit disorder' as a product of our collective self-indulgence, invented to disguise our failure to discipline ourselves, and our children."

His own symptoms, Jim said, began when he was four, with daydreaming, disorganization, and ferocious outbursts. "Any frustration would set me off," he said. But ADD was not an available explanation for what Diana and Lionel always called "The Problem" with their son. He was either "hyperactive" or "difficult." Jim noted that drugs for ADD have been available since 1930 (although the disorder wasn't named as such until the 1970s) and that Diana and Lionel had often taken Dexamyl, which contained barbiturate and amphetamine components and was actually one of the early ADD remedies. His parents had used the drugs for anxiety and depression, and Jim wishes his father had remained on the drug, but he didn't. (Instead, Lionel self-medicated with a drink every night.)

When Jim was an adult, he was prescribed a relatively new ADD drug—Ritalin—"with spectacular success."

He recognizes that whether or not his father had ADD "has become both academic and technically insoluble," and Jim acknowledges that "there is always a risk of vulgarity in diagnosing the famous dead." But he judges it "a risk worth taking. . . . I showed that my father succeeded in spite of ADD."

Among Lionel Trilling's symptoms were his frequent rages at Diana, his blaming her for a host of sins, his reckless body movements, and his not being careful about his surroundings, as when he swam without lifting his head out of the water to see where he was heading. Among others were his frenzied tennis playing; his careless driving, frequently shifting between lanes for no reason; and his sometimes not taking in information. Paramount was his trouble getting down to writing.

As soon as Jim recognized ADD in himself, he also saw it in his father, as well as his grandfather, David Trilling. Jim writes of "the scanty but compelling" evidence of his grandfather "botching the reading at his Bar Mitzvah."

Two other well-known symptoms of ADD are a sense of underachievement, which Lionel Trilling, in his journal, often wrote about experiencing, and depression, which can and could have contributed to sexual problems. In fact a symptom of ADD in adults is often said to be impotence, although not all experts agree, and most of the evidence is anecdotal, often found in blog posts. Natalie Weder, MD, of the Child Mind Institute, the leading group in child mental health research, reports that there is "no evidence of this that is worth noting." But the idea of ADD and impotence persists and will continue until more research is completed.

Sarah Gray Gund, a leading clinician with forty years' experience teaching children with learning difficulties and problems with attention, as well as supervising teachers, says that after reading Jim Trilling's article, she believes that there is little doubt that Lionel Trilling had attention deficit disorder.

Anne Fadiman,* the editor of *The American Scholar* who bought Jim's "quite convincing" article, said that many people thought it was an insult to his father. But, she said, the "notion that Jim had knocked his august father off some pedestal is ridiculous." He got "completely slammed," she said, adding that it was also "the most controversial event in her own career." In fact, Paul R. McHugh, MD, the psychiatrist-in-chief at Johns Hopkins Hospital, quit the journal's board over Jim's article, saying that "it is a clumsily written, meanly written article about a defenseless father" and that it was full of "sophisticated name-calling."

---

* She is the daughter of the Trillings' good friend Kip (Clifton) Fadiman.

Dr. McHugh added that Jim Trilling "uses psychiatric principles to settle personal scores." Two decades earlier, in 1978, Diana Trilling herself left *The American Scholar*'s board in protest over an article by William Chace about Lionel she thought unfair in the way it characterized her husband—as "besieged by doubts," among other things having to do with both literature and his peers. Criticism of Jim's article poured in. Leon Wieseltier, in *The New Republic*, called the article "banal and low" and an "exercise in filio-porn." Gertrude Himmelfarb wrote in *Commentary* that she deplored everything about the article and accused Jim of using "a pseudo-medical" diagnosis on his famous father.

Sarah Gund says that "the hard part about [Jim's] article is the way in which he talks about his father in their relationship, and I can see why that got him into trouble with this beloved name in literary criticism— that he had all these problems that nobody on the outside perceived." She continued: "But I think that just shows how well socialized he was. You can handle it—you learn to handle it—by covering it up—by not putting yourself in interactions—by the kind of life you choose to lead." And she stressed:

> I thought it was fascinating the way he talked about his father not creating anything new but always being able to see ambiguity and nuance of difference in other people's critique. And I think that was incredibly perceptive of Jim, the son, and perhaps quite true of some ADD people, and the kind of mind they have. I mean you also have the whole spectrum of intelligence—some people are exceedingly bright and have it and some people are average or below . . . and then you're just in trouble all the time. You're not doing anything that's very creative intellectually.

Gund said she thought it was also "fascinating the way the mother-in-law told Diana to be careful of these rages. . . . And blaming other people is another big characteristic [of ADD]. . . . Temper is one of the primary characteristics. . . . You do blame it on other things because you're not really doing it willfully," she said. "You just can't hold it in anymore. And so if you are well socialized you hold it in at work and when you get home you have to let it out somehow, and you can trust that environment at home." So Lionel blamed Diana for everything he felt wrong with his life.

Lionel was always able to make his ADD work to his advantage. He rarely let any of the symptoms be seen by anyone outside his family, masking them with his well-known reserve and aloofness. Diana always understood that her husband, like her father, had the power of mind over body. As Gund explained, "One learns to handle ADD by covering it up, by not putting oneself in interactions." Diana always protected him. Diana did for her husband what he could not do for himself. His work was always her work.

Speaking of writing in general, as well as getting rid of all the drafts with Diana's editing on them, Sarah Gund said that it could be that he was uncomfortable about needing so much help, "and maybe he didn't want to destroy a facade which he had created for himself by showing how much help he needed, from his wife, in this case. Most people would get help from their editor—is that more honorable than having your wife do it?" she asked.

She added that "another aspect of ADD is . . . you can certainly have an idea and have trouble putting that idea into words. So that could be a very subtle feature of his particular ADD." Diana understood Lionel's mind like no one else and was able to put his ideas into words that were very much his own.

Jim writes about his father's "extravagant contempt for his colleagues," and Lionel's journal often complains about having to deal with graduate students. Gund says that "it's interesting that [Lionel] worked alone a lot. And that he didn't [really understand] his relationship with graduate students, how fundamentally wrong that was [to be remote]. But I think that's something that's often true of ADD people. . . . They have inter-personal relationships—they don't necessarily show it in an extreme way, but every once in a while they cross a line that is absolutely obvious to everyone else."

Stephen Koch said that he and his wife, Franny Cohen (her father was Lionel's cousin), "were among the minority who believed what Jim was saying." He went on to acknowledge that "I did not know Lionel; I never even met him. I cannot say anything from personal observation. But as a sufferer from ADD myself, I found Jim's arguments plausible." He said that after his wife read Jim's article, "she immediately knew, intuitively, that it was true . . . and even though at the time she had never observed symptoms in Lionel, nonetheless, she said, 'Jim's account is consistent with her memories.'" Koch also said that he "thinks that if and when the literary public learns that Lionel Trilling himself had ADD, the revelation can only be a force for the good."

Koch says that "Diana always knew something was wrong with Lionel but didn't know what. She pulled the words out of him." Moreover, Koch, who says his ADD "is an issue I deal with every day" (he takes Ritalin)—has been able to find success as a writer in spite of the disorder and says that "every syllable of Jim's piece about it was correct."

Lionel could successfully work around his ADD, not only because of Diana but because of his strong will and sense of responsibility and his need to do "right." He knew instinctively that he needed to find a woman who could safeguard him. Persons with ADD are often exceptionally intelligent, perceptive, charismatic, and verbally advanced; after all, ADD is a neurobiological syndrome affecting the wiring of the brain and is not anything abnormal, just something different. Trilling's hero Ernest Hemingway is suspected by some people to have had ADD/ADHD, as did perhaps Leo Tolstoy, Edgar Allen Poe, F. Scott Fitzgerald, and Robert Frost.

Sarah Gund speculates that ADD could have been a factor in keeping Lionel from writing the novels he wanted to write and Diana wished him to write. She wrote in a draft of *The Beginning of the Journey* that "why he turned as fully as he did from fiction to criticism is finally as difficult to explain—reliably explain—as his choice of me as a wife. The clues are many but the mystery will always remain."

The chances Diana would have accepted an ADD diagnosis are small—neurosis was her verdict of choice. After all, as Gund says, "Freud was sweeping the world. Everyone thought everything was psychological. . . . So we had to live through that and get to now where everything is mostly physiological and it's almost that [the] psychological has taken a backseat."

Lynn Weiss writes in her book about adult ADD that "the family of an unrecognized ADD person suffers most, perhaps. Marital conflict, seemingly constant disruption in the household, and spouse or child abuse are all fallouts from trying to maintain relationships with an adult with unrecognized ADD. Codependency problems run rampant. The human heartache is enormous."

Diana, as Deborah Wagnell, a character full of heartache and conflict, writes in her unpublished novel, "I Was in Arcadia Too," that "the existence of fiction is what leads us to believe in the existence of its opposite, truth, but fiction is in a curious way *more* truthful; certainly it gives more of an appearance of truth, than does real life." Diana had worlds opened to her when she was the fiction reviewer for *The Nation*. The job changed the course of her life and offered her a coping stratagem for "the constant disruption" in her household. Writing criticism was never the "sorcerer's art" her father had said it was.

Diana, still as Deborah, writes in her journal:

> I've made a career for myself, successful enough. I've had a successful marriage, successful motherhood. I'm even being a successful widow . . . and I burden no one. I'm to be envied. As myself, not merely as John's wife. But were I asked to what extent I had used my energies in the living of my life, all the energies at my disposal, all that had been given me by nature, I'd have to say—what, fifty percent? Forty percent? Less? . . . I'm not talking about laziness. But suppose I'd been endowed as Balzac, say, was endowed: would I have been able to give myself the permission to use my talent to its fullest, as he did? I'm not complaining about anything I did put on paper; it's what I *didn't* put on paper, but might have, that matters, the truth I didn't feel permitted to tell, the force I didn't feel permitted to assert—and not alone as a writer but as a person—that stands to the discredit of the culture which bred me, or perhaps only to my personal discredit because I lacked courage.

She concludes: "Only in timidity—cowardice would be the more precise word—are my personal and professional lives tied like blood sisters, and this bears in on me more and more heavily since John's death, or perhaps only as I grow older. I think of myself approaching the end of my life carrying a burden of undelivered ideas, undelivered tenderness, undelivered understanding, undelivered generosities, undelivered desire (yes, desire too can be undelivered), undelivered love. . . . I always wanted to be on the stage, maybe that's why; it's the only way I know which might have relieved me of my unlived life."

ACKNOWLEDGMENTS

I t probably isn't possible to thank properly the person who has been at my side and on my side for fifty years. My husband, Christopher, has read draft after draft after draft of this book. Lucky, lucky, me.

I am especially appreciative to Diana Trilling's son, Jim, for his support, wisdom, and good humor throughout. Dore Levy, Jim's wife, was a wonderful resource and provided me with many anecdotes. I thank her for greatly enhancing my narrative.

The librarians, curators, and archivists at Columbia University's Rare Books and Manuscript Library (as well as the Oral History Research Office) are a wonderful group of people! I will list many of them, although some I just never got to know, or they have left for other positions, or have retired.

Thank you to:

Gerald Cloud
Tara Craig
Jane Gorjevsky
Susan G. Hamson
Carrie Elise Hintz
Christopher Laico

Tom McCutchon
Elizabeth Pope
Cathy Ricciardi
Michael Ryan
Corie Trancho-Robie
Eric Wakin
Jocelyn Wilk
And thank you, too, to the many student employees who
  dragged box after box over to the table where I was working.

Thank you to Columbia University Press!
I am especially grateful to:
Jennifer Crewe, associate provost and director
Jonathan Fiedler, assistant editor
Julia Kushnirsky, art director
Marisa Pagano, senior copywriter and catalog manager
Leslie Kriesel, assistant managing editor
Justine Evans, rights and permissions
Derek Warker, publicity
Joe Abbott, copy editor
Heather Jones, indexer
Also thanks to Joanna Summerscales and Linda Steinman

I am also grateful to the following people who agreed to be inter-
viewed for this book:
Jonathan Alter
Brom Anderson
Jacques Barzun
Marguerite Barzun
Carroll Beichman
Patricia Bosworth, with special thanks for allowing me to use a
  photograph of Diana Trilling taken by her late husband,
  Tom Palumbo
Oliver Conant
Midge Decter

Morris Dickstein
Lore Dickstein
Jason Epstein
Ann Fadiman
Gray Foy
Jules Feiffer
Alexis Gelber
Jerome Gentes
Robert Gottlieb
Sarah Gund
Richard Howard
Beth Karas
Joel Kaye
Stephen Koch
Steven Kurtz
Richard Locke
Peter Manso
Edward Mendelson
Daphne Merkin
Patricia O'Toole
Catherine Park
Norman Podhoretz
Peter Pouncey
Lucy Rosenthal
Michael Rosenthal
Elisabeth Sifton
Fritz Stern
Sam Tanenhaus
Benjamin Taylor
Phyllis Theroux
Lina Skucas Vlavianos
Natalie Weder
Larry Weisman
Mary Lou Weisman
Drenka Willen

Christopher Zinn
Harriet Zuckerman.

I thank the following people for listening to ideas, or digging up material, or offering suggestions, or sharing thoughts, or just providing encouragement:

Randy Abreu
Marcia Allina
Steven Aronson
Carolyn Baldwin
Carole Baron
Barbara Barrie
Charles Beichman
Amy Bendeca
Joe Caldwell
Lisa Chichelo
Karen Clarke
Denise Daly
Liz Darhansoff
Shelly Dattner
Changchun Deng, MD
Heather Dials
Angela DiMango, MD
Matthew Fink, MD
Robin Goland, MD
Dan Green
Jane Green
Yuko Hagiwara
Dalma Heyn
Lone Jones
Daniel Kevles
Elizabeth Cooke Levy
Kit Lukas
Richard Marek
Angie Marrero

Angela Martinez

Elaine McGann

Greg Mears, MD

Jay Meltzer, MD

Cheryl Mendelson

Lester Migdal

Amy Militar

Helen Milonas

Leo Milonas

Victor Navasky

the late Hugh Nissenson

Marilyn Nissenson

Kathy O'Brien

Owen O'Conner, MD

Mary O'Neil

Cecilia Paasche

Franz Paasche

Vita Paladino (director of the Howard Gotlieb Archival
     Research Center—also Sean Noel, associate director; and
     Ryan Hendrickson, assistant director for mss.)

Kathleen Paratis

Alison Pavia

Letty Cottin Pogrebin

Andrea Rabinovitch

Elsa Rush

Norman Rush

Joanne Scabila

Peggy Shapiro

Selma Shapiro

Ronnie Scharfman

James H. Silberman

David C. Sperling, MD

Marilyn Taveras

Joseph Tenenbaum, MD

Barbara Trilling

Carolyn Trois
Phyllis Wender
Lynn Zivin

I have probably left people off this list who belong here, and I hope I am forgiven for any oversights.

SOURCE NOTES

The Diana Trilling Papers, 1921–1996, at the Rare Book and Manuscript Library at Columbia University were my primary and most important research tool in the writing of this book. The collection contains sixty hefty boxes of documents—letters, notes, drafts, diaries, books, reviews, interviews, tapes, articles, poems, and photographs. I also relied on much material found in the Lionel Trilling Papers, 1899–1987, especially LT's journals, held at the same library. I also consulted material from the Oral History Research Office, although most of the transcribed interviews eventually became part of the Diana Trilling Papers.

In my chapter notes I use the abbreviation "DTP" for the Diana Trilling Papers, and the abbreviation "LTP" for the Lionel Trilling Papers. The box number where the material is found will be listed and, if required, the title and description of any documents as well.

I am forever grateful to the staff at the library for their guidance, patience, and expertise during the years of my research. (Some names will be listed in my acknowledgments, but there are so many people I just didn't get a chance to know. I extend my thanks to them—all of them—for their efforts on my behalf.)

I also thank the many, many people who agreed to be interviewed for this book. Some are listed in the chapter notes as well as in the acknowledgments.

PREFACE

Information in the preface was drawn from the following:

DTP: Box 12, Folder 1, Edna Rubin to DT, August 10, 1960; Box 13, Folder 12, DT to Dr. Norman Reider, Oct. 4, 1965; Box 21, Folder 2, draft of "The Education of a Woman," by DT; Box 21, Folder 6, "Radcliffe"; and Box 38, Folders 14 and 15.

BOOKS, ARTICLES, AND OTHER RESOURCES

Natalie Robins, *Alien Ink* (New York: William Morrow, 1992), 76.
Natalie Robins, *Living in the Lightning* (New Brunswick, NJ: Rutgers University Press, 1999).
Diana Trilling, *The Beginning of the Journey* (New York: Harcourt, Brace, 1993).
Stephen Koch, "Journey's Beginning: A Talk with Diana Trilling," *New York Times*, Feb. 19, 1989.
Patricia Bosworth, draft of *Partisan Review* interview of DT, Howard Gotlieb Archival Research Center, Boston University.
Natalie Robins, FBI interviews Box 27, Folder 14, and Box 20, Howard Gotlieb Archival Research Center, Boston University.
Glenn Horowitz Bookseller, "From The Library of Lionel and Diana Trilling."
Some descriptions of 35 Claremont Avenue come from the following people: Patricia Bosworth, Christopher Lehmann-Haupt, Natalie Robins, and James Trilling.

1. ESCAPE INTO FICTION

Information in this chapter was drawn from the following:
DTP: Box 1, Folder 1, application forms; Box 1, Folder 8, Diaries, 1922; Box 10, Folder 3, DT to Priscilla Cohen, Editor, *Radcliffe News*, Oct 23, 1944; Box 18, Folder 6, Leah Salisbury to DT, May 13, 1930, and Sept. 2, 1931, also letter to Leah Salisbury from the story editor at Columbia Pictures; Box 19, Folder 3, drafts of childhood memoir; Box 19, Bettina Mikol Sinclair marriage note in *Wisconsin Alumni Magazine*, Nov. 1928; Box 19, Folder 3, drafts of *Beginning of the Journey*; Box 20, Folders 4, 7, and 8, childhood memoir; Box 21, Folder 4; Box 21, Folder 6, more information on Radcliffe; Box 22, Folders 6 and 7, drafts of childhood memoir; Box 22, Folder 6, undated draft of "Memoir of a Marriage"; Box 31, Folder 7, draft of "The Education of a Woman"; Box 36, Folder 3, "*Snitkin.*" All the transcripts of the tapes between DT and Christopher Zinn (the "oral history" component) are located in Boxes 38, 39, 40, and 41; Box 60, Folders 1, 2, and 3, drafts of "Biography of a Marriage."

ARTICLE

Diana Trilling, "The Girls of Camp Lenore," *New Yorker*, August 12, 1996.

2. UNDERTAKINGS

Information in this chapter was drawn from the following:
LTP: Box 2, Folders 7 and 8, Journals: undated and Sept. 1926–Spring 1929.

DTP: Box 1, Folder 3, Engagement book 1928; Box 17, Folder 4, Harriet Trilling Schwartz to DT, June 30, 1978; Box 18, Folder One, DT to Joanna and Dan Rose, April 13, 1979; Box 19, Folder 3, draft of childhood memoir, p. 34; Box 20, Folder 7, draft of childhood memoir; Box 21, Folder 3, draft of childhood memoir; Box 22, Folder 6, information on LT; Box 31, Folder 17, draft of childhood memoir; Box 37, Folder 24, memoir; Box 44, Folder 1, interview with Kip Fadiman; Box 47, Folder 7, oral history, Elsa and Jim Grossman; Box 53, Folder 6, oral history, Quentin and Thelma Anderson; Box 60, Folders 1 and 2, draft of "Biography of a Marriage"; Box 69, Folder 3, draft of memoir of a marriage.

BOOKS, ARTICLES, AND OTHER RESOURCES

Michael L. Grace, "The Grace Line History," Dec. 1, 2009, http://cruiselinehistory. com/the-grace-line/).

John Rodden, "The Trilling Family Romance Report of a Psychoanalytic Autopsy," *Modern Age*, Summer 2006.

James Trilling, "My Father and the Weak-Eyed Devils," *American Scholar*, March 22, 1999 (re: Cecilia Rubin's Tourette Syndrome).

Lucy Rosenthal, interview by Natalie Robins, on lunches between her father and DT and her mother and LT.

3. PROLEGOMENON

Information in this chapter was drawn from the following:

LTP: Box 2, Folder 8, Journals: Sept. 1926–Spring 1929; Box 2, Folder 11, 1938–43.

DTP: Box 18, Folder 5, Malcolm Cowley to DT, Oct. 13, 1931; Box 19, Folder 3, draft of childhood memoir; Box 19, Folder 3, draft of *The Beginning of the Journey*; Box 22, Folder 6; Box 31, Folder 5, undated short story (possibly the story DT wrote on her honeymoon); Box 31, Folder 7, draft of "The Education of a Woman"; Box 46, Folder 4, oral history, Steven Donadio, 1976; Box 50, Folder 3, oral history, Michael Rosenthal; Box 53, Folder 6, oral history, Quentin Anderson; Box 60, Folder 2, draft of "Biography of a Marriage"; Box 60, Folder 1, "Bobolinka's Neighbor," *Vanity Fair*, May 1983.

BOOKS AND ARTICLES

Diana Trilling, *The Beginning of the Journey*, 120–28, 171–76.

Village Voice: Dec. 18, 2007 (information on One Bank Street).

4. ISOLATION AND DESPERATION

Information in this chapter was drawn from the following:
LTP: Box 2, Folder 9, Journals, 1930–31; Box 2, Folder 10, 1934–36; Box 3, Folder 11, late 1930s to 1941.

DTP: Box 5, Folder 6, Elizabeth Ames to LT, April 3, 1931, and; Elizabeth Ames to DT, April 8, 1931; Box 16, Folder 3, Sidney Hook to DT, Jan. 10, 1976; Box 17, Folder 1, DT to Richard Parker, Jan. 24, 1977; Box 18, Folder 5, Malcolm Cowley to DT, Oct. 13, 1931; Box 18, Folder 6, Leah Salisbury to DT, March 21, 1931; Box 38, Folder 9, DT, interview by Dr. Sarah Alpern, June 21, 1983; Box 48, Folder 3, oral history, Elinor Hays; Box 46, Folder 4, oral history, Steven Donadio, p. 20; Box 53, Folder 6, oral history, Quentin and Thelma Anderson; Box 60, Folder 2, draft of "Biography of a Marriage."

BOOKS AND ARTICLES

Diana Trilling, *The Beginning of the Journey*, 171–87.
Natalie Robins, *Alien Ink*, 299.
Alan Wald, *The New York Intellectuals* (Chapel Hill: University of North Carolina Press, 1987), 58–59.
"About Books," *Junior Bazaar*, Sept. 1946 (DT on *Partisan Review*).
"Forbidden Tunnels Guard CU History," *Columbia Spectator*, March 27, 2003.
Alan Blinder, "Pardon for the Last 'Scottsboro Boys,'" *New York Times*, Nov. 22, 2012.

5. THE REST OF OUR LIVES

Information in this chapter was drawn from the following:
LTP: Box 2, Folder 7, undated journals; also folder 8, Sept. 1926–spring 1929.

DTP: Box 2, Folder 10; Box 17, Folder 3, information on LT at Hunter and DT letters to Mrs. J. R. Spurling, Jan. 16, 1978; Box 19, Folder 3, draft of *The Beginning of the Journey*; Box 20, Folders 2 and 3, misc. notes; Box 21, Folder 2, childhood memoir and handwritten notes; Box 22, Folder 6, draft of memoir of a marriage; Box 53, Folder 6, oral history, Quentin and Thelma Anderson.

BOOKS, ARTICLES, AND OTHER RESOURCES

Lawrence R. Samuel, *Shrink: A Cultural History of Psychoanalysis*, (Lincoln: University of Nebraska Press, 2013), 2. (re: the term *psychoanalysis*, first used by Freud c. 1895).
Diana Trilling, *The Beginning of the Journey*, 259, 229–30.
Diana Trilling, "The Girls of Camp Lenore," *New Yorker*, August 12, 1996.

DT in conversation with Christopher Lehmann-Haupt, early 1990s (re: LT in despair over DT's criticism).

6. THE GREATEST SERVICE

Information in this chapter was drawn from the following:
LTP: Box 3, Folder 7, 1952–55.
DTP: Box 1, Folder 1, 1921–30: rejection letter with personal note to DT from *The Southern Review*; Box 3, Folder 4, Kip Fadiman to DT, May 28, 1940; Box 10, Folder 2, Bettina Sinclair to DT, 1935; Box 20, Folder 2, notes; Box 60, Folder 2, draft of "Memoir of a Marriage"; Box 22, Folder 6; Box 34, Folders 10 and 12; Box 30, Folder 14, "Beppo: The Canary Who Sang Muh"; Box 35, Folder 15, simplified *Wind in the Willows*; Box 51, Folder 2, oral history, Steven Donadio; Box 60, Folder 2, draft of "Biography of a Marriage."

BOOKS AND ARTICLES

Diana Trilling, *The Beginning of the Journey*, 317 (re: Norton as publisher of *Matthew Arnold*), also 244, 318.
Jacques Barzun, "Remembering Lionel Trilling," *Encounter*, Sept. 1976, 82.
James Gutman, "The Columbia College Colloquium," *CU Quarterly* 1937.
F. R. Leavis, "Arnold's Thought," review of LT's *Matthew Arnold*, *Scrutiny*, June 1939.
Edward Rothstein, Jacques Barzun obituary, *New York Times*, Oct. 26, 2012.
Edmund Wilson, "Uncle Matthew," review of LT's *Matthew Arnold*, *New Republic*, March 21, 1939.

7. *THE NATION* CALLS

Information in this chapter was drawn from the following:
LTP: Box 3, Folder 7, 1952–55.
DTP: Box 4, Folder 3, William Maxwell to DT; Box 4, Folder 4, "Dear Diana, affectionately, Peggy," August 27, 1947; Box 4, Folder 6, DT to David Riesman, June 30, 1976; Box 4, Folder 6, Katherine Anne Porter to DT, Sept.8, 1942; Box 5, Folder 2, Mark Van Doren to DT, 1943; Box 10, Folder 2, *New Yorker* to DT, Feb. 13, 1941; Box 10, Folder 2, Eliseo Vivas to DT; also Anita Berenbach to DT, *PM Daily*, Nov. 1, 1943; also Nanine Joseph to DT, March 13, 1940; Box 10, Folder 4, re: *Junior Bazaar*, Box 10, Folder 4, Leo Lerman to DT and LT, June 1946; Box 10, Folder 3, Pascal Covici, Viking Press, to DT, August 25, 1943, Jan. 16, 1945, and June 14, 1945; Box 10, Folder 4, Rev. Roddey Reid Jr. to DT; Box 12, Folder 3, Ken McCormick, Editor-in-Chief of Doubleday, to DT, May 24, 1962; Box 12, Folder 4, DT to Fred Warburg; Box 18, Folder

1, DT to *Current Biography,* Feb. 7, 1979; Box 22, Folder 5, DT, interview by John Horder, May 29, 1965, in *The Scotsman*; Box 23, Folder 2, interview about Jean Harris; Box 32, Folder 24, "Reading Out of Season," *Junior Bazaar,* July 1946, Feb., 1946, April 1947; Box 33, Folder 9, "Fiction in Review," May 8, 1943 (DT's review of *Gideon Planish,* by Sinclair Lewis); Box 33, Folder 9, "Fiction in Review," May 5, 1945 (DT's review of *The Ghostly Lover,* by Elizabeth Hardwick); Box 35, Folder 11, reviews; Box 35, Folder17, "The Sale of a Work of Art"; Box 38, Folder 9, DT, interview by Dr. Sarah Alpern, June 21, 1983; Box 60, draft of "Biography of a Marriage."

BOOKS AND ARTICLES

Diana Trilling, *The Beginning of the Journey,* 125, 224, 328, 330, 337.

David Laskin, *Partisans: Marriage, Politics, and Betrayal Among the New York Intellectuals* (Chicago: University of Chicago Press, 2000), 45, 190.

Diana Trilling, *Reviewing the Forties,* introduction by Paul Fussell (New York: Harcourt Brace Jovanovich, 1978), 5, 28 (review of John Cheever, April 10, 1943).

Patricia Bosworth, draft of *Partisan Review* interview of DT at Howard Gotlieb Archival Research Center, Boston University.

Koch, "Journey's Beginning."

Christopher Lehmann-Haupt, Elizabeth Hardwick obituary, *New York Times,* Dec. 4, 2007.

Nation, DT's review of *Tilda,* by Mark Van Doren, May 8, 1943; also DT's review of *Memoirs of Hecate County,* by Edmond Wilson, March 30, 1946.

Paris Review, Winter 1993.

8. NOT MERELY A CRITIC'S WIFE

Information in this chapter was drawn from the following:

LTP: Box 3, Folder 2, Oct. 1944–Sept. 1945; Box 3, Folder 6, Sept. 1948–April 1952.

DTP: Box 1 Folder 1, Quentin Anderson to DT, n.d.; Box 4, Folder 3, DT to Mr. Laughlin, June 23, 1946; Box 6, Folder 4, DT to Susan Moore, August 10, 1982; Box 6, Folder 5, DT to Norman Mailer (c. 1976); Box 10, Folder 3, Pascal Covici to DT, June 14, 1945, also March 4, 1947; Box 10, Folder 4, unsigned letter from unnamed editor at *Vogue* to DT, Nov. 1946; Box 20, Folder 3, re: Mary McCarthy and Dwight McDonald; Box 31, Folder 7, draft of "The Education of a Woman"; Box 32, Folder 24, various DT book columns in *Junior Bazaar,* 1946–47; Box 33, Folder 3, "The Marriage of Elsie and John," by "Margaret Sayles" (DT pseudonym); Box 35, Folder 4, "The Psychology of Plenty," by DT (penciled note at top of ms. by DT: "I think this was never published."); Box 35, Folder 11, review of *Gentleman's Agreement, Commentary,* March 1947; Box 51, Folder 1, oral history with Jack and Susan Thompson conducted by DT, Feb. 1976; Box 53, Folder 2: "Before Bandwagons," by Leo Lerman, *Vogue,* May 11,1944

(a special thanks to Carrie Hintz, head of Archive Processing at the Rare Book and Manuscript Library, for locating this column for me); Box 53, Folder 6, oral history, Quentin and Thelma Anderson

BOOKS, ARTICLES, AND OTHER RESOURCES

The Beginning of the Journey, 337 (on Leo Lerman).
Leo Lerman, *The Grand Surprise: The Journals of Leo Lerman* (New York: Alfred A. Knopf, 2007), 3n.
Lionel Trilling, *E. M. Forster,* preface to the 2nd ed., 3.
"Acne Paper #10," story by Joan Juliet Buck "Chez Leo and Gray."
Nicholas Rasmussan: "America's First Amphetamine Epidemic," *American Journal of Public Health* (June 2008): 974–85.
Review of *The Portable D. H. Lawrence, Kirkus Reviews,* Jan. 3, 1946.
Paul Woolridge, "Lionel Trilling and the Periodical Imagination," *American Periodicals* 23 (Nov. 2013): 43–59 (re: *Harper's Bazaar* and LT's short story).
Louis Menand, "The Culture Club," *New Yorker,* Oct. 15, 2001.
Liesl Schillinger, "Life of the Party," review of *The Grand Surprise: The Journals of Leo Lerman,* edited by Stephen Pascal, *New York Times Book Review,* April 22, 2007.
Amanda Fortini, "So You Want to Be a Star? Leo Lerman's Gossipy Journals Offer Lessons on Fame," *Slate,* July 2, 2007, www.slate.com/articles/arts/culturebox /2007/07/so_you_want_to_be_a_star.html.

9. GLOWING

Information in this chapter was drawn from the following:
LTP: Box 3, Folder 4, Sept. 1946–Sept. 1948; Box 3, Folder 6, journals Sept. 1948– April 1952.

DTP: Box 3, Folder 1, DT to Newton Arvin, March 18, 1949; Box 4, Folder 6, DT to Evie and David Riesman, May 12, 1949; Box 5, Folder 1, May Sarton to DT, March 22, 1948, also April 3, 1948; Box 5, Folder 1, "The Baby Nurses," by DT; Box 5, Folder 1, William Shawn to DT, May 5, 1952; Box 9, Folder 3, DT to Dr. Marjorie Rosenberg, June 19, 1987; Box 10, Folder 5, Bettina Sinclair Hartenbach to DT, Jan. 15, 1948; Box 10, Folder 5, Betsy Moulton, Feature Assistant, *Mademoiselle,* to DT, Nov. 29, 1948; Box 11, Folder 2, nursery school report, Jan. 1953; Box 11, Folder 5, re: James T's fear of elevators; Box 20, Folder 2, notes re: "Biography of a Marriage"; Box 21, Folder 2, DT to Dr. Morris Greenberg, May 21, 1955, and Dr. Greenberg to DT, May 29 and June 5, 1955; Box 22, Folder 3, "Virginia Woolf: A Special Instance," by DT in *New York Times Book Review,* March 21, 1948; Box 31, Folder 17, draft of "The Education of a Woman"; Box 31, Folder 21, "Footnote to My Life as a Critic," by DT, a version of an essay that appeared in *Explorations* magazine, 1998; Box 34, Folder 1, *Fiction in Review*, Jan. 31, 1948, DT's review of Truman Capote's *Other Voices, Other Rooms*; Box 38, Folder 9, DT, interview by Dr. Sarah Alpern, June 21, 1983; Box 53, Folder 6, oral history, Quentin and Thelma Anderson.

BOOKS, ARTICLES, AND OTHER RESOURCES

The Beginning of the Journey, 192, 248–49, 413–15.

The Collected Letters of Thomas and Jane Welsh Carlyle, 1999, Duke-Edinburgh Edition, http://carlyleletters.dukeupress.edu.

"Living Legacies," *Columbia Alumni Magazine*, Summer 2001 (re: Lionel Trilling at Columbia).

Koch, "Journey's Beginning."

Midge Decter and Norman Podhoretz, interview by Natalie Robins, Oct. 25, 2011. I am grateful to the Oral History Office for letting me read MD's interview. I later discovered a letter in DT's archives in which MD angrily asked DT to remove the interview from her proposed book, but DT never did.

Edward Mendelson, interviews by Natalie Robins, April 2012, June 2012, Oct. 2012, Feb. 2013.

10. OH BE BRAVE

Information in this chapter was drawn from the following:

LTP: Box 2, Folder 11, 1938–43; Box 4, Folder 5, undated note, also Norman Mailer quote: March 1959–July 1961.

DTP: Box 4, Folder 4, Marianne Moore to DT April 17, 1950; Box 4, Folder 4, Karl A. Menninger, MD, to DT, April 14 and April, 28, 1950; Box 4, Folder 4, DT to Norman Mailer, June 18, 1959, and Norman Mailer to DT, June 30, 1959; Box 11, Folder 1, S. F. Rubin to DT, June 26, 1951; Box 11, Folder 1, Monroe Engel to DT, date noted only as 1950, with no further details; Box 12, Folder 1, DT to *Look* magazine; Box 16, Folder 4, DT to Bettye Rubin Turitto, April 16, 1976; Box 19, Folder 3, Draft of "This Is a Chapter About Money"; Box 20, Folder 3, draft of "Education of a Woman"; Box 22, Folder 5, A. Alvarez, review of DT's *Claremont Essays*; Box 51, Folder 2, oral history, Steven Donadio; Box 53, Folder 6, oral history, Quentin and Thelma Anderson.

BOOKS, ARTICLES, AND OTHER RESOURCES

Lerman, *The Grand Surprise.*

Lionel Trilling, *Freud and the Crisis of Our Culture* (Boston: Beacon, 1955).

Lionel Trilling, *The Opposing Self* (New York: Viking, 1955).

Peter Manso, *Mailer* (New York: Simon and Schuster, 1985), 287.

Margaret Mead, *Male and Female* (New York: William Morrow, 1949).
John Rodden, *Lionel Trilling and the Critics: Opposing Selves* (Lincoln: University of Nebraska Press, 1999).
Morris Dickstein, foreword to *Lionel Trilling and the Critics: Opposing Selves* (Lincoln: University of Nebraska Press, 1999).
Michael Rosenthal, interview by Natalie Robins, April 24, 2012 (re: foyer of Trilling's apartment on Claremont Avenue).
Stephen Koch, interview by Natalie Robins, Nov. 12, 2013.

11. GUILT MAKES US HUMAN

Information in this chapter was drawn from the following:
LTP: Box 22, Folder 11, 1938–53; Box 5, Folder 3, 1973.
DTP: Box 4, Folder 4, Bernard Malamud to DT, Dec. 16, 1954, and April 30, 1955; Box 4, Folder 4, Norman Mailer to DT, Dec. 8, 1960; Box 4, Folder 5, John O'Hara to DT, Jan. 24, 1957; Box 10, Folder 1, DT to Peter Shaw, re: DT's Oppenheimer essay; Box 11, Folder 1, Pearl Kluger, Executive Secretary of American Committee for Cultural Freedom, to DT, May 23, 1951; Box 11, Folder 2, DT to Sidney Hook, Oct. 15, 1955; Box 14, Folder 5, list of all members of "The Family" by S. A. Longstaff; Box 16, Folder 5, DT to Professor Arthur Edelstein, Department of English and American Literature, Brandeis University, Nov. 12, 1976; Box 20, Folder 2, DT notes for "X11, 32–33"; Box 31, Folder 1, DT to Cary Grayson, Carnegie Corporation of New York, July 12, 1956; Box 36, Folder 23, minutes for Planning Conference ACCF, March 1952; Box 37, Folder 14, "Draft of a Statement of Policy by the American Committee for Cultural Freedom; Box 38, Folder 11, DT, interview by Alan Kaufman, *Jewish Frontier*, May-June 1998; Box 60, Folder 1, draft of "Biography of a Marriage."

BOOKS, ARTICLES, AND OTHER RESOURCES

Alexander Bloom, *Prodigal Sons: The New York Intellectuals and Their World* (New York: Oxford University Press, 1987), 283 (re: Rahv's politics).
Diana Trilling, *The Beginning of the Journey*, 182 (re: Committee for Cultural Freedom).
Norman Podhoretz, *Ex-Friends* (New York: Free Press, 1999).
Manso, *Mailer*, 264.
William Barrett, "The Authentic Lionel Trilling," *Commentary*, Feb. 1, 1982.
Elizabeth Janeway, "In Earthquake Country," *New York Times*, Jan. 3, 1960.
Delmore Schwartz, "The Duchess' Red Shoes," *Partisan Review*, Jan.-Feb. 1953.
Gilbert Seldes, review of *But We Were Born Free*, *Saturday Review*, Feb. 13, 1954.
Dawn B. Sova, *Literature Suppressed on Sexual Grounds* (New York: Facts on File, 2006).
Norman Podhoretz, interview by Natalie Robins, Oct. 25, 2011.

Michael Rosenthal, interview by Natalie Robins, April 24, 2012.
Elisabeth Sifton, interview by Natalie Robins, May 8, 2013.

12. WEAVING

Information in this chapter was drawn from the following:
LTP: Box 3, Folder 7, 1952–55; Box 4, Folder 7, March–August 1960.
DTP: Box 3, Folder 2, Arnold Beichman to DT, Jan. 23, 1955, also DT to Arnold
Beichman, Oct. 19, 1960, and Feb. 29, 1968; Box 4, Folder 2, Allen Ginsberg to DT, Jan.
15, 1976; Box 4, Folder 3, "For Publication by DT"; Box 4, Folder 5, DT to William
Phillips (in this letter DT does not change a typo—she typed "1869" when she clearly
meant 1969); Box 4, Folder 6, DT to David Riesman, Jan. 18, 1955, and David Riesman
to DT, May 29, 1949; Box 4, Folder 6, DT to Evie and David Riesman, May 21, 1949,
also David Riesman to DT and LT, Feb. 16, 1953, and David Riesman to DT, Feb. 16, 1955;
Box 4, Folder 7, Ginsberg to DT, May 7, 1959; Box 5, Folder 2, DT to LT, May 26, 1962;
Box 6, Folder 5, DT to William Phillips, Jan. 2, 1980; Box 11, Folder2, Marjorie Harley to
DT, July 13, 1955; Box 11, Folder 2, various correspondence between Francis Brown and
DT—March 21, 28, 31, 1955; Box 12, Folder 1, Leon Skir to DT, Dec. 13, 1959; Box 12, Folder
3, DT to Editors of *Encounter*, Sept. 1967; Box 20, Folder 2, DT notes for a memoir; Box
36, Folder 1, DT lecture: "The Self as Subject," Feb. 23, 1983; Box 36, Folder 9, statement
read by DT to Board of Directors of the American Committee for Cultural Freedom,
Jan. 10, 1961; Box 36, Folder 23, American Committee for Cultural Freedom list of suggestions for members of the National Advisory Board, April 12, 1956; Box 37, Folder14,
DT to James T. Farrell, Oct. 3, 1956; Box 51, Folder 2, oral history, Steven Donadio.

BOOKS, ARTICLES, AND OTHER RESOURCES

Bloom, *Prodigal Sons*, 261 (re: Norman Mailer at Waldorf conference).
Podhoretz, *Ex-Friends*, 23, 74, 96.
Diana Trilling, "The Other Night at Columbia: A Report," in *Claremont Essays* (New
York: Harcourt, Brace and World, 1964).
Diana Trilling, ed., *The Selected Letters of D. H. Lawrence*, 1; also "Letter to a Young
Critic," xiv–xlii.
Hugh Wilford, *The Mighty Wurlitzer: How the CIA Played America* (Cambridge, MA:
Harvard University Press, 2008), 95.
Patricia Bosworth, complete transcript of *Paris Review* interview of DT, 29.
Lis Harris, "Di and Li," *New Yorker*, Sept. 23, 1993.
Terry Teachout, "Going Highbrow at the CIA," *Commentary*, March 2008.
Diana Trilling, "The Case for American Women," *Look*, March 3, 1959.
Diana Trilling, "A Symbol of Reason," review of *A Train of Powder*, by Rebecca West,
New York Times Book Review, March 20, 1955.

Lina Vlaviovos, telephone interview by Natalie Robins, Nov. 13, 2013.
Lore Dickstein and Morris Dickstein, interview by Natalie Robins, Spring 2013.

13. SUBVERSIVE SEX

Information in this chapter was drawn from the following:
LTP: Box 3, Folder 7, 1952–55; Box 4, Folders 5 and 7.
DTP: Box 6, Folder 4, DT to Daphne Merkin, re: carrot soup recipe, August 3, 1982 (proper cooking of corn is from a conversation NR had with DT); Box 8, Folder 5, DT to Bea Crystal (Gertrude Himmelfarb), July 5. 1994; Box 9, Folder 3, DT to Carl Rollyson, May 28, 1991; Box 12, Folder 1, Evan Thomas to DT, 1960; Box 22, Folder 5, DT interview by John Horder, *Scotsman*, May 29, 1965; Box 49, Folder 5, oral history, Steven Marcus; Box 53, Folder 6, oral history, Quentin and Thelma Anderson; Box 60, folder 1, draft of "Biography of a Marriage."

BOOKS, ARTICLES, AND OTHER RESOURCES

Diana Trilling: *The Beginning of the Journey*, 372.
Steven Marcus, *The Other Victorians: A Study of Sexuality and Pornography in Mid-Nineteenth-Century England* (New York: Basic Books, 1964), xvi–xvii.
Laskin, *The Partisans*, 22.
Lionel Trilling, *The Moral Obligation to Be Intelligent: Selected Essays* (New York: Farrar, Straus and Giroux, 2000), 354.
Diana Trilling, interview by Patricia Bosworth, *Paris Review*, Winter 1993.
Kathleen Hill, "Reading with Diana," *Yale Review*, July 1998.
Thomas Mallon, "Transfigured," *New Yorker*, April 5, 2010.
Evan Osnos, "Meet Dr. Freud," *New Yorker*, Jan. 10, 2011.
Lionel Trilling, "Snake Story," *Kenyon Review*, Fall 2011.
Brom Anderson, interview by Natalie Robins, May and June 2012.
Carroll Beichman, telephone interviews by Natalie Robins, April 19, 20, 23, May 4, June 21, 2012.
Gray Foy, telephone interview by Natalie Robins, April 12, 2012.
Michael Rosenthal, interview by Natalie Robins, April 24, 2012.

14. A LIMITED KIND OF CELEBRITY

Information in this chapter was drawn from the following:
LTP: Box 4, Folder 3; Box 5, Folder 5 (undated letter from LT to DT).
DTP: Box 2, Folder 12, Thelma Anderson to DT, Jan. 8, 1965; Box 2, Folder 12, DT to Quentin Anderson, March 19, 1965; Box 3, Folder3, DT to Bill Beutel, Feb. 13, 1968,

and Bill Beutel to DT, May 21, 1968; Box 3, Folder 5, DT to Elsa Grossman, May 9, 1965; Box 4, Folder 2, DT to Elinor Hays, correspondence, 1964–65; Box 4, Folder 3, DT to Melvin Lasky, May 21, 1962, also DT to Irving Kristol, May 25, 1967; Box 4, Folder 4, Norman Mailer to DT, August 30 (year not on letter but most likely c. 1962–64), also Norman Mailer to DT, Feb. 25, 1965; Box 4, Folder 5, correspondence between DT and William Phillips, winter 1965; Box 5, Folder 1, Robert Silvers to DT, Feb. 1962, Jan. 20, 1964, March 26, 1964, and April 14, 1967, also DT to Robert Silvers, May 4, 1967; Box 5, Folder 2, C. P. Snow to DT Feb. 4, 1963; Box 12, Folder 2, DT to Edward Morrow, May 18, 1961; Box 12, Folder 3, DT to J. M. Rizzo, Collier Books, Sept. 28, 1962; Box 12, Folder 5, DT to Linnie W. Schafer, Administrative Assistant Inter-University Committee on the Superior Student, April 10, 1964; Box 13, Folder 2, DT to Dr. Reider, Oct. 4, 1965, and Dr. Reider to DT, Oct. 6, 1965; Box 13, Folder 1, G. S. Fraser to DT, March 13, 1965; Box 14, Folder 1, Gertrude Himmelfarb to DT, June 4, 1965; Box 22, Folder 5, Stanley Edgar Hyman, review of *Claremont Essays* in *New York Review of Books*, April 16, 1964; Box 22, Folder 5, review of *Claremont Essays* in *Saturday Review*, March 14, 1964, also review by Arnold Beichman of *Claremont Essays*, also G. M. Pepper, a review of *Claremont Essays* in *National Review*, April 21, 1964; Box 32, Folder 10, "The Image of Woman in Contemporary Literature," by DT; Box 33, Folder 6, Byron Dobell to DT, July 23, 1963; Box 35, Folder 14, "The Riddle of *Who's Afraid of Virginia Woolf?*" by DT; Box 36, Folder 6, notes and draft of "A Visit to Camelot," by DT; Box 53, Folder 6, oral history, Quentin and Thelma Anderson; Box 60, Folder 2, draft of "Biography of a Marriage."

BOOKS, ARTICLES, AND OTHER RESOURCES

Gerald Clarke, *Capote: A Biography* (New York: Simon and Schuster, 2010).

Carolyn Heilbrun, *When Men Were the Only Models We Had: My Teachers Barzun, Fadiman, Trilling* (Philadelphia: University of Pennsylvania Press, 2002).

Lerman, *The Grand Surprise*, 503 (re: Jim Trilling's cello).

Michael Lennon, *Norman Mailer: A Double Life* (New York: Simon and Schuster, 2013), 354.

Diana Trilling, *The Beginning of the Journey*, 350, also 374 (Robert Lowell) and 335 (Alfred Karin).

Diana Trilling, "The Moral Radicalism of Norman Mailer," in *Claremont Essays*, 175–202.

Podhoretz, *Ex-Friends*, 102n.

Manso, *Mailer*, 350.

Alfred Kazin's America: Critical and Personal Writings, edited and with an introduction by Ted Solotaroff (New York: Harper Perennial, 2003), 175.

Larry Andrews, "The Wisdom of Our Elders: Honors Discussions—The Superior Student," *Journal of the National Collegiate Honors Council* (Fall-Winter 2011).

Richard Bernstein, obituary of Melvin Lasky, *New York Times*, May 22, 2004.

Martin Gross, letter to the editor, *New York Review of Books*, May 28, 1964.
Stanley Edgar Hyman, review of *Claremont Essays*, *New York Review of Books*, April 16, 1964.
Robert Mazzocco, review of *Beyond Culture*, *New York Review of Books*, Dec. 9, 1965.
Diana Trilling, "A Visit to Camelot," *New Yorker*, June 2, 1997.
Edward Mendelson, interview by Natalie Robins, May 2, 2012.

15. AT A TABLE

Information in this chapter was drawn from the following:
LTP: Box 4, Folder 12; Box 5, Folder 1, 1970–74.
DTP: Box 3, Folder 4, Midge Decter to DT August 6, 1968; Box 4, Folder 1, DT to Mrs. Beaujous, n.d.; Box 4, Folder 2, DT to Elinor Hays, n.d.; Box 5, Folder 1, DT to William Shawn, August 19, 1968; Box 12, Folder 2, DT to Editor of the *New York Times*, Feb. 1, 1961; Box 14, Folder 1, DT to *New York Review of Books*, Sept. 20, 1920 (marked by DT as "Letter Not Sent"); Box 21, Folder 2, DT to William Goodman, Harcourt, March 18, 1971, also Sept. 14, 1972, Oct. 6, 1972, Oct. 16, 1972; Box 22, Folder 2, "On the Politicalizing of Culture," by DT; Box 32, Folder 18, "Letter from Abroad: An American Looks at British TV," by DT; Box 34, Folder 3, notes; Box 34, Folder 8, DT to *Commentary*; Box 60, Folder1, "Biography of a Marriage."

BOOKS, ARTICLES, AND OTHER RESOURCES

Paul Fussell, introduction to *Reviewing the Forties*, by Diana Trilling.
Diana Trilling, *The Beginning of the Journey*, 132.
Diana Trilling, "On the Steps of Low Library," in *We Must March My Darlings: A Critical Decade* (New York: Harcourt Brace Jovanovich, 1977).
Diana Trilling et al., "Germany Through American Eyes," *Atlantic*, May1967.
Lewis P. Simpson, "Imagining Our Time: The Vocation of Diana Trilling," *Explorations: The Twentieth Century* (blog), Oct. 4, 2012, https://explorations20th.word press.com/2012/10/04/imagining-our-time-the-vocation-of-diana-trilling/.
Midge Decter and Norman Podhoretz, interview by Natalie Robins, Oct. 25, 2011; also an email exchange between Natalie Robins and Midge Decter, July 11, 2012, re: DT and Dachau Concentration Camp.

16. JUST CLOSE YOUR EYES

Information in this chapter was drawn from the following:
LTP: Box 4, Folder 6, journals; Box 5, Folder 1, notes 1970–71 ("going to be so nice to be dead").

DTP: Box 3, Folder 3, DT to Aline and Isaiah Berlin, Jan. 10, 1977; Box 4, Folder 2, DT to Lillian Hellman, June 1952 and assorted letters; Box 4, Folder 4, Norman Mailer to DT, Sept. 9, 1977, and DT to Norman Mailer, May 22, 1977, August 2, 1977, and Dec. 22, 1977; Box 8, Folder 2, Robert Gorham Davis to DT, June 25, 1986; Box 10, Folder 2, Nanine Joseph to DT, March 13, 1940; Box 15, Folder 4, DT to Mortimer Ostow, Dec. 23, 1975; Box 15, Folder 5, DT to Riesmans, Jan. 12, 1976, also DT to David R. Jacoby, Jan. 26, 1976; Box16, Folder 3, DT to Jacques [sic] Trilling, Jan. 12, 1976, also DT to Emma Lou Benignus, Jan. 15, 1976; Box 16, Folder 5, DT to Pearl Bell, Dec. 2, 1976; Box 30, Folder 9, tentative outlines for a series of articles on the American female; Box 31, Folder 20, "Feminism and Women's Liberation: Continuity or Conflict?" a lecture by DT; Box 35, Folder 2, LT seminars (list); Box 42, Folder 5, DT to William Jovanovich, August 5, 1977; Box 43, Folder 17, "The Liberated Heroine," also William Shawn to DT, May 3, 1978; Box 49, Folder 5, Steven Marcus, oral history; Box 51, Folder 1, oral history, Jack and Susan Thompson; Box 53, Folder 6, oral history, Quentin and Thelma Anderson; Box 54, Folder1, list of reserved seats at LT's funeral.

BOOKS, ARTICLES, AND OTHER RESOURCES

Deirdre Carmody, "Trilling Case Sparks Publisher Loyalty Debate," *New York Times*, Sept. 30, 1976.

Laura Cottingham, *Seeing Through the Seventies: Essays on Feminism and Art* (New York: Routledge, 2006).

Koch, "Journey's Beginning."

Lerman, *The Grand Surprise*, 418.

Manso, *Mailer*, 584.

Podhoretz, *Ex-Friends*, 94, 95.

Diana Trilling, *The Beginning of the Journey*, 220 (re: "Pumpkin Papers").

Diana Trilling, *We Must March My Darlings*, 45.

Diana Trilling, Goronwy—and Others: A Remembrance of England, *Partisan Review*, 1996.

Midge Decter and Norman Podhoretz, interview by Natalie Robins, Oct. 25, 2011.

Drenka Willen, interview by Natalie Robins, Feb. 12, 2012.

17. NOT GIVING A DAMN

Information in this chapter was drawn from the following:

DTP: Box 2, Folder 9, DT to Patty O'Toole, Sept. 2, 1992; Box 3, Folder 1, DT to Jacques Barzun, July 5, 1977, also DT to Lester Migdal ("eyes kicking up"), Jan. 2, 1977; Box 3, Folder 2, DT to Arnold Beichman, and Arnold Beichman to DT, June 11, 19765, to March 16, 1994; Box 3, Folder 4, DT to Kip Fadiman, April 3, 1979, also Kip Fadiman to DT, Nov. 8, 1975; Box 4, Folder 6, DT to David Riesman, May 30, 1978; Box 8, Folder 3, DT to Kip Fadiman, Oct. 4, 1991; Box 16, Folder 1, Howard Mumford Jones to DT Nov. 6, 1975; Box 17, Folder 1, DT to Pat Goodheart, Jan. 2, 1977; Box 21, Folder 2, childhood memoir (thoughts on Jewishness); Box 29, Folder 4, review by Emile Capoya in *The Nation*; Box 42, Folder 8, DT to Bill Jovanovich, June 5, 1977: also assorted letters in Box 60, Folder 1; Box 42, Folder 8, DT to Norman Podhoretz, June 25, 1977; Box 60, Folder 1, DT to Bill Jovanovich, Nov. 8, 1977; Box 60, Folder 2, draft of "Biography of a Marriage."

BOOKS, ARTICLES, AND OTHER RESOURCES

William Jovanovich, *The Temper of the West*, a memoir (Columbia: University of South Carolina Press, 2003), 285–86.
Leo Lerman, *The Grand Surprise*, 437 (re: Alfred Kazin).
Diana Trilling, *We Must March My Darlings*, 47 (quotations re: *Scoundrel Time*).
Diana Trilling, interview by John Firth, *Saturday Review*, May 28, 1977, 22–25.
Diana Trilling, "Lionel Trilling: A Jew At Columbia," *Commentary*, March 1, 1979.

18. HER OWN PLACE

Information in this chapter was drawn from the following:

DTP: Box 5, Folder 1, DT to Sargent Shriver, June 22, 1971; Box 6, Folder 1, Kip Fadiman to DT Oct. 2, 1981; Box 6, Folder 3, DT to Mark Krupnick; Box 6, Folder 5, Midge Decter to DT Jan. 25, 1980; Box 10, Folder 1, DT letter to Christopher Zinn, June 21, 1987; Box 16, Folder 3, DT to Morris Dickstein, Feb. 13, 1976; Box 16, Folder 4, DT to Lydia Bronte at the Rockefeller Foundation; Box 17, Folder 1, Harriet Trilling Schwartz to DT, Oct. 9, 1977; Box 17, Folder 1, DT to Bernard Cohen, Sept. 1977; Box 17, Folder 1, DT to Elenore Lester, April 6, 1977; Box 17, Folder 4, Daphne Merkin to DT, April 7, 1978; Box 18, Folder 1, DT to John Gross, Feb. 15, 1979, also May 12, 1980; Box 18, Folder 1, DT to *Harvard Educational Review*, June 6, 11, and 14, 1979; Box 23, assorted material re: *Mrs. Harris*; Box 26, Folder 2, Christopher Sinclair-Stevenson, Hamish Hamilton Ltd., to DT, April 17, 1982; Box 28, Folder 6, Dannye Romani, "Respectable Headmistress Respectable Murder," *Charlotte Observer*, May 11, 1980; Box 28, Folder 7, "Three Racing To Tell Tarnower Story," *New York Post*," May 12, 1981; Box 28, Folder1, assorted *Mrs. Harris* publicity materials; Box 42, Folder 8, DT to Bill Jovanovich, May 31, 1978 and June 19, 1978, and DT to Bill Jovanovich, May 1, 1978; Box 44, Folder 4, DT to Norman Mailer Nov. 7, 1979, also Norman Mailer to DT, Nov. 27, 1979; Box 53, Folder 14, DT to Ted Solotaroff, Oct. 28, 1977, and Phillip Lopate to DT, March 31, 1981; Box 56, Folder 1, *Washington Post Book World* announcement of *A Respectable Murder*."

BOOKS, ARTICLES, AND OTHER RESOURCES

Diana Trilling, interview by Patricia Bosworth, *Paris Review*, Winter 1993.

Koch, "Journey's Beginning."

Mark Krupnick, "The Trillings: A Marriage of Two Minds," *Salmagundi*, no. 103 (Summer 1994).

Phillip Lopate, "Remembering Lionel Trilling," in *Bachelorhood: Tales of the Metropolis*, 161.

"Confesses He Gave Poison to His Wife," *New York Times* article (April 25, 1924) sent to DT by Beth Karas, June 28, 1995.

Interviews by Natalie Robins: Patricia Bosworth, May 29, 2012; Jules Feiffer, June 11, 2012 (telephone interview); Stephen Koch, Nov. 12, 2013; Daphne Merkin, Oct. 5, 2012; Peter Pouncey, former dean of Columbia and former president of Amherst College, May 2, 2012 (telephone interview); Michael Rosenthal, April 24, 2012; Elisabeth Sifton, May 8, 2013; Phyllis Theroux, June 18, 2013.

Morris Dickstein, email to Natalie Robins, Feb. 3, 2014.

19. RE-CREATION AND IMAGINATION

Information in this chapter was drawn from the following:

DTP: Box 3, Folder 1, DT to Hannah Robinson, Harvest Books Marketing Director, Jan. 11, 1996; Box 3, Folder 4, DT to Judy Rosenthal, Oct. 4, 1994; Box 5, Folder 3, DT to Anatole Broyard, Dec. 27, 1981; Box 6, Folder 4, Norman Mailer to DT, n.d.; Box 7, Folder 1, typed review of *Mrs. Harris* by Peter Shaw with "by DT" at top and "Written for PR but he asked that it be returned"; Box 7, Folder 6, DT to Georges Borchardt, March 4, 1994, also Georges Borchardt to DT, several letters; Box 7, Folder 6, Jacques Barzun to DT, Nov. 19, 1993; Box 8, Folder 1, DT to Susan Moore, Oct. 2, 1987; Box 8, Folder 3, DT to Kip Fadiman, Jan. 29, 1993; Box 8, Folder 5, Gertrude Himmelfarb to DT, July 8, 1994, and DT to Gertrude Himmelfarb, July 28, 1994; Box 8, Folder 6, DT to Gene Marcus, May 6, 1995, and Feb. 26, 1996; Box 9, Folder 4, DT to James Seaton, Department of English, Michigan State University, Nov. 9, 1995; Box 18, Folder 3, DT to Dr. Arnold Lisio, n.d. (but sometime in 1996); Box 20, Folder 2, DT notes on *Mrs. Harris*; Box 20, Folder 5, assorted reviews of *The Beginning of the Journey*; Box 23, Folder 3, interview by Steven M. L. Aronson in *Interview* magazine; Box 23, Folder 4, DT to Bill Jovanovich, April 18, 1981; Box 23, Folder 5, DT to Edward Klein, April 3, 1981; Box 28, Folder 3, "Penguin's Using Two Covers for Selling *Mrs. Harris*," *Publisher's Weekly*, July 30, 1982; Box 23, Folder 6, DT to Joyce Slater, Dec. 5, 1982, also several other letters mentioned in chapter; Box 28, Folder 3, *All Things Considered*, Oct. 22, 1981; Box 28, Folder 4, Michael Sovern to DT, Feb. 26, 1982, also "Hollywood Connection," by Hank Grant, July 1982; Box 28, Folder 5, "Hard Time in Hard-Cover Country," *Time*, March 22, 1982; Box 28, Folder 8, Martin Amis, "A Critic in the Courtroom," *Observer*, May 2, 1982; Box 28, Folder 8, Rebecca West in

The Sunday Telegraph, May 9, 1982, also Anita Brookner, *London Review of Books*, May 9, 1982, and several other book reviews mentioned in chapter by Christopher Lehmann-Haupt; George V. Higgins, R. Z. Sheppard, Joseph Adelman, Elizabeth Pochoda, Dorothy Rabinowitz, and Michiko Kakatani; Box 31, Folder 221, "Footnote to My Life as a Critic," by DT; Box 32, Folder 5, Cressida Leyshon at *The New Yorker* to DT, July 28, 1995; also DT to Tina Brown, n.d.; Box 34, Folder 4, "Notes on the Trial of the Century," by DT, *New Republic*, Oct. 30, 1995, also DT to Editors of the *New Republic*, Oct. 16, 1995; Box 37, Folder 7, Sally Jacobs, "Diana Trilling Readies for the Next Political Battle," *Boston Globe*, Sept. 19, 1995, and DT to Sally Jacobs, Sept. 28, 1995; Box 37, Folder 12, DT, "Reading By Ear," *Civilization*, Nov./Dec. 1994; Box 42, Folder 6, Guggenheim material; Box 42, Folder 8, assorted letters from DT to Bill Jovanovich; Box 43, Folder 1, DT to Bill Jovanovich, April 20, 1994; Box 43, Folder 9, DT to Jim Hyde, May 30, 1996; Box 53, Folder 11, DT to Edward Said, Sept. 15, 1986.

BOOKS, ARTICLES, AND OTHER RESOURCES

Diana Trilling, *The Beginning of the Journey*, 405.
Natalie Robins, *Living in the Lightning*, 62–63.
Patricia Bosworth, "A Life of Significant Contention," *New York Times*, Dec. 29, 1996.
Diana Trilling, interview by Patricia Bosworth, *Paris Review*, Winter 1993.
Lis Harris, "Di and Li," *New Yorker*. Sept. 13, 1993.
Kathleen Hill, "Reading with Diana," *Yale Review* 86, no. 3 (1998): 1–29.
Koch, "Journey's Beginning."
Michael Norman, DT's obituary in *The New York Times*, Oct. 25, 1996.
Assorted tapes with DT made by Brom Anderson.
Fritz Stern, telephone interview by Natalie Robins, Feb. 26, 2015.
Patricia O'Toole, telephone interview by Natalie Robins, June 16, 2012.
Daphne Merkin, interview by Natalie Robins, Oct. 15, 2012.
Peter Manso, interview by Natalie Robins, March 30, 2016.
Dore Levy, email exchange, April 16, 2016.
Oliver Conant, telephone interview by Natalie Robins, June 23, 2016.

EPILOGUE: ARCADIA

BOOKS, ARTICLES, AND OTHER RESOURCES

Lynn Weiss, *Attention Deficit Disorder in Adults*, foreword by Kenneth A. Bonnett (Boulder, CO: Taylor Trade, 2005).
Sarah Boxer, "Doctor Resigns over Trilling Diagnosis," *New York Times*, May 29, 1999.

Gertrude Himmelfarb, "A Man's Own Household His Enemies," *Commentary*, July 1, 1999.

Daphne Merkin, "A Passion for Order," *New York Times*, Nov. 17, 1996.

James Trilling, "My Father and the Weak-Eyed Devils."

John Rodden, "The Trilling Family 'Romance': Report of a Psychoanalytic Autopsy," *Modern Age*, Summer 2006.

Gloria Steinem, "The Woman Who Will Not Die," 1986 (from "Marilyn Monroe: Still Life," *America Masters*, season 20, episode 4, aired July 19, 2006.

Description of ADD as part of ADHD is from Steven Kurtz of the Child Mind Institute and Natalie Robins's email exchange with Dr. Natalie Weber of the Child Mind Institute, Sept. 25, 2013.

Sarah Gund, interview by Natalie Robins, Oct. 26, 2012.

Dore Levy, email exchange with Natalie Robins, May 12, 2016.

"Dreary Details About My Funeral," from Dore Levy.

SELECTED BIBLIOGRAPHY

BOOKS BY OR EDITED BY DIANA TRILLING

The Portable D. H. Lawrence (editor). New York: Viking, 1947.
The Selected Letters of D. H. Lawrence (editor). New York: Doubleday, 1961.
Claremont Essays. New York: Harcourt, Brace and World, 1964.
We Must March My Darlings: A Critical Decade. New York: Harcourt Brace Jovanovich, 1977.
Reviewing the Forties. New York: Harcourt Brace Jovanovich, 1978.
The Last Decade: Essays and Reviews, 1965–1975, by Lionel Trilling (editor). New York: Harcourt, Brace and World, 1979.
Of This Time, of That Place, and Other Stories, by Lionel Trilling (compiler). New York: Harcourt, Brace, 1979.
Speaking of Literature and Society, by Lionel Trilling (editor). New York: Harcourt Brace Jovanovich, 1980.
Mrs. Harris: The Death of the Scarsdale Diet Doctor. New York: Harcourt Brace Jovanovich, 1981.
The Beginning of the Journey: The Marriage of Diana and Lionel Trilling. New York: Harcourt Brace, 1993.

BOOKS BY LIONEL TRILLING

Matthew Arnold. New York: Norton, 1939.
E. M. Forster. Norfolk, CT: New Directions, 1943.
The Middle of the Journey. New York: Viking, 1947.

The Liberal Imagination: Essays on Literature and Society. New York: Viking, 1950.
The Opposing Self: Nine Essays in Criticism. New York: Viking, 1955.
Freud and the Crisis of Our Culture. Boston: Beacon, 1955.
Gathering of Fugitives. Boston: Beacon, 1956.
Beyond Culture: Essays on Literature and Learning. Cambridge, MA: Harvard University Press, 1972.
Sincerity and Authenticity. Cambridge, MA: Harvard University Press, 1972.
Mind in the Modern World: The 1972 Thomas Jefferson Lecture in the Humanities. New York: Viking, 1973.
The Moral Obligation to Be Intelligent: Selected Essays. Edited by Leon Wieseltier. New York: Farrar, Straus and Giroux, 2000.
The Journey Abandoned: The Unfinished Novel. Edited by Geraldine Murphy. New York: Columbia University Press: 2008.

GENERAL SOURCES

American Psychiatric Association. *Diagnostic Criteria from DSM-IV.* Washington, DC: APA, 2005.
Brenner, Marie. *Great Dames: What I Learned from Older Women.* New York: Crown, 2000.
Bloom, Alexander. *Prodigal Sons: The New York Intellectuals and Their World.* New York: Oxford University Press, 1986.
Brightman, Carol. *Writing Dangerously: Mary McCarthy and Her World.* New York: Harcourt Brace, 1992.
Chambers, Whittaker. *Witness.* Washington, DC: Regnery, 1952, 1980.
Clarke, Gerald. *Capote: A Biography.* New York: Simon and Schuster, 1988.
Cooney, Terry A. *The Rise of the New York Intellectuals: "Partisan Review" and Its Circle, 1934–1945.* Madison: University of Wisconsin Press, 2004.
Heilbrun, Carolyn G. *When Men Were the Only Models We Had: My Teachers—Fadiman, Barzun, Trilling.* Philadelphia: University of Pennsylvania Press, 2001.
Jacoby, Russell. *The Last Intellectuals: American Culture in the Age of Academe.* New York: Basic Books, 1987.
Jovanovich, William. *The Temper of the West.* Columbia: University of South Carolina Press, 2003.
Kirsch, Adam. *Why Trilling Matters.* New Haven, CT: Yale University Press, 2011.
Kristol, Irving. *The Neoconservative Persuasion: Selected Essays 1942–2009.* New York: Basic Books, 2001.
Krupnick, Mark. *Lionel Trilling and the Fate of Cultural Criticism.* Evanston, IL: Northwestern University Press, 1986.
Krystal, Arthur, editor. *A Company of Readers: Uncollected Writings of W. H. Auden, Jacques Barzun, and Lionel Trilling from the Readers' Subscription and Mid-Century Book Clubs.* New York: Free Press, 2001.

Kurzweil, Edith. *Full Circle: A Memoir*. London: Transaction, 2007.

Laskin, David. *Partisans: Marriage, Politics, and Betrayal Among the New York Intellectuals*. Chicago: University of Chicago Press, 2001.

Lerman, Leo. *The Grand Surprise: The Journals of Leo Lerman*. New York: Alfred A. Knopf, 2007.

Lopate, Phillip. *Bachelorhood: Tales of the Metropolis*. New York: Poseidon, 1989.

Manso, Peter. *Mailer: His Life and Times*. New York: Washington Square Press, 2008.

Marcus, Steven. *The Other Victorians: A Study of Sexuality and Pornography in Mid-Nineteenth-Century England*. New York: Basic Books, 1966; New Brunswick, NJ: Transaction, 2011.

Phillips, William. *A Partisan View: Five Decades in the Politics of Literature*. New York: Stein and Day, 1983.

Podhoretz, Norman. *Ex-Friends: Falling Out with Allen Ginsberg, Lionel and Diana Trilling, Lillian Hellman, Hannah Arendt, and Norman Mailer*. New York: Free Press, 1999.

Rodden, John, and Morris Dickstein. *Lionel Trilling and the Critics: Opposing Selves*. Lincoln: University of Nebraska Press, 1999.

Trilling, James. *The Language of Ornament*. New York: Thames and Hudson, 2001.

Shoben, Edward Joseph, Jr. *Lionel Trilling*. New York: Frederick Ungar, 1981.

Taylor, Benjamin. *Saul Bellow Letters*. New York, Viking-Penguin, 2010.

Taylor, Benjamin. *Into the Open: Reflection on Genius and Modernity*. New York: New York University Press, 1995.

Wald, Alan M. *The New York Intellectuals: The Rise and Decline of the Anti-Stalinist Left from the 1930s to the 1980s*. Chapel Hill: University of North Carolina Press, 1987.

Weiss, Lynn. *Attention Deficit Disorder in Adults: A Different Way of Thinking*. New York: Taylor Trade, 1997 (rev. ed. 2005).

INDEX

Note: Diana and Lionel Trilling are referred to as DT and LT in the subheadings below.

Lawrence, Frieda, 124, 259
Leary, Timothy, 232
Leavis, F. R., 87, 89
Lehmann, Rosamond, 120
Lehmann-Haupt, Christopher, 323, 333–34
Lenzer, Gertrud, 214
Lerman, Leo, 130, 151; DT's statements to, 271–72; friendship with the Trillings, 119–21, 197–98; and Jim Trilling's music studies, 239; and Kazin's *A New York Jew*, 290; and LT's funeral, 274
Lerner, Max, 61
Levy, Dore, 326, 327, 345–46
Lewin, Bertram, 77
Lewis, Sinclair, 108
The Liberal Imagination (L. Trilling), 140–41
The Life and Work of Sigmund Freud (Jones), 207
Lindbergh, Anne Morrow, 275–76
Lionel Trilling and the Fate of Cultural Criticism (Krupnick), 313
Lionel Trilling Book Award, 336–37
Lisio, Arnold, 342–43
Literary Guild, 118–19
Little, Brown, 278–80, 282, 284
London Review of Books, 155, 323
Look magazine, 183–84
Lopate, Phillip, 311
Los Angeles Times Book Review, 301
Lowell, Robert, 219, 256
Lowenstein, Rudolph, 95, 139
Lowes, John Livingston, 8
Lynch, James J., 232

MacDonald, Dwight, 245
Mademoiselle, 135
Mailer, Adele, 173, 239–40
Mailer, Norman, 208; and blurb for DT's *We Must March My Darlings*, 281; and Columbia protests of 1968, 255; DT's essay on, 217, 219–20; and DT's feud with Lillian Hellman, 281–82; and DT's

Mrs. Harris, 320; friendship with DT, 171–76, 220–22, 282; and the "new journalism," 222; and New York Intellectual Family, 176; and panel on women's liberation (1971), 263–64; potential romance with DT, 173–74; *The Prisoner of Sex*, 263–64; and proposed memoir of LT, 303; and visit to Oxford, 239–40
Making It (Podhoretz), 247, 304, 321
Malamud, Ann, 327
Malamud, Bernard, 163–64, 327
Male and Female (Mead), 148–49
Man-Eaters of Kumaon (Corbett), 118
Mansfield, Katherine, 76
Manso, Peter, 170–71, 173, 219–20, 282
Marcus, Gene, 201–2, 206, 208, 210, 337, 340, 341
Marcus, Stephen, 200–202, 223, 230; collaboration with LT, 207–9; DT's attachment to, 207–11, 214–15; falling out with DT, 214; and Fraser's review of *Claremont Essays*, 233; as friend and protégé of the Trillings, 200–202; and LT's death, 271
Markham, Beryl, 203–4
Marling Hall (Thurkill), 106
Marlowe, Sylvia, 166
marriage of Diana and Lionel Trilling: and childlessness, 95–96, 121; and "compulsive doubt," 45; DT as collaborator and editor for LT, 80–83, 85, 91, 101, 114, 125, 141, 155, 257, 334; and DT's career, 91, 95, 104–11, 114, 142, 199, 218–19; and DT's phobias and anxieties, 56–57, 75, 77, 121, 242; early married life, 40–53, 55–69; and emotional dependence, 41, 128, 242; engagement, 37; and feelings of guilt, 40, 121; finances, 45–50, 57, 58, 63, 76, 95, 157–59; financial assistance from friends and relations, 48, 157, 227; friendships and love affairs of middle age, 197–215; and